0-07-020359-8	Feit	*SNMP: A Guide to Network Management*
0-07-004674-3	Bates	*Wireless Networked Communications: Concepts, Technology, and Implementation*
0-07-042588-4	Minoli	*Imaging in Corporate Environments*
0-07-005089-9	Baker	*Networking the Enterprise: How to Build Client/Server Systems That Work*
0-07-004194-6	Bates	*Disaster Recovery for LANs: A Planning and Action Guide*
0-07-046461-8	Naugle	*Network Protocol Handbook*
0-07-046322-0	Nemzow	*FDDI Networking: Planning, Installation, and Management*
0-07-042586-8	Minoli	*1st, 2nd, and Next Generation LANs*
0-07-037936-X	Lindberg	*Digital Broadband Networks and Services*
0-07-034247-4	Kessler	*ISDN: Concepts, Facilities, and Services, 2/e*
0-07-063263-4	Taylor	*McGraw-Hill Internetworking Handbook*
0-07-005730-3	Blakeley	*Messaging and Queuing Using the MQI*
0-07-069416-8	Summers	*ISDN Implementor's Guide*
0-07-063638-9	Terplan	*Benchmarking for Effective Network Management*
0-07-057634-3	Simonds	*Network Security: Data and Voice Communications*
0-07-060362-6	McDysan/Spohn	*ATM: Theory and Application*
0-07-707883-7	Deniz	*ISDN and Its Application to LAN Interconnection*
0-07-024842-7	Grinberg	*Computer/Telecom Integration: The SCAI Solution*
0-07-035968-7	Kumar	*Broadband Communications: A Professional's Guide to ATM, Frame Relay, SMDS, SONET, and B-ISDN*
0-07-049663-3	Peterson	*TCP/IP Networking: A Guide to the IBM Environment*
0-07-911857-7	Ananthaswamy	*Data Communications Using Object-Oriented Design and C++*
0-07-020056-4	Fatah	*Electronic Mail Systems: A Network Manager's Guide*
0-07-005203-4	Berson/Anderson	*SYBASE and Client/Server Computing*

D1617268

Introduction to
ATM Networking

Introduction to ATM Networking

Walter J. Goralski

McGraw-Hill, Inc.

New York   San Francisco   Washington, D.C.   Auckland   Bogotá
Caracas   Lisbon   London   Madrid   Mexico City   Milan
Montreal   New Delhi   San Juan   Singapore
Sydney   Tokyo   Toronto

Library of Congress Cataloging-in-Publication Data

Goralski, Walter J.
    Introduction to ATM networking / Walter J. Goralski.
        p.   cm.
    Includes index.
    ISBN 0-07-024043-4 (acid-free paper)
    1. Asynchronous transfer mode.   I. Title.
TK5105.35.067
004.6'6—dc20   94-4017
                                                 CIP

1 2 3 4 5 6 7 8 9 0   DOC/DOC   9 0 0 9 8 7 6 5

ISBN 0-07-024043-4

*The sponsoring editor for this book was Jerry Papke, the editing super-
visor was Bernard Onken, and the production supervisor was Suzanne
Rapcavage. It was set in Century Schoolbook by Ron Painter of
McGraw-Hill's Professional Book Group composition unit.*

Printed and bound by R. R. Donnelley & Sons Company.

McGraw-Hill books are available at special quantity discounts to use
as premiums and sales promotions, or for use in corporate training programs. For more information, please write to the Director of Special
Sales, McGraw-Hill, Inc., 11 West 19th Street, New York, NY 10011.
Or contact your local bookstore.

This book is printed on recycled, acid-free paper containing 10%
postconsumer waste.

Contents

Preface

ATM is not only the promise of a new networking architecture, it is also the promise of *the* new networking architecture. Not only for now, but for all time. Part 1 of this book makes this clear.

This kind of transition has happened before, and breathtakingly fast. The original "communications technology" in the United States, and hence the world, was the telegraph. This "telegraph transfer mode" network lasted until the telephone was invented. Since the telephone was an evident improvement over the telegraph, it did not take long before the network became "telephone transfer mode."

This gave way in time to "synchronous transfer mode" and will soon become "asynchronous transfer mode." Since this process is supposed to end with ATM, it may be instructive to detail these network transitions with an eye on the possible time frame for ATM transition. Also, since the process is supposed to halt with ATM as the "ultimate network," it may be worthwhile to review the economic and social factors that fueled these changes. Will these factors really cease to operate under ATM? Or will the pace of technological change continue to generate pressure that will eventually build up to force transition to some unforeseen "transfer mode" in the future? This is the topic of Chapter 1.

Having explored ATM as a natural progression of national network technology, Chapter 2 details the capabilities of ATM as an answer to the proliferation of networks and services that are threatening to overwhelm network implementers today. Instead of building a series of specialized networks, as designers have done in the past, ATM offers a way of building a "generic" network that may be used in different ways to satisfy different user communities. Some of these communities are outlined here, especially the data users who are currently taxing the resources of the most advanced networks currently available. The ATM cell is introduced here, as well as the particular ATM multiplexing techniques that make it all possible.

Part 2 forms the heart of the text and gives a detailed, byte-by-byte introduction to just how ATM works. Chapter 3 details the relationship of the ATM protocol stack to the Open Systems Interconnect Reference Model (OSI-RM). It also introduces some key concepts as to how ATM functions. Of course, to be a true networking architecture, more is needed than just a method of transferring user data. ATM signaling is introduced, as well as the concept of ATM traffic control and network management. And if ATM is to be the *only* network that exists in the future, what will happen to other networks that exist now, such as SMDS (switched multimegabit data services), frame relay, and even IBM's SNA (System Network Architecture)? These issues are raised in Chapter 3 as well.

Chapter 4 deals with the lower layers of the ATM protocol stack: the physical layer and the transmission convergence layer. Physical transport media currently supported by the ATM Forum are detailed, as well as current specifications for ATM premises wiring. The rest of the chapter deals with exactly how an "asynchronous" transport network such as ATM can package up cells for transmission over framed transmission systems (which most are and will remain). The touchy issue of ATM over T-1 [a digital transmission link running at 1.544 million bits per second (Mbps)] is dealt with here in considerable detail, given the importance of T-1 in current networks.

Chapter 5 is a full-scale treatment of the key layer of ATM: the ATM layer itself. The ATM cell field functions are detailed, as well as the concept of ATM flow control. ATM flow control is a critical area, due to the fact that it must work not only for data applications but also potentially for voice and video applications. There is a discussion of current and future ATM switching systems, which will, of course, form the key ingredient of an ATM network. Chapter 5 also deals with more detailed information on specialized cells for ATM network management and signaling.

Chapter 6 closes out the ATM architecture layers with a treatment of the ATM adaptation layers (AALs). These are important to ATM network acceptance because the AALs must work as well as (if not better than) the existing network schemes ATM wishes to eventually supplant. AAL classes and types are discussed, as well as the newer ATM Forum proposals. The chapter closes with a look at the services ATM provides to end users, all of which *must* ensure acceptable quality of service to these users.

Part 3 puts the information contained in Part 2 to work. Chapter 7 points out that ATM networks are different from any networks ever built and that performance is critical for user acceptance. Issues affecting these performance aspects are discussed, as well as the practical issue of managing an ATM network with existing methods.

Chapter 8 considers other high-speed networking architectures and methods. Perhaps ATM is not the only game in town. Are there other networking schemes that may be just as good as or even better than ATM? The chapter closes with a look at the relationship of B-ISDN (Broadband–Integrated Services Digital Network) with ATM and a look at the ATM Forum's plans for the next few years.

Chapter 9 explores the promise of ATM not only from the perspective of builders of private networks but also from the point of view of public service providers. It closes the book with a look at the kinds of networks and services that will be built for and offered to users over the next several years.

Walter J. Goralski

Acronym List

AA	Administrative authority
AAL	ATM adaptation layer
ABR	Available bit rate
AFI	Authority and format identifier
AIS	Alarm indication signal
AL	Alignment field
AlGaAs	Aluminum-gallium-arsenide (chipset)
ANSI	American National Standards Institute
API	Application program interface
APS	Automatic protection switching
AREA	Area identifier
ATM	Asynchronous transfer mode
AToMMIB	ATM management information base (BellCore)
AVI	Audiovisual interleaved
B-ICI	Broadband intercarrier interface
B-ISDN	Broadband integrated services digital network
B-ISUP	Broadband interim signaling user protocol
B-NT1	Broadband network termination type 1
B-NT2	Broadband network termination type 2
BAsize	Buffer allocation size
BECN	Backward explicit congestion notification
BER	Bit-error rate
BEtag	Beginning end tag
Btag	Beginning tag
BICMOS	Bipolar complementary metallic-oxide semiconductor
BIP	Bit interleaved parity
BOD	Bandwidth on demand
BOM	Beginning of message
BSS	Broadcast switching system
BSVCI	Broadcast signaling virtual channel identifier
BW	Bandwidth
CAC	Connection admission control
CAP	Competitive access provider
CAU	Cause
CBDS	Connectionless broadband data services
CBR	Constant bit rate

CCITT	Consultative Committee for International Telephone and Telegraph
CD	Compact disk
CDV	Cell delay variation
CL	Connectionless
CLNAP	Connectionless network access protocol
CLNS	Connectionless network services
CLP	Cell loss priority
CMOS	Complementary metallic-oxide semiconductor
CO	Connection oriented
COCF	Connection-oriented convergence function
COM	Continuation of message
CPCS	Common part convergence sublayer
CPE	Customer premises equipment
CPI	Common part indicator
CPU	Central processing unit
CRC	Cyclical redundancy check
CS	Convergence sublayer
CSMA/CD	Carrier sense multiple access with collision detection
CSU	Channel service unit
DAS	Dual attached station
DCC	Data communications channel
DCC	Data country code (ATM addressing)
DCE	Data circuit-terminating equipment
DCLI	Data connection link identifiers
DCS	Digital crossconnect system
DDD	Direct digit dialing
DE	Discard eligibility
DFI	DSP format identifier
DLCI	Data link connection identifier
DMPDU	Derived MAC protocol data unit
DOD	Department of Defense
DOS	Disk operating system
DPG	Dedicated packet group
DQDB	Distributed-queue dual bus
DS-0	Digital signal 0 level (64 kbps)
DS-1	Digital signal 1 level (1.544 Mbps)
DS-3	Digital signal 3 level (45 Mbps)
DSP	Domain-specific part
DSU	Digital service unit
DTE	Data terminal equipment
DXI	Data exchange interface
E-1	ETSI level 1 digital carrier trunk (2.048 Mbps)
E-2	ETSI level 2 digital carrier trunk (4.096 Mbps)
E-3	ETSI level 3 digital carrier trunk (34 Mbps)
E-4	ETSI level 4 digital carrier trunk (140 Mbps)
ECL	Emitter-coupled logic
EFCI	Explicit forward congestion indicator
EFI	Errored frame indicator
EN	Ethernet

ENR	Enterprise network roundtable
EOM	End of message
ESF	Extended superframe
ESI	End-system identifier
ESS	Electronic switching system
ET	End termination
Etag	End tag
ETSI	European Telecommunications Standards Institute
FA1	Frame alignment byte 1
FA2	Frame alignment byte 2
FDDI	Fiber distributed data interface
FDM	Frequency division multiplexing
FEBE	Far end block error
FECN	Forward explicit congestion notification
FERF	Far end receive failure
FOT	Fiberoptic termination
FR	Frame relay
FRBS	Frame relay bearer service
FT-1	Fractional first level T-carrier digital trunk
FT-3C	Fiber third level T-carrier digital trunk combined (2 T-3s)
GaAs	Gallium-arsenide (chipsets)
GCRA	Generic cell rate algorithm
GFC	Generic flow control
GUI	Graphical user interface, e.g., Microsoft Windows
HDLC	High-level data link control
HDTV	High-definition television
HE	Header extension
HEC	Header error control
HLPI	Higher-layer protocol identifier
HPPI	High-performance parallel interface
HSSI	High-speed serial interface
ICD	International code designator
ICF	Isochronous convergence function
IDI	Initial domain identifier
IDNX	Integrated digital network exchange
IE	Information element
IEC	Interexchange carrier
IETF	Internet Engineering Task Force
IISP	Interim interswitch signaling protocol
ILMI	Interim local management interface
IMPDU	Initial MAC protocol data unit
IP	Internet protocol
IPX	Internetwork packet exchange
ISDN	Integrated services digital network
ISO	International Standards Organization
IT	Information type
ITU-T	International Telecommunications Union—Telecommunications Standardization Sector
IWF	Interworking function
IWU	Interworking unit

IXC	Interexchange carrier
JPEG	Joint Photographers Expert Group
LAN	Local area network
LAP-B	Link access protocol, balanced
LAP-D	Link access protocol, D channel
LAP-F	Link access protocol, Frame Relay
LATA	Local access and transport area
LCF	Link congregation function
LEC	Local exchange carrier
LEN	Local exchange node
LES	LAN emulation services
LI	Length indicator
LLC	Logical link control
LME	Layer management entity
L-NNI	LAN emulation network-node interface
LT	Line termination
LUNI	LAN emulation user network interface
MA&E	Marketing awareness and education
MAC	Media access control
MAN	Metropolitan area network, e.g., 802.6
MCF	Media access control convergence function
MCP	Media access control convergence protocol
MF	Management function
MIB	Management information base
MID	Multiplexing identifier
MPEG 1	Motion Picture Editor's Group compression alogrithm 1
MPEG 2	Motion Picture Editor's Group compression alogrithm 2
MPEG 3	Motion Picture Editor's Group compression alogrithm 3
MSS	Metropolitan switching system
MSVC	Metasignaling virtual channel
MT	Message type
N-ISDN	Narrowband integrated services digital network
NIC	Network interface card
NM	Network management
NNI	Network-node interface
NSAP	Network service access point
NVP	Nominal velocity of propagation
OAM	Operations and maintenance
OA&M	Operations, administration, and maintenance
OAM&P	Operations, administration, maintenance, and provisioning
OC-n	Optical carrier level n ($n = 1...256$)
OSI	Open systems interconnect
OSI-RM	Open systems interconnect reference model
PARIS	Packetized automatic routing integrated system
PAS	Packetized elementary stream
PBX	Private branch exchange
PC	Personal computer
PCM	Pulse-code modulation
PCR	Peak cell rate
PD	Protocol discriminator

PDH	Pleisochronous digital hierarchy, e.g., T-carrier
PDU	Protocol data unit
PHY	Physical layer
PLCP	Physical layer convergence protocol
PLOAM	Physical layer operations and maintenance
PLP	Packet layer protocol
PM	Physical media
PMD	Physical media dependent
Pn64	(n multiple ISDN 64-kbps channels)
P-NNI	Private network-node interface
POH	Path overhead
POI	Path overhead indicator
POTS	Plain old telephone service
PS	Program stream
PSVCI	Point-to-point signaling virtual channel identifier
PT	Payload type
PTI	Payload type indicator
PVC	Permanent virtual circuit
Px64	(x multiple ISDN 64-kbps channels)
QOS	Quality of service
RAI	Remote alarm indicator
RAM	Random access memory
RD	Routing domain
RI	Reference indicator
RISC	Reduced instruction set computer
RES	Reserved
SAA	Service aspects and applications
SAAL	Signaling ATM adaptation layer
SAP	Service access point
SAR	Segmentation and reassembly
SCR	Sustainable cell rate
SDH	Synchronous digital hierarchy
SDLC	Synchronous data link control
SDT	Structured data transfer
SDU	Service data unit
SEAL	Simple and efficient adaptation layer
SEL	Selector (NSAP)
SECDED	Single-error correction/double-error detection
SIG	Signaling
SIP	SMDS interface protocol
SMDS	Switched multimegabit data services
SMI	Structure of management information
SN	Sequence number
SNA	Systems network architecture
SNAP	Subnetwork access protocol
SNI	Subscriber-network interface
SNMP	Simple network management protocol
SNP	Sequence number protection
SONET	Synchronous optical network
SPANS	Simple protocol for ATM network signaling

SPE	Synchronous payload envelope
SPID	Service profile identifier
SRTS	Synchronous residual time stamp
SS7	Signaling system number 7
SSCOP	Service-specific connection-oriented protocol
SSCS	Service-specific convergence sublayer
SSM	Single-segment message
ST	Segment type
STM	Synchronous transfer mode
STM-1	Synchronous transfer module level 1 (155.52 Mbps)
STM-2	Synchronous transfer module level 2 (311.04 Mbps)
STM-4	Synchronous transfer module level 1 (622.08 Mbps)
STM-16	Synchronous transfer module level 2 (2488.32 Mbps)
STS	Synchronous transfer signal
STS-1	Synchronous transfer signal level 1 (51.84 Mbps)
STS-2	Synchronous transfer signal level 2 (103.68 Mbps)
STS-3	Synchronous transfer signal level 3 (155.52 Mbps)
STS-3c	Synchronous transfer signal level 3 concatenated
STS-6	Synchronous transfer signal level 6 (311.04 Mbps)
STS-12	Synchronous transfer signal level 12 (622.08 Mbps)
STS-48	Synchronous transfer signal level 48 (2488.32 Mbps)
STS-256	Synchronous transfer signal level 256 (13271.04 Mbps)
STSX-n	Synchronous transfer signal on coax cable level n
SVC	Switched virtual channel or switched virtual circuits
SWG	Subcommittee working group
T-1	First-level T-carrier digital trunk
T-3	Third-level T-carrier digital trunk
TC	Transmission convergence
TCP/IP	Transmission control protocol/internetwork protocol
TDM	Time-division multiplexing
TOH	Transport overhead
TR	Token Ring
TS	Transport stream
TTC	Telecommunications Technical Committee (Japan)
UDP	User datagram protocol
ULP	Upper layer protocol
UNI	User-network interface
UPC	Usage parameter control
UU	User-user interface
VBR	Variable bit rate
VC	Virtual channel
VCC	Virtual channel connection
VCI	Virtual channel identifier
VGA	Videographics adapter
VP	Virtual path
VPC	Virtual path connection
VPI	Virtual path identifier
VPN	Virtual private network
VSTEP	Vertical-to-surface transmission electrophotonic
WAN	Wide area network

Introduction

Technology, Economics, and Society

This book is a complete technical introduction to asynchronous transfer mode (ATM) networks. While there has been an enormous amount of publicity and literature about ATM over the past 2 years, many networking books have not focused on ATM itself. In many cases, ATM is reduced to a chapter or so as part of an overall discussion of "broadband networks" or "fast packet switching," of which ATM is indeed only a part. Even books dedicated to ATM frequently describe ATM from an overview standpoint or, worse, an outdated perspective.

ATM is certainly deserving of a volume all its own. ATM has the promise to be a "transforming technology," one that makes it hard to imagine life in a world without it. However, this usually becomes apparent only in retrospect. Technology is only part of the story of such transforming technologies. They must appear in a context that supports their use and growth. ATM does seem to be appearing at a time that is ripe for change.

The structure of the national network is changing. The term *national network* is not a precise term but rather one used loosely to describe the network that communications carriers have built up over the years from coast to coast. It includes not only the national phone network (both local and interstate) but also such components as private lines leased from these carriers (T1s, T3s, etc.) and other specialty portions such as a public X.25 packet-switched network. The evidence is all around. Pacbell has planned a $20 billion rebuilding of its network, with $5 billion earmarked for AT&T to provide switching equipment based on ATM technology. Phone companies are busily courting cable TV companies, and vice versa. Bell South is installing more fiberoptic cable bandwidth each week than the entire bandwidth of its entire network before fiber.

1

There must be an underlying reason for all these fundamental changes to the structure of the national network. Such a fundamental change must mean that there are fundamental shortcomings and limitations to the network itself. In fact, there are. These shortcomings are technical, but they affect economic and social factors as well. Perhaps it might be best to explore one major aspect of this fundamental change with an analogy.

Suppose you have a friend who decides to start a transportation business. Not just any kind of transportation business: Your friend's motto is "We carry anything!" Your friend calls the business the Synchronous Transfer Mode Company (STM Co.). STM Co. starts out with a fleet of 10 taxis and makes a good profit transporting people to work, shopping, and home again. However, one day there is a customer who needs to take larger groups of people cross-country. A tour group, maybe. Now, 10 taxis in a row is not the best way to transport groups of people, so your friend buys a couple of buses. Then another customer wants to use STM Co. to deliver appliances. Large, bulky goods like refrigerators and stoves will not fit well in taxis or buses, but a couple of trucks will fit the bill.

So far, all seems well at STM Co. A conversation with your friend and several of his customers, however, reveals some limitations to this way of transportation. There are 10 taxis, but most of the time only two or three are in use, so your friend complains that they cannot be used for delivering stoves. Sometimes all 10 are in use, and then customers complain that STM Co. sometimes sends a truck to take them to work. And, of course, if all the buses are on the road, there is no way to take a tour group on a truck and make them happy.

Your friend, as a "service provider," is unhappy because there is no way to shift idle capacity in trucks to the taxi fleet, or to the buses, and so on. Customers, as "service consumers," are unhappy because they frequently cannot get the type of transport that best suits their needs from STM Co.

Maybe there is a better way that addresses these limitations. Therefore, you found Asynchronous Transfer Mode Company (ATM Co.) as a completely different way of transporting anything. At ATM Co., there are no taxis or buses or trucks. There are only four-wheel chassis around the lot, but there are a lot of them. Instead of taxi bodies, bus bodies, or truck bodies, there are a huge number of identical "building blocks," enough for all the wheelbases.

ATM Co. works like this: Whenever a customer calls, depending on whether he or she needs a taxi, a bus, or a truck, you just assemble the parts to make a body that *looks like* a taxi, a bus, or a truck. You place this on a chassis, and off it goes to deliver a person, a group, or a refrigerator. You get maximum use out of the fleet you have, and customers are happier as well. If you ever run out of vehicles, you just order more parts. They are cheap, identical, and interchangeable.

Customers flock to ATM Co., and the company is a great success. Even though STM Co. is still around, when they need an extra bus or truck, they come to ATM Co. and get one. Eventually, of course, all transportation companies will have to model themselves on ATM Co. It just does not make sense to do it anyway else.

This analogy, between synchronous transfer mode (STM) networks and asynchronous transfer mode (ATM) networks, is not precise, but it is not misleading. Later on it will be shown that STM Co. represents a way of building *channelized* networks (the taxis and buses and trucks) and ATM Co. represents a way of building *unchannelized* (there are just "vehicles") networks.

Of course, the analogy presented the technology behind the changes to the national network. There are actually three components present in all these changes and plans. There is the factor of technological capabilities (as above), the factor of economic feasibility, and the important factor of social acceptance. All three factors must be present to justify any radical change in the way things were done before. Whether the change involves motorcars, airplanes, or VCRs, the same three components determine the success of any new invention or industry.

It is not enough to merely have a new technology. Airplanes were wonderful to behold, but it required much more hard work and imagination to eventually lead to frequent flyer clubs and business class travelers. However, technology has the capability of transforming the way people live their lives and may do so to such an extent that people cannot imagine how their parents lived their lives before television, or radio, or electric light. And a transforming technology means that there is no going back, by definition.

The economic factor, however, must always be considered as well. Many promising technologies have languished because the cost remained too high for large-scale deployment without extensive government subsides or incentives. Even electricity, as radical and welcomed a technology as any before or since, needed federal funding to help reach into rural areas on a meaningful scale. And the economics are not only a factor on the retail side. The economic incentive must exist on the side of the technology provider as well. There must be a way of employing the technology in a fashion that both maximizes the profits of service providers and minimizes the expense of service consumers.

The third factor, social acceptance, is the most crucial to the success of any promising transforming technology. The benefits of technology would seem to make this a nonissue. Every technology, every change, has a social price to be paid, however. Sometimes the price is obvious. Automobiles are accepted by the public in despite some 50,000 or so deaths per year. Airplanes fly despite highly publicized plane crashes. Sometimes the price is not so obvious. The use of food preservatives means that not many people are killed by something they eat, but the price is that people will never taste really fresh food again.

There is a disturbing trend toward thinking that social acceptance of a new technology can be won by marketing. Marketing means many things to many people, but the sense employed here is marketing as the art of creating a perceived need for a product or service in the public consciousness. The key word is *perceived*. The public may in fact *not* want nor need the service, but it is nonetheless the job of marketing to generate this need. And it must be generated in sufficient quantity to help the product or service along with the economic feasibility portion of the equation.

The danger lies in the fact that marketing is a notoriously fickle tool. All the marketing hype in the world did not lead to social acceptance of nuclear power plants. The archetypical example in the computer/communications world is Xerox. Xerox pioneered the personal computer (PC), the laser printer, the local area network (LAN), the windows interface, and the mouse. Yet somehow Xerox never managed to make much money at all with any of these transforming technologies.

The lesson of Xerox is also that one technology feeds another, and they may become so entangled that they end up merging into one seamless whole. The PC was a technology for extending the power of a computer to a single user (they were much too expensive previously for just *one* person to use). The laser printer was essentially a Xerox machine without the glass. Since users were now isolated on their PCs, the LAN was invented to tie them together. The PC was still a powerful multiprocessor box, but there was only one monitor. Windowed interfaces allowed more than one program to be displayed. There was only one keyboard as well, so pointing and clicking became a way to focus the keyboard input on a particular window.

The three factors are always at work in bringing or withholding potential transforming technologies from the public.

Thus this transformation of the national network is not surprising. It is natural; it is inevitable. The three factors of change are hard at work today. The technological capability is irresistible. In 1985, Compaq could put on the desktop a PC that was as powerful in terms of instructions per second, memory, and disk storage as the high-end IBM mainframe of 1979. And now there are PC-based supercomputers. It was only a matter of time before the PC revolution began to be applied to the national network as a whole.

The economic factor is feeding off the potential merger of telephone, television, and information networks. Whether this should be called the "information superhighway," video dial tone, or the Sega Channel, the result will be the same. Anyone will be able the watch a movie, play a game, or do their banking through the exact same simple and inexpensive device.

The social factor remains a wild card. The public generally does not demand services so much as adopt them. This is rather like saying that the telephone was invented so that people could make phone calls. Nobody demands movies shown any time of day or night. If such services are available, however, the public may take to them *if* they are not prohibitively expensive or restricted. Technology developers are historically poor marketeers. Digital watches were initially made by computer chip manufacturers, who quickly left the field when they churned out the same numbers of watches month after month and they went unsold. Traditional, analog watchmakers had long ago learned that watches sell only two times a year: graduation and Christmas. They had adjusted production to this schedule long ago.

ATM is the only current technology that has at least two of these three items on its agenda. The technology is there, if still evolving in a standards sense. The economics are there, in the capability of mixing voice, video, and data on the same unchannelized physical network. The social element, with the risky marketing factor, remains problematic for any new technology, not just ATM.

Although ATM networking involves more than just technology, without the technology there is nothing to talk about. This book will address the technology in detail and bring in the economic factors as a side issue. The social acceptability of ATM remains an unknown. In fact, ATM has sometimes been accused of *Field of Dreams* marketing: "If you build it, they will come." This book will help in understanding how ATM networks will work when they are built.

Standards Organizations

This book will describe the technology of ATM, but not just any ATM. It describes the current state of the ATM Forum's ATM standards and proposals. This is an important point.

Several standards organizations have worked over the years to formulate ATM. Among these are the American National Standards Institute (ANSI), which has been active in adapting the ATM protocols and architecture for use in the United States. Much of the work of ANSI somewhat overlaps and in many cases extends the work of other standards organizations. However, the most crucial standards organization for ATM technology has been the Consultative Committee for International Telegraph and Telephone (CCITT).

ATM is based on a series of international standards that first appeared in 1988 as part of the CCITT "Blue Books." The CCITT has recently been renamed the International Telecommunications Union–

Telecommunications Standardization Sector (ITU-TSS), but most people still loosely refer to ATM as a CCITT standard, especially since the change was recent. ATM was the transport mechanism for B-ISDN services, as outlined in a series of "I Standards."

The CCITT met every 4 years. Their standards were then published as a set of manuals with distinctive colors (red for 1984, blue for 1988, etc.). They were a standards organization based on consensus, meaning that all member countries (entire countries, not vendors, are members of the ITU-TSS) had to vote "yes" before a particular protocol became an international standard. If a member country objected to an item in a standard, the objection had to be dealt with, and the entire member community had to repeat the approval process with the changed standard. There was no time limit on this process. There were cases where a country held onto a draft proposal for a standard for 6 months, and then ultimately rejected it because of the spelling in the document.

This pace was all right for the 1970s and 1980s, but the pace of change in computing and communications has accelerated too much in the 1990s. Chip manufacturing giant Intel plans on coming out with a new chip technology every 2 years or so until the year 2000 (386, 486, Pentium, and so on). What ran on a 4-Meg RAM machine last year needs 8 Meg this year. A 120-Meg hard drive must be 200. And the 9600-bps FAX/modem board must be 14,400.

Clearly, if ATM is so good for so many situations, there must be a faster procedure for filling in the gaps of the currently published standards. Perhaps if all the major potential vendors of ATM equipment got together and agreed to flesh out the existing "I Standards" (and the existing ANSI standards as well) in a mutually beneficial way, then the ITU-TSS would catch up later on. There had been mixed success with this approach before. On the one hand, why should the ITU-TSS reinvent the wheel, if everyone is doing it one way already? On the other hand, there is no pressure that can be applied to the ITU-TSS to make sure that the popular way is the way that becomes the standard.

In any case, a small group of potential vendors felt that it had little choice but to go ahead and speed up the standards process in this way.

The ATM Forum

The ATM Forum was founded in October 1991 by four companies who wished to manufacture and sell products compliant with international ATM standards. Unfortunately, the international standards were not very helpful in this regard. Accordingly, these four companies— Adaptive, Cisco, NTI, and US Sprint—decided to take a more active role in the standardization process than with previous technologies. They adapted the simple democratic formula of "majority rules" for adapting specifications. If there are 30 members present and the issue is up for a vote, a "show of hands" suffices. If 16 members vote "yes," 10 vote "no," and 4 abstain, then the motion is carried.

As a consortium of vendors, the ATM Forum is not a standards-making body in the traditional sense. Their charter is "to accelerate the use of ATM products and services through the rapid convergence of interoperability specifications, promotion of industry cooperation, and other activities." This "rapid convergence" involves the proposal, discussion, and adaptation of ATM-related protocols and procedures, which are then applied by the member organizations and proposed to the appropriate international standards-making bodies.

The ATM Forum has grown remarkably in the past 3 years. There are three classes or membership: principal, auditing, and user. There are over 550 member organizations today. The principal members (over 100) are mostly equipment vendors looking to market ATM-compliant products. They vote, attend meetings, and participate in the standardization process. Auditing members (nearly 400) have access to documents generated by the ATM Forum but may not attend meetings, nor can they vote on issues and proposed documents. The user members (relatively new and small in number) are organizations interested in proposing requirements for ATM products and standards.

Although founded in the United States, the ATM Forum is truly an international body. Many European and Japanese corporations are members, and special branches of the Marketing Awareness and Education (MA&E) Committee were formed to address the interests and concerns of these European and Asian companies.

For the most part, ATM Forum documentation is not available to the general public. There are three important exceptions. Late in 1993, the ATM Forum approved three documents for general release, for a modest cost, to anyone who requested them. These three documents are (1) the *ATM User-Network Interface* (UNI) specification, Version 3.0, (2) the *ATM Data eXchange Interface* (DXI) specification, Version 1.0, and (3) the *ATM Broadband-ISDN Inter-Carrier Interface* (B-ICI) specification, Version 1.0. All three will be dealt with at some length in this book.

Although not technically a standards organization, the ATM Forum is organized along the lines of one (see Figure 1). The seven-member board of directors oversees the work of the Technical Committee, the Market Awareness and Education (MA&E) Committee, and the Enterprise Network Roundtable (ENR) Committee. The ENR Committee handles the details of the requirements submitted through the user members and has its own Education Group besides. The three ENR Working Groups provide ATM users with a means of expressing requirements for ATM technology. They also enable ATM users with a venue to collaborate and share experiences in migrating to ATM equipment and platforms. The

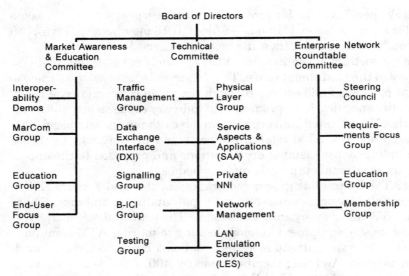

Figure 1 ATM Forum organization.

MA&E Committee deals with the promotion and demonstration of ATM as a workable technology. As such, the MA&E Committee is mainly responsible for organizing and implementing many ATM technology demonstrations at conferences and trade shows, as well as all public relations. The committee also provides market research results to ATM Forum members on industry needs for ATM and stages interoperability demos.

The great bulk of the actual proposal work, and to many the main reason that the ATM Forum exists, is done by the Technical Committee Working Groups. There are currently 10 major Subcommittee Working Groups (SWGs). The 10 groups are:

1. The Physical Layer (PHY) Group, in charge of all specifications regarding the sending of ATM information over physical media such as fiberoptic cable, unshielded twisted-pair cable, and the like.

2. The Service Aspects and Applications (SAA or SA&A) Group, in charge of all specifications regarding the services that ATM networks must provide to users.

3. The Private Network Node Interface (P-NNI) Group, in charge of all specifications regarding the interfaces between ATM equipment operating without the need for a public ATM network (e.g., on a single-customer premises).

4. The Network Management (NM) Group, in charge of all specifications regarding the structure and operation of network management software and hardware in an ATM network.

5. The Traffic Management (TRAFFIC) Group, in charge of all specifications regarding the handling of connections and congestion in an ATM network.

6. The Data eXchange Interface (DXI) Group, in charge of all specifications regarding the DXI arrangement, a means of dividing the task of connecting to an ATM network between several pieces of equipment.

7. The Signaling (SIG) Group, in charge of all specifications regarding the establishment and use of a standard protocol for signaling between all types of ATM equipment.

8. The Testing (TEST) Group, in charge of all specifications regarding the compliance of vendor's equipment with ATM standards and the testing of this equipment for interoperability.

9. The Broadband-ISDN Inter-Carrier Interface (B-ICI) Group, in charge of all specifications regarding the interoperability and connectivity requirements between ATM networks operated by different public network service providers.

10. The Local Area Network (LAN) Emulation Services (LES) Group, in charge of all specifications regarding the use of ATM networks, both public and private, for LAN connectivity.

In practice, all the groups share information and results with each other. There is considerable overlap between the several groups' activities. For instance, it is hard to specify testing suites without knowing exactly what media (e.g., cable) are supported or not at the physical layer.

This book will emphasize the activities of the ATM Forum in general and the Technical Committees specifically. In this case it differs from previous ATM books that have traditionally emphasized ITU-TSS (formerly CCITT) activities and standards. With the ATM Forum assuming a leadership role, however, this seems the only feasible approach today.

Networking and ATM Networking

Channelized Networking

When a person picks up the telephone, he or she gets a dial tone. He or she dials a number, and the phone at the other end rings.

Other times people may access a data network. In a corporation, the personal computer (PC) on an employee's desk may be attached to a local area network (LAN, e.g., an Ethernet LAN), and all the LANs in the corporation may be connected through an internetwork of routers using leased lines. At home, the employee may dial in through a PC to a service such as Compuserve or Prodigy and access the Internet to send and get electronic mail.

In the evening, many people may sit back and enjoy television, either through the broadcast networks or, increasingly, through a cable TV connection.

Whether an employee of a corporation or a person at home, people seldom think about the massive amount of equipment, computing power, and personnel that are required to build and operate such networks to give such cheap and reliable service.

In the past, such networks have always been built separately. There is a voice network, and a data network, and a TV network. Even when a corporation needs to link the company PBXs (private branch exchanges) together, or build a client-server data network for their LANs, or support videoconferencing between cities, all these networks are built, operated, and controlled individually.

This can lead to enormous duplications of effort and cost outlays. The most common way of building networks today in a corporate environment is with T-1 leased lines running at 1.544 megabits per second (Mbps), channelized into 24 channels running at 64 kilobits per second (kbps) (DS-0). These channels are completely isolated from each other. Typically, some corporate planning group will lease a T-1 circuit to a building and then parcel out the channels among the users.

For example, the 24 DS-0s may be assigned as follows. Six channels may be given to the PBXs for tie lines in the corporation. Six channels may be given to the data network to link the site's routers together to form a LAN internetwork. Six channels may be used for videoconferencing. The final six channels may be used to support the corporate System Network Architecture (SNA) network or may be reserved for future growth of network applications.

Another important aspect of building networks like this, especially when contrasted with how ATM networks are built, is the fact that these networks are built for peak-load conditions. Someone had to decide that six channels is the right number for the tie lines or for the data networks. Data networks are configured for "busy hour" traffic. This is the time of day when 20 percent or more of the work may be done and the network is usually pushed to its limit. Depending on the industry, there may be two busy hours per day (e.g., 9 to 10 a.m. and then 4 to 5 p.m.) and even busy days or weeks (e.g., last week of a quarter). The voice network in America is designed for the busiest day of the year—Mother's Day. Whether voice or data, this means that most of the time large amounts of bandwidth sit idle. But they still must be purchased and maintained.

There is nothing wrong with building networks this way, but the duplication of effort and waste of monetary resources can quickly become apparent. There are very few people on the phone at 3 o'clock in the morning, but the night shift is busily backing up the network servers over the router-based network. Yet there is no easy way of taking these channels and their assigned bandwidth from the PBX tie-line network and giving it the router network to use. The same holds true for the video-conferencing channels. And when there are a number of

employees on the phone from site to site and yet little data traffic on the router network, there is no easy way to reassign the
data channels to the voice network.

Clearly, in such a situation there may be an economic incentive to find a way for assigning bandwidth on an "as needed"
basis. If the channels are in use only 50 percent of the time,
only half the total bandwidth (12 channels instead of 24) is
needed. The problem is that no easy way exists today to
"dynamically" assign the bandwidth in this way. If bandwidth
is assigned dynamically, this is known as flexible bandwidth
allocation. (Many times the term bandwidth on demand is
used, but this implies the creation of bandwidth where none
exists.) In the channelized networks of today, the bandwidth
the channels represent is assigned in a "static" fashion. If a
channel is idle, a special idle bit pattern is sent in the channel.

The corporation is billed by the bandwidth it purchased, not
the usage of this bandwidth. Less bandwidth needed translates into a cost savings. And the service provider has an
incentive as well. More customers can be supported on a given
link, which will maximize their revenues. Running new facilities is a major expense for service providers.

ATM networking is a sophisticated way of letting both companies and service providers build unchannelized networks to
make more efficient use of the underlying bandwidth on the
network. It is not magic, it is not hype—it is very real.

And if the current environment of service providers for voice
networks, data networks, and TV networks changes to one of
combined voice/data/video service providers, then this is just
an added incentive. As a general rule, whenever there are network devices that must support many different services and
user communities at the same time, ATM can provide a cost-
effective way of doing so.

Almost all networks today are built up from channelized,
point-to-point, leased digital T-1 links. There are observers
who argue that ATM is not needed to provide the economic
benefit of unchannelized bandwidth allocation. What is really
needed, they say, is extremely cheap bandwidth. They cannot
see the need for essentially rebuilding this national network of
T-1s that has been slowly built up over the past 30 years.

However, the network has always been rebuilt. There is
nothing sacred about the national network of T-1s in place
today. It is merely the "transfer mode" of the network most pro-
fessionals have grown up with and feel most comfortable working with. But there have been others before, and ATM may
only be the next.

ATM Networking

ATM stands for asynchronous transfer mode. *The* asynchronous *has little to do with the term* asynchronous *as applied to
PC modem communication. (The term* asynchronous *has more
meanings in networking than almost any other.) The* asynchronous *in ATM just refers to the way in which ATM achieves
its unchannelized bandwidth allocation.*

*The official definition of ATM from the CCITT Blue Books is
"a multiplexing technique in which a transmission capability
is organized in undedicated slots filled with cells with respect
to each application's instantaneous real need" (CCITT I.113, p.
2). There's actually more, but this is the main point. The
"undedicated slots" are specifically meant to contrast with the
channels of "circuit transfer mode."* Circuit transfer mode *is
defined as "a transfer mode in which transmission and switching functions are achieved by permanent allocation of chan-
nels/bandwidth between the connections" (CCITT I.113, p. 2).
This circuit transfer mode is the essence of the way networks
are built today with channelized T-1 links. The circuit switches are very fast, since all they do is take every bit from an input
port to an output in the least amount of time.*

*Another benefit of ATM networks is that the network no
longer needs to be configured for peak load. In the preceding
example of channelized networking, the six channels assigned
were a maximum, hit perhaps once or twice a day (in fact,
some networks are designed to never hit the maximum, thus
providing built-in "spare capacity").*

*ATM provides a way to build these networks not based on
the peak traffic demand but on some other, lesser value, closer
to the average. The task now becomes just what value below
the peak to build the network for, but at least this becomes possible with ATM.*

*Thus ATM networking is the technology that enables infor-
mation to be transported from place to place in these "undedicated slots filled with cells" as opposed to the older technology
with "permanent allocation of channels/bandwidth."*

*While this helps to explain what ATM is, it does not help
much to explain where ATM came from or why it is a natural
evolution of past networks. The key term for understanding the
evolution of ATM networking is the* transfer mode *part. Just
what is a transfer mode?*

Older "Transfer Mode" Networks

The 1988 I-series standard recommendation from CCITT included a document named *Vocabulary Terms for Broadband Aspects of ISDN* (I.113). While the term *asynchronous transfer mode* is defined, the definition emphasizes the *asynchronous* aspect of ATM. In Section 2.2 ("Interfaces, Channels and Transfer Modes"), term 202 defines ATM as "a transfer mode in which the information is organized into cells; it is asynchronous in the sense that the recurrence of cells containing information from an individual user is not necessarily periodic." The term *transfer mode* is never defined by itself in the document.

This has meant that the term means slightly different things to different people. For example, DePrycker (DePrycker, 1994, p. 48) defines a transfer mode as a "technique used in a telecommunications network, covering aspects related to transmission, multiplexing and switching." He then proceeds to define circuit switching (dedicated, point-to-point paths), packet switching (multiplexed paths for packetized data), and so forth as examples of "transfer modes."

Handel and Huber (Handel and Huber, 1994, p. 14) take a slightly different approach. To them, a transfer mode is a "specific way of transmission and switching information in a network." They then proceed to break transfer modes down into asynchronous (ATM) and synchronous (STM).

Other authors have more or less followed one or the other of these interpretations. For instance, to one (Onvural, 1994, p. 13) it is a "technique used for transmission, multiplexing, and switching aspects of communications networks." To me this means circuit switching, message switching, and packet switching in broad terms.

The point is that ATM is not the only transfer mode possible. And obviously, there is a great deal of interpretation when seeking examples for the term. For the moment, the term *transfer mode* will be defined as a technique used in a telecommunications network for transmission and switching that defines just how information must be packaged, sent, and received on the network. And as examples of different transfer modes, the "telegraph transfer mode" and the "telephone transfer mode," as well the synchronous transfer mode (STM) and the asynchronous transfer mode (ATM), will be considered.

These four technologies form a natural evolution of networks from the 1840s to the 1990s and beyond. ATM promises to be to STM what jet planes were to propeller aircraft. And many of the same issues that were addressed in the transitional periods from one technology to another will be addressed with regard to ATM as well.

Imagine an all-digital, unchannelized, national network that people may use to sell their goods and services to others and even pay their bills. The network is much faster than anything that has ever existed and is used for both business and private citizens. It was enormously expensive to build, so extensive government funds were employed to keep deployment costs down. Even so, it was hard for the operators of the network to make any profit at all initially, until several "killer applications" came along. These applications, uses for the network that were dreamed of but never really demanded in any sense by the public, so transformed American life that it was hard to imagine a world before the network existed.

This network does not exist, but it does not exist because it has not been built. It does not exist because it has been built, enjoyed a long and productive life, and then was replaced by new technology. This has not been a description of the Internet, nor the "information superhighway," nor a national ATM network. *This was the telegraph.*

1.1   The "Telegraph Transfer Mode" Network

The first national network built in the United States for telecommunications purposes was the telegraph network. It was built on the principles of Samuel Finley Breese Morse, but it was not the first national telecommunications network in the world.

The first national telecommunications networks were built in Europe during the late 1700s and early 1800s. These were true data networks and were commonly known as "optical telegraph" networks. These optical telegraphs were sophisticated semaphore systems capable of sending messages across hundreds of kilometers in an hour or so. The message speeds were limited by the need to relay the messages from tower to tower along the route and the complexity of the encoded message. But these systems were much faster than any other form of communications available.

The most elaborate systems were built in France and Sweden. Although similar in function and concept, the two differed greatly in appearance. The French system of Claude Chappe consisted of crossarms and pulleys. Demonstrated publicly on March 2, 1791, it could take 4 minutes to transmit a message such as "If you succeed, you will bask in glory." The messages were sent as a series of numbers, which had to be looked up in code books and written down. Nonetheless, the French government enthusiastically embraced the system, and by 1810 it had spread out from Paris to the borders of Italy, Germany, Belgium, and the Atlantic Coast.

By 1799, the code books had grown to three volumes with 25,392 entries. This clearly pointed out the need for a system that was based not on codes but on alphabetical representations, but this possibility was never explored. Besides, the use of code numbers provided a measure of security for what was essentially a broadcast medium. By 1800, the maximum speed attainable for a message was about 20 characters per minute, or 160 bits per second (bps) in modern terms. At its peak, in 1852, the French system linked 29 cities, consisted of 556 stations, and comprised 4800 km of "lines."

The Swedish system was deployed partly because of the success of the French. In fact, by 1840 almost every European country was employing some form of optical telegraph for military or governmental communication. The Swedish system was based on a system of shutters instead of crossarms, but the elaborate codings remained a constant. The prime mover was the nobleman Abraham Edelcrantz. While not as widely deployed as the French system, the Swedish system did eventually cover some 200 km by 1809.

Several important concepts and advances came out of these first data networks. The idea of compressing information (the code books) was proven to be a vital and viable concept. The whole area of error recovery and flow control (a sender must never overwhelm a receiver) was pioneered in these early systems. And the concept of encrypting sensitive information was first used on a large and systematic scale on these networks.

England, Germany, and even Russia had similar optical telegraph systems, but none achieved the penetration of the French and Swedish systems. By 1881, however, with the demise of the last three signaling towers in the Swedish system, the era came to an end. The towers were neglected and forgotten, and even the important role of the optical telegraph in data networking faded from memory.

The attention of the industry shifted to the electrical telegraph.

The first practical electrical telegraphs merely translated the codings of the optical systems to a new medium. The semaphore towers were replaced by pole-mounted strands of copper and iron (cheaper and stronger) wire.

As soon as electricity was shown to be a predictable physical entity by scientists such as Michael Faraday, engineers began working on schemes to use it to send messages over the wires. One of the earliest proposals was by William Sturgeon, the inventor of the practical electromagnet using copper wire. In 1822, Francis Ronalds approached the British Admiralty with a design for an "electric telegraph" (as opposed to "optical") based on Sturgeon's electromagnet. Electrodes were used to point to letters or numbers at each end. Ronalds ran 8 miles of wire around his estate at Hammersmith for demonstrations. Ultimately, however, the Admiralty decided that the electric telegraph was "wholly unnecessary," since Britain was well served by the existing optical system begun in 1796, closely modeled on the French system.

One important side effect of this activity was the exposure of people to this new technology. In 1824, a New York University art professor named Samuel Finley Breese Morse attended a lecture on electromagnetism, which set his mind in motion, as so many others. The limitations of communication over distance were made painfully obvious to Morse in the following year. His wife died when he was out of town, and it took days for him to learn of it.

In 1831, Joseph Henry set up a 1-mile-long electromagnetic telegraph in Albany, New York. Henry's device used clicks and bell rings to show that a sender was present, but he never filed for a patent nor explored more practical uses for his device. In fact, Henry never even bothered to encode the signals sent by his device. Remote bell ringing remained its sole accomplishment. Morse's thoughts on telegraph systems became more determined and clearer in 1832 when he was returning from Europe. The shipboard talk revolved more and more around communication by means of electric signals over wire, and Morse was inspired to pursue his ideas in a more systematic fashion. By 1837, his ideas had reached the patentable stage. He had strung 1700 feet of wire around his room at New York University. That same year, he staged a public demonstration of his device.

Also in 1837, in England, Charles Wheatstone and William Cooke combined their independent efforts and set up a British electric telegraph. With Joseph Henry as a visitor, the two Englishmen developed what came to be known as the "ABC telegraph." It employed five "needles" to point to letters and numbers on cards under the needles. This synchronized rotation limited the speed at which the device could operate, and this soon became the most serious obstacle to large-scale deployment.

Morse also had grappled with this problem in the United States. His associate and assistant, Alfred Vail, soon hit on an ideal solution. Instead of transferring coded letters and numbers, which had to be looked up in voluminous code books, Vail represented simple text by means of dots and dashes, where a dash was defined as three times the duration of a dot. A spool of paper at the receiver printed out the dots and dashes as they were sent. This Morse code telegraph seriously challenged the British five-needle telegraphic system both in terms of speed and ease of use. By 1845, when Wheatstone and Cooke quarreled over who had invented what, the American Morse code became the de facto universal standard for electrical telegraph systems.

Having now demonstrated a practical digital communications system, where the dots and dashes could be easily thought of as the 0s and 1s of modern binary codes, Morse took the next logical step. He approached the federal government, naturally assuming that such a system of nearly instantaneous communication would be of interest to a country that was rapidly expanding to continental dimensions. He was right.

In 1838, Morse demonstrated a working telegraph to a congressional committee in the Capitol building in Washington, D.C. By this time, the telegraph was working over 10 miles of wire filling the room. After some delay and bickering, including seriously proposed amendments for funding to study hypnotism and the possibility of the end of the world in 1844, in March of 1843, Congress approved $30,000 for a telegraph line to be run between Washington, D.C., and Baltimore, Maryland. This 40-mile run would be a true test of the technology's capabilities.

The project did not proceed smoothly. Morse tried to lay the insulated telegraph wire inside a pipe run alongside the right-of-way of the Baltimore and Ohio railroad, but the spring rains and defective wire conspired to end the project with only a few miles installed. Down to his last $7,000, and aware that the future of his invention depended on the success of the project, Morse reluctantly pulled up the wire and ran it on poles alongside the tracks instead.

Even before the project was completed, Morse had the opportunity to demonstrate the telegraph's "killer application," a use so unique that the telegraph became a requirement and not merely an expensive luxury to most Americans. In the spring of 1844, both major political parties in the United States at the time, the Whigs and the Democrats, had their nominating conventions for the presidential elections that year in Baltimore. When the Whigs gathered in May, the telegraph had only reached Annapolis Junction, about halfway from Washington. Morse, desperate to show the utility of his invention, arranged for Alfred Vail to meet the train from Baltimore back to Washington there. As the train passed by, Vail asked who had been nominated. "Clay and Frelinghuysen!" one of the delegates shouted back.

Henry Clay for president was no surprise, but the nomination of Theodore Frelinghuysen for vice-president was a real shock. Vail tapped out the news to Morse at the Capitol, and when the delegates arrived with their astonishing news, they were the ones who were surprised instead. Everyone had already heard the news. This first application of "electronic mail" made a lasting impression on many influential people.

The first official "telegram" was sent on May 24, 1844, between Vail at the Baltimore and Ohio Mount Clare railroad station and Morse in the Supreme Court chamber of the Capitol. The famous message "What hath God wrought?" was not a Morse inspiration. To prevent possible collusion, the assembled dignitaries in Washington decided to go along with Morse's suggestion that a spur-of-the-moment message be sent and returned. The expression was selected by Annie Ellsworth, daughter of a government official who was a longtime friend of Morse. Vail immediately echoed it back, and the witnesses cheered.

If there was any doubt as to the utility of the telegraph, they were laid to rest when the Democrats met in Baltimore that summer. This time, the vice-presidential nominee was not even in Baltimore but remained in Washington. When the telegraph clicked out that Senator Silas Wright was to be the running mate of James K. Polk, Wright astonished one and all by refusing. The telegraph was still so new that when word of Wright's decision was telegraphed back to Baltimore, the convention halted while a delegation was dispatched by train to verify the message's content. No one doubted the telegraph after that. The two national conventions of 1844 became the defining moment of the telegraph as a transforming technology.

So far Morse's telegraph had passed two tests with flying colors. It was a viable technology, and it was socially acceptable. The question of economic viability, however, was still an issue. The line was paid for, true enough, and the batteries only added minimally to operating expenses. The main expense was in personnel to operate the telegraph equipment at each end.

Morse tried to sell the whole thing to the government for a fixed price of $100,000, but the deal fell through. The Washington end of the line was moved to the city post office building, and it operated for free to the public for almost a year. Finally, on April 1, 1845, a charge of 1 cent for every 4 characters sent was imposed by Morse's Magnetic Telegraph Company. The public, which had been playing chess games over the wire, immediately found alternate means of communication adequate. Total revenue for the first 4 business days was 1 cent.

Business soon picked up again, and by the end of April, the telegraph had taken in a sum total of $21.23. At that rate, the original investment would be recovered in 118 years. In fact, by October, the total revenue of $413 barely cut into the $3925 of operating expenses. The postmaster general, Cave Johnson, in his annual report, was under the impression that whatever the rate, the telegraph would never be profitable.

Morse was not discouraged. By May of 1845, he had extended the line to Philadelphia. It cost about $50 per mile to build a telegraph line, so expanding service was not an enormous burden. Other telegraph companies sprung up, linking Buffalo, New York, and Boston, Massachusetts, by 1846. In 1847, the lines stretched west all the way to St. Louis,

Missouri. New York and Chicago were linked the same year. Newspapers in both cities decided to use the line to share information, and so the Associated Press was formed. Many newspapers took on the designation *Daily Telegraph* to emphasize the origin of their news. Business use of the telegraph far outstripped personal use.

Rates remained based on message size. In England, by contrast, two networks had been set up by September of 1847. The rate structure of the Electric Telegraph Company was based on distance, and this proved too expensive for most potential customers. By 1850, a maximum rate of 10s was imposed, and this was dropped to 2s by 1860.

Message transfer remained slow, mostly due to the laborious task of interpreting the paper-tape dots and dashes into letters and words. In 1848, a 15-year-old boy in Louisville, Kentucky, became a celebrity of sorts when he demonstrated the odd ability to interpret Morse code directly by ear alone. Soon this became common, and speeds of 25 to 30 words per minute were achievable. Figuring a 5-character word, this rate of almost 20 "bits" per second is impressive for its day. It compares very favorably with the 2.67-bits-per-second rate of optical telegraphs. By 1858, newer mechanical senders and receivers boosted the rate on the telegraph lines up to 267 bits per second.

Data compression was used on the telegraph lines as well. There was no systematic code use, but an ad hoc abbreviated writing taken from the newspaper industry was widely used. Known as *Phillips code,* after the Associated Press' Walter P. Phillips, operators could tap out "Wr u ben?" for "Where have you been?" and even "gx" for "great excitement." The code was only used internally, and customers were still charged by the word.

There were exceptions to the basic rates, especially on "special" lines. When the first transcontinental link was opened in 1861 between New York and San Francisco (on Telegraph Hill, of course), the government subsidized the link to keep the cost down to $3 for 10 words. But the company immediately charged $1 a word, claiming cost overruns.

By 1873, Western Union, an amalgam of many smaller telegraph companies, was handling 90 percent of all telegrams. Their assets were close to $40 million, an enormous amount for the day. Western Union had increased its capital by 11,000 percent in the preceding 10 years. They were adding about 19,000 miles of wire per year to the network, at a cost now of between $100 and $150 per mile.

The success of the telegraph spawned a whole new kind of business as well. In 1886, a young telegraph operator named Richard Sears took possession of a shipment of watches refused by a local jeweler. Using his telegraph, he soon sold them all to fellow operators and railroad employees. In 6 months, he had made $5,000, quit his job, and founded the company that later became Sears, Roebuck, and Company. Another "killer application" had been found.

The telegraph implemented its own transfer mode. The wires were manufactured and installed to be optimal for telegraph signaling. The end equipment, senders and receivers, was universally adapted to Morse code. The only way information moved around the network was by means of dots and dashes. Everything had to conform to this transfer mode.

This was the national network in the 1870s—an all-digital, unchannelized national network that the public used to sell goods as well as to communicate. The initial deployment expenses were kept down by government funding, but the "killer applications" of messaging and telegraphic marketing quickly became sources of profit to the operators. The country would never be the same again.

1.2   The "Telephone Transfer Mode" Network

Even as the telegraph was becoming an indispensable part of all citizens' lives, the public began to look beyond the telegraph. If a telegraph could send messages by clicks and taps, which were just sounds after all, why not just send the whole voice? As early as 1854, suggestions were made to make this possible. Perhaps silver and zinc plates could be held in the mouth and hooked up to a telegraph line. Then the receiver might produce voice instead of dots and dashes.

The extent of excitement of the public imagination was illustrated in 1866, when a series of articles chronicling the exploits of one Joshua Coppersmith appeared in many New York City newspapers. Supposedly, this gentleman was convicted of fraud for exhibiting a device he called a "telephone," which adapted the principles of the electric telegraph for the sending of human voice through a wire. The problem was that no one named Joshua Coppersmith was ever proven to have existed, and no record of such a court action was ever found. This whole incident was a legend, but one that served the same function as legends today: It outlined a story that, even if not true, people firmly believed and desired to be true.

Thus the social acceptance of voice communication was established long before a young teacher of the deaf named Alexander Graham Bell sat down in an office in Boston and tried to solve a problem that had been vexing the telegraph for years. The problem was that telegraph lines were inherently unchannelized. That is, only one telegraph message could be transmitted at a time. The others had to wait until the operator finished tapping out the current message. If some way could be found to multiplex the telegraph signals on the wire, then many messages could be sent simultaneously. This would make more effective use of the single strand of telegraph wire, and short messages would not have to be delayed until longer ones were finished.

Bell ultimately failed. Tuning forks seemed promising, but to work they required enough bandwidth in the wire to respond to different signal frequencies. In seeking to expand the available bandwidth of the telegraph circuit to accommodate many simultaneous signals, he accidentally tightened a screw too tight and ended up with an arrangement that would send human speech across the wire.

Bell's invention of the "harmonic telegraph" in 1876 hardly measured up to Joshua Coppersmith's legend. Only Bell could speak loudly enough to be heard at any distance, and only the enthusiasm of Emperor Dom Pedro of Brazil at Bell's exhibit at the Centennial Exposition in Philadelphia convinced Bell's backers to continue their financial support. Better transmitters soon helped the volume problem.

Very early in the history of the telephone, in 1877, Bell's backers, eager to make good on their investment, offered the Bell telephone patents to the Western Union Telegraph Company for $100,000. The Western Union president refused. Later that year, Bell replaced his Patent Association with his own Bell Telephone Company. By 1878, the whole system had grown to 1000 phones, and the first switch was installed in Hartford, Connecticut.

Connections were made by hand by the switchboard operators. Young men were used as operators until their tobacco-chewing, foul-mouthed ways and relaxed work ethic forced their replacement by more sweet-voiced and tractable young women. For years, the only respectable work a young lady could find was at the local Bell system office. Connections were requested by the subscribers, by name. It soon grew difficult to keep track of the growing client list, so the connectors on the operators' switchboards were numbered sequentially. At first some customers resisted, but once the advantage of fewer wrong connections became obvious, telephone numbers were accepted by the public in 1879.

The economics of the telephone worked differently than the telegraph. The telegraph was never intended by its developers to extend to residential use. Everyone could not be expected to learn Morse code, and there was no real equivalent of the switch in the telegraph world. There was no easy way to take a telegraph message from one source and send it out to one of several possible destinations. This was all done by manually relaying messages through the system.

Everybody could talk, however. Bell at first targeted the telephone for business use. He saw it as an easy way for retailers to contact suppliers, much as the telegraph was used. The general public wrote letters to communicate. The telegraph was only needed for situations of a particular urgency. Most areas had two mail deliveries per day, one in the morning and one again in the afternoon, just in case someone had written in the meantime. Others saw much more potential for the telephone than just for businesses.

Bell's company leased the telephones to users. They would have otherwise been prohibitively expensive, it was felt, and this emphasized the company's "service" position. The charge was set at $40 per year for business use and $20 per year for home. The distinction was based on anticipated utility and ability to pay. A residence had few users, but a business had many more potential users of the telephone.

So far the telephone hardly seemed a threat to the telegraph. Bought mostly by the well-to-do and technically curious, it still seemed that most communications situations were best handled by going down to the local Western Union office and sending a telegram. Local messengers rushed off to the home of the recipient.

In January of 1878, the "killer application" for the telephone arrived. A serious train wreck occurred near Tariffville, Connecticut, just outside Hartford. The local druggist had phone lines available directly to all the local doctors, in the business use model that Bell had championed. In this case, the druggist was able to summon all the doctors to the crash site almost immediately. The obvious advantage of direct voice communication over a messaging service was dramatically pointed out.

By 1880, there were some 50,000 telephones in the United States. There also were nagging technical problems that threatened to limit telephone use to local areas. Early telephone systems used rented telegraph wires. Naturally, these were "telegraph transfer mode" links, consisting of a single strand of copper or iron wire with what was known as a *ground return*. While quite efficient for the intermittent dots and dashes of the telegraph, these circuits formed long antennas when converted to telephone use. Every rumble of thunder within 30 miles caused the voice on the circuit to dissolve in a burst of static. When adjacent wires were chattering with telegraph signals, the phone users heard this too, through a phenomena known as *cross talk* caused by electromagnetic induction.

The problem was solved in 1881 when a technician named John Carty, exasperated by the poor sound quality on a wire running the 45 miles from Providence to Boston, accidentally hooked up two wires between the telephones. By not disconnecting the first telegraph wire before trying the second to check for a better voice connection, Carty invented the *isolated metallic ground* circuit that dramatically reduced noise.

Another sticky problem was the use of iron wire. Much cheaper and stronger than copper wire, iron wire was used extensively in the telegraph network. Although quickly covered with a layer of rust, "open" (uninsulated) iron wire remained the medium of choice for many telegraph runs. However, copper wire seemed much better for the newer two-wire "paired" voice circuits. Fortunately, in 1884, a new method of hard-drawing copper resulted in a copper wire that was as strong as iron and yet cheap enough to run economically just for voice networks.

The use of copper soon made longer runs, such as from New York to Boston (292 miles), possible.

Soon afterwards, it was discovered that twisting the two wires in a pair virtually eliminated the annoying crosstalk among closely packed wires. The newer twisted-pair wire made cables (specially constructed packages with many wire pairs) possible. And cables made deployment of multiple-voice paths more efficient and therefore less expensive. Cables were more protected from environmental damage as well.

These two developments, the use of twisted-wire pairs for voice and the use of copper in that wire, marked the first physical differences between transmission networks built for telegraph and those built for voice. The "telephone transfer mode" was slowly evolving.

By 1890, the number of telephones had grown to 250,000. New York and Chicago were linked by 1892. Nebraska, Minnesota, and Texas had service by 1897. The nation was crossed in 1915. Again, San Francisco and New York were linked. Telephone use exploded with the expiration of Bell's original patents in the early 1900s. Now anyone could build and operate a phone company, and many people did. The telephone had arrived.

The first calls from New York to San Francisco took 23 minutes to switch by hand from switchboard to switchboard and cost $20.70. It seemed expensive, even then, and it was. The Bell system really had little idea how much to charge for phone service, and local rates varied widely. At late as 1923, the Bell system followed 206 different local rate structures, with some places being charged three times what others were for the same basic service. Rates were set based on the community's ability to pay, historical reasons, and sometimes just simple greed. Candidly, many executives admitted that telephone service was overpriced. The vast profits fueled further network expansion and research into improved equipment.

The technology of the telephone network continued to advance. Dial phones replaced hand cranks, and switches became automated to break strikes by the unionized operators. By the 1930s, the situation of the telegraph and telephone companies had completely reversed itself. The national network was now based on the telephone transmission and switching system instead of the telegraph. Ownership passed to telephone operating companies, and instead of phones over rented telegraph lines, telegrams now rode over rented voice lines from the phone companies. The "telephone transfer mode" network was in place. No information flowed without keeping the transmission and switching techniques of the voice network in mind.

The network was now analog, not digital, as was the telegraph network. Analog signals vary continuously and not discretely. A receiver must not just distinguish between a 0 (or dot) and a 1 (or dash) but among an infinite number of possible values (was it 0.1342 or 0.1343?). This did not seem like much of a limitation in the early part of the century. By 1939, however, forces were gathering to push the next great evolution in the national network to the forefront.

1.3   The Digital and Fiber Revolution

Between 1939 and 1945, the economy of the United States doubled, fueled by the urgent needs of production for World War II. Things hardly paused after the war, and between 1945 and 1960, the economy doubled again. This quadrupling of the gross national product in 21 years had two lasting effects. First, it caused a whole generation to look on the 1950s in America as a kind of "Golden Age," which it was. Second, it resulted in a tremendous pressure on social institutions, government agencies, and service corporations to expand their facilities to handle the growth, which, of course, was assumed in the 1960s to be the way things should be.

One of the most seriously affected service companies was the phone company. In 1939, only some 40 percent of households had telephones. The percentage was higher among businesses, but most families, especially working-class families, simply did not see the need to expend scarce monetary resources on a telephone. However, by 1960, almost everyone had a telephone, and the newfound wealth of America fed the demand.

The service demand led to a revolution of sorts in the telephone transfer mode national network. Strangely, it was not the end-user phone subscribers who were affected at all. They continued to pick up the phone, dial, and talk just as they always had. The difference was in the way the voice was transported and switched within the network itself.

In 1939, in England, an engineer named Alec Reeves invented a method for converting analog voice signals into digital signals represented by a string of 0s and 1s. He did so mainly to try to overcome the limitations of analog receiving equipment in the presence of noise (an unwanted, interfering signal). Digital receivers proved more resilient with higher noise levels on the link. There were other advantages as well, but of lesser importance. The method came to be known as *pulse-code modulation* (PCM) and was not exactly embraced initially.

An analog voice conversation had to be "sampled," "quantized," and "coded." In other words, the continuously varying input signals had to be measured at frequent intervals, the signal strength expressed as a number, and then the number represented as a string of 0s and 1s. This string was then transmitted sequentially, one bit a time, to the receiver unit, where the electronic equivalent of graphing was done to reproduce the string of numbers as a continuously varying voice signal once again. This whole process proved slow and expensive with available vacuum tube technology, and the resulting 0s and 1s required much more bandwidth than the original analog signal occupied. However, if bandwidth and equipment could be made cheap enough, all the advantages of digital communication would make PCM an attractive method for transmitting voice.

The economic environment of the 1960s in America provided both. The vacuum tube had been replaced by the ubiquitous and cheap transistor, itself the product of the Bell system. Transistors were used more and more frequently in new devices known as *computers,* named not for their computational abilities (which mathematicians sneered at) but because they replaced the GI job description of "computer" with a machine.

The computer and PCM contributed greatly to the next step in the evolving national network. Two huge problems had sprung up in trying to expand the telephone network facilities fast enough to keep pace with the growing economy. The first problem involved a need for capacity. Obviously, more phones meant more people *on* the phone. This was fine, since it generated more revenue, but it generated a high demand on the links between switching offices, the "trunks" of the phone network. Typically, the number of trunks installed between two offices was based on a statistical analysis of the potential "traffic" between them. If, for example, it was determined that revenues would be maximized between two offices if six trunks for six simultaneous voice conversations were installed, then that was done. Cable was installed, either above ground on poles or, increasingly in urban areas, below ground in conduits.

Care was taken to ensure that the traffic analysis was correct, for if the trunk demand for service exceeded the supply, revenues were lost until more trunks could be run.

By the mid-1960s, urban areas were literally saturated with telephone cable. There was nowhere left to run more wire or more cable or more conduit. The streets were pretty well full. And even if more streets were dug up, or dug deeper, this merely postponed the problem, which was to find a way to get more capacity out of existing wires. And for future expansion, a medium would be welcomed that took up less space than the bulky cables currently in use.

The digital PCM method offered a possible solution. It turned out that newer transmission equipment could not only efficiently convert analog signals to 0s and 1s and back again, but the 0s and 1s could be sent on two pairs of copper wires. And not just one voice conversation, but many. They could be interleaved by a method known as *time-division multiplexing* (TDM), which divided the transmission path into a number of "channels" based on these time slots.

Now, analog multiplexing techniques had been used before. These divided the bandwidth available not by time but by a means of *fre-*

quency-division multiplexing (FDM), exactly as television channels are organized today. These multiplexing schemes were known as *carrier systems* and came out of Bell Labs on a fairly regular basis.

A system called *N-carrier* put 12 simultaneous voice conversation on 2 pairs of copper wire. Another known as *L-carrier* put even more on coaxial cable. As they were tried out and perfected by Bell Labs, all these multiplexing techniques received letter designations. The digital TDM method using PCM voice was designated *T-carrier*. It was wildly successful.

The T-carrier system was a whole family of TDM methods. The first level of the hierarchy, T-1, could take the PCM voice from 24 simultaneous conversations and put it on 2 pairs of copper wire. The attraction was that a phone company switching office, for the price of new sending and receiving equipment, could double the capacity of their existing N-carrier (12 voice channels with N-carrier, 24 with T-carrier) without running new wire between the offices. The increased revenue and the cost savings for new cable would theoretically cover the cost of the end equipment.

Another 1960s development affected capacity as well. For new trunks in urban areas, phone companies began to run a new kind of cable made out of optical fiber. This extremely pure glass was light and small, thinner than a human hair in its raw form. It could snake through congested conduits with the greatest of ease, and the bandwidth fiber offered was virtually unlimited. Fiber was expensive but deemed worth it both for the savings it offered in installation of new trunks and for the bandwidth it made available for the higher levels of the T-carrier hierarchy.

Of course, the signals on the new fiber and T-carrier networks were all digital. This brings up the second problem, which was the ability of the switching systems to handle and process (and bill for!) the huge number of new phone calls the suddenly affluent Americans were making in the 1960s.

Older mechanical switching systems had been analog, of course. They were controlled by interpreting the "pulses" from the rotary phone dial as instructions to a vast assembly of spindles and rotors that actually moved to provide electrical pathways through the switch. The switches filled entire buildings and resembled giant Tinker-Toy contraptions. They required a small army of technicians to maintain, repair, and troubleshoot.

After World War II, modern digital computers began to be applied to making these electromechanical switches more reliable, faster, and more efficient. At first, the computer merely controlled the switch fabric itself, which remained totally analog. With the development of integrated circuits in the late 1960s, it became possible and economically feasible for these computer chips to actually become the entire switch itself.

In the *electronic switching system* (ESS), voice from an analog local loop was digitized at the interface board of the switch itself. The voice was switched as a string of 0s and 1s, transmitted on a digital T-carrier trunking system as a string of 0s and 1s, and only reanaloged as needed at the destination local loop.

This system was elegant and practical. It resulted in a total revolution in the way the national phone network was organized and operated. Older, rotary pulse dial phones suitable for electromechanical switches gave way to "touch tone" dial phones better suited to the computers controlling the solid-state electronic switches. The added intelligence of the individual switches lead to the deployment of *direct digital dialing* (DDD) service, where the use of "area codes" meant that almost anyone could dial almost anyone else in the country without the intervention of a long-distance operator.

The retention of the analog local loop was the only drawback. The investment in twisted-pair copper to each residence ran into the billions. Nevertheless, by 1984, ambitious plans were developed to replace every analog phone with a digital unit that would digitize voice directly in the telephone handset itself. It was to be called the *integrated services digital network* (ISDN).

Only here did the digital revolution falter. The features that were supposed to make the general public enthusiastic enough about the new all-digital network were seen as nonessential or even trivial. Some features, such as advanced data services through X.25 packet networks, were just not needed in every home, especially in these pre-PC days. Others, such as the display of the caller's phone number on the ringing phone, were actually challenged in court by irate subscribers. And no one liked the idea of paying more for phone service that was just fine the way it was.

So ISDN failed the social acceptability test miserably. The technology was sound, but the lack of social acceptance meant that even if deployed, the prices to the few interested subscribers would remain so high that more potential customers would be discouraged. And the high initial investments demanded a rate structure to support the economic feasibility issue. (It was not supposed to be this way: Telephone companies' own studies repeatedly showed that ISDN would sell well if priced at about 1.5 times traditional voice service. But the anxiety over short-term revenues kept the pricing for ISDN in many cases above twice the older rates for voice services.)

However, the all-digital network employing computer-based switches and digital trunks made so much sense that the phone companies decided to try again. This time they concentrated on services and features that were so good and so farsighted that surely everyone would see the benefit at once.

1.4   ATM and the "Next Generation" Network

Seen against this background of evolution from digital telegraph to analog telephone to digital telephone, the origin of ATM networks is obvious and natural. ATM is the culmination of the application of computer technology to the digital telephone network. As such, ATM is not a technology that needs to answer the question "Why?" but only "When?" and "How?"

In 1988, the CCITT Blue Books contained a description of ATM as a switching technology based on unchannelized, high-speed digital links. The links themselves were all fiber-based, point-to-point trunks arranged in a hierarchy of speeds well into the gigabit per second (1000 Mbps) range. Known in the United States as SONET (synchronous optical network), these fiber links were to be coupled with the ATM switches to form a new generation of network to be called *broadband ISDN* (B-ISDN). The older, "plain" ISDN is now called *narrowband ISDN* (N-ISDN).

Lately, the term *B-ISDN* has been downplayed, probably due to the bad associations of the term *ISDN* in the mind of the public. The term *broadband services,* or *broadband network,* is much preferred.

The Capabilities of ATM

This chapter will be more specific in exploring the reasons that asynchronous transfer mode (ATM) has attracted such a huge following among vendors as diverse as 10BaseT LAN hub manufacturers to router vendors to cable TV companies. And it has happened in a relatively short time period.

To understand this, it is necessary to look at the limitations of current network schemes and technologies and show exactly how ATM networks will attempt to address them. For this is the attraction of ATM: No business is interested in technology but rather in gaining a *competitive edge* over its business rivals. Then it is not a matter of "The company cannot afford to do it," but "The company cannot afford *not* to do it, because the competition is."

2.1 ATM as an "Asynchronous" Technology

This chapter first takes a detailed look at the *cell*, the core of ATM networks. Next, it explores how ATM works its "magic" in its potential ability to mix the different kinds of networks (voice, video, data) into one big *unchannelized* physical network. This method of multiplexing the ATM cells defines the concept of an *asynchronous* transfer mode. In this context, *asynchronous* refers to the ability of the ATM network to send only the data associated with a connection when there are actual live data to send. This is in contrast again to channelized networks, where even if a channel is idle, a special bit pattern (called, naturally, the *idle* or *keep alive* bit pattern) must be sent in every time slot representing the channel. Otherwise, the receiver would not be able to recover the information present in the other time slots. This is the essence of *synchronous* transfer mode networks.

2.2   Problems Addressed by ATM

A *transfer mode* has been defined previously as the main technique of transmitting, multiplexing, switching, and receiving information in a network. This term was looked at in Chapter 1 as it applies in a historical sense, but most observers use it in a more restrictive fashion. In this usage, every communications technology from telephone to broadcast television has had its own "transfer mode," although people seldom talk about it in these terms because it is so obvious. *Circuit mode* is for voice: Pick up the phone (terminal device) and dial the number (network address). *Packet mode* is for data: Take the user's data from a LAN client (terminal device) and add a header with destination information (network address) for connectionless services, or a circuit identifier for connection-oriented services. It is all the same, but until now, the network transfer mode was specialized for network functions. This is the key to understanding just what ATM is for. A network could not be built using voice packets, since this "transfer mode" was developed and optimized for data. Of course, this tends to be a very inefficient resource (bandwidth, etc.) usage. And putting the voice and data on the same *channelized* T-1 does not really help; it just shifts the problem.

All these methods involve *synchronous* use of the network. ATM, by contrast, is structured to work in an *asynchronous* manner. The terms *synchronous* and *asynchronous,* as applied to transfer modes, refer to the scheme of multiplexing: mixing traffic from many sources together on the *same* physical network path. In a synchronous transfer mode, each source is assigned a fixed bandwidth based on *position:* a frequency band in FDM or a time slot in TDM. ATM is *not* based on position in the data stream at all; a header identifies *whose* traffic it is and *where* it goes. *All* traffic is sent based on demand; no traffic, no bandwidth drain. Therefore, an ATM network is *not* service-dependent; it works well for voice and video as well as data. It is *not* inflexible; as bandwidth requirements for video decrease (the blue VCR "idle" screen, for example), ATM networks can easily adjust. It is *not* inefficient; resources assigned for now to a voice connection can be used later for data traffic. Everything in ATM is done based on *connections,* not *channels,* as is done in traditional time-division multiplexing.

2.2.1   Too many networks

One of the biggest problems with networks today is that there are too many of them. Corporations built SNA networks in the 1970s for their mainframe data needs and followed them with router-based networks for their LAN connectivity needs. The need to provide the company with low-cost voice services led to the purchase of private branch exchanges (PBXs) and then to the deployment of a private tie-line (point-to-point voice channel) network to connect the PBXs. Videoconferencing needs were addressed with still another network, and as more and more services become necessary for a corporation to remain competitive, this list will only grow longer.

Besides the duplication of effort, there are the limitations to building these many networks out of channelized T-1s. Spare capacity cannot easily be taken from one network and used on another. Each network is designed for the *busy-hour/busy-day* capacity. There is a need to accommodate "bursts" of usage and peak demand. No network is immune. The national voice network is built around Mother's Day traffic demand. This is enormously wasteful, since the typical residential phone is in use only 40 minutes per day. Since there is no way to predict exactly when a subscriber may pick up the phone, the voice network must be available to each user 24 hours a day, 7 days a week, 52 weeks a year. The capacity is there whether it is in use or not.

Peak business phone usage is during normal business hours. The cable TV network has peak usage during the evening hours. Today, these are completely separate channelized networks (e.g., channel 46 is present if it is watched or not). Clearly, there would be an advantage to a service provider if there could be one network that could be used for voice during the day and cable TV service in the evening.

Yet it is not so simple a matter as merging the physical paths used by all these networks. There is the matter of service-parameter differences as well.

2.2.2 Too many services

All these various networks are based on different *service parameters,* such as bit rate and delay variation tolerance (Fig. 2.1). Connectionless services are those in which the receiver does not have to be contacted in some way prior to communication. Information is merely packaged and

TELEPHONE	DATA	CABLE TV	VIDEO CONF.
CONN-OR	CONN-LESS OR CONN-OR	CONN-LESS	CONN-OR
DELAY VAR SENSITIVE	DELAY VAR INSENSITIVE	DELAY VAR SENSITIVE	DELAY VAR SENSITIVE
LOW BW	LOW/HIGH BW	HIGH BW	LOW/HIGH BW
CBR	VBR	CBR	CBR & VBR

Figure 2.1   Too many services and too many networks.

sent as it is made available to the sender. Connection-oriented services require the establishment of a "connection" between sender and receiver. *Delay variation sensitivity* deals with the issue of how long data may be delayed within the network. Typically, this value will vary with the amount of traffic in the network itself. When the network is busy, things are slower. The variation sensitivity of the receiver is an indication of how much this delay can vary (from 10 to 100 ms, for instance) before the receiver will think there is something wrong. *Bandwidth* just refers to the required bit rate of the service, which is highly dependent on whether some bit compression coding is used or not.

Some services are always sending bits at a constant rate: *constant-bit-rate (CBR) services*. Some send bits in bursts: *variable-bit-rate (VBR) services*. Some networks offer the possibility of multiple *quality of service* (QOS) parameters that users may want at various times. The challenge of ATM is to make *one* physical network for *all* previous networks and services and be immune to changes in service demands in the future. Just as houses could be built out of "house walls" and office buildings out of "office walls," it is better if they are all built out of "bricks." This is the way it is with ATM. No existing network technology can handle it all, which is why things are like they are today. Thus ATM invents the "brick" to build any kind of network needed or wanted.

The brick of ATM networks is the *cell*.

2.3   ATM Solutions: The ATM Cell

All ATM networking is based on the *cell* as the unit of data exchange (Fig. 2.2). A *cell* is defined as a fixed-length block of information. Previous networks all used a simple stream of 0s and 1s that were organized into different structures depending on the service and networks. This organization is still done with ATM networks, but at the endpoints of the network. At the physical (bit) level, everything is sent and received as cells: a fixed-sized packet of bits.

This is actually more efficient; just as a PC will be more efficient with a 32-bit bus than an older 8-bit bus, so it is with ATM. Although ATM

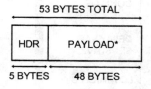

53 BYTES TOTAL

HDR | PAYLOAD*

5 BYTES   48 BYTES

* PAYLOAD MAY INCLUDE SOME
OVERHEAD BYTES AS WELL AS DATA

Figure 2.2 The ATM cell.

networks are capable of integrating voice and video, the initial driving force will be the need for increased bandwidth and LAN interconnectivity. This is an important point that cannot be overlooked.

It is the data users who will initially deploy, or initially purchase, ATM networking services. The explosive growth of PC power and networking needs has left many organizations with no current technology to link their PC applications together. There are newer technologies available that will address these needs, but *only* ATM will ultimately offer a means to merge voice and video services onto the *same* network in the future.

The implications of this situation are serious. It means that ATM must perform adequately for data applications from its inception, or else the data users will look elsewhere for solutions. It also means that even if the details of voice and video transmission on an ATM network are not available immediately, this may not be a serious handicap. It also means that voice channel banks and T-1 voice channels will be around for a long time, since there is no financial, technical, or social incentive to migrate these services to ATM networks. When it comes to the networking needs for data, rather than voice and video, ATM is designed to meet three main areas.

The first area is LAN interconnect bandwidth. As LANs run at higher and higher speeds and distributed computing becomes more common, existing digital speeds will become even more of a bottleneck. Related to this is the second area of LAN networking efficiency in terms of the number of links needed to connect multiple LANs. Lastly, image and graphics applications pose their own problems due to the large sizes of these files that must cross the network.

2.3.1 LAN interconnect bandwidth

Consider two Ethernet LANs running at 10 Mbps bridged with a 9.6-kbps digital link. The ratio of the two speeds is 10,000/10, or 1000:1. At 64 kbps (a T-1 channel), it is about 10,000/64, or 160:1. Even at 1.5 Mbps, it remains about 6:1. Clearly, this is a bottleneck for LAN-to-LAN communication.

Even in terms of raw speed, it is slow. A full screen of information under DOS (character-based) is $25 \times 80 = 2000$ characters. Each character is usually loaded as 16 bits (attribute and character). Thus $16 \times 2000 = 32$ kbits must be transferred. At 64 kbps, this takes 1/2 s $(32/64 = 0.5)$.

With a graphical user interface (GUI) such as Windows, the problem is even worse. Most VGA screens are at least 1 megapixel, with 24 bits representing colors and data for the point. This is 24 Mbits per screen. At 64 kbps, it would take about 6 min to load.

Of course, when 100-Mbps LANs [fiber distributed data interface (FDDI) or Ethernet or even Token Ring] come along in a big way, things will only get worse.

2.3.2 LAN network efficiency

This problem deals with connecting multiple LANs at many sites with point-to-point links. The ideal situation would be to connect each LAN to every other LAN—but this quickly becomes much too expensive. For example, $N(N - 1)/2$ connections are required to fully mesh connect N LANs. For 10 LANs, this is $10(9)/2 = 45$ links. And even if point-to-point dedicated links happen to be cheap enough to make this scheme feasible, each node on the network would require $N - 1$ access ports—boards with network connectors—into the network. For 10 LANs, this is 9 ports per LAN, an enormously expensive proposition. Instead, many LANs have routers for remote access attached to only some LANs. If the LANs are grouped by twos, only $5(4)/2 = 10$ links are needed.

Now, however, there is a delay in getting traffic to the proper LAN to be routed. In other words, these routers themselves tend to become bottlenecks, since they find themselves handling more and more traffic for LANs that are not directly connected to them. With a full-mesh network, routers are very effective, since every LAN on the network is at most one hop (link) away.

If LAN traffic switching were faster, only *one* link per LAN would be needed. The router would not work so quickly that plenty of LANs could connect to these very fast machines. Most of the delay on such a network would be propagation delay, the delay that all networks (no matter how fast) must deal with just because the speed of electricity in wire, or through space, is limited by the speed of light itself.

There is an argument that one nice benefit of a full-mesh network, or even a partial-mesh network, is that it is very tolerant of link failures. Indeed, a full-mesh network may tolerate many of the links failing and continue to function. With only one network interface and link per LAN, an ATM network would be easily disrupted by link failures. However, if the link is *very* stable and offers some form of "protection switching" to activate a backup link when needed, this argument loses some force. Of course, for truly critical applications, there is no reason why multiple links could not still exist. With ATM, however, this need is not as great for performance reasons.

2.3.3 Multimedia and image/graphics transfers

Transfer of image and graphics information around a network is becoming more and more commonplace. It would be more useful if it was not so slow. Faxing medical x-rays is a tedious process and very slow. A 4K × 4K pixel x-ray, with 8 bits per pixel, takes up 128 Mbits per image. Data-compression algorithms exist, of course, but the really effective ones rely on what is known as *lossy* compression. Lossy compression means that image details are not necessarily preserved during the compression/decompression (expansion) process. This may be okay for advertising graphics photographs and the like, but the medical profession is generally nervous about lossy data compression. Effective data-compression algorithms can easily compress the medical x-ray from 128 to 12.8 Mbits, a 10:1 compression ratio. Even so, it is a large file.

Suppose a network could be built that runs at 155 Mbps. At 155 Mbps, the full, uncompressed 128-Mbit image could be sent in less than 1 second. In the field of electronic publishing, an 8½ × 11-in image at 500 dots per inch (dpi) (color) and 24 bits per pixel occupies about 550 Mbits. This would be sent in 3.5 s. Even at magazine quality (2000 dpi) with a size of 9000 Mbits (9 Gbits, an astonishing number), it could be done in about 60 s. Even more important to computer specialists is the fact that a 2-Gbyte disk drive (2000 Meg) could be backed up across a network in a little more than 100 s.

Lately, a lot has been written about the growing importance of multimedia applications. Definitions of *multimedia* are varied and many, but most observers agree that multimedia involves the mixing of graphics, animation, sound, and video into very sophisticated Windows-based applications that move and play music and even tell users what button to push next. There are multimedia applications today, but most exist on a high-speed CD-ROM attached directly to the PC or workstation. There is nothing wrong with this, of course, but these applications would be more effective to use if the video were on a video server on a network, the audio on an audio server, and so on. The trouble is that today's networks are much too slow to deliver the data representing the video or audio fast enough, and consistently enough, to display the frames or play the sound without serious distortion and errors.

For example, a simple quarter-screen video and audio sequence of the space shuttle lifting off lasting about 60 seconds occupies 24 Mbytes on a hard drive or CD-ROM. This file conforms to the Microsoft ".AVI" (audiovisual interleaved) format. Multimedia is sometimes called the "killer application" that will someday "kill" off the older networks and become the application that no one can live without. And this means new networks, not only with very large capacities but also with very low end-to-end delays.

ATM networks can deliver all these LAN and data solutions. It is not magic. It is the cell.

2.4   ATM Cell Structure

Asynchronous transfer mode (ATM) is easy to understand; it is simply a method of transferring information as it is generated by a source using fixed-length cells. The *asynchronous* part refers to the "as it arrives" phrase in the definition. *Cells* are related to the concept of "cell relay." Much of the cell technology in ATM is closely related to packet-switching systems. That is, it is a connection-oriented network method based on switches as network nodes, not routers.

This is not the place to go into a long discussion of routers versus switches, but suffice it to say that both are network devices that perform essentially the same function: Get a data unit from an input port, look it up in some table based on some field in the header, and put the data unit out on the output port indicated. The difference is in the way the table is set up and what is in the header field. In a router, it is a destination address; in a switch, it is a connection identifier. It is not too much of a stretch to say that a router is a connectionless switch and a switch is a connection-oriented router.

In an ATM network, the network nodes (switches) switch ATM cells. The ATM cell structure consists of 53 bytes. They are usually called *octets* in ATM literature, but it means the same today. The 53 bytes are divided into a 5-byte *header* and a 48-byte information section known as the *payload*. The bytes are sent out on the network 1 byte at a time in sequence, from byte 1 to byte 53 (Fig. 2.3). Since "ownership" of cells is *not* determined by position in the data stream, determination of this ownership is one function of the cell header.

The structure of the ATM cell header is shown in Fig. 2.4. Officially, it is the *B-ISDN user-network interface (UNI) cell header*. The UNI

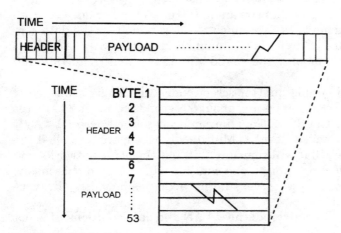

Figure 2.3   ATM cell structure.

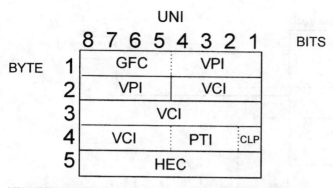

Figure 2.4 ATM cell header.

header has a number of fields that will be examined in more detail later on. For now, it is enough to note that the bits in each byte are numbered 8 to 1, left to right. Bit 8 is the most significant bit, meaning it has the highest value when expressed as a binary (base 2) number. Bytes are sent on the ATM network from most significant bit (bit 8) to least significant bit (bit 1), or from left to right on the page. Also, most of the bits in the header, 24 of 40, are used for a hierarchical network connection identifier [the VPI/VCI (virtual path identifier/virtual connection identifier) field].

It has been stated that the *asynchronous* in ATM refers to the sending of data on the network "as they arrive." Data are packaged into the fixed-sized cells and sent out onto the network. It is this use of cells by data "as they arrive" that has led to the label "bandwidth on demand" being applied to ATM. Of course, it cannot make bandwidth out of nothing, but it does make the most flexible use of the available bandwidth when shared by a number of users. The term *flexible bandwidth allocation* is technically more accurate, but "bandwidth on demand" remains entrenched even in ATM Forum circles.

The cell stream leaving a network node may be filled by the same user's data or different user's data. Most likely, it will be a combination of many users taking up varying amounts of cells at different times: bandwidth on demand.

ATM is sometimes referred to as *label multiplexing* or even *asynchronous time-division multiplexing* in older documentation. Both terms were used to refer to ATM when the standards were still under development. The *label* is the connection identifier that tells the receiver which connection the cell is to be associated with.

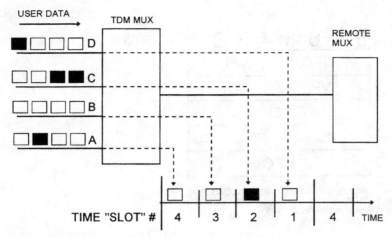

Figure 2.5 Time-division multiplexing.

2.4.1 Time-division multiplexing

Figure 2.5 shows how traditional time-division multiplexing (TDM) works. As the most efficient strategy for multiplexing digital signals, as opposed to analog signals, it is very commonly deployed in digital T-1 networks and elsewhere. TDM works by having a fixed-length time slot assigned to each user input. This is therefore synchronous transfer mode (STM), since each slot is synchronized to a user input time slot.

There is no need to identify the user bits in the data stream; if it is time X, these are user Y's bits. In STM, the ownership of bits is determined by position in the data stream. However, if no user bits have arrived to fill the time slot, it *cannot* be given to another user. A special "idle" bit pattern must be sent on each channel (i.e., in each time slot) to keep the sender and receiver synchronized. Therefore, this method can result is a great deal of idle bandwidth, and User C in Fig. 2.5 must wait until the next time slot to send data, although none from other users are ready to go.

Obviously, there is no way in STM to assign "bandwidth on demand" to individual users or to send data "as they arrive." Everything must be parceled out based on the available time slots.

2.4.2 ATM multiplexing

In contrast, ATM multiplexing is shown in Fig. 2.6. ATM multiplexing works by having a fixed number of cells per unit time available for user data. Each cell has the 5-byte header whose primary purpose is to identify cells belonging to the same "virtual channel" or connection. Notice that the ATM cell header determines the identity of the data and *not*

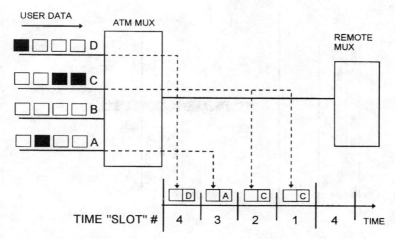

USER DATA

ATM MUX

REMOTE MUX

D

C

B

A

TIME "SLOT" #   4   3   2   1   4   TIME

D   A   C   C

Figure 2.6   ATM multiplexing.

the time-slot position, as in straight time-division multiplexing. Note also that cells are transmitted according to what is called in ATM the user's *instantaneous real need.* The idle patterns and STM channels have been eliminated, to the benefit of both the user (who gets to send data faster) and the network service provider (who gets more efficient use of the network bandwidth). It is easy to see in Fig. 2.6 that User *C* gets two cells and that User *B* gets none at all—for now. All the ATM multiplexer does is take the data and add the header. Finally, the link to the local exchange node (network node) may be fiber-based, but it also may be copper, coaxial cable, or anything else.

The cell length in ATM is only 53 bytes. By contrast, the smallest allowable frame size on an Ethernet LAN is 64 bytes. The cell length in ATM is set so small for a number of reasons. It is basically a compromise between the needs of voice and the needs of data applications such as file transfer. The whole idea is to avoid the long and unpredictable delays in waiting for long packets to finish transmission. This scheme gives acceptable voice delay—but it can be very inefficient for data transfer at less than T-3 (45-Mbps) speeds. (The reason will be explained later.)

The short cell length also allows *circuit emulation* for DS-0 at 64 kbps, DS-1 at 1.544 Mbps, DS-3 at 45 Mbps, and digitized video at various bit rates, depending on the compression standard. ATM is aimed primarily at networks built on links running at 155 Mbps, known as *STS-3c speed.* At this speed, a 53-byte cell lasts only about 2.7 μs: (53 bytes × 8 bits/byte)/155.52 Mbps = 2.726 μs. (A microsecond is one-millionth of a second.) Thus any delay while a cell is being transmitted is very short.

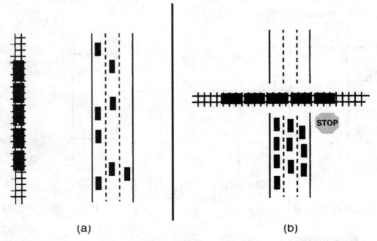

Figure 2.7 Mixing voice and data. (*a*) Separate "channels"; (*b*) "unchannelized" voice and data.

It may not be obvious why long, variable-length data packets may be detrimental to short, fixed-length pulse-code modulation (PCM)–type voice samples when they are mixed on an unchannelized link. Why bother to make cells at all? Here is a simple analogy.

In the United States today, railroads are still in use for moving large, bulky loads of freight. Railroad engines pull variable-length trains of boxcars, up to 200 or so, on special "networks" of railroad tracks. Highways were built as another special kind of network, but this time for fixed-length cars that are optimized for carrying people. As long as the networks are separate—and the trains stay on the tracks and the cars stay on the roads—the networks both work fine. This situation is shown in Fig. 2.7*a*.

The problem arises when the railroad tracks must cross the highway. At a railroad crossing, once the train starts across the highway, the cars all must stop. They have to wait until the entire train is across the intersection. This causes a delay, which may be a long one, considering the number of boxcars that may be in the train. The cars must be "buffered" until the train is past. And even when the train is clear of the crossing, the backup of automobile traffic still takes a while to make its way through the crossing. This is the situation shown in Fig. 2.7*b*.

In this analogy, the train is the large, variable-length data frame, and the cars are the smaller, but more numerous, fixed-length PCM voice samples. The entirely separate railroad tracks and highways are the channelized time-division multiplexed networks commonly built today. The crossing situation represents an attempt to mix the data and delay sensitive voice samples on the same unchannelized network, but without ATM cells as a possibility.

Clearly, this causes a problem. The backup of voice traffic will cause the receiver to think that something is wrong if the absence of "cars" arriving persists too long. Exactly how long it will persist, however, depends on the length of the train.

There are actually two potential solutions to this problem. First, if the engine pulling the train runs very much faster than usual, the delay for the cars waiting for the train to pass will be correspondingly shorter. That is, if the train runs twice as fast, the wait is half as long. If it runs ten times as fast, the wait is one-tenth as long, and so on. The point is that if the train runs fast enough, the time that the cars have to wait, and the number built up at the crossing, can be made almost insignificant. The solution is then to make an unchannelized network that runs much faster than ever before, and trains to run on it. This solution is considered in Fig. 2.8a.

There is a drawback to this approach, however. It has been shown that data requirements have grown in leaps and bounds in the past, and the trend is upward. Files today are larger than the entire DOS partition (32-Meg limit with DOS 3.2) was not too long ago. It is not unusual to have 16 Meg of RAM on a PC today, larger than the most common hard drive size 10 years ago (10 Meg). The trains keep getting longer and longer. Rebuilding the railroad to stay ahead of the trend may be a self-defeating proposition in the long run. Faster railroads may actually encourage longer trains.

Maybe there is another solution. What if each boxcar were a self-propelled unit about the same size as a car. Now if a "train" starts across

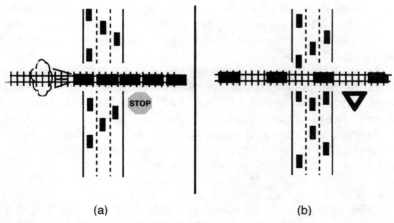

(a)   (b)

Figure 2.8 Possible solutions to mixing voice and data. (a) "Fast train" approach; (b) ATM approach.

the intersection and a car arrives, there is only a very short delay before the boxcar is through the crossing and the car may pass. It is much simpler than the previous solution and requires no reengineering of the railroad or the highway. This is illustrated in Fig. 2.8*b*. This is the ATM solution, with the boxcars and cars becoming cells.

2.4.3 Cell allocation and bandwidth

So what is the "trick" of ATM? How can different services with different data rates all use the same physical data stream? Before looking at some examples, some explanation is in order. Most networks today employ a digital data link technology over some kind of cable to transfer data. There are exceptions, such as wireless LANs, but the vast majority still use cable. Most digital links today are *framed* transports, which means that there are some overhead bits or bytes added to the raw data to be transported. These *payload* bits plus the overhead bits form a unit known as a *frame,* which is different from other data units also known as frames, such as Token Ring frames or Ethernet frames.

One major difference is that frames used on LANs such as Token Ring or Ethernet only send a data frame when one is generated. The frames may carry protocol-specific management information or user data, but the point is that there is no requirement to generate these frames unless there is a reason. The frames used for wide-area transport of digital data (e.g., T-1 frames, T-3 frames) are different. These frames must be packed head to tail on the physical link—be it coaxial cable or some other medium—in order for the sender and receiver to stay in synchronization and be sure that the link is available.

Data are packed into these transport frames, if available, or else a special idle pattern is generated by the sender and essentially discarded by the receiver. Various kinds of data may be packed into these transport frames. The only real requirement is that the receiver know what the sender is sending. One of the possible contents of the transport frames is ATM cells.

The frames themselves are generated at a standard rate in most cases. Usually, this is 8000 frames per second, or one frame every 125 µs (thousandths of a second: $1/8000$ s $= 0.125$ s). Since ATM technology is geared toward higher-speed networks than exist today, ATM is geared toward higher-speed data links than those commonly found today. In fact, ATM is based on a family of digital data links known in the United States as SONET (synchronous optical network). SONET links run on fiberoptic cable at speeds of 51.84 Mbps and above. This is known as a *STS-1.* In the example below, STS-1 is mentioned along with STS-3c, which is a digital link running at 155.52 Mbps. In an STS-1 frame, about 15 ATM cells will fit (with some bits left over), packed head to tail in the payload section of the transport frame. In an STS-3c frame, about 44 ATM cells will fit.

SONET will be explored in more detail later, but for this discussion, all that is important is that the SONET frames are generated 8000 times per second by a sender and the SONET frame payload may consist of ATM cells. In a perfect world, an even (integer) number of cells would fit into a SONET frame with no bits left over, but unfortunately, this is not the case in the real world. Thus numbers have been somewhat rounded off here for illustration purposes.

The whole point is to show how a single high-speed link can still be used with ATM cells to carry an arbitrarily small bandwidth from user to user. These cell flows form a *connection* in ATM, rather than the *channels* formed in other transport frames, such as T-1s.

Here is how ATM will allocate bandwidth for different services all on the same physical link in an unchannelized fashion.

Example 1   For video signals, ATM may assign *all* available cells to *one* user. This gives a bandwidth (over an STS-3 running at about 155 Mbps) of about 135.168 Mbps:

44 cells/frame × 8000 frames/second × 48 bytes/cell × 8 bits/byte

There is an overhead associated with ATM as well (5 bytes per cell for the cell header). This works out to 14.08 Mbps:

44 cells/frame × 8000 frames/second × 5 bytes/cell × 8 bits/byte

Example 2   If the ATM cells are over an STS-1 running at about 51 Mbps, users will get about 43 Mbps:

14 cells/frame × 8000 frames/second × 48 bytes/cell × 8 bits/byte

And the associated overhead in this case will be about 4.48 Mbps:

14 cells/frame × 8000 frames/second × 5 bytes/cell × 8 bits/byte

Since the new HDTV (high-definition TV) with MPEG (Motion Picture Experts Group) 3 compression needs about 30 Mbps, this should be fine.

Of course, all cells do not have to be assigned to one user. This is the essence of any multiplexing scheme. Suppose that a digital transport generates 8000 transport frames per second, and one cell per frame is assigned to each user. One frame every eight-thousandth of a second is one frame every 125 μs (one-millionth of a second). It does not really matter what the data rate is, because all transports faster that a few megabits per second will accommodate more than one cell per frame.

Example 3   If the user gets one cell per frame, 8000 times per second, then the users would get 3.072 Mbps:

$$8000 \text{ frames/second} \times 48 \text{ bytes/cell} \times 8 \text{ bits/byte}$$

And the associated overhead would be 320 kbps:

$$8000 \text{ frames/second} \times 5 \text{ bytes/cell} \times 8 \text{ bits/byte}$$

Not much network equipment operates at 3.072 Mbps, but even lower bandwidths may be allocated. There is no requirement that a user get a cell every transport frame, most of which will be generated at a rate of 8000 frames per second.

Example 4 If User A sends a cell every second frame (*any* data rate, but the number of potential users will vary) and User B sends a cell every fourth frame, the data rates are

User A:

$$1.536 \text{ Mbps } (3.072 \text{ Mbps/2}) \quad \text{(T-1 support)}$$

User B:

$$0.768 \text{ Mbps } (3.072 \text{ Mbps/4}) \quad \text{(FT-1 support)}$$

This is illustrated in Fig. 2.9.

How low can this method go? ATM is supposed to be good for everything, from high speeds to low. What about voice? Suppose User C sends a cell every forty-eighth frame. This works out to 64 kbps bandwidth, or just 3.072 Mbps/48. This just happens to be the PCM DS-0 voice channel bandwidth.

Of course, the cells are *only* sent once every 6000 μs, which is 48 × 125 μs, or 6 ms (milliseconds, one-thousandth of a second). Also, the cell has 48 bytes of information. Thus many PCM words have to be put into one cell. A DS-0 voice channel generates 1 byte in 125 μs (8000 per second). To fill a cell (remember, it is the size that is fixed), however, the network needs to accumulate 48 bytes, or 48 voice samples. This will take 48 × 125 μs = 6000 μs = 6 ms. In ATM, this is known as the voice *packetization delay*. This is shown in Fig. 2.10.

```
IF:  USER A SENDS A CELL EVERY 2ND FRAME
     USER B SENDS A CELL EVERY 4TH FRAME

THEN: USER A HAS 1.536 Mbps
      USER B HAS 0.768 Mbps
```

Figure 2.9 Cell allocation: low bandwidth.

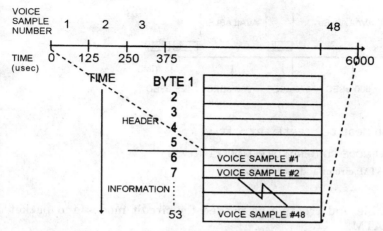

Figure 2.10 ATM for voice transport (simplest case*).

Therefore, users have to wait *at least* 6 ms to send any voice. The round trip delay is *at least* 12 ms (2 × 6). Of course, the bandwidth is still 64 kbps (3.072 Mbps/48), but this *delay* in the voice has one big result. The propagation delay on the network itself must be added to the round-trip packetization delay. Therefore, the delay on voice circuits over ATM will be higher than it has been in the past on straight voice channels, but it should still be acceptable. However, this effect will be magnified by many packetizations and depacketizations if non-ATM and ATM networks are joined back to back for voice.

2.4.4 ATM circuit and packet mode

What good is ATM if cells must be assigned to users at a constant and known rate? Where's the "bandwidth on demand?" The answer is that ATM can allow users to operate in either circuit mode or packet mode. *Circuit mode* (of which voice is an example) is also known as *continuous bit rate (CBR)*. *Packet mode* (just about all data) is a *variable bit rate (VBR)*. The whole point to supporting both circuit mode and packet mode is for backward compatibility with existing network equipment and network services.

The example in Fig. 2.11 shows User *A* running at 1.536 Mbps (DS-1 rate, 24 × 64 kbps) circuit mode by being *guaranteed* a cell every second frame. User *B* is running at 0.768 Mbps (a fractional T-1 rate) circuit mode by being *guaranteed* a cell every fourth frame.

The rest of the bandwidth (and it is huge) is available for contention among other users. These users are running packet mode. Users can

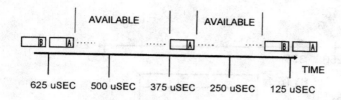

CIRCUIT MODE: CELL SENT EVERY "X" FRAMES

PACKET MODE: CONTEND FOR REMAINING FRAMES

Figure 2.11   ATM: circuit and packet modes.

be as flexible and creative as needed for circuit modes and packet modes in ATM.

2.5 Summary

This chapter has defined ATM networks both in terms of *asynchronous* and *transfer mode*. The *asynchronous* refers to ATM's capability to send user data only when they are presented to the network. The *transfer mode* just means that ATM forms its own unique way of sending, switching, and receiving all forms of traffic.

This chapter also described how ATM attempts to address the limitations of channelized networks by replacing the channels with connections. In addition, these connections are run over physical transports that offer much higher bit rates and much lower delay than other network technologies.

ATM is more than just a way of sending bits. This chapter showed how ATM networks include a multiplexing technique for mixing voice, video, and data in a manner that gives acceptable performance for all of them. ATM cells and ATM multiplexing, both in packet mode and circuit mode, give a new networking paradigm that may ultimately become the accepted way to build networks in the near future.

The ATM Protocol Stack

The second part of this book is a top-to-bottom tour of the ATM protocol stack. A protocol stack *is nothing more than a collection of layers that address networking by dividing the communications functions into specific tasks spread among the layers. A set of layers that incorporates the standards of one body or another at each layer is known as a protocol stack. There are many different kinds of protocol stacks. IBM's System Network Architecture (SNA) is a layered protocol stack, but a proprietary one. A proprietary protocol stack is one wholly developed and owned by a private company, and the company is under no obligation to reveal the internal details of its functioning to anyone, even customers who purchase the products based on the protocol.*

Other protocol stacks may be implemented based on documentation available to everyone. The Open Systems Interconnection Reference Model (OSI-RM) is a seven-layer protocol stack based on documentation from the International Standards Organization (ISO). The popular Transmission Control Protocol / Internetwork Protocol (TCP / IP) protocol stack is a four-layer model based on documentation available from a variety of sources. All these models bridge the gap between the connector on the back of a PC or communications board (the lowest layer) and the applications program running in the local memory of the PC or network device (the highest layer). The task of interfacing software (the applications pro-

gram) and hardware (the connector) is the job of the protocol stack. Note that layers may be implemented in hardware (i.e., on a chip on a board) or in software [i.e., a terminate and stay resident (TSR) program on a PC].

Protocol stacks such as TCP/IP and OSI-RM are open. *The term* open *means many different things to many people, but for the purposes of our discussion of ATM,* open *will refer to protocols that have the following characteristics:*

1. *They are fully published.*

2. *They are available from a number of vendors.*

3. *They are available at a competitive price.*

4. *They are not subject to royalties.*

5. *They are all technically equal.*

The "fully published" characteristic excludes most proprietary protocols on this ground alone. Open standards are implemented by a number of vendors, and for this reason, their price is usually much lower than that of proprietary protocols. Even if a company chooses to just purchase the documentation and then implement its own hardware and software products, the company never owes anyone royalties on the sale of the resulting product, whether it sells one copy or a million.

It is the last point that is really the key. Protocols based on open standards may be implemented equally by any vendor or individual. Everyone is entitled to say "mine is as good as yours" when it comes to standard protocol products.

ATM is an open standard, based on documentation from the ITU-TSS and the ATM Forum. It is a three-layered protocol stack for communications over a high-speed network where voice, video, audio, and data are sent in cells in an unchannelized fashion.

However, there is more to building and operating a network than just having hardware and software to send bits around in a standard manner. To be a complete network architecture, a protocol stack must include various components to make the protocol a complete solution for the user's networking problems. These components must include a signaling protocol for controlling the network, a method of monitoring network performance, a means of managing the resources and traffic on the network, and even a way to internetwork with older networking technologies. ATM includes all these and more.

The chapters in Part 2 reflect this. Rather than just present the ATM layers and begin detailing the function and options of each, Chapter 3 provides an overview of the components of the ATM architecture. It attempts to fit the ATM protocol stack in with the protocol stacks encountered in other network architectures. However, the emphasis is on the special needs and unique features of ATM networks. ATM is nothing if not a very ambitious network architecture that includes support for not just data, but other services such as voice and video. As such, it is essential that the signaling, management, and so forth operate not only in a data networking environment but also in an equally efficient manner for all possible services.

Chapter 4 begins a more detailed look at the components of the lower layers of the ATM model. This includes not only a look at which physical transports ATM networks may be built on but also a look at exactly how ATM cells will be packaged to be sent on these links and transports. These various transports are allowed for cell "mappings" in various configurations by the ATM Forum, and these will be detailed as well.

Chapter 5 is a look at the ATM layer itself, the heart of the ATM model. ATM networks, being connection-oriented networks (similar to the telephone network), have network nodes that are switches, not routers, as in networks used today for local area network (LAN) interconnectivity. LAN internetworks tend to be connectionless, as are the LANs themselves (similar to the postal network). These switches, or network nodes, are considered in depth, and different architectures for building these devices are explored. Signaling is an important function of these network nodes, and this topic is explored in Chapter 5 as well.

Chapter 6 considers the higher layers of the ATM protocol stack. This is where the different services offered by ATM networks must interface with the layers delivering traffic to the ATM network. Traffic, whether voice or video or data, must be "adapted" to make it suitable for transport over an ATM network. Both the adaptation process and a more detailed look at the ATM network services will be explored in this chapter.

ATM Network Concepts and Architecture

ATM is a new network architecture, but it is still very much a complete architecture. As such, it must address issues and implement functions common to networks since the early days of SNA and X.25. This chapter takes a look at the overall structure of ATM networks, giving a solid foundation for details later. Rather than just plunging into the layers of the ATM protocol stack, this chapter will introduce the layers and detail their functions, as opposed to the actual implementation of these functions through various mechanisms. These mechanisms will be dealt with in later chapters.

This chapter looks at ATM as an outgrowth of the trend toward "leaner and meaner" network models and protocols. This is stretched to the limit in ATM, meaning the Open Systems International (OSI) model is no longer a complete match, or even a good match, to the layers of the ATM architecture. However, it is still layered. Circuits and physical channels have given way to connections called *virtual paths* and *virtual channels*. This chapter will look at how ATM networks must still address the issues of signaling, network performance, and traffic control, just as all network architectures have had to in the past. ATM will require many more capabilities in these areas, since networks in the past mainly looked to solve these problems from a data perspective. ATM adds the requirement of addressing functions such as signaling, performance, and the like from a more general perspective. ATM signaling, for instance, must work for voice connections as well as point-to-multipoint video connections and even multipoint-to-multipoint connections for videoconferencing services.

Lastly, this chapter will look at how ATM networks must handle the old problem of operations and maintenance (and administration will have to be added for billing purposes). The main goal of this chapter is

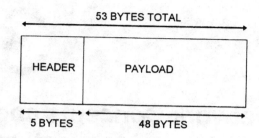

CELL: A FIXED LENGTH BLOCK FOR
       MULTIPLE BIT RATE SERVICES

Figure 3.1   Focus of ATM: the cell.

to become familiar with ATM terms and concepts. Many of these terms and concepts are unique to ATM networks and have only peripheral relevance to more familiar older networking terminology.

ATM is founded on the concept of a *cell* as the unit of information transfer (Fig. 3.1). A *cell* is defined as a *small* fixed-length block, as opposed to the variable-length packets (up to some more or less arbitrary maximum) most data services use. The fixed length makes the cell useful for transferring other services such as voice and video at the same time over the same (high-speed) links. In fact, it would not be misleading to define a *cell* as "a fixed-length block for supporting multiple quality-of-service parameters to different users over the same unchannelized physical network." *Quality-of-service parameters* mean such things as error rate, network delay, and bit rate—in short, all the parameters that distinguish one network service (voice, video) from another.

ATM is still essentially a connection-oriented system, like the phone network, although it is intended that data services that are traditionally connectionless, such as LAN-to-LAN interconnectivity, will be able to use ATM as a transport easily. In fact, many initial ATM services, such as SMDS and LAN emulation, are likely to be connectionless.

3.1   ATM's Position in the OSI Reference Model

The Open Systems Interconnect Reference Model (OSI-RM) was established by the International Standards Organization (ISO) in 1979. Originally conceived as a seven-layer model for communications over a wide area network (WAN), it was soon modified for functioning over a local area network (LAN) as well. The problem was that the original data link layer (layer 2) specification worked only between *adjacent* systems, that is, systems connected directly to each other over a single-hop, point-to-point link. Actually, a *multipoint* link was supported as well, but only from a single primary to a limited number of secondaries on the link. In this limited context, the OSI-RM data link layer only needed a very few addresses for the *frames,* or protocol data units (PDUs), at layer 2.

The invention of LANs meant that there were no longer a small number of adjacent systems. Rather, *every* system on a LAN was adjacent to all the other systems due to the shared media nature inherent in LANs. This meant that with a LAN such as Ethernet, with up to 1024 adjacent systems, the available layer 2 addresses in the original WAN OSI-RM were quickly exhausted long before anything like 1024 systems could be attached. The model had to be modified to provide a solution. This modification consisted of dividing the data link layer (layer 2) into an upper and lower portion: Layer 2b became the logical link control (LLC) sublayer, and layer 2a became the media access control (MAC) sublayer. This splitting of layers is not uncommon and can be extremely useful in the implementation of these protocols in hardware and software. Layer 2b, the logical link control, retained the functions of the original WAN data link layer, which now became the "logical" link, since there were no longer any physical adjacent links needed for LANs. Under layer 2b, layer 2a (the MAC sublayer) generated the proper frame structure and protocol for the various LAN technologies being developed in the early 1980s. For example, the 802.3 MAC generated Ethernet-type frames, and the 802.5 MAC generated Token Ring frames (and the token as well). Figure 3.2 shows the relationship of these layered architectures.

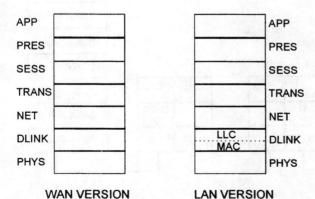

Figure 3.2   The OSI Reference Model (OSI-RM).

A thin "upper crust" of the LLC sublayer is known as the *subnetwork access protocol (SNAP) sublayer,* which is also used in some LAN protocols (e.g., Token Ring).

3.1.1. Router-based networking

The most common paradigm for networking today is the concept of *router-based networking.* In this scheme, all networks are connected by routers rather than other network connectivity devices such as bridges or gateways.

Bridges and gateways are used for connectivity in many situations, but routers have a unique position in the OSI-RM. Many different types of networks may be connected, with the routing of messages between them done by special relaying/switching devices. If these devices operate at layer 3 of the OSI-RM and use layer 3c to perform the routing (called the *internetworking* function), then this device is a router.

These devices handle layer 3 protocol data units (PDUs) known as *packets* if the network service is connection-oriented and *datagrams* if the network service is connectionless. These services are distinguished by the need in connection-oriented networks for a signaling protocol to establish the connections in the network before data can flow from a sender to a receiver. No signaling is needed for a datagram service. It is common today to refer to layer 3 network devices that handle packets as *switches* and to call layer 3 network devices that handle datagrams as *routers.*

The architecture of a router-based network is shown in Fig. 3.3. It shows two networks connected with a router network. Usually, the

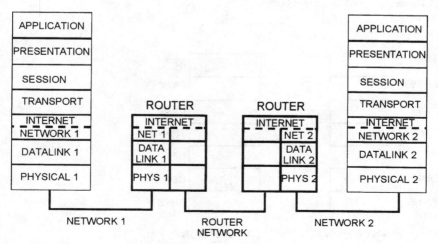

Figure 3.3 Router-based networking.

routers on network 1 and network 2 will have a network interface card (NIC) for the LAN connectivity and a WAN board for the router network connection. There is no need for the LAN networks to be the same; they may just as easily be two Ethernets or Token Rings as one Ethernet and one Token Ring. As long as the datagram format and structure are the same from one end system to the other, the router network will work. Of course, real-world router networks may have many LAN attachments and more than one WAN connection, but this is just a model of router functions.

Notice several things about Fig. 3.3. First, the transport layer (layer 4) forms the end-to-end (user-to-user) layer in the model. This means that layer 4 is found nowhere in the network on the routers. It is only present on the origin and destination systems. Second, the routers have no users on them; they merely look up the network addresses in the datagrams in a table and forward the traffic hop by hop through the network. Actually, routers do a lot more than just look up addresses, but this is their essential function. Lastly, the structure and protocols used on the *router network* between the routers is entirely open: Almost anything can be used. That is, there is nothing to prevent a vendor or user from using any wide-area protocol available, providing that all routers understand the protocol used on the router network.

This is still a long way from picturing an ATM network. Router networks are usually connectionless, and ATM is connection-oriented. Here is what a connection-oriented network based on the OSI-RM would look like.

3.1.2 X.25 packet-switched network

Many users may be familiar with traditional WAN delivery of packets between sites. Use of the term *packets* usually indicates a connection-oriented network service. The older (1984) X.25 standard describes a network architecture that looks very much like router-based networking.

This is no surprise, since there is very little difference today between a router and a switch and between switching and routing as a way of getting packets through a network of layer 3 PDU relaying devices. In X.25, an X.21 connector specifies the physical layer. Link access protocol–balanced (LAP-B), a part of high-level data link control (HDLC, very similar to SDLC) forms the data link layer. The X.25 packet layer protocol (PLP) is the network layer.

The packet-switched network is shown in Fig. 3.4. Keep in mind that the switching function shown as a "layer" in the packet-switch device is not really a layer at all. It is really the overall function of the switch and is included merely to provide a correspondence to the routing function of a router.

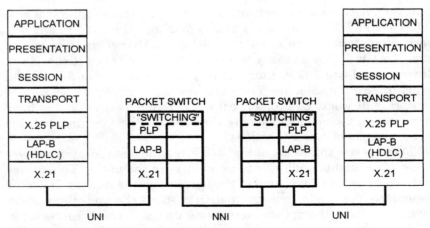

Figure 3.4   X.25 packet-switched network.

There is a switching function in the packet switch, and the internals of the packet network are left blank, as with the router network before. As before, the transport layer (layer 4) forms the end-to-end layer through the network. The user-to-network portion is known as the *user-to-network interface (UNI)*, and the network-to-network device portion is known as the *network node interface (NNI)*. Both are important in the ATM model.

3.1.3   Switching versus routing

The differences between router-based networking and switched-based networking are more in terms of operation than in architecture. Both network nodes operate at the bottom three layers of the OSI-RM; both involve taking in a layer 3 PDU from an input port, looking it up in a table, and forwarding it through the network to the next network node, and so on. The differences are not in the architecture but in the fact that routers are connectionless and switches are connection-oriented. This is the crucial difference in understanding how LAN interconnection with ATM switches will differ from LAN interconnection with routers.

Routers route datagrams (connectionless layer 3 PDUs), and switches switch packets (connection-oriented layer 3 PDUs). All layer 3 PDUs have similar structures. That is, there is a layer 4 PDU inside, with some layer 3 header attached. They differ only in the specifics of fields and lengths. A packet is a connection-oriented datagram, and a datagram is a connectionless packet. And by extension, a switch is a connection-oriented router, and a router is a connectionless switch. Today, most network nodes are "switchlike" or "routerlike," since many prod-

- SWITCHING:
  "PATH" SET UP AT CONNECTION TIME
  SIMPLE TABLE LOOKUP
  TABLE MAINTENANCE VIA SIGNALING
  NO OUT OF SEQUENCE DELIVERY
  LOST PATH MAY LOSE CONNECTIONS
  MUCH FASTER THAN PURE ROUTING

- ROUTING:
  CAN WORK FULLY CONNECTIONLESS
  COMPLEX ROUTING ALGORITHM
  TABLE MAINTENANCE VIA PROTOCOL
  OUT OF SEQUENCE DELIVERY LIKELY
  VERY ROBUST: NO CONNECTIONS LOST
  SIGNIFIGANT PROCESSING DELAY

Figure 3.5 Switching versus routing.

ucts combine the features of both, much like bridges and routers did before. However, ATM network nodes are switches.

Routers and switches do differ significantly in operation. These differences are summarized in Fig. 3.5. Switches set up *paths* through the network at connection time. This connection time may be done by contract at service provision time or upon processing the first datagram for connectionless services. Both switches and router may deliver connectionless and/or connection-oriented *services,* but it is more efficient to do so on the "native" mode of the network. That is, connection-oriented switches will always be able to offer connection-oriented services in a simpler, more efficient, and more economical fashion. This path also may be set up using a special protocol designed just for the purpose: the *signaling protocol.*

Once the connection is set up, all traffic follows the same path through the network. There is only a simple table lookup needed to switch traffic to the correct output port. The table entries are established and maintained by the signaling protocol. Because all traffic follows the same path, there can be no out-of-sequence delivery. This has an important effect. It means that if a destination receives packet 1 and then packet 3 from the source at the other end of the connection, the receiver knows that packet 2 is not coming and can take immediate steps to correct the situation.

However, a lost path may mean that all connections using that path may be lost. And even if the switches can somehow move the connections to a new path, the signaling protocol must be fast enough to update all the affected tables without losing much data. The drawback is balanced by the fact that switches are much faster internally than routers, due primarily to the simpler processing rules internally.

A router can work in a totally connectionless manner. This requires a full *routing algorithm,* or set of rules, to follow at each network node. These rules will be followed to determined which one of several outputs will be used to send the datagram on its way. Even if 99 datagrams have followed the same route to a destination, the one-hundredth datagram may not. Router tables are more complex than switch tables because they must take these possibilities into account.

Unlike switches, these router tables are maintained by a full routing protocol that runs between each adjacent router in the network (and users also in many cases). Signaling protocols tend to be very rudimentary compared with routing protocols, but routers gain the ability to dynamically route traffic around failed links.

This has a price, however. Routers deliver datagrams out of sequence all the time, since the actual route a datagram takes may vary from minute to minute on a router-based network. Unfortunately, this means that a receiver that has gotten datagram 1 and datagram 3 can make no assumptions at all about datagram 2. It may still be on its way by a longer route, or it may never arrive. Delays are added at the destination to deal with these situations. And, of course, as soon as the destination notifies the sender to resend datagram 2, the missing datagram 2 shows up.

All these characteristics combine to make router-based networks significantly slower than switch-based networks in terms of both nodal delay and end-to-end network delay. Again, however, many network devices today combine aspects of switches and routers as designers seek to take advantage of the pluses of both.

3.1.4   Frame-relay network

What if network nodes did not have to extract the layer 3 packets from the layer 2 frames in order to process (switch/route) them? Then the network node would not be switching packets around the network but relaying frames. This is the philosophy behind frame-relay networks.

Frame-relay networks take the functions of X.25, which include full error control and flow control hop by hop—between switches—through the network, and strip them down to the bear essentials—routing. Error control and flow control move to the "edges" of the network, which is actually to the end-user customer premises equipment. This makes possible the rapid transmission that is characteristic of frame-relay networks, using LAP-F (for frame relay) and the high-speed serial interface (HSSI) at layers 2 and 1 (other standards are possible).

Frame relay is therefore a version of X.25 for the 1990s. Instead of the normal nine processing steps that an X.25 switch must take to move a packet through a switch or network node, frame-relay network nodes take only two processing steps. This makes the nodal processing delay much less than in an X.25 network, making frame relay much more suitable for the high-speed networks needed today. A frame-relay protocol stack is shown in Fig. 3.6.

Notice, however, the similarities frame-relay networks have with both routers and X.25 networks; the NNI is very permissive, and rout-

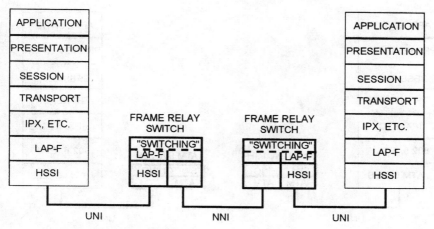

Figure 3.6 Frame-relay network.

ing/switching must still be done somehow in the network. In frame relay there is a *logical connection,* an identifier included in the frame, but it is a connection nonetheless. This is the data link connection identifier (DLCI) in frame relay, a composite field made up of two separate fields from the original high-layer data link control (HDLC) frame structure that forms the basis for frame relay.

Most important, this now makes layer 3, the network layer, the *end-to-end layer* in the network. While this gives the chance to use Novell's IPX or other protocols (anything with packets) over the frame-relay network, has this modified the OSI-RM? In other words, if the end-to-end layer of the network is layer 4 by definition, is layer 3 in a frame-relay network now "promoted" to layer 4, again by definition? And does it really matter?

These questions will be answered shortly. But first, since the removal of layer 3 in the network node seems to have had such good effects in terms of efficiency and speed, maybe the same trick will work again.

3.1.5 Cell-relay (ATM) network

As it turns out, there is still another layer to play around with. If a network node can relay frames instead of switching packets, cannot the network node relay bits around the network even more quickly? Yes, it can. There is a problem, however. There is no unit at the physical layer to process at a network node. Other than bits, pure 0s and 1s, there is no structure at all.

What cell relay and ATM do is invent a structure: the cell. Now the network nodes are relaying cells around the network, and layer 2 becomes the *end-to-end layer*. This is shown in Fig. 3.7. This is nice for

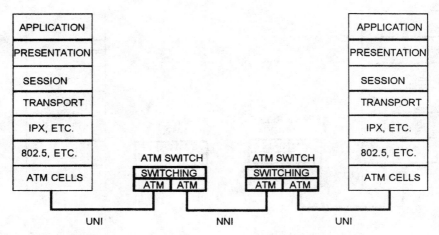

Figure 3.7 Cell-relay (ATM) network.

a number of reasons, because now it does not matter if the user networks are running Token Ring (802.5), Ethernet (really 802.3), or whatever. It is the perfect LAN interconnection technology. Notice, however, that switching still takes place. This is still very much a connection-oriented network.

Also, the NNI portion is part of the standard. This is something new. Usually, switch vendors are allowed to implement almost anything they please on the NNI. The only requirement is that the switches understand each other. The problem is that this tends to lock customers into a specific vendor, since the products from other switch vendors will almost certainly *not* work together with those of the original vendor. ATM standards are more conscious of interoperability requirements.

But is not a cell defined as a fixed-length *block?* Has the frame now been made the end-to-end unit of the network, and not the packet? Yes to both. Has this process really stripped off layers and functions of the OSI-RM, or is something else going on?

The discussion so far has brought problems trying to fit ATM into a strict interpretation of the OSI-RM. Either the physical layer has gotten very smart and function-rich, or there is more going on than meets the eye. Purists demand that the end-to-end layer is, by definition, layer 4, and what is routed or switched is, by definition, a layer 3 packet. They have added fuel to the debate by consistently defining a cell as a fixed-length packet rather than the more noncommittal fixed-length block. Keep in mind that a model is not reality. It is a useful tool for understanding reality but really no more than that. In ATM, the reality is that the network nodes still need to route or switch cells between end systems, and more than just physical layer activity is needed to make this happen. Whether this means that several new layers have been slid under layer 2 or that the functions of some other layers have been "promoted" to higher levels of the OSI-RM really depends on how it is looked at. In the model of ATM as a physical layer entity, ATM is a network for connecting routers. The traditional routing function is performed at the network layer. The bottom line is that for the present, the exact relationship of the ATM layers to the OSI-RM layers is undefined.

3.1.6 The six necessary cell functions

Whatever a cell is in regard to the OSI-RM, the ATM network exists to move cells around the network. What needs to be done to transport cells across a network can be expressed as a list of six essential elements. All networks that are cell-based, and ATM is only one possible implementation of cell-based networks, must process their cells in each network node according to these six necessary cell functions.

The layers of the ATM protocol stack implement each of these functions:

1. *Routing of cells must occur in a connectionless manner.* This is not done with all cells on all connections, so this function is not needed in all cases. Even though ATM is a logical outgrowth of older connection-oriented protocols, ATM networks must still provide connectionless services to users who require them. In ATM networks, a separate layer is needed to establish tables in the ATM switches to associate logical end-system destination addresses with network node connections. This is a complex task that will be dealt with in more detail in a later chapter. And even in the case of connectionless services, all the cells must still follow the same connection path through the ATM network.

2. *Housekeeping tasks must be done to establish and maintain ATM connections and handle the different service requirements of voice, video, and data.* This task is usually described as *adaptation* because this term emphasizes the fact that services as diverse as voice (with its constant generation of small voice samples) and video (with its high bit rate and complex compression needs) must be adapted to a cell stream that will all be mixed together with data cells on the ATM network.

3. *Segmenting and reassembly must be done to break down frames or packets or other data units into cells at the sender and build them up again at the receiver.* Within the ATM network, they will generally remain cells, although this may not always be true for some services.

4. *Cell handling, or ATM switching, must be done hop by hop through the network in an exact analogy of what our routers/switches*

did before.   At the end systems, this layer must multiplex the various types of service connections into a single cell stream that preserves the service requirements of the connection. This layer constructs the cell headers at the sending system and interprets them at the receiving system. In each network node or switch, this layer must examine the cell headers and make switching decisions based on these header field values. It also may modify the cell header field contents. This layer forms the very heart of ATM.

5. *Convergence must be provided so that different types of physical transport media for cells can be supported.*   Cells may not be sent directly out on a link (although this is allowed), since most physical transport media today are *framed* transports. This terminology should not be confused with layer 2 protocol data unit *frames,* as in "Token Ring frames." *Physical transport frames,* as in "T-1 frames," refer to very low-level structures not covered by the OSI-RM. This model and all models of communications protocol stacks essentially stop at the connector at the back of the end system or network node. However, cells must still be packaged inside transport frames at the sender and unpacked at each network node. The network node must repackage the cells for the next link and so on to the destination.

6. *The sending of the physical bits as 1s and 0s over the physical media transport must be done.*   Cells or frames or packets, all bits must be sent on most network links as a sequential series of 0s and 1s. This layer must generate the proper line coding to represent the 0s and 1s in a manner understood by the receiver.

All six of these functions are done in ATM networks. How they are split into layers, what the layers are called, and how they are implemented are the proper activities of various standards organizations.

For instance, the ITU-TSS has split five of the functions into three main layers for ATM: the physical layer, the ATM layer, and the AAL (ATM adaptation layer). The topmost function, for connectionless services, is a separate layer altogether. Other splits are possible. Bellcore has developed a split for their switched multimegabit data service (SMDS) based on yet another cell-based protocol known as *distributed queue dual bus (DQDB),* which uses cells for connectionless LAN interconnectivity. In SMDS, the cell functions are split into three layers called SMDS *interface protocol (SIP) layers* that map very well into the ATM architecture layers. In the case of SMDS connectionless services over an ATM network, the network must have CLNAP at the topmost layer (really it is CLNS, connectionless network services). These layerings as illustrated in Fig. 3.8.

Keep in mind that these are all models, and they should not be stretched to the breaking point to fit them to older models that never envisioned the capabilities or requirements of ATM networks.

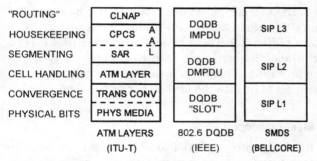

"ROUTING"	CLNAP		DQDB IMPDU	SIP L3
HOUSEKEEPING	CPCS	A A L		
SEGMENTING	SAR		DQDB DMPDU	SIP L2
CELL HANDLING	ATM LAYER			
CONVERGENCE	TRANS CONV		DQDB "SLOT"	SIP L1
PHYSICAL BITS	PHYS MEDIA			
	ATM LAYERS (ITU-T)		802.6 DQDB (IEEE)	SMDS (BELLCORE)

Figure 3.8 Implementing the six cell functions.

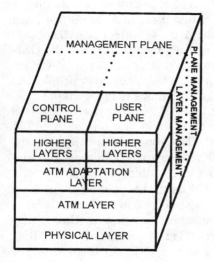

Figure 3.9 B-ISDN protocol reference model.

3.2 B-ISDN Protocol Reference Model

ATM is included under the umbrella idea of the broadband integrated services digital network (B-ISDN), a logical extension of older ISDN methods to the new world of higher-speed networks (to ITU-TSS, broadband equals faster than T-1/E-1 speeds of 1.544 or 2.048 Mbps). Models such as this use the concept of planes. *Planes* are just another way of visualizing the multiple needs a model addresses (Fig. 3.9). The *user plane* is concerned with the transfer of bits through the network, while the *control plane* sets up connections, maps table entries, and does various other signaling chores. The *management plane* is split into plane management and layer management, both concerned with resources and performance of the network. Network implementers speak of OAM (operations and maintenance) functions in Europe and OAM (operations, administration,

and maintenance) or even OAM&P (operations, administration, maintenance, and provisioning) functions here in the United States.

Notice the main point of Fig. 3.9: There are no longer OSI-RM layers.
They are masked by the label "higher layers," which is a polite way of saying that they could be anything. This is an idea that is worth exploring
in more detail. How *can* ATM fit into the OSI-RM, and how *should* it?

3.2.1   ATM as a MAC layer protocol

Since ATM does not fit easily into the OSI-RM, it can basically be fit in
anywhere implementers want it to. All that really changes much is
exactly where the interface between OSI layers and ATM is located.
However, this will enhance or restrict ATM capabilities depending on
where cells are available for services. For instance, an ATM network can
easily be built that uses ATM as a Media Access Control (MAC) sublayer protocol. That is, it uses only ATM as the physical layer of the OSI-
RM, exactly as it has been developed to this point and as many writers
have depicted it. There is no need for a LAN MAC sublayer at all (it is
not a LAN), so Logical Link Control (LLC) frames may be mapped directly into ATM cells and sent out (Fig. 3.10). This is the position SMDS
basically takes in ATM networks. In fact, a working group of the ATM
Forum—the LAN Emulation Services (LES) Group—is working to standardize this process for all IEEE LANs. There are advantages and disadvantages to using ATM networks as a MAC sublayer, of course.

The advantages of implementing ATM as a MAC sublayer protocol
(some call it a *virtual LAN,* since it now spans wide areas but still functions as a single LAN) are that ATM now becomes just another transport method, like Token Ring or Ethernet. It now extends the OSI-RM,
mainly by adding the ATM sublayers to the physical layer. And, of
course, the ATM network access is totally transparent to the user.
There are disadvantages as well. There is obviously no broadcast capability, since ATM is connection-oriented. There is no access to QOS

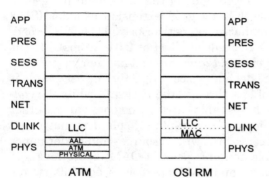

Figure 3.10   ATM as a layer
protocol.

parameters by a user, since these are employed at higher layers in the OSI-RM. Most seriously, the router function that "true" internetworks do so well is missing. Frames from Token Ring, for example, *cannot* be taken to true Ethernets directly. The LLC and SNAP frame structures are *different* in each case. Routers do this but *not* ATM switches. More important, this is not "really" ATM at all. All the nice features of ATM (flexible bandwidth, multimedia transport, and so on) are completely hidden from the users. ATM just becomes a (poor?) substitute for a router-based TCP/IP network.

3.2.2 ATM as a link layer protocol

However, there is nothing to stop us from implementing ATM as a data link layer protocol either. Now network layer packets (e.g., IP datagrams) may be loaded into cells and sent across the ATM networks. There is no need for any other data link layer protocols at all. The LLC and MAC sublayers are not needed (Fig. 3.11). This is the proposal of the position of ATM in a TCP/IP network, as put forward by the Internet Engineering Task Force (IETF).

There are advantages and disadvantages here as well. We still have two of the three advantages listed before, with ATM offering transparent user access and extending the OSI-RM. But ATM is no longer just another transport method because of the way the network layer interacts with the data link layer. That is, the unique network address exists at the network layer [e.g., the IP address, the ISO NSAP (network service access point)], but frames are sent based on the link layer address [e.g., the globally unique network interface card (NIC) address in LANs, the locally unique HDLC (high-level data link control) identifier in WANs, etc.]. Network layer PDUs must be sent as link layer PDUs based on the link layer address. All protocols, but especially TCP/IP, must "map" the network layer address to a link layer address. The protocol developed to do this in TCP/IP, known as the *address res-*

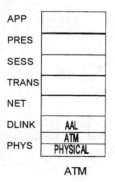

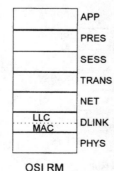

Figure 3.11 ATM as a link layer protocol.

olution protocol (ARP), which uses broadcasts, will not work with ATM as a link layer protocol.

However, there is also an additional disadvantage, namely, that the network layer protocol (e.g., IP) has to be modified somewhat. ATM is a new way of doing networking, not just different. IP and other older protocols will have to be changed a little (or maybe a lot) to work with ATM as a data link protocol. The IETF has proposed "InARP" as one modification to TCP/IP for this purpose, but more may be needed. Serious proposals to actually scrap TCP/IP and merge them into one protocol just for ATM networks have been made. After all, TCP and IP are not really separate protocols to begin with. (In the real world, no layer 3/4 protocols function totally independently.)

3.2.3   ATM as a network layer protocol

Given the problems with ATM as a data link and MAC sublayer, perhaps it fits in better at the network layer. Now ATM can interface directly with the end-to-end layer: the transport layer (e.g., TCP). ATM now forms the entire transport network from one endpoint to the other (Fig. 3.12). The transport layer "address" is used, *not* the network layer address (e.g., IP address). There is no need for it, or even a way to express it, anymore in this model of an ATM network. ATM forming the entire transport network seems completely natural, and the popular convention of defining a cell as a fixed-length packet seems to identify ATM cells with layer 3 (network layer) PDUs (packets). Unfortunately, because TCP is so tied up with IP, this approach is next to impossible with existing TCP/IP implementations. And the same argument extends to all popular layer 3 and layer 4 protocols, which *should* function just fine without each other but in reality just do not.

Therefore, this move introduces a whole new set of problems. This arrangement is anything but "transparent." It puts ATM right in the user's face. However, it does mean that only one universal network

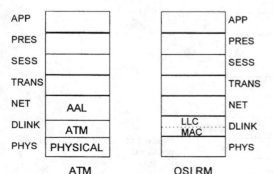

Figure 3.12 ATM as a network layer protocol.

address is needed. It offers hope for direct connectivity anywhere on the ATM network (i.e., there are no "subnets" anymore; there is *only* ATM). And only one routing method is needed: ATM routing. No more "multiprotocol routers" exist on this version of the network.

However, this cuts both ways: The transport layer must be modified for an ATM interface. Not only that, this scheme does away with the whole concept of router-based networking. There must be connections across the network. And, most critically, this is totally incompatible with the installed base. Fortunately, no group has seriously proposed this approach.

3.2.4 ATM as a transport layer protocol

Of course, it is possible to place ATM as high up in the OSI-RM as possible: at the transport layer itself. [It would not fit any higher; the upper layers (5, 6, and 7) exist for specific functions and applications, not for general networking tasks.] Now *all* applications are ATM applications. Programs will send and receive cells directly. There will be one Application Program Interface (API) for all applications: an ATM API (this has been proposed by the ATM Forum) (Fig. 3.13). In fact, there is nothing to preclude its use as an *internal* "protocol"; the monitor of a PC is no more than a video screen, and memory could be seen as a data transfer across a very short network (the memory bus). Why not use ATM inside the computer as well? Surely this is the best place for ATM after all.

Unfortunately, even this does not solve all the problems. True, there are advantages, such as direct application access to ATM and real QOS access for multimedia and video, and it does make the most effective and efficient use of ATM networks, but there are other considerations. This requires major changes to existing program APIs and methodologies. ATM requirements and networking paradigms are poorly understood by today's program writers and multimedia authors. Also, ATM

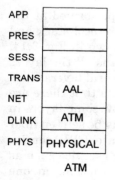

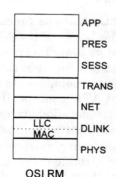

Figure 3.13 ATM as a transport layer protocol.

would mesh poorly with existing operating systems' network interfaces. These expect variable-sized packets, as before, and may not work efficiently with ATM.

However, it is important to point out that this is essentially what full B-ISDN does: ATM is the transport network, while B-ISDN forms the upper (user) layers.

3.2.5   ATM and the OSI-RM

The discussion in this entire section is to emphasize one essential point: that ATM networking is different from any kind of networking ever developed previously. Even such clear-cut issues as "Where does it fit in with the OSI-RM?" are not given to obvious and easy answers. Added to this are purists' demands that the cell is a packet and that the layers connected at end systems by networks must be transport layers.

The only reason any ATM implementer needs to be concerned with these arguments is just this: What if Vendor A builds ATM networks and products viewing ATM as a link layer, and Vendor B builds ATM networks and products viewing ATM as a network layer? What happens to interoperability?

It may even be possible for customers hooked up to the same ATM network *not* to be able to communicate at all, because one uses the ATM network as a transport layer and the other uses ATM as a network layer. These customers may not be happy with this situation.

Does this mean that providers of ATM networking services must support *all* combinations of ATM layerings and interfaces? Perhaps, but this does raise the issue of why a company spends millions of dollars to go from a "too many networks" problem to a "too many ATMs" problem.

The bottom line is that a model is not reality. It is a useful tool for understanding reality but no more than that. For the present, the exact relationship of the ATM layers to the OSI layers is *undefined*.

3.3   ATM Functions and Layers

This section is a first look at the various functions performed at the ATM layers in more detail. The layers of the ATM protocol stack and the major functions performed at these layers are shown in Fig. 3.14. Notice that layer management is a function that spans all the layers and the use of various convergence components in several layers.

Convergence is an important ATM concept. It means that there are multiple options that may be employed above or below some layers in the model. Bits may be framed or sent "raw." They may be sent on fiber or coaxial cable. They may come from a constant-bit-rate (CBR) service such as voice or from a bursty variable-bit-rate (VBR) service such as LAN interconnection routers. Whatever the diverse options at one

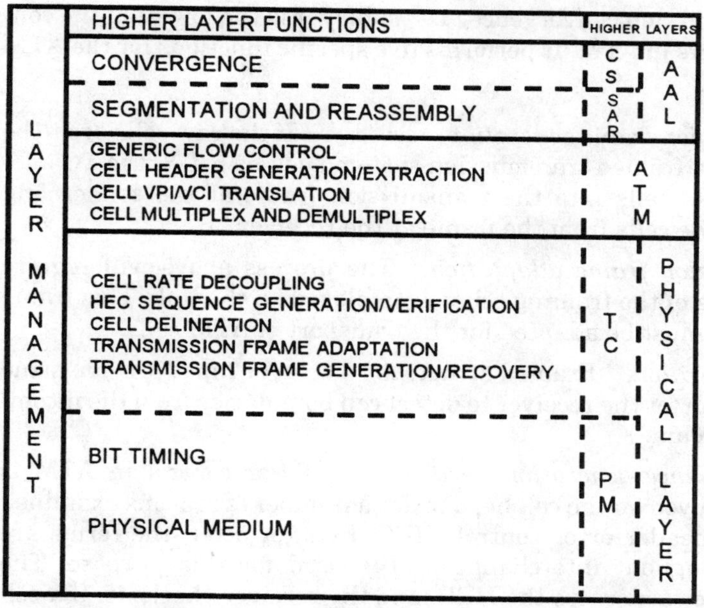

Figure 3.14 ATM functions and layers.

layer or another, however, the convergence layers help to present a uniform interface to other adjacent layers, just to make it easier for implementers.

The lowest layer of the ATM model is the physical layer, divided into two sublayers: the transmission convergence (TC) sublayer and the physical medium (PM) sublayer. The physical (PHY) layer is concerned only with functions that are completely dependent on the physical medium itself. These physical medium–dependent (PMD) functions include all bit transmission and bit alignment functions for transmitting 0s and 1s across the link. The line coding is therefore done here, and if the electric signal from the device is being sent over an optical link, this conversion is provided here as well.

Many physical media require Manchester coding or other schemes to provide bit timing and clocking from sender to receiver. If needed, this bit timing information is provided by this layer. Notice that various media such as optical fiber, coaxial cable, or even unshielded twisted-pair wire may be supported in various network configurations with ATM. As originally conceived by the CCITT in 1988, ATM was closely aligned with very high-speed fiber networks. As long-distance fiber networks running at these high speeds failed to materialize, the ATM Forum essentially decoupled the dependence of the ATM physical layer on fiber networks.

The transmission convergence (TC) sublayer is the lowest of the convergence layers in ATM. It performs five specific functions for the ATM layer above it:

1. *Transmission frame generation/recovery.*   If the raw cells are to be sent over a framed transmission system such as a T-3, the TC sublayer packs cells into the transmission frame at the sender and unpacks the cells from the frame at the receiver.

2. *Transmission frame adaptation.*   The process above will require knowledge of the framing scheme employed on the link. This frame structure must be adapted for the transport of ATM cells.

3. *Cell delineation.*   Framed or not, the TC layer must provide some mechanism for the receiver to detect cell boundaries from the incoming bit stream.

4. *HEC sequence generation/verification.*   Error control in ATM is only employed on the cell header (for a number of reasons examined later). A header error control (HEC) byte (or octet; the terms are used throughout interchangeably) is used for this purpose. The transmitter generates the HEC, and the receiver checks it. If a cell fails the HEC check, it is discarded to prevent the cell from being switched to the wrong destination.

5. *Cell rate decoupling.*   A bursty data service may spend a lot of time idle and then attempt to send a lot of data all at once. During these idle periods, the TC layer will insert special "idle" cells at the sender and remove them at the receiver. *Only* "nonidle" cells are passed up to the ATM layer itself.

The ATM layer is the heart of the ATM network. Its functions define what most people think an ATM network is all about:

1. The ATM layer multiplexes (mixes) cells over the same physical link. The multiplexed cells are distinguished by the network nodes (ATM switches) and at the destination by means of header fields that identify virtual paths (VPs) and virtual channels (VCs). (More on these two important ATM concepts soon.)

2. The ATM layer must translate the incoming VP identifier (VPI) and VC identifier (VCI) on a link to the proper VCI/VPI pair for the output link. These new pairs are placed in the cell header when the cell is switched to the output link. The values are obtained from a table in the switch. This table is built at connection time by signaling protocol messages on the management plane of ATM. (This is the main distinction between a switch and a router; routers do not deal with connections as such.)

3. At the endpoints of the networks, the ATM layer generates and interprets the cell headers. *Only* the payload field of an ATM cell is ever passed up to the layers above.

4. On the UNI side of the network only, the ATM layer provides a generic flow control (GFC) mechanism for media access. The GFC function is neither available nor defined on the network node interface (NNI) between ATM switches.

The ATM adaptation layer (AAL) is required on end systems but is not always required on internal network nodes, such as the ATM switches themselves. The AAL is divided into two sublayers: the segmentation and reassembly (SAR) sublayer and the convergence sublayer (CS).

The SAR sublayer supplies a "bookend" function so that the receiver can associate a sequence of cells into the original frame or other data unit the sender broke down into cells. The CS provides the mechanism for mixing the different requirements of voice, video, and data by defining a number of *classes of service,* each with the appropriate parameters for the service. These are used to provide the proper quality-of-service (QOS) parameters on that connection. The four classes of service currently defined are mapped onto six "types" of AALs for ATM implementation.

The four AAL service classes are defined by three parameters that the higher layers may require of the transport:

1. *Timing relation between the source and destination.* Also known as *real-time applications,* traffic such as 64-kbps digitized voice must retain the timing relation across ATM. This timing relation is essential in voice and other constant-bit-rate (CBR) applications. CBR applications will not function correctly if a sender is generating 64 kbps in each second, but the ATM network delivers 32 kbps and then 96 kbps to the receiver, even though the gross number of bits sent and received is the same.

2. *Bit rate.* Some services have a constant bit rate; others have a variable bit rate (VBR) over time. These CBR applications include uncompressed digitized voice and video. It is important to note that CBR services will automatically become VBR services with the addition of compression.

3. *Connection mode.* Some services, such as voice, are always connection-oriented. That is, a connection must be established across the network with the destination before any data transfer can take place. Some services are connectionless. Data transfer may be attempted at any time. Others, including many kinds of data services, may be either.

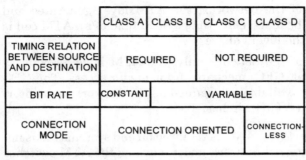

	CLASS A	CLASS B	CLASS C	CLASS D
TIMING RELATION BETWEEN SOURCE AND DESTINATION	REQUIRED		NOT REQUIRED	
BIT RATE	CONSTANT	VARIABLE		
CONNECTION MODE	CONNECTION ORIENTED			CONNECTION-LESS

Figure 3.15 The four AAL service classes.

The established AAL service classes established by the ITU and AAL types are shown in Fig. 3.15. Typical services using these classes might be

Class A: Circuit emulation, constant-bit-rate voice and video

Class B: Variable-bit-rate audio and video (compressed)

Class C: Connection-oriented data transfer

Class D: Connectionless data transfer

The six types of AALs that use these services will be covered in detail later. It should be noted that these service classes have been modified somewhat by the ATM Forum. The ATM Forum now recognizes five AAL service "categories." These also will be dealt with in detail later.

3.3.1 ATM virtual channels and paths

As has already been pointed out, ATM is a network architecture that uses unchannelized network transports. Of course, traffic still must be identified as voice, video, or data if for no other reason than to preserve the required QOS parameters for each separate service. Since there are no physical channels to distinguish the traffic in an ATM network, their place is taken by logical connections. Instead of voice or video channels, ATM networks have voice or video connections. In ATM networks, these logical connections are established and maintained by means of a two-part identifier structure: the virtual channel and virtual path.

Virtual channels (VCs) and virtual paths (VPs) are a part of the overall architecture of broadband ISDN (B-ISDN). ATM is the network transport for B-ISDN, and VCs and VPs form the ATM layer transport functions on a logical level, as opposed to the physical level transport functions of sending bits over a specific medium. A *virtual channel* is "a concept used to describe unidirectional transport of ATM cells associated by a common unique identifier value" (CCITT I.113). This unique

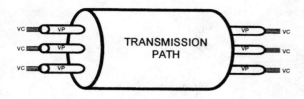

VC = VIRTUAL CHANNEL
VP = VIRTUAL PATH

Figure 3.16 Relation of VCs and VPs.

identifier is the VCI. Note that the VCI is valid in one direction. A *virtual path* is "a concept used to describe unidirectional transport of cells belonging to virtual channels that are associated by a common identifier value" (CCITT I.113). This is the VPI. Note that the VPI is also valid in one direction.

VCIs and VPIs are in cell headers and are hierarchical. Many VCs may make up a VP. Cells flow along the transmission path in an ATM network (Fig. 3.16). In the cell header are VCI and VPI fields. The transmission path itself may comprise several VPs, although this is not necessarily true. These VPs may in turn be comprised of several VCs. What is the purpose of the VCs and the VPs? Besides forming a useful way of distinguishing types of traffic (but not the only way) and various destinations, they form a method for establishing and using two other concepts in ATM: the idea of a virtual link and a virtual connection.

A *virtual channel link* is a unidirectional transport of cells from the place where a VCI is assigned to the place where it is translated (switched) or removed. In the same way, a *virtual path link* is bounded by the points in the network where the VPI value is assigned or translated or removed. Thus links on VCs or VPs are just the paths on the ATM network where the VCI or VPI values stay the same. The places where they change establish the endpoints of the link.

Obviously, user end systems will be separated by more than one VC link and VP link in most cases. In these instances, the concatenation of these virtual channel links is called a *virtual channel connection (VCC)*, and a concatenation of virtual path links is called a *virtual path connection (VPC)*. Thus a connection in an ATM network guides all cells along the same path on the ATM network, and each connection consists of a series of links, all of which have a consistent value of the VPI or VCI field in the cell header. A connection has many consecutive VPI and VCI field values in its cells' headers but always the same series as they make their way across the network. Multiplexing and switching in ATM are *always* done on VPs first and *then* on VCs. This is based on their hierarchical relationship.

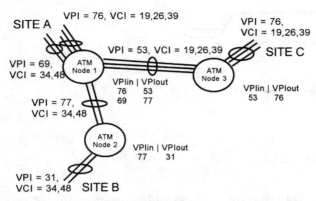

Figure 3.17 ATM VCI and VPI usage.

This is all well and good, but what are VCs and VPs used for in an ATM network? Basically, the VCI field identifies *dynamically* allocated connections, and the VPI field identifies *statically* allocated connections.

In the connection-oriented ATM network, a VCI is assigned at call setup time via a signaling channel. It has only local significance on the link between ATM switches (meaning other switches may be using the same connection values on other links) and is translated switch by switch by table lookups in the network. When the connection is released, the VCI value may be reused by other connections. However, B-ISDN allows for semipermanent connections between endpoints as well. Another name for virtual path seen in older ITU documentation is *virtual network*. ATM nodes will use the VPI values assigned to customers to switch traffic between ATM customer sites. In this way, it will be easier for the ATM node to switch a whole path between customer sites rather than merely channel by channel. Typical use of VPI and VCI values is shown in Fig. 3.17.

The figure shows an ATM network consisting of three ATM network nodes (switches) and three customer sites. Naturally, there may be many more customers attached to each ATM switch and many more ATM switches in the entire network, but this is a simplified picture. As such, the figure does not even show the physical links between the network nodes but only the logical VPI/VCI links.

The figure shows the relevant network node VPI/VCI translation table in each switch. There are many more potential table entries, but again, this is extremely simplified. In fact, the entire network shows the VPI/VCI values and translation tables from a specific point of view. This is a user's perspective from Site A of the network, on the outbound side only. *Outbound* refers to the fact that the figure is accurate only when a user at Site A is sending cells. Looking at the connections from any other user's point of view, or inbound traffic, would changes things radically.

This is how the ATM network uses the VPI/VCI values in a cell header to deliver traffic through the ATM network. The network service provider has agreed with users at Site A, either at the time the ATM service was first provided or by means of a signaling protocol, that when Site A sends cells to Site B, Site A generates cells with the VPI field in the cell header set to 69. Also, the service provider has set up the network (again, either by prearrangement or by a signaling protocol) so that cells generated by users at Site A with VPI = 76 will be delivered to Site C. Therefore, the connections indicated in the VPI fields take the place of physical channel destinations. This is the equivalent of a permanent virtual circuit (PVC) in a packet-switched network.

The channels themselves are represented by the VCI field values. VCI values may be set up by signaling or prearrangement, as are the VPIs. However, since VCIs are to represent *dynamic* resources, it is more likely that in ATM Forum networks VPIs will be set up at service provision time (PVCs, permanent virtual circuits), and VCIs will be set up by a signaling protocol (SVCs, switched virtual circuits). Note that the terms *PVC* and *SVC* are not ATM terms per se but are useful analogies to the actual ATM connection arrangements. In Fig. 3.17, Site A currently has defined VCI = 34 and 38 as contained within VPI = 69 and running to Site B. Site A also has defined VCI = 19, 26, and 39 within VPI = 76, and these terminate at Site C.

Here is how the cells sent with any established VPI and VCI combination find their way through the network to Sites B and C. ATM node 1 will process all the cells received from Site A on the physical link. The table shown (VPI$_{in}$/VPI$_{out}$) is a very abbreviated table of the kind of information associated with the physical link to Site A at ATM node 1. The ATM switch will translate the VPI field of the cell coming in from Site A based on the table and output the cell on the proper output link. In this case, a cell with VPI = 76, regardless of VCI field value, will be output on the link to ATM node 3 with VPI = 53. At ATM node 3, the cell with VPI = 53 will be output to Site C with VPI = 76, as shown in its table. It this case, Site C will recognize that cells arriving with VPI = 76 are coming for Site A.

The same process occurs when Site A sends cells to Site B. In this case, cells are sent to ATM node 1 with VPI = 69. These cells are sent on the output port to ATM node 2 with VPI = 77. ATM node 2 will translate the cells with VPI = 77 to VPI = 31 and send them to Site B. Notice that there is no requirement to match the sending VPI with the receiving VPI. No switching or processing was done on the VCI fields at all. They simply went along for the ride, based on the VPI switching.

This example was very simple. The ATM nodes did not change the VCI field, for example. It would be possible to send VPI = 76 and VCI = 26 cells not to Site C, as is done here, but to Site B. But this would involve a second table lookup and translation. VPI switching is very powerful and fast. The VPIs themselves have local significance only, meaning that many ATM nodes may have a VPI = 77 assigned, as long as they serve different input or output links.

There are limitations, however. For example, there will be many links from user sites coming in to ATM node 1 (and all the others as well), but the VPI field is only 8 bits wide, giving only 256 possible unique VPI values. Any more and a second link must be installed. And it is not the sites attached to a particular switch that is the issue but the number of destinations. For instance, if Site A has a very large network and needs connectivity to 300 remote sites, one link will not be sufficient, because only 256 unique sites can be addressed with VPIs. VCIs have more flexibility, since the VCI field is 16 bits wide, giving about 64,000 unique VCI connections from site to site. Thus one possibility is to use subsets of VCI to connect larger numbers of sites (e.g., 1 to 1000 for Site B, 1001 to 2000 for Site C, etc.). A second possibility is to allow the VPIs themselves to be switched (i.e., established with a signaling protocol like VCIs). They may still be viewed as "semipermanent," but the network nodes have much more work to do to establish these site paths dynamically. For now, both the ATM Forum and the ITU limit VPI usage to site connectivity without switching capability.

Another limitation is the fact that between the network nodes the VPI field is expanded, but only to 12 bits. This gives 4096 VPIs between ATM network nodes, but no more. Since many user network interfaces will be attached to one ATM network node, this is necessary. Otherwise, there would have to be one switch-to-switch link for every user link, each carrying only 256 VPIs. To avoid this, the VPI field is expanded to 4096 and so can carry the VPIs for up to 16 ($16 \times 256 = 4096$) user-network interface links. However, is 16 adequate for large ATM networks? Again, switching would provide a possible solution but increase the processing load on the ATM network nodes. More details on the operation of ATM switches will be explored in a later chapter.

3.3.2   ATM switching concepts

The preceding network diagram showed the ATM network nodes acting as virtual path switches. In this case, although the VPIs changed on a node-by-node basis, the VCIs did not. The VPI translation was done by a simple table lookup at each ATM network node.

These *VP switches* terminate the previously defined VP links and therefore must translate the incoming VPIs to the outgoing VPIs. This is sometimes referred to as a *virtual network* because the assignment and use of virtual channels are up to the end users, and the ATM network provides connectivity between site locations. This can be useful for LAN-to-LAN or client-server, router-based networked applications. A VP switch is shown in Fig. 3.18.

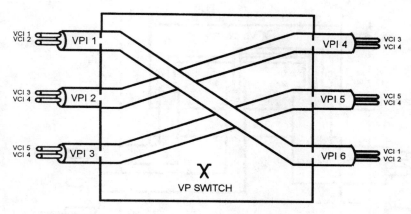

VCI = VIRTUAL CHANNEL IDENTIFIER
VP = VIRTUAL PATH
VPI = VIRTUAL PATH IDENTIFIER

Figure 3.18   VP switching.

However, VP switching is not the only possibility for an ATM net-work node. These network nodes also may switch virtual channels, although this function must be built on top of a virtual path switch function. These VC and VP switches terminate both VC links and (of course) VP links (otherwise we could not get at the virtual channels). Now VCI translation is possible, again based on a table lookup, usual-ly in a completely separate table. It is important to note that *all* cells associated with a particular VPI/VCI value in a cell header are trans-ported along the *same path* (so cell sequence—first sent, first re-ceived—is preserved). There is *no* dynamic routing on a cell-by-cell basis. (This function, cell-by-cell routing, must be provided by a sepa-rate mechanism in the ATM switch if it is to be provided at all.) While dynamic routing might be good for data (especially connectionless data), it would cause havoc among the cells set aside for voice/video/audio, where elaborate bit sequencing mechanisms do not exist in end-user equipment. This is an important point that must not be over-looked or minimized. The fact remains that networks based on ATM standards make extraordinary efforts to afford consistent delays and sequential delivery for CBR applications such as uncompressed audio, video, and voice. A full VPI/VCI switch is shown in Fig. 3.19.

Although it is not expected to be common because its application is not obvious, it is nevertheless allowed to have a pure VC switch in an ATM network. That is, the VP switch function exists but is just a "pass through" while the VCIs are reassigned. This device is shown in Fig. 3.20. The network will have more to say about VCIs and VPIs when considering the ATM layer in more detail later.

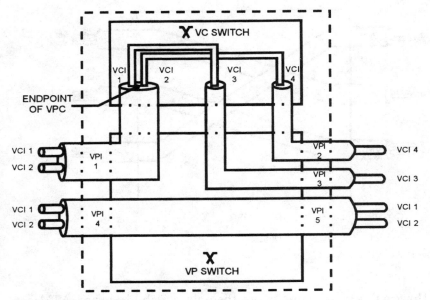

Figure 3.19 VP and VC switching.

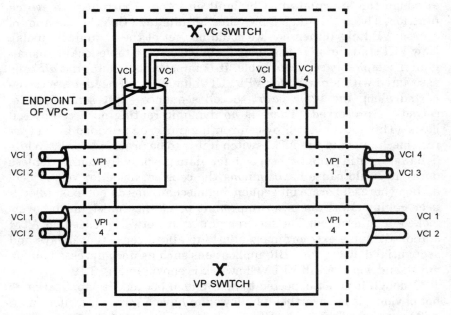

Figure 3.20 VC switching.

When discussing ATM switches, it is always a good idea to keep in mind that these devices are switches, not routers. Recall that the difference in *routing* is that all hop-by-hop output link decisions are made based on information included in the packet header, and each packet is sent repeatedly through the routing process at each node. In *switching*, all hop-by-hop link decisions are made *ahead of time,* and resources are allocated at this point. Thereafter, *no* other decisions are necessary other than a quick table lookup. Header information may be kept to a minimum.

The other advantage that switch-based networks have is with the use of sequential delivery. If delivery of data is not guaranteed to be sequential, as with connectionless, router-based networks, if a destination receives packet 1 and 3 but not packet 2, the destination must wait to see if packet 2 shows up. This means that an additional delay must be built into the destination to allow for this. On the other hand, packet 2 may be "lost" in the network (a link or router fails, etc.) and never arrive. Thus the "timeout" interval must be balanced between the need to wait for an out-of-sequence packet and the need to request the sender to resend the missing packet.

Connection-oriented, switch-based networks have no limitation. With sequential delivery guaranteed, if the destination receives packet 1 and then packet 3, packet 2 must be missing in action in the network itself. Immediate steps may be taken by the destination to correct this error condition, which may involve notifying the sender that a retransmission is needed, but not necessarily.

Thus ATM switches make decisions based on the information in a VPI/VCI table. But how does the ATM switch VPI/VCI table information get there in the first place? There are actually several ways.

3.4   ATM Signaling Principles

Connectionless networks employ a sophisticated routing protocol to update tables stored in their network nodes, such as OSPF (open shortest path first). These protocols may add a large amount of traffic to the network and essentially run independently of the users of the network itself.

In ATM switch networks, things are different. The information on virtual channels stored in the ATM network nodes gets there from the users themselves. There are several ways a user can inform the ATM network what connections, either VPCs or VCCs, need to be set up on the ATM network. This whole process is known as *call control,* where a *call* is any connection on the ATM network.

The simplest way is to do it by hand. That is, the user of the ATM network service simply writes down all the connections needed on a piece of paper and hands it to the service representation of the ATM network service provider. The ATM network service provider may then configure the tables in the network and inform the user: "When cells are to be sent to the Boston videoconference site, use VPI 45 and VCI 186." (It may be up to the individual user to configure the site software to generate cell headers with these VPI/VCI field values, or the service provider may actually do it.) This whole process is known as setting up the connections at *service provision time* and has the advantage of being a straightforward process. These connections may be changed in the future, but this tends to be a slow process, relying as it does on the manual coordination of several parties.

Alternatively, there may be a signaling protocol that runs between the customer premises equipment (CPE) at the user's site and the ATM network node. This protocol must be a standard way for the devices themselves to set up, maintain, change, and terminate connections across the ATM network. In this scenario, the CPE sends a message to the local network node (the one that it is directly attached to) requesting a connection with Boston. The ATM network nodes set up the path, and if the connection is acceptable to the network (e.g., the destination will accept the connection), another message is sent back to the originator along the lines of "Connection OK, use VPI = 45, VCI = 186."

It is also possible to take a *hybrid* approach. It this case, VPIs may be assigned at service provision time on a per-site basis, and VCIs may be set up by means of some kind of signaling protocol. Current ITU standard ATM network implementations use VPIs in this "permanent" way for site connectivity (i.e., one VPI per building) and VCIs for "dynamic" connections between users at these sites.

Recall that VCs are dynamically assigned between users on the virtual path connections (virtual networks). ATM uses the same out-of-band signaling concept (i.e., no signaling is done over a channel used for traffic) that is used in narrowband ISDN. But instead of a *physical* "D channel" for signaling, ATM (and B-ISDN) uses a *logical* signaling channel. This signaling is done in ATM by cells sent from the user to the network and back again.

Of course, the signaling that needs to be done in an ATM network is much more complex than in a point-to-point connected voice or data network. ATM is designed to meet the broadband requirements of *all* network services. As such, ATM must support such connection types as point to multipoint (for video services where one cell sent into the network is delivered to a number of endpoints) and even multipoint to multipoint (for complex voice or video conferencing arrangements).

3.4.1 Required ATM signaling capabilities

Because of the wide-ranging capabilities of ATM networks, ATM signaling must be capable of doing a number of things. It must be able to establish, maintain, and release the actual user VCCs and even the static VPCs for information to flow across. It must be able to negotiate (and perhaps even renegotiate) the proper traffic and service characteristics of a connection. These are fairly obvious functions, but others are more subtle.

ATM allows multiconnection calls between users, transferring voice, image, and data simultaneously. These connections can be set up "on the fly," when needed, during a call connection. Conferencing is needed in some applications, and video will usually require multiple endpoints. Video is also highly "asymmetrical," with many bits outbound and few (if any) inbound.

ATM signaling standards must be capable of providing for all of these. Not much work has been done on a standard ATM signaling protocol at the ITU level. Most of the work is being done by the ATM Forum. Their current status will be dealt with in a later section.

3.4.2 ATM signaling virtual channels

At the user-network interface (UNI), signaling is handled by dedicated virtual channels used for signaling messages. Four different types have been specified, each serving a different purpose for the various types of traffic and connections. One of these signaling virtual channels (SVCs) is indispensable; there is only one permanent metasignaling virtual channel (MSVC) per user interface. That is, all users (and there may be up to 256) on the local network node link use the MSVC for signaling.

At the network node interface (NNI), the signaling plan is still being developed. Most likely it will adapt UNI signal principles onto existing national telephone signaling networks. Although more complete at the UNI level, the ATM signaling scheme has many possible forms of implementation, even as to whether some will be in the ATM end device (terminal) or in the ATM PBX customer premises equipment or even both.

The four types of SVCs start off with the metasignaling virtual channel (MSVC). It is *bidirectional,* meaning both the user may signal the network and the network may signal the user. It can use one and only one SVC. Metasignaling is a very new concept, and many early implementations of ATM networks (including those based on ATM Forum standards) will *not* include the use of metasignaling and MSVCs.

There are also two broadcast SVCs: general and selective. They are both *unidirectional,* meaning the network will only signal the user over these SVCs. The general broadcast SVC is a quick means for the network to send a signal to *all* signaling endpoints at the user interface. Therefore, only one SVC is needed (and in fact required). The selective broadcast SVCs may be many and are used for the network to signal *all* endpoints fitting the same "service profile category" (CCITT Q.932),

SVC TYPE	DIRECTIONALITY	NUMBER OF SVCs
META-SIGNALING CHANNEL	BIDIRECTIONAL	1
GENERAL BROADCAST SVC	UNIDIRECTIONAL	1
SELECTIVE BROADCAST SVC	UNIDIRECTIONAL	SEVERAL POSSIBLE
POINT-TO-POINT SVC	BIDIRECTIONAL	ONE PER SIGNALING ENDPOINT

Figure 3.21   ATM UNI signaling VCs.

e.g., all video endpoints. Thus general broadcast SVCs are used by the ATM network node for "here is something everybody should know"–type messages, and selective broadcast SVCs are used for "here is something all the voice users should know"–type messages. There may be several selective broadcast SVCs on a UNI, depending on the services supported on that link by the ATM network node.

Last of all, the point-to-point SVCs are the general way endpoints signal the network (and vice versa) to handle the VCCs and VPCs for data transfer [although VPCs will probably be established *statically* (by hand), at least in initial ATM implementations]. There will be many point-to-point SVCs that will handle the protocol messages between users and local network nodes on an ATM network. The four types of ATM UNI signaling SVCs are detailed in Fig. 3.21.

3.5   ATM Performance: Merging Voice, Audio, Data, and Video

An ATM network built for simultaneous transport of voice, audio, video, and data must have acceptable performance characteristics for each kind of service. Unfortunately, they all have different requirements with regard to a number of crucial parameters. Some of these parameters are shown in Fig. 3.22. Therefore, it will not be easy. It is not just a bandwidth problem; it is many problems. In terms of the effects of delay, error tolerance, and the "burstiness" of data, each service has its own distinctive requirements. And compressed voice, audio, and video now become "bursty" themselves. This does not help the problem; it just moves it. ATM has defined a number of performance parameters that will make the performance of the ATM layer acceptable for all these different services.

ATTRIBUTE:	VOICE	DATA	VIDEO
BANDWIDTH	LOW	VARIES	HIGH
DELAY TOLERANCE	LOW	VARIES	MEDIUM
ERROR TOLERANCE	HIGH	LOW	MEDIUM LOW(*)
BURSTS	NONE	MANY	NONE MANY(*)

* IF COMPRESSION IS USED

Figure 3.22 Merging voice, data, and video.

3.5.1 ATM layer network performance

In an ATM network, the performance ATM delivers is separate from the performance of the underlying transport. Bit errors may occur, and delays may vary from physical medium to physical medium, but the ATM cell offers some error detection and correction. This section will focus on the performance of the ATM layer itself.

A cell with an bit error (e.g., a 0 bit sent but a 1 bit received) in it is not the only possible bad outcome on an ATM network. Cell errors that are not detected in the header may result in misdirected cells turning up on the wrong connections. While cell transfer delay is a very important parameter, especially for real-time voice and video services, the delay variation is actually more important. Some ATM layer parameters for performance are defined as a ratio (good ones/bad ones); others are defined as a rate (number of occurrences per unit of time).

ITU-TSS (CCITT) Recommendation I.35B (for broadband) defines four possible things that may happen when a cell enters an ATM network:

1. *Successfully delivered cell.*   Cell arrives at the destination with less than time T cell delay. No error implications are made on the *information* in the cell, only the header. Note that a cell, to be considered successfully delivered, must arrive within a specified period and not just without any errors.

2. *Errored cell.*   Cell arrives with at least one detected bit error in the *information* in the cell. Another possibility is a *severely errored cell,* with information field bit errors equal to N ($N>1$, not specified by ITU yet, but most likely value $N = 2$).

3. *Lost cell.*   Cell either never arrives, or it arrives after the time T cell delay, in which case it is discarded at the destination.

4. *Inserted cell.*   Cell contains an undetected header error or is misdirected by ATM node and therefore shows up at the wrong destination.

3.5.2 ATM cell transfer delay and delay variation

Since it is not much of an exaggeration to say that the main purpose of ATM is to give acceptable traffic delay patterns for voice, video, and data over the same physical network, here is exactly what is meant by *acceptable*.

A cell is sent from a source *A* (*cell entry event* in ATM standards language) and arrives at a destination *B* (*cell exit event*). In between, there are links and network nodes. The links have a characteristic propagation delay (called the *nominal velocity of propagation,* or *NVP*), and the network nodes have a widely varying processing delay (due to switch processing time). If the effects of all these are combined, the time from the *first bit sent* from source *A* until the *last bit arrives* at destination *B* is the *cell transfer delay.* If this exceeds the time *T* after which a cell is supposed to be delivered, the arriving cell is discarded by the receiver, whether in error or not. This is illustrated in Fig. 3.23. *What is the maximum value of T?* No one knows for sure, and no one will know until large ATM networks are built and become common. Early ATM networks will almost certainly set the maximum allowable value of *T* so high that it will be extremely unlikely that any cell will be discarded at the destination due to exceeded time *T*. However, the more important parameter may be the cell delay *variation*.

The *cell delay variation (CDV)* in an ATM network refers to the fact that some cells will be switched very rapidly through the ATM network, but other cells may take longer, due to such effects as network nodal congestion. This will have a noticeable effect on constant-bit-rate (CBR) applications.

For example, digitized voice most commonly has a constant bit rate of 64 kbps. These bits are always flowing at this rate on a voice channel in a T-1 network. As long as it is a point-to-point dedicated channel, no delay variation exists (this is not strictly true, but processing delays

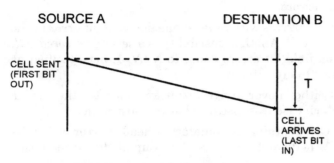

Figure 3.23 ATM cell transfer delay.

are limited by the ITU to less than 450 µs per circuit switch, not significant enough for this discussion).

CDV means that it is possible, when this digitized voice is sent over an ATM network, that a cell containing the digitized voice is delayed a variable amount of time when sent across the ATM network. However, receiving equipment in a digitized voice network will process the voice samples received based on a constant arrival pattern to the samples. Voice is distorted if the cells arrive at larger and larger intervals (called *dispersion*) or shorter and shorter intervals (called *clumping*). Therefore, a consistent delay across the ATM network is absolutely crucial for providing acceptable voice services.

The mechanism for providing this consistent delay on a widely variable delay ATM network is known as *ATM network conditioning*. It has the potential to be a critical aspect for ATM network acceptance among data users. As such, it will be dealt with in greater detail later on.

3.5.3 ATM performance parameters

The following parameters will fully characterize the performance of any ATM network. This means that by finding the values of these parameters through measurement on an ATM network, a network manager has all the information needed to make decisions about how the ATM network is currently performing. These decisions involve taking action to ensure network availability to users and that all current connections are receiving adequate service based on the class of service.

1. *Cell loss ratio.* The cell loss ratio is the ratio of the number of lost cells to the sum of the number of lost and successfully delivered cells.

2. *Cell insertion rate.* The cell insertion rate is the number of cells inserted (a *cell entry event,* defined in Sec. 3.5.2) into an ATM network within a specified time period (or perhaps per connection second). This is the performance parameter officially defined by the ITU. The ATM Forum, realizing the difficulty in defining a standard time period for all ATM networks, has redefined the cell insertion rate as a ratio. Now this cell insertion ratio is measured as the total number of misdelivered cells on a connection divided by the total number of misdelivered cells plus the total number of cells sent on the connection.

3. *Severely errored cell ratio.* The severely errored cell ratio is the ratio of severely errored cells (perhaps defined as cells with more than 1 bit error in the header; see Sec. 3.5.1) to the number of successfully delivered cells.

4. *Cell transfer capacity.* The cell transfer capacity is the maximum number of successfully delivered cells occurring over a specified ATM connection during a unit of time (probably a second).

5. *Cell transfer delay.* The cell transfer delay has two components: the mean cell transfer delay and the arithmetic average of a specified number of cell delays. The cell delay variation (CDV) is more critical and has been explained in Sec. 3.5.2. This is the difference between a specific cell delay observation and the average. It will be shown that this causes the most problems, especially with real-time voice and video (in fact, any constant-bit-rate application or service) requirements.

The ATM Forum Network Management Working Group has taken these ITU parameters and proposed several further modifications along the lines of the cell insertion ratio modification. None of these has currently reached the status of the cell insertion ratio change, however. The ATM Forum also has proposed extensions to these parameters for specific services, i.e., videoconferencing service.

3.6   ATM Traffic Control

In order to deliver the required performance outlined above, the ITU has defined a set of traffic control capabilities for ATM networks. *Traffic control* refers to the necessity for ATM networks to monitor traffic (cells) entering the network to ensure that the network is still capable of delivering the promised connection performance parameters to the users. If necessary, the ATM network must have the capability to scale back the rate at which cells enter the ATM network and even the ability to discard cells that have already entered the network. The whole task of traffic control in any network is a crucial function of network management.

This traffic control mechanism is much harder to implement in ATM networks than it sounds. Traffic control is well understood in data networks, where elaborate flow control and congestion control mechanisms have evolved in the protocols used there over the years. An ATM network, however, is more than a data network. Whatever is used for ATM traffic control must work not only for data connections but also for voice and video connections. How can a constant-bit-rate application such as uncompressed video be informed by the ATM network not to send any cells for a while? It really cannot, and this is a problem being explored by many standards organizations.

The ITU, in Recommendation I.311, has defined a set of functions that all ATM networks must implement to perform traffic control. These currently are

1. *Connection admission control.* ATM networks must set aside the proper amount of resources (e.g., to provide bandwidth or a bounded transmission delay) to service a connection. This is done at connec-

tion time, whether a connection is set up at service provision time on a semipermanent basis or by means of a signaling protocol on a dynamic basis. If the connection cannot be given these resources, the ATM network will not accept it.

2. *Usage parameter control.* ATM networks must "police" the user-network interface (UNI) to make sure cell traffic volumes and so forth do not affect overall network performance. For example, if a connection is granted on the ATM network based on a certain maximum cell insertion rate, or bandwidth, the ATM network itself must monitor that connection to make sure the accepted rate is not exceeded.

3. *Priority control.* ATM networks must adequately service buffers in the network nodes under all kinds of conditions. Under congested conditions, when there are just too many cells in the network, a priority mechanism can be used to remedy the congestion situation. That is, some cells can be discarded under congested conditions. Some method must exist for the ATM network nodes to quickly identify cells that are candidates for discarding and those which should not be discarded except under the most extreme conditions. (It is always more desirable to discard some traffic than to risk crashing the network and losing *all* traffic for a period of time until the network can be brought back up again.)

4. *Congestion control.* ATM networks must prevent congested conditions from spreading throughout the network. Congestion is a widely misunderstood concept in networking circles. While related to flow control, it is not "just" flow control. *Flow control* refers to the idea that a sender should never be able to send faster than a receiver can receive. *Congestion,* on the other hand, is a global property of the network itself, not a property of any individual user. No sender may be overwhelming any receiver, but the network may still be hopelessly congested; there is just too much traffic in it.

All these concepts are important enough for ATM network traffic control that they each deserve a closer look at the specifics.

3.6.1   ATM connection admission

ATM connection admission is performed at call setup time, when a VCC or VPC is established. The ATM network will only accept a call if the network has the resources to deliver the user's requested quality of service (QOS) end to end through the ATM network. This is important. The local network node at the sender's end of the network may have the resources, and the local network node at the receiver's end of the network may have the resources, but every possible path through the internal, or backbone, ATM network nodes cannot provide the request-ed QOS. The connection cannot be accepted at all.

The most critical aspect of QOS is to determine the source traffic characteristics: What exactly is required of the network? This source traffic can be characterized by four parameters. The first is the *average bit rate* at which the source operates, which is just an arithmetic mean over time (interval unspecified). The second is the *peak bit rate* at which the source is capable of sending (notice these are usually two different rates).

These two combine to form an important concept in ATM networks: burstiness, or burst ratio. The term *burstiness* is used for the ratio of peak to average bit rate. It may vary from 1 to 100 to 1000 for voice to compressed video to LAN data and is vital to know ahead of time. There is no standard definition of burstiness because there is currently no standard definition for the time period over which the average bit rate is to be computed. Clearly, network traffic on a connection averaged over a minute will be vastly different from network traffic averaged over a full day.

The third parameter is the *physical bit rate* of the link from the user to the local ATM network node. The average, peak, and physical bit rates a user declares as QOS parameters to the network may all differ, may all be the same, or may even all be zero. In the case that they are zero, the ATM Forum has defined a connection of this type to be *available-bit-rate (ABR) service*. This means that the connection is assigned whatever bit rate the ATM network connection admission procedure has determined to be available at the particular time.

The last parameter is peak duration. *Peak duration* is a measure of how long the source is capable of maintaining the peak bit rate. Again, this is absolutely necessary to know *before* a connection is accepted. Knowing the peak duration along with the other parameters enables the ATM network node to determine the maximum number of cells that may enter the network from a given connection during any time interval. A standard value for peak duration has been proposed, at least in ATM Forum implementations. It is currently defined in proposals as $\frac{1}{2}$ s, $\frac{3}{4}$ s, 1 s, $1\frac{1}{4}$ s, or $1\frac{1}{2}$ s. These values are taken from current frame-relay network values. Given these four values and the user's class of service, the ATM network has all the information it needs to decide whether a connection should be granted or not on the network. ATM Forum proposals allow these values to be negotiated between the user and the local network node at connection setup time. In other words, a connection that has been rejected with a peak bit rate request of 10 Mbps can try to get a connection with a revised peak bit rate of 5 Mbps. All the parameters detailed above are candidates for negotiation.

3.6.2 ATM usage parameter control

Once a connection has been accepted based on the parameters of source traffic, problems still remain for the ATM network. What is there to prevent a user from claiming to need only a low bit rate and then dumping things into the network at a very high bit rate, either unintentionally ("software bug") or even intentionally ("try and stop me")? This is especially tempting when a connection has been accepted after a negotiation process. Once the connection has been accepted at 5-Mbps peak bit rate, the user may try to increase the peak bit rate up to the desired 10 Mbps and hope the network does not notice or take exception.

ATM traffic usage parameter control is designed to protect the ATM network from this, monitoring the traffic volume from the user and checking the validity of VPI/VCI values. It takes up where connection control leaves off. The function occurs purely during the data transfer phase of a connection.

What should the network do with "violations"? The ATM network is allowed to simply discard the violating cells and even drop a connection that is repeatedly "guilty" of violating the source traffic characteristics. However, providers of ATM network services will not be pleased with rejecting potential paying customers. "Nice" networks may simply flag the violating cells and send them if they pose no serious degradation of service on the ATM network as a whole. This can be a dangerous strategy in the long run. Once users realize that their connections are violating connection parameters and still functioning, they may be tempted to continue to do so as a standard operating procedure. This poses congestion threats for the entire network. It may be a better strategy to charge users that violate connection parameters a surcharge for delivering the excess cells and inform the user of the violation. The surcharge should be steep enough to encourage compliance with connection parameters.

3.6.3 ATM priority control

As cells are switched through an ATM network, queues will develop as a natural consequence of propagation delays (too many cells to send out on an output link) and processing delays (in the network nodes) coupled with high user loads. The cells in the queues must be buffered until they can be dealt with. But some cells may have to be discarded in order to service the rest with their correct QOS parameters. To allow for this, the cell header has a bit called the *cell loss priority (CLP) bit*. This single bit allows for only two states: The cell is eligible for discarding, or it is not.

How should the ATM network maintain buffers to make this process of finding and discarding eligible cells most efficient? Several mechanisms have been proposed, but none are standardized. In the common buffer with a pushout mechanism, cells all go into a single buffer. If the buffer is full and a cell that cannot be discarded arrives, one that can be discarded is found in the buffer and "pushed out" (discarded). This is a complex process that can take some time.

In another scheme called *buffer separation,* two separate buffers are used for each CLP possibility. Then cells with the CLP bit equal to 1 can easily be found and discarded. However, cells will be guaranteed to be delivered in sequence only if they all have the same priority on a connection path. This is not always possible to ensure on an ATM network connection.

The most promising strategy is known as *partial buffer sharing*; "low-priority" cells will only be accepted if the buffer is less than X percent full. This is easy and efficient to implement. The decision to discard a cell can be made before it is even buffered. The only question that needs to be answered is what is the value of X? This may be given an initial value and changed over time.

3.6.4   ATM congestion control

Congestion control has been the focus of traffic control in traditional networks of the past. It holds a special place in ATM networks because of the traffic mix (voice/video/data) and cell concept. Some mechanism must exist in ATM networks to try to prevent congestion from occurring and to alleviate it if and when it does occur. No further or more detailed mechanisms have been standardized beyond the use of ATM connection control and usage control. In fact, ATM congestion control may never be standardized.

This may come as a surprise to some, but the goal is to give network implementers maximum flexibility and room to be creative in developing more and more efficient and effective congestion control mechanisms. Unfortunately, most implementers will respond by taking the easy way out: congestion control based on restricted utilization, i.e., allowing the use of only 70 percent or so of the available bandwidth. While this makes congestion control easier, it is wasteful in the long run. ATM congestion control remains an area for much more work to be done.

3.7   ATM Operation and Maintenance

ATM has a set of actions that must be performed to make sure that the components of the network function properly. They are known as *operations and maintenance (OAM) functions* or sometimes *operations, administration, and maintenance* (still abbreviated *OAM*) *functions*. These functions are implemented by special ATM cells that flow periodically on the ATM network between the various components of the network.

It is tempting to call these OAM cell flows network management functions and let it go at that, but this would be an oversimplification of ATM OAM functions. Remember that ATM networks are not just data networks or just video networks and so forth. Therefore, ATM networks cannot be managed as networks have been in the past. Traditional LANs and WANs have been built and then network management hardware and/or software added on as almost an afterthought. Even with the prevalence today of the simple network management protocol (SNMP) for managing everything from routers to multiplexers, it is still possible to build elaborate networks without any network management at all. While this is not a good idea, nothing prevents it.

ATM networks are different. An ATM network simply cannot be built without network management. The OAM functions are part and parcel of the ATM network definition. Rather than building an ATM network and adding on network management for data and network management for video services, an ATM network has OAM built in. A network management package "taps in" to the flow of OAM cells that is always present on the ATM network. This package may be bought from a third party, from the provider of the network equipment, or simply written by a programmer for the user.

3.7.1   OAM functions

Five functions have been defined for the OAM cell flows on an ATM network:

1. *Performance monitoring.*   Performance monitoring ensures normal functioning by periodic checking of ATM network entities.

2. *Defect and failure detection.*   Defect and failure detection produces alarms (e.g., link failure conditions) as required.

3. *System protection.*   System protection excludes the failed component from the network to prevent the problem from spreading.

4. *Failure or performance information.*   Failure or performance information is actually error codes or reports that respond to network management requests and process the alarm indications.

5. *Fault localization.*   Fault localization runs internal or external diagnostics on suspect network components.

3.7.2   OAM network layering

Not surprisingly, ATM OAM is layered, as is the ATM model itself. Five levels of OAM *information flow* are defined at the physical and ATM layers. They correspond to such concepts as the virtual path and virtual channel.

Outlined in CCITT Recommendation I.610, much work remains to be done on the OAM information flows that are bidirectional, meaning they flow in both directions between equipment on the network. Levels F1, F2, and F3 are concerned with things like cell header errors or loss of cell delineation (distinction) altogether. These flows are concerned with the physical transport and only the fiber-based synchronous digital hierarchy (SDH) in particular. Since ATM is no longer tied to SDH fiber networks, the future of F1, F2, and F3 OAM flows is in question.

For this discussion, F4 and F5 are most vital. They perform the five OAM functions at the ATM layer itself. As such, they follow the VPC and VCC portion of the network, respectively. A VCC in an ATM network consists of a concatenation of VCLs (virtual channel links), and the F5 OAM flows are of two types. One type follows the VCC end to end through the network, and the other type follows the VCL across each link, known in OAM documentation as a *segment*. The F4 OAM flows have two types that flow end to end and along a segment for VPCs and VPLs as well. These OAM flows are shown in Fig. 3.24.

The F4 OAM flow may indicate that the virtual path is not available. This would trigger a system protection action when received by other

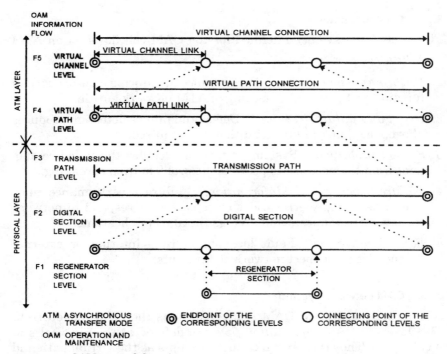

Figure 3.24 OAM network layering.

pieces of equipment on the ATM network. Either the F4 or F5 flow may indicate degraded performance. This may be caused by cell loss, cell insertion, or high information bit error rates. More details on OAM flows will be presented later.

3.8 ATM Reference Configurations

Standard diagrams of ATM network components tend not to be very enlightening. As part of the process of creating B-ISDN, the ITU took the standard components and interfaces from N-ISDN and just added a *B* for broadband to things like the network termination type 2 (B-NT2) and the "T" interface (T_B). These are shown in Fig. 3.25. There are many variations allowed on these basic diagrams. They all involve various *functional groupings* (the boxes like B-NT2) and *reference points* (the lines between the boxes). Reference points include descriptions of bit rate and frame formats as well. The ITU standards for ATM will only specify the T and S interfaces.

It is a little more helpful to realize that the B-NT1 functional grouping is where the ATM transport (e.g., SONET) link is terminated. This forms the physical (bottom) layer of the B-ISDN reference model. The B-NT2 functional grouping is where the functions of the ATM layer and AAL will be implemented. These two layers are the next two layers of the B-ISDN reference model, as shown in Fig. 3.9. The B-TE1 implements the higher layers of the reference model. A workstation

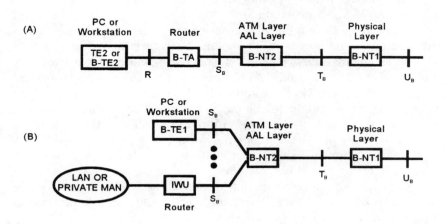

B-NT NETWORK TERMINATION FOR B-ISDN   B-TE TERMINAL EQUIPMENT FOR B-ISDN
B-TA TERMINAL ADAPTOR FOR B-ISDN   LAN LOCAL AREA NETWORK
IWU INTERNETWORKING UNIT   MAN METROPOLITAN AREA NETWORK

Figure 3.25 ATM reference configurations (many others possible).

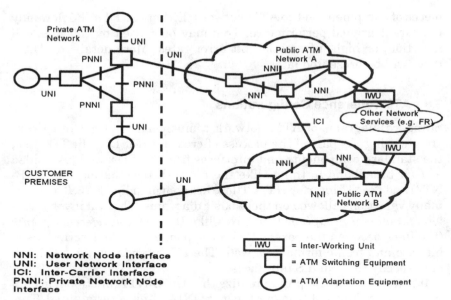

NNI: Network Node Interface
UNI: User Network Interface
ICI: Inter-Carrier Interface
PNNI: Private Network Node
Interface

IWU = Inter-Working Unit
☐ = ATM Switching Equipment
◯ = ATM Adaptation Equipment

Figure 3.26 ATM Forum networks.

with an ATM board generating ATM cells directly would be a B-TE1 device. A workstation attached to a router, with the router having an ATM interface, would form a TE2 (the workstation) and B-TA (the router) arrangement. Again, while a necessary part of the standardization process, these diagrams are not too helpful in visualizing just what an ATM network would look like.

It is probably more helpful to describe the network components and interfaces defined by the ATM Forum. These are shown in Fig. 3.26. The ATM Forum envisions that most ATM services over a wide area will be provided by a public ATM network. (A *public* network is characterized by the ability of any subscriber to connect with any other subscriber, e.g., the public telephone network.) There may be several providers of public long-distance (inter-LATA) ATM network services, exactly as in the public telephone network. These public network ATM switches will connect using the *intercarrier interface (ICI) protocol,* as standardized by the ATM Forum. This will ensure that users will always be able to interconnect in a standard fashion. Within the public ATM network, switches will exchange cells and control information with the network node interface (NNI).

On a customer premises, user equipment will interface with noncell (variable-frame) equipment on one side and the ATM network node on the other. This ATM adaptation equipment will communicate with the local ATM network node over the user network interface (UNI). But this is not the only possibility. A user may buy ATM equipment privately and build its own ATM network within its own organization. There will still be a standard UNI (although perhaps not exactly the same as the public UNI), but the switches on the customer premises will use a different interface, the private network node interface (PNNI or P-NNI). The main differences between the PNNI and the public NNI are in terms of physical media supported, distances, and bit rates. These differences will be detailed later.

Currently, the only way to interface a private ATM network with a public ATM network is with the UNI. However, extensions to the public NNI to enable its use between the private NNI network are being considered.

ATM networks will have to be used in conjunction with other types of networks; otherwise, there is little point to it. No one expects ATM networks to replace other networking technologies overnight, and few expect it even ultimately. The attraction for linking other kinds of networks with ATM is simple: Since ATM is a "network of networks" technology, there is no need to extend only the frame-relay network or LAN internetwork. Both may be extended to wherever they are needed over an ATM network, which does not care if the cells it carries contain frame-relay data or LAN frames.

An ATM network implementation may be driven by pure bandwidth considerations (e.g., 155 Mbps data transfer). More likely, they will be used for consolidation of at least two types of previously separate backbone corporate networks: LAN router-based internetworks and private T-1 networks. An interworking unit (IWU) will provide attachment to the ATM from either network type. For LANs, this will likely be a board in a LAN switch hub or (less likely) in a router. The IWU for a T-1 multiplexer may be a separate box altogether.

The best fit for a standard IWU is an IEEE 802.6 MAN (metropolitan area network) running a protocol known as DQDB (distributed queue dual bus). (A DQDB "slot" even looks pretty much like a cell.) Unfortunately, these MANs are extremely rare and will probably not multiply even as a connection mechanism for ATM networks.

3.8.1   ATM networks and LANs

Router-based networks consisting of routers connected by leased T-1 channels (or even unchannelized T-1s running at a full 1.544 Mbps) have been built for LAN interconnectivity for a number of years. But there are good reasons to connect LANs with ATM networks instead. Besides the high bandwidth available, a bandwidth much closer to LAN bit rates than commonplace internetwork possibilities, the low delay through an ATM network makes it attractive for all client-server applications.

The ATM Forum has acknowledged this by establishing a LAN emulation service (LES) for ATM networks. LES will allow existing Ethernet or Token Ring LANs to internetwork transparently. That is, the LANs linked by the ATM network will not even know of the existence of the ATM network between them. This makes it possible to create a *virtual LAN* with all the clients on one LAN and all the servers on another LAN separated over a wide area. As envisioned by the ATM Forum, LES will be a class C service (connection-oriented, data transfer) delivered with AAL-5. This entire topic will be dealt with in considerable detail in a later chapter.

3.8.2 ATM networks and frame-relay networks

Frame relay has been described as "X.25 packet switching for the 1990s," and the description fits very well. Instead of switching packets, frame-relay networks relay frames through the network nodes, which are still switches. Because frame-relay networks are connection-oriented and are another form of fast packet switching, it seems as if it would be an easy matter to link two widely separated frame-relay networks over an ATM network.

In truth, it is not so simple. There are many features of frame-relay networks that must be preserved over the intervening ATM network. But it is not obvious how ATM networks should implement these frame-relay features (such as forward explicit congestion notification, or FECN). Both the ITU and the ATM Forum have begun the process of standardizing the IWU for frame relay to ATM networks.

Frame-relay traffic will be carried on an ATM network as a class C, connection-oriented data service using AAL-5. More details on frame relay to ATM network arrangements will be discussed later.

3.8.3 ATM networks and SMDS networks

SMDS poses a special challenge to ATM networks. SMDS was created by Bellcore [the R&D arm of the Regional Bell Operating Companies (RBOCs)] as an early implementation of ATM. SMDS has sometimes been called the "first ATM service," and this is true enough, with one important distinction. Although the distinctions between connection-oriented networks and connectionless networks have tended to become blurred, there are still important differences. SMDS is the only currently defined full service that ATM networks can carry in a connectionless fashion. [There are, of course, connectionless *protocols* that ATM networks will carry, but many of these protocols, like IP, are still connection-oriented at their higher layers (e.g., TCP).] SMDS will be carried on ATM networks as a class D connectionless data service using

AAL-3/4. AAL-3/4 has the highest overhead of any ATM service, approaching 20 percent, and for this reason alone has been criticized as unnecessary. This will be detailed later.

For now, it is enough to point out the essential problem: If ATM is connection-oriented form top to bottom, and no cells can flow without a connection, then what is the connection for connectionless services? Clearly, there must be a connection, and if all users share one connection number for SMDS services, then what will be used to distinguish one cell from another?

There is an answer, of course, but the answer means that SMDS will always have higher overhead than other services on an ATM network and that ATM networks will always have more work to do to switch connectionless cells than connection-oriented cells. Does this mean that connectionless ATM services (like SMDS) will be more expensive than connection-oriented ATM services (like frame relay)? Many observers think so.

The expense may be more than balanced by the considerable robustness of connectionless networks and services in terms of routing around failures and congestion. The flexibility will most likely attract users concerned about possible bandwidth limitations on the ATM network's connection-oriented virtual channels.

The ATM Protocol Stack:
The Lower Layers

In a very real sense, the essence of all data communications is the art of sending 0s and 1s from point A to point B. Thus the means of getting information in digital form through some physical medium is an important part of any data communications protocol and technology. ATM may be a very sophisticated protocol and technology, but its goal must be very simple: the transmission of this digital information through physical media.

Many different kinds of media have been employed for this purpose, from the open iron wire of early telegraph networks to the pervasive unshielded twisted-pair copper wire of the telephone network. Bandwidth limitations have been dealt with by using other media. Coaxial cable has been employed, as well as broadcast media such as microwave towers and earth-orbiting satellites. These last two have an added advantage of not being restricted to some guiding medium, such as the wire itself. Microwave and satellite networks do not require the owner or installer of the bandwidth to acquire a right-of-way to run the cable between two separated points.

Today the usefulness and importance of all other forms of media, from copper wire to satellites, have been lessened by the application of fiberoptic cable to modern networks. Fiberoptic cable, made of thin strands of glass or even plastic, offers unprecedented economic and technical advantages over all other forms of transmission media, including satellites.

The question remains for this discussion, What will be the physical medium for ATM networks? Several other questions need to be answered once this has been determined. What other media, if any, should be allowed? What speed in terms of bits per second should be allowed? Are multiple speeds permitted? Will every situation and need be covered?

Answering these initial questions will lead to a discussion of another kind. Most physical transports in common use today for data communications are *framed transports*. That is, the digital information these transports carry is organized into a series of patterned bits called *frames*. These transmission frames are not to be confused with the layer 2 PDU, also called a *frame,* as in frame relay. Transmission frames exist below the physical layer of the OSI reference model (OSI-RM) and are part of the physical network itself.

ATM cells are also serially transmitted patterns of bits. Thus the question immediately becomes, How should ATM cells be packaged inside physical transmission frames? Again, any answer here leads to more questions. Is there a single best way? Are others allowed at all? And are framed transports even necessary for the transmission of ATM cells, which form their own unit?

These topics are all explored in this chapter. The latest recommendations and thinking from the ATM Forum along these lines are discussed, as well as possible future developments.

4.1 Fiber-Based Networks

At the bottom of the ATM protocol reference model is the ATM physical layer. It is this layer that transmits the ATM cells as a sequence of bits link by link through the ATM network. This layer performs the following functions for the higher layers of the model:

1. *Bit timing:* The definition and distinction of 0 and 1 bits as represented on the link, including distinction of strings of multiple 0s and 1s.

2. *Line coding:* The actual technique for representing these 0 and 1 bits over the physical medium.

3. *Electrical or optical transmission:* The coding of 0 and 1 bits for transmission and receiving over the medium, either electrically or optically.

In short, this layer performs all physical media–dependent (PMD) functions. Many different existing and proposed media types have been considered for ATM networks. Some are obviously more important than others. This section will detail the most important. The currently supported standards from the ATM Forum are treated at length, as well as others that are under consideration.

Not all physical media are appropriate in an ATM network for all possible interfaces. Thus the anticipated use of each one is discussed as well.

It should be noted that the original transport for ATM was developed as part of the ITU-T (then CCITT) B-ISDN architecture in the late 1980s. This transport was a fiber-based, scalable, high-speed network scheme called the *synchronous digital hierarchy* (SDH). The SDH is standardized for use in the United States by the American National Standards Institute (ANSI), where it is known as the *synchronous optical network,* or *SONET.* Ironically, SONET was initiated by Bellcore in the United States and then transferred to ANSI. SONET and SDH were parallel efforts by ANSI and the ITU-T that diverged primarily due to transport speed support (the United States wanted 51.84-Mbps support, which the ITU-T rejected).

While there are important differences between SDH and SONET, the most obvious ones involve terminology. That is, the same bit pattern in SDH has a different name in the SONET standard terminology. Rather than add confusion by attempting to explain both sets of words, this chapter will employ the SONET terms in common use today in the United States.

Therefore, the original medium for ATM cells was high-speed fiberoptic cable. Indeed, it was the *only* medium prescribed for the ATM network in 1988. And in a perfect world, there would be plenty of SONET available to build ATM networks on and run ATM cells across. Alas, by 1992 it became obvious that if ATM networks waited for SONET fiber to run on, there would be very few ATM network for years to come. And what about private ATM networks? Did a company that bought ATM switches and equipment have to run fiber to connect them with? SONET-compliant fiber?

It was the ATM Forum that addressed these issues and declared that ATM did not have to wait for SONET-based fiber. Other media were possible for ATM networks, especially private ATM networks. This neatly solved the waiting-for-SONET problem but opened up another series of issues that have still not been resolved.

The fact remained, for example, that ATM was *designed* to run on fiber-based networks. Several important features of the ATM architecture presume that the transport medium will be fiber and nothing else. These features include, but are not necessarily limited to, the small 53-byte cell size, the employment of error checking in the network only on the header field, and the exclusive use of connections. There are others, but these three are the main features that indicate that the ATM networking architecture is *optimized for fiber.*

Before looking at these three features in detail, it would be a good idea to explore the attractiveness of fiber as a medium for modern telecommunications networks. The simple fact of the matter is that fiber has many characteristics that make it the medium of choice for network designers and implementers today. Then, with these characteristics in mind, it can be shown how ATM was designed to operate hand in hand with this fiber network. The debate today revolves around whether other media are close enough to fiber in these essential characteristics to allow ATM to operate in an unmodified fashion across such network transports as coaxial cable.

4.2   Fiber-Based Network Advantages

It is not an exaggeration to state that in the near future fiber-based networks will be as pervasive in their own right as open-wire telegraph networks or copper-based twisted-pair telephone networks. Whether fiber will penetrate every home, every lab, every classroom, and every office by 2015, as the federal government seems to believe, is probably wildly overoptimistic. However, it really makes little sense in many cases to design and build networks with anything else, especially networks needing high-bit-rate data transfer.

Networks based on optical fiber technology have numerous advantages over the older coaxial cable, twisted-pair, and microwave networks. ATM is expected ultimately to run on a fiber network. In fact, as mentioned, many of the design issues of ATM were settled on the basis of fiber network characteristics. Thus it is well worth looking at fiber in detail.

Figure 4.1 is a list of the advantages of fiberoptic cable for use in communications networks. Each will be examined in a little more detail because of the importance of fiber for ATM networks. Many sources that discuss the reasons for building fiberoptic networks sometimes mention three or four of these. This particular list is meant to be as exhaustive as possible. Some network designers and implementers will seize on one or two to justify building the entire network out of fiber, while others may downplay the same factors.

The seven advantages of fiber-based networks are higher bandwidth, longer distances without repeaters (actually regenerators), immunity from electromagnetic interference, enhanced security, fewer and lower maintenance costs, small size and weight, and bandwidth upgrades that are possible on the same fiber.

The first three are mainly technical, and the fourth has some appeal to network managers. The fifth and sixth are most important to carriers (or other service providers) and private network implementers. The seventh appeals to both end users and carriers alike. In combination, they form a potent argument for fiber as the transmission medium of choice.

Before looking at each advantage in detail, it is necessary to give a brief description of just how fiberoptic transmission of digital data

- HIGHER BANDWIDTH
- LONGER DISTANCES WITHOUT REPEATERS
- IMMUNITY FROM INTERFERENCE
- SECURITY
- LESS MAINTENANCE COSTS
- SMALL SIZE AND WEIGHT
- BANDWIDTH UPGRADES ON SAME FIBER

Figure 4.1   Fiber-based networks.

actually works. The transmission of digital data on a fiberoptic cable works because of the physical principle of "total" internal reflection in a long tube of glass or plastic. The quotes are used because impurities in the fiber manufacturing process make "total" impossible, but most of the signal loss still comes from injecting a light source into the fiber.

All fiberoptic cable has two parts: an inner core and an outer cladding. These have different indices of refraction. An *index of refraction* is just a measure of the difference of the velocity of light in different media. For example, the different index of refraction in air and water is what makes a spoon appear bent in a glass of water. Light is bent when traveling from a material with one index of refraction into another material with a different index of refraction. The more the difference, the more the bend. A light signal is reflected back and forth down the fiber—which is just a very narrow and very long tube—until it emerges. The core is of glass and ranges from 5 to 50 μm (a millionth of a meter) in diameter. The cladding, which may be of glass or plastic, is usually about 120 μm in diameter—about the size of a human hair (140 μm).

4.2.1 High bandwidth

The formula for determining the bandwidth of a communications channel is given by $f = c/\lambda$ (Greek lambda). (Actually, it is a range of f, but this is good enough.) In the formula, f is the frequency given in cycles per second (Hz), c is the speed of light (300,000 km/s), and λ is the wavelength (about 1 μm for visible light).

Plugging these numbers into the equation gives us a frequency potential of 300 THz (terahertz), which is 300,000 GHz (gigahertz), or 300,000,000 MHz (megahertz). Of course, frequency is an analog measurement (Hz), and digital transmission speeds are rated in digital bandwidth terms such as megabits per second (Mbps). Moreover, there are many schemes for representing bits on an analog transmission path, as used in modern modems, for instance. However, even the simplest of these schemes allows one cycle per second (1 Hz) to represent a 0 or a 1 bit. Therefore, 300 terabits per second (Tbps) is not impossible for a fiberoptic cable, and this may go higher with other techniques.

No one has ever been able to generate a signal fast enough *not* to be carried on fiber cable. In fact, fiber is so good that no other medium is even being investigated in a university laboratory or research department as a serious competitor to fiberoptic cable. In other words, there is bandwidth to spare in a fiber cable.

4.2.2 Long distance without repeaters

Any signal sent over a wire gets weaker with distance. Eventually, the signal is so weak that it can no longer be detected at the far end at all.

Signal losses are measured in decibels (dB), a special scale used for expressing the ratio of the input signal strength to the received signal strength. This loss, called *attenuation,* requires periodic repeating or regeneration of the signal by special network components after a specific distance over a link. This distance depends on the medium itself and the initial strength of the signal. Alternatively, raising the power of the transmitter may help, but this usually requires some monetary investment. Obviously, the longer the cable without these components and the weaker the original signal needs to be for a specific distance, the more attractive this particular cable will be for network use.

Fiber has very low loss characteristics. They are as low as 0.2 dB/km in many cases. This compares with ordinary unshielded twisted-pair cable, which can have losses as high as 10 dB/1000 ft, or 30 dB/km. Because of the way the decibel scale works (it is a logarithmic scale), a 0.2-dB signal loss corresponds to about a 5 percent signal loss. The 10.0-dB signal loss for UTP corresponds to a signal loss of 90 percent. Lower signal losses translate to longer distances between repeaters (really regenerators) or lower transmitter power.

4.2.3 Immunity from interference

Interference is basically a spurious signal. It is noise that intrudes into a transmission system. In older analog transmission systems, this noise or interference appears at the receiving end of the network as static or crosstalk (*crosstalk* means someone on the telephone hears another conversation in the background). In digital systems, the interference shows up as bit errors.

Fiber is essentially immune to outside interference from electrical storms, power sources, or stray microwave signals. The bandwidths of these electromagnetic interference sources do not overlap with fiberoptic bandwidths. Fiber is a guided medium, which means the signals are confined to a physical path and do not radiate. Most other cables, even coaxial cable, are essentially very long antennas, and they radiate some signals into nearby cables.

This is one reason why a personal computer (PC) needs a Federal Communications Commission (FCC) sticker: The data bus radiates into the surrounding area and may interfere with television or radio reception. This is also why the airlines require passengers to shut off all electronic devices during takeoff and landing. Power companies are large users of fiberoptic cable for this reason as well. No other medium can run alongside very high-voltage power lines and still work well. The power grid in the United States is interlaced with fiberoptic cable for coordinating power distribution substations.

Because of this immunity to electromagnetic interference, fiber has a very low bit error rate (BER). It is around 10^{-10} bits, or one per

10,000,000,000 (10 billion) bits. The benefit from improved bit error rates (BER) is considerable in itself. Each increase in a bit error rate from one power of ten to another is 10 times better than the one below it. Thus a BER of 10^{-10} is 10 times better than a BER of 10^{-9}.

The advantages of the low BERs of fiber networks cannot be underestimated. Early X.25 networks on voice-grade copper data circuits ran with bit error rates of about 10^{-6}. Even at only 64 kbps, this meant users could expect a bit error every 16 seconds or so. With a fiber-based ATM network, the rate should be down to at least one per 4.3 *hours* (with a BER of 10^{-9}) and maybe even one per 6 *months* (with a BER of 10^{-12}). This is one reason it is no longer desirable or even necessary for the *network* to do error checking and recovery. End nodes and users, of course, will still perform these functions, but doing error checking in the network node merely slows down the end-to-end performance of the network. There are very few errors to detect.

At ATM speeds, fiber better be good. Even on fiber cable, at 135 Mbps, the ATM payload rate on SONET OC-3, users can expect a bit error every 7.4 seconds or so with a BER of 10^{-9}. One every 2 hours will be much better, as on a fiber network with a BER of 10^{-12}, but there will be serious decisions to make before running ATM on old T-3s, with errors every 22 ms (characteristic of a BER of 10^{-6}).

As mentioned, the ATM network does no error checking on the cell contents (payload) or retransmissions for errored cells between ATM network nodes. The cell headers are checked for errors, but not for the purposes of retransmissions. Instead, errored cells are generally thrown away, with one exception: when there is a single bit in error in the ATM cell header. This single-bit error is correctable. The reason for this behavior is that ATM is designed to run on the low BER links that fiber networks provide. If ATM networks are built on other media besides fiber, care must be taken to ensure that the BER on these links is adequate for ATM cells.

Another important point when discussing fiber and other media bit error rates is the fact that the vast majority of errors on fiber networks (94 percent) are single-bit errors. That is, if the BER is 10^{-9}, which is one bit in error out of a billion bits sent, the chances are vanishingly small that two consecutive bits will be in error. And it is even less likely that many consecutive bits will be in error. On fiber, therefore, the bit errors are fairly well spaced out, meaning that most cells with errors on a fiberoptic ATM network have only single-bit errors.

Things are different on other media. Copper-based media that operate with electromagnetic signals are subject to *impulse noise* such as lightning strikes and/or adjacent power line surges. These impulses last for a few milliseconds or more and thus result in a large "block" of bits being errored. At moderate speeds, it is not unusual for a lightning strike to wipe out 90 or so consecutive bits. These are *burst* errors. Older network protocols expected this and allowed for this possibility.

In fact, the very language used for error rates on older networks reflects this higher likelihood that one bit in error will have an adjacent bit in error. Since a bit error rate is an "average" of the number of bit errors over time, the use of BERs to express burst errors is misleading. Instead, the concept of *error-free seconds* is used. This acknowledges that there will be many consecutive seconds of network operation without any bit errors at all but that when they occur, they are concentrated in bursts that are generally confined to fractions of a second. Thus error-free seconds is a much better measure of bit errors on nonfiber networks than raw BERs.

Older error-detection mechanisms such as cyclical redundancy checks (CRCs) were designed to catch these error bursts. For example, a CRC-16 (a 16-bit CRC calculated over some variable amount of data) will catch *all* error burst less than or equal to 16 consecutive bits, 99.997 percent of all 17-consecutive-bit-error bursts, and 99.998 percent of all 18-or-longer-consecutive-bit-error bursts.

ATM networks will require different, and simpler, mechanisms.

4.2.4 Security

As mentioned earlier, fiber is a guided medium. Since it does not radiate ("total" internal reflection), its signals cannot be picked up by nearby listening equipment. This means that it is tougher to "tap" (intercept the signal without being detected) than other media based on electromagnetic signals. (The wire is a long antenna, remember.) And even if it were tapped (not too complex: bend the fiber, scrape off the cladding, add an optical receiver), the resulting signal loss would be easily detectable at the receiving end of the run.

The key to using fiber for secure networks is to constantly monitor the end-to-end signal loss (attenuation). If it changes by about 0.5 dB or more over a short time period, something has happened. It may be physical: The fiber was tripped over or a connector was yanked too hard; or it may be a security issue: The fiber has been tapped.

This makes fiber very attractive for security-sensitive organizations: banks, governments, and big business.

4.2.5 Lower maintenance costs

This is really an indirect benefit derived from the advantage of being able to transmit over long distance without repeaters, as discussed earlier. The fact that fiber needs fewer repeaters or regenerators, which are active components, means that a fiberoptic cable run needs much less time and energy devoted to maintenance that other media.

Fiber is impervious to corrosion (glass does not weather) and can be made impervious to water. However, installers should not directly bury nonoutdoor fiber. Groundwater will eventually fill up microscopic pores in the fiber, and then it will stop working. In fact, once fiber is properly in place, not much can go wrong. Some carriers even bury the fiber under poured concrete painted red or orange on top. This prevents backhoes from damaging it. The point is, however, that installers do not do this to cable they need to access frequently for maintenance purposes. Modern fiberoptic cable runs can be designed for a mean time to failure (MTTF, a measure of how long the component might be expected to work before failure) of 25 *years*.

4.2.6   Small size and weight

The small size and weight of fiberoptic cable mean that fewer cables need to be run to achieve the same overall bandwidth (bit rate). In fact, this was the reason fiber was first deployed in the 1960s rather than any other factor. The conduits under many city streets were just too congested to run enough copper-based cable for the bandwidth increases needed.

One duplex fiberoptic cable running SONET OC-48 will carry 2.48 Gbps. The same aggregate bandwidth using DS-3 over coaxial cable requires 96 cables. And for DS-1 over UTP, this amount of bandwidth would need 2688 unshielded twisted-pair copper wires. Compared with the size and weight of a single duplex fiber, 2700-pair UTP cable is 3.38 in in diameter (about the size of a fire hose) and weighs almost 7 lb/ft. A 1000-ft reel of such cable weighs close to 4 tons and is not easily installed. Fiber can easily be strung across the most delicately installed hung ceilings and the most stringent load-bearing floors.

4.2.7   Bandwidth upgrades on the same fiber

Upgrading the bit rate or bandwidth on a digital link in the past was difficult. For instance, going from a T-1 link to a T-3 link requires new media to be run, since T-1 is defined only on UTP and T-3 is defined on coaxial cable and fiber. The same applied to local area networks (LANs) as well. It was not unusual for a company to install unshielded twisted-pair wire for a 4-Mbps Token Ring, then shielded twisted-pair wire (less attenuation and crosstalk) for a 16-Mbps Token Ring, and finally fiber cable for a high-speed 100-Mbps LAN. The medium will only support so much bandwidth.

In a fiber network, however, the cable bandwidth is not the limiting factor at all. Once the fiber is run, it can easily be upgraded to run at higher speeds just by changing the end electronics and components. The transmitter and receiver are changed, and then a 155-Mbps fiber link may run at 622 Mbps. This is not true across all speeds and all distances, but at least it is possible with fiber cable.

In fact, fiber's bandwidth and advantages are so overwhelming that no other medium is being seriously researched today as a future "fiber replacement." Microwave and satellite technologies may always have their places, but fiber will be the first choice of implementers.

4.3 Fiber Modes

Many of the advantages that fiber-based networks provide (e.g., longer distances between repeaters, easier bandwidth upgrades) depend on the "kind" of fiber installed. Since ATM networks will be built on both kinds, this is the best time to look at the differences between single-mode and multimode fiberoptic cable.

A *mode*, as it applies to fiberoptics, is one of a severely limited numbers of ways a light source of a specific wavelength can be sent down a fiber of given core diameter without severe signal loss. Modes correspond to a limited number of angles of incidence for the injected light source (known as *theta*). The proper angle gives constructive rather than destructive interference between the incident and reflected rays in the fiber. Two strategies for exploiting these modes have been developed and are in common use in fiber networks: multimode fiber transmission and single-mode fiber transmission.

4.3.1 Multimode fiber transmission

With multimode fiber transmission, there are multiple paths a light wave can follow through the fiber. The core diameter is about 50 μm (millionths of a meter), meaning it is much larger than the optical signal wavelength [usually measured in nanometers (nm), billionths of a meter]. This is what allows multiple paths. The signal is injected with a light-emitting diode (LED) setup, which is cheap and easy to implement on a board or in a separate network interface device. The typical wavelength is 1300 nm (1.3 μm).

Detection is done by either a P-intrinsic N-diode (PIN) or an avalanche photodiode (APD). The typical arrangement of a link in a multimode fiber cable is shown in Fig. 4.2.

4.3.2 Single-mode fiber transmission

With single-mode fiber, the core is smaller. In fact, it is *tuned* to the light source wavelength of about 1300 nm. However, this time the light source must be a laser (*l*ight *a*mplification by *s*timulated *e*mission of *r*adiation). A set of mirrors is properly spaced to form a *tuned cavity* where the light is injected into the fiber. Loss is lower, so transmission distance is greater, bandwidth is higher, and bit errors are fewer.

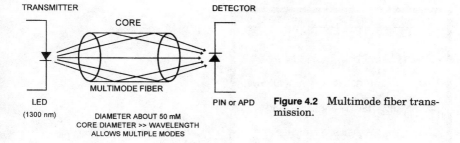

TRANSMITTER   DETECTOR

LED   PIN or APD   **Figure 4.2** Multimode fiber trans-
(1300 nm)   DIAMETER ABOUT 50 mM   mission.
            CORE DIAMETER >> WAVELENGTH
               ALLOWS MULTIPLE MODES

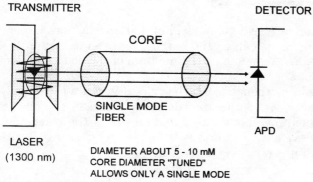

Figure 4.3 Single-mode fiber transmission.

Detection must be done with an APD in this case (PINs will be destroyed by even the lowest-power laser). A typical single-mode fiber link is shown in Fig. 4.3.

Single-mode fiber is more expensive to make than multimode, and lasers are not cheap either. Also, there are strict government rules about placing lasers in general office spaces or buildings. The lasers used for data communications are very low-powered, but the human eye is a very effective lens that can focus enough of the laser's energy on the eye's retina to cause permanent damage.

4.3.3 Single mode versus multimode

Figure 4.4 compares single-mode with multimode fiber, at least as far as the types of fiber for general use. In specialized situations, such as an undersea fiberoptic cable run without any repeaters, single-mode *dispersion-shifted* fiber may be used to span the Atlantic Ocean at 4.8 Gbps (OC-96).

Single mode requires a tuned laser, while multimode just needs an LED. And single mode requires an APD detector, while multimode may use either an APD or a PIN (cheaper).

	SINGLE	MULTIMODE
TRANS:	LASER	LED
DETECT:	APD	PIN or ADP
SPEED:	HIGHER BW	LOWER BW
DISTANCE:	100 GB-KM	1 GB-KM
COST:	EXPENSIVE	CHEAPER
USAGE:	TELCO	PREMISE

Figure 4.4 Single-mode versus multi-mode fiber.

Bandwidths are higher for single mode, but distance is more important: At 1 Gbps, single mode can go 100 km to a repeater, while multimode will only go 1 km. This makes it the medium of choice for outside plant/telco applications.

Multimode fiber is less expensive, but the price difference is decreasing every day. However, it remains the choice for premises use and is called for in 100-Mbps fiber networks. Single mode is the choice for SONET, which can have a BER as low as 10^{-13} (one bit error in 10 trillion bits sent, or one bit error every 5 years at 64 kbps).

4.3.4 Fiberoptic limits

Do not get the impression that fiber is perfect. Fiber does have its limitations. The links in fiber-based networks are still limited by errors, distance, and speed, just as in any other network.

Errors are a limit because of the weakest link in a fiberoptic network. This means that although BERs of 10^{-12} on fiber are attainable, in practice, many fiber networks still exhibit BERs of about 10^{-9} or even 10^{-8}. It is always worth remembering that in any network, the end-to-end BER experienced will always be equal to the BER of the worst link. This means that even if a 10-link fiber network from point A to point B has 9 links with a BER of 10^{-12}, and only 1 link with a BER of 10^{-8}, the overall BER end to end from A to B will be 10^{-8}. It must be, since the better links cannot "clean up" the bit errors from the weaker link. Some networks that are supposedly fiber from end to end pass through short copper links, greatly reducing the BER benefit anticipated from using fiber in the first place.

Distance is limited by signal loss (attenuation). There is a real limit to how weak the light signal can get and still be detected at the remote end. Poor connectorization can severely limit fiber distances due to signal loss. The detection limit is about 15 photons in a given sample period.

Speed is limited by signal dispersion. There is a limit to how "spread out" a light pulse can become and still be distinguished from adjacent pulses. The two main kinds of dispersion are modal and chromatic. *Modal dispersion* only affects multimode fiber (the various modes interfere with each other). *Chromatic dispersion* affects both and is also of two types. *Material dispersion* is caused by impurities in the glass, and *waveguide dispersion* is caused by the cladding-core structure. There are two ways to combat dispersion: Either decrease the distance between the regenerators or decrease the maximum bit rate (time between pulses increases). The second is difficult in practice because lasers have a characteristic "risetime" such that small changes in pulse times have larger bit-rate effects. Newer dispersion-shifted fiber can be used in many cases to counteract these effects.

Research is continual in all areas. More sophisticated end electronics are produced every year to improve these parameters. In general, fiberoptic bit rates have increased fourfold every 2 years in the recent past.

4.4   ATM Physical Layer Media

The ITU-T, in the B-ISDN material regarding ATM, specified only two physical transports for ATM cells. The first is for transmission of ATM cells on two separate 75-Ω coaxial cables, one for transmit and one for receive, at 155.520 Mbps (the STS-3c rate of SONET). The second is for transmission of ATM cells over two single-mode fibers running at 622.080 Mbps (the STS-12c rate of SONET). Neither is very helpful for use when trying to build ATM networks today. The data rates are very high, and SONET-compliant links, while becoming more and more prevalent in major metropolitan areas, remain expensive.

In the interim, the ATM Forum has approved four high-speed standard physical layer transport mechanisms for ATM cells. Others operate at lower speeds and will be used mainly on "access nodes" to concentrate traffic onto an ATM network backbone. Even more will definitely be allowed in the future, but the high-speed transports chosen represent an overall philosophy about what an ATM network should be. First, an ATM network should be fast, and second, ATM networks should have orders of magnitude fewer errors than other, older networks. Last, and most important, the transports should be readily available.

The four standard high-speed ATM cell transports are

1. 155.520 Mbps running on single-mode or multimode fiber (STS-3c SONET)

2. 155.520 Mbps running on multimode fiber or shielded twisted pair (STP) using 8B/10B encoding (based on the ANSI "Fibre Channel" architecture)

3. 100 Mbps running on multimode fiber using 4B/5B encoding (based on the IEEE and ANSI FDDI architecture, usually known to the

- Multi-Mode Fiber:
  155 Mbps SONET STS-3c (Single Mode also)
  155 Mbps Fibre Channel
  100 Mbps FDDI (TAXI)

- Shielded Twisted Pair (copper)
  155 Mbps Fibre Channel

- Coaxial Cable:
  45 Mbps DS-3

- Newly Standardized in UNI 3.1:
  52 Mbps Category 3 Unshielded Twisted Pair
  155 Mbps Category 5 Unshielded Twisted Pair
  34.368 Mbps E3 and 139.264 E4
  1.544 Mbps T1 and 2.048 Mbps E1

Figure 4.5   ATM Forum physical transports.

ATM Forum as TAXI (transparent asynchronous exchange interface)

4. 44.736 Mbps running on coaxial cable (DS-3, universally known as 45 Mbps or T-3)

It is perhaps more informative to group the allowed transports by medium rather than by technology, since ATM is meant to be an unchannelized network giving many different speeds for connections to different users. Some of the transports are meant to be used only in private ATM networks, and some are anticipated for use only in public ATM networks. In this framework, the ATM Forum transports are listed in Fig. 4.5.

Over multimode fiber, public ATM networks may offer access at 155 Mbps, and even single mode. For private ATM networks, multimode fiber may support 155 Mbps with the Fibre Channel encoding or 100 Mbps with the FDDI encoding. Over shielded twisted pair, private ATM networks may run at 155 Mbps using the same Fibre Channel encoding as on multimode fiber. And over coaxial cable, public ATM networks may offer access at 45 Mbps over DS-3. It also should be noted that 155-Mbps transport may be offered over coaxial cable, but only for short distances. Sometimes known as the STSX-3 interface, this coaxial interface is primarily envisioned as a "tail end" to the fiber link itself.

The ATM Forum has given serious consideration to lower-speed transports as well. The ones currently defined are 51.840-Mbps category 3 unshielded twisted pair (for private ATM networks and premises use), 155.520-Mbps category 5 unshielded twisted pair (also for private network and premises use), European standard rates of 34.368 Mbps (E3) and 139.264 Mbps (E4) (for public networks), and even the relatively very slow 1.544 Mbps (DS-1 or T-1) and 2.048 Mbps (E1). The last two will be for public networks, but probably they will only be recommended for limited use to the previously mentioned access nodes or "concentration points" where the higher-speed transports will actually access the ATM network itself.

Of course, it is important to remember that ATM was designed to run on fiber-based networks. In fact, ATM was designed to run on a very specific kind of fiber network, known to the ITU as synchronous digital hierarchy (SDH) and to ANSI in the United States as SONET. SDH is not the same as SONET, but the differences are mainly in terminology. Thus before detailing the functions and structure of the other physical layer transports for ATM, a closer look at SONET is in order.

4.4.1 SONET

This is only an overview—but a detailed overview—of SONET itself. SONET is a recreation of the digital transmission hierarchy (e.g., T-1, T-3) with framing and pointers in place for easier access to lower-speed channels. It is still very much a channelized network, but SONET is a whole new family of channels, all running on fiberoptic cable, with few exceptions. The speeds initially run from 51.84 Mbps in the United States (although this is mainly a concession for backward compatibility with T-3) through 2.4 Gbps (2400 Mbps). This high end will be extended in the future to about 13 Gbps. The European carriers will not use the SONET hierarchy, although they will use the same technology. They number from 155 Mbps, or the SONET STS-3 rate, which is known in SDH as STM-1. SDH increments by 155-Mbps units. Any SONET level number divisible by 3 will give an STM; for example, STS-48 = STM-16.

It has sometimes been stated that SONET is to B-ISDN and ATM networks what T-1 was to digital data services (DDS). That is, DDS (56 kbps on digital links) was a service that required a T-1 network (1.544-Mbps digital links with twenty-four 56-kbps channels). Extending this concept to B-ISDN, it can be said that B-ISDN is a system of services, ATM is the transport, switching, and multiplexing cell technology for these services, and SONET is the physical trunking point-to-point transmission network for ATM cells.

It is important to remember that SONET, like the T-carrier system, is a trunk, point-to-point transmission system. Switching is not a part of the definition or function of SONET. This is what ATM itself provides, along with much, much more.

Synchronized multiplexing. SONET is a *synchronous optical network*. The word *synchronous* refers to the multiplexing method used to combine channels on a SONET network. Synchronous multiplexing is achieved in SONET by making sure that the clocks on the input side of the multiplexer are all within a certain tolerance, a tolerance that is much better than defined today for T-1 networks. This clocking allows SONET to be byte-multiplexed throughout the hierarchy, as opposed to the existing T-carrier networks, which are only byte-multiplexed at the T-1 level. T-3s multiplex at the *bit* level, meaning a single bit from an input stream is taken and interleaved with a single bit from another input stream.

All levels of SONET use byte-interleaved multiplexing. The input streams are sent through a byte-interleaved multiplexer with some overhead added. This overhead consists of framing and pointers for finding the input streams quickly and easily. The most important point is that the output stream is exactly three times the input stream (3 × 51.84 = 155.52 Mbps). This is generally true throughout SONET; higher layers add *no* additional overhead to the input streams. This is certainly not true of the T-carrier system.

The SONET hierarchy. Figure 4.6 introduces the SONET family of standard, high-speed, synchronous, digital channels. The electrical specification (for signal generation) uses the prefix *STS* (synchronous transport signal level) and refers to the data stream generated by an input device. The optical specification uses the prefix *OC* (optical carrier level) and refers to the signal transported through the fiberoptic carrier system.

The line rates are easy to compute. They are all just simple multiples of the basic STS-1 level: 51.84 Mbps. There is *never* any additional overhead (it is about 3.3 percent at all levels). Levels up to STS-256 (13.271 Gbps) are currently possible.

Figure 4.7 shows the most common SONET channel speeds. These are all slated for near-term (1995+) implementation. We can compare them with the existing T-carrier system. The new "T-1" will be STS-3, running at 155.52 Mbps, about 100 times faster than the T-1s of today. This will be the main building block of SONET, STS-1 being put in mostly for easy T-3 service migration. STS-12 and STS-48 will be for

ELECTRICAL	LINE RATE (Mbps)	OPTICAL	SDH (CCITT)
STS-1	51.840	OC-1	
STS-2	103.680	OC-2	
STS-3	155.520	OC-3	STM-1
:	:	:	
STS-6	311.040	OC-6	STM-2
:	:	:	
STS-n	n X 51.840	OC-n	(n \ 3)
:	:	:	
STS-256	13271.040	OC-256	

Figure 4.6 SONET hierarchy.

STS LEVEL	LINE RATE (Mbps)	OC LEVEL	# 64 kB VCs	STM
STS-1	51.84	OC-1	672	--
STS-3	155.52	OC-3	2016	STM-1
STS-12	622.08	OC-12	8064	STM-4
STS-24	1244.16	OC-24	16128	STM-8
STS-48	2488.32	OC-48	32256	STM-16

Figure 4.7   Near-term SONET channel speeds.

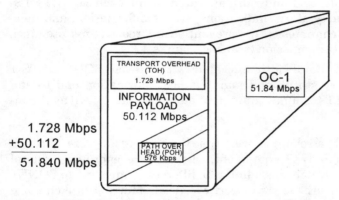

Figure 4.8   STS-1 channel structure.

higher-speed backbones and for sophisticated video and distributed operating system applications.

As bandwidth needs grow and service providers begin offering STS-1 and STS-3 to customers, these network service providers will start to deploy more and more high-speed fiber on their own backbones. A major fiber manufacturer has projected that by the end of the decade, most fiber deployed will be at OC-96 (4.8 Gbps) and OC-192 (9.6 Gbps) speeds.

STS-1 channel structure.   Figure 4.8 shows the structure of the STS-1 channel, the lowest level of the SONET hierarchy. This level is not directly supported for ATM yet, although the ATM Forum private UTP interface will most likely be very similar to this. The frame is always shown this way: as an array of 90 columns and 9 rows. Each intersection is an 8-bit byte, for a total of 810 bytes per frame. Frames are sent 8000 times per second (125 μs per frame). Bytes are sent sequentially, left to right, from row 1, column 1 to row 9, column 90. The basic rate of 51.84 Mbps comes from 810 bytes per frame times 8 bits per byte times 8000 frames per second. Notice that there is some overhead—mainly transport overhead. This runs at 1.728 Mbps (yes, the *overhead* in SONET is more than a T-1 today), but it does much more than the poor 193rd framing could ever do. It is known as *transport overhead* (TOH). The rest, 50.112 Mbps, is information payload. Embedded within the payload is another overhead, not strictly part of the SONET structure. This is known as *path overhead* (POH).

The various components of the STS-1 channel structure are defined as follows:

Information payload: Bandwidth allocated within each SONET STS-1 channel to carry user information end to end.

Transport overhead: Bandwidth allocated within each SONET STS-1 channel to carry alarm indications, status information, and message-signaling channels for the preventive and reactive maintenance of the SONET transmission (transport) links.

Path overhead: Bandwidth allocated within each SONET STS-1 channel to carry status and maintenance information end to end between SONET terminal equipment along the same path as the information payload.

Transport overhead changes every time the STS signal passes through an active piece of SONET equipment, whether a regenerator, a digital crossconnect, or a switch. Each link is a different "transport" to SONET and gets its own overhead. Transport overhead is further broken down into line and section overhead. (A *section* is defined as any fiber link between two termination points on a SONET path, even a fiber regenerator, and a *line* is defined as any link between two "active components" such as a digital crossconnect and a terminal.)

Path overhead, on the other hand, is generated once at each end of the network and passes unchanged along the same path as the user information. Its function supports the end user.

The frame is always broken down into 9 rows of 90 bytes (810 bytes total) because of this overhead. The first 3 bytes of each row is the transport overhead. This leaves 87 bytes per row for the payload. This means that the transport overhead bytes are dispersed throughout the frame. Only by showing the frame as a 9 by 90 two-dimensional array will the transport overhead bytes line up correctly.

It may be instructive to compare STS-1 with T-1 at this point. Both send 8000 frames per second, but the similarity ends there. While T-1 sends only 193 bits in 125 μs, STS-1 sends 6480 bits (810 × 8), or more than 30 times as much. While T-1 has only 0.518 percent overhead (1 in 193 bits), STS-1 has 3.3 percent transport overhead (27 bytes in 810 bytes). Of course, the transport overhead in STS-1 is asked to do a lot more than the 193rd bit was.

STS-N/OC-N channel structures.   The idea of higher rates is easy to understand given the synchronous nature of SONET. Multiplexers can build up to any layer of the STS-N/OC-N hierarchy by simply multiplexing together *N* STS-1 signals at the basic 51.84 Mbps rate. And this multiplexing could not be easier. All that is needed is to byte-interleave them together. That is, take one byte from each input stream at a time. The STS-1 level gives a basic data rate of 51.84 Mbps. Since all the transport overhead is included, byte interleaving allows multiplexing without additional overhead at higher layers. This is why all that is ever needed to find a higher-level data rate is to multiply *N* times 51.84 Mbps.

An STS-3 would contain three STS-1 payloads. Each one would have its own TOH and POH. The aggregate data rate for the OC-3 would be 155.52 Mbps. However, this only gives us three 51.84-Mbps channels. For the transport of ATM cells at a raw bit rate of 155.52 Mbps, it is necessary to concatenate the three STS-1 channels. The method for doing this will be shown shortly. First, here is the STS-3 frame structure.

Figure 4.9 shows the format of an STS-3 frame with three embedded STS-1s. The easiest way to picture the whole STS family is to keep the

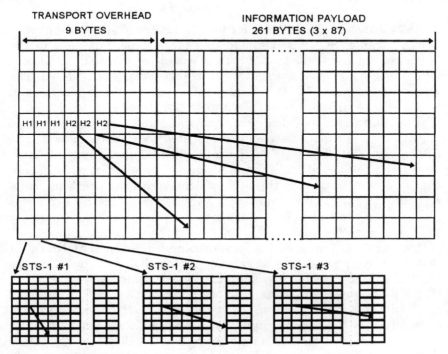

Figure 4.9 STS-3 channel structure.

9 rows and adjust the number of columns. Since the whole thing is byte-interleaved, the device can just start interleaving the three STS-1s, starting with the 3 columns of transport overhead and continuing with the 87 columns of information payload. The STS-3 thus consists of 9 columns of transport overhead and 261 columns (3×87) of information payload. It is important to realize that the whole STS-3 frame is still sent at 8000 per second, and frame time is still 125 µs. The constituent STS-1s are also shown in the figure. But what about using all 155.52 Mbps in *one* channel for ATM cell transport?

STS-3c is the designation for 155.52-Mbps service with no subchannel structure. It is achieved by setting a "concatenation" indicator and using only one path overhead bit stream. There are still three separate sets of TOH columns, however, although for many functions only the first set is active. STS-3c is anticipated to be the basic unit of SONET—the T-1 of B-ISDN—mainly because of its versatility. It can be used for three DS-3s running at 44.736 Mbps in North America. In Europe, four E3s running at 34.368 Mbps can be accommodated. It can carry three NTSC-quality television signals or one compressed high-definition television (HDTV) signal. It is also the method of choice to carry FDDI 100-Mbps LAN traffic over wide areas. Also, once the IEEE standardized 100-Mbps Ethernet is available, STS-3c seems a logical choice for carrying this traffic as well.

SONET overhead. This is a brief look at the overhead present in a SONET frame. SONET overhead is a large topic, but most of the fields are not used when ATM cells are sent over the SONET links. Only those fields used with ATM cell transport will be detailed. The transport overhead (TOH) is divided into section overhead (SOH) and line overhead (LOH). The path overhead (POH) is in the payload portion of the frame, specifically in the synchronous payload envelope (SPE). Various functions are even repeated in all three places. The SPE is also the location of the path overhead bytes. This path overhead flows end to end through the network. Therefore, it makes sense that it is associated with the SPE, which carries the user's information end to end. It does, however, subtract from the 50.112 Mbps available to the end user, reducing the net bit rate by 576 kbps to 49.536 Mbps.

It is an effect of the use of synchronous multiplexing in SONET that the SPE may begin literally anywhere within a SONET frame. Because SONET equipment will be synchronized to the same network clock, all SONET equipment will attempt to begin sending a frame at the same time, within a small tolerance. However, because light waves are still constrained by the speed of light, bytes from different remote sources located at different distances from the SONET multiplexer will arrive at slightly different times. Instead of buffering the bytes until the start

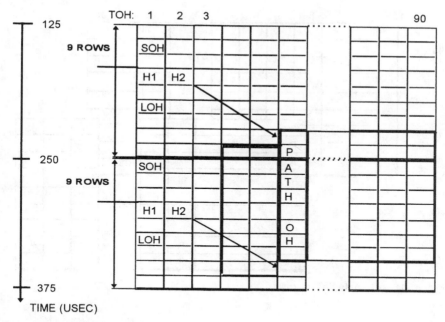

Figure 4.10 STS-1 payload.

of a frame, SONET allows bytes to be transferred from an input port to an output port anytime during the 125-μs frame duration. Of course, the receiver must be able to detect where the sender has placed the SPE in the frame. Special overhead bytes, H1 and H2, are set by the sender to indicate this. This offset location of the SPE, which thus spans two SONET frames, is shown in Fig. 4.10.

Figure 4.11 shows a simplified but more typical picture of the relationship between the STS-1 frame and the SPE. Here the special H1 and H2 pointer bytes point to an "exploded" SPE. SPEs still run at 50.112 Mbps, and the path overhead is still there, but it is easier to "see" the SPE this way. Just keep in mind that it is *not* a separate set of bytes but a subset of the SONET frame itself (actually, taken from two successive SONET frames).

The path overhead (POH) "floats" with the SPE within the STS-1 frame. The POH is found by the receiver by examining the H1 and H2 pointer bytes, which form the first 2 bytes of the line overhead (LOH), row 4, columns 1 and 2. It is important to realize that the SPE is located by pointers in the LOH, *not* the SOH. This means that the section equipment (i.e., regenerators) has no way of adjusting the location of the SPE within an STS-1. The first byte of the POH is pointed at directly by the H1 and H2 pointers. After that, the POH bytes are interleaved every 87 columns by the SONET equipment.

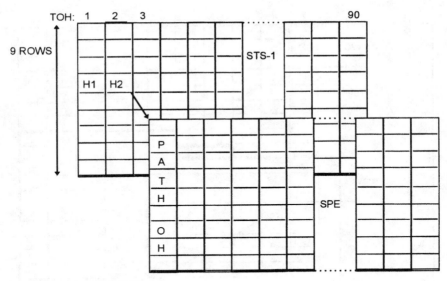

Figure 4.11 Alternate SPE picture.

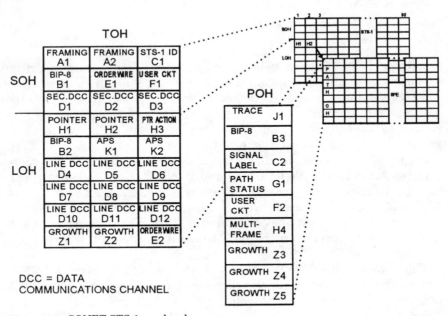

Figure 4.12 SONET STS-1 overhead.

Figure 4.12 shows all the transport and path overhead all at once. Some of the elements have already been mentioned (H1 and H2), and some are self-explanatory (growth −Z bytes), but a brief explanation of their function is in order. Where elements are present in all three over-heads (BIP-8), they will be discussed all at the same time.

Section overhead. *A1, A2 framing:* Two bytes provide the SONET framing pattern, a repeating F8 26 hex pattern (1111 0110 00101000) the receivers lock on to delimit the incoming frames.

C1 STS-1 ID: This byte identifies the STS-N signal set within a channelized SONET frame. This byte is provided in all STS-1s within an STS-N, with the first being assigned the number 1.

B1 BIP-8: BIP stands for *bit-interleaved parity*. Fiber networks need different bit error detection procedures than those provided for other media. Instead of CRCs on the frames, SONET provides bit-position-by-bit-position parity checking across various SONET frame components. In addition to directly checking for single-bit errors, the use of BIP-8s has a further benefit: BIP counts can easily be trans-lated directly to BERs by a simple table lookup, thus doing away with the need to disable a link to perform a separate BER test on it. Indeed, the equipment itself can detect degradation of the link and take appropriate action while notifying a remote network control center. The B1 BIP is calculated over all bytes of the previous SONET frame.

E1 orderwire: This byte provides a 64-kbps voice channel for techni-cians working on problems between regenerators and other SONET equipment. For STS-Ns, this channel is only defined for the first STS-1.

F1 user circuit: This byte provides a 64-kbps data channel for the user (actually, the vendor) of the SONET equipment. A vendor may use this channel to download revised firmware to a device, but there is no standard usage set. For STS-Ns, this channel is only defined for the first STS-1.

D1-D3 section DCC: These 3 bytes form a 192-kbps data communi-cation channel (DCC) between section equipment (such as regenera-tors) on a SONET link. This is to be used with a message protocol for alarm, maintenance, administration, monitoring, and other needs. Again, in an STS-N, this channel is only defined for the first STS-1.

Line overhead. *H1, H2, and H3 pointer bytes:* These 3 bytes are used to locate the start of the SPE (specifically, the first path overhead byte) within the SONET frame. These are active for all STS-1s within an STS-N, except for an STS-Nc (concatenated STS-N).

B2 BIP-8: This byte is a line BIP check for all bits of the line over-head and previous SONET STS-1 frame (i.e., all but the 9 section over-head bytes).

K1, K2 automatic protection switching (APS): These 2 bytes provide signaling between line-terminating equipment. It enables SONET equipment to automatically route around path failures if necessary. Note that there is no APS for each individual STS-1 in an STS-N. All must be switched or none. These bytes are therefore defined only for the first STS-1 in an STS-N.

D4-D12 line DCC: These 9 bytes form a 576-kbps data communication channel (DCC) between line equipment on a SONET link. This is also to be used with a message protocol for alarm, maintenance, administration, monitoring, and other needs. In an STS-N, this channel is only defined for the first STS-1.

Z1, Z2 growth: These 2 bytes are reserved for future functions not yet defined in SONET.

E2 orderwire: This byte provides another 64-kbps voice channel between line-termination equipment. It is only defined for the first STS-1 channel of an STS-N.

Path overhead. *J1 path trace:* This byte is to be used to repetitively transmit a 64-byte, fixed-length string that represents the network address of the originator of the SPE payload. The presence of this pattern indicates to the receiver that the source of the signal is still connected to the receiver.

B3 BIP-8: The byte is a path BIP check for all bits of the previous SPE. It is not tied to the SONET frame contents.

C2 signal label: This byte identifies the SPE within an STS-N. It is assigned one of 256 possible values.

G1 path status: This byte is used for status information fed back through the network to the sender. That is, it is used to indicate problems and performance of the reverse channel on the SONET link. This allows the state and performance of the two-way path to be monitored at any point along the path or at either end.

F2 user channel: This byte provides a 64-kbps data channel for the user (actually, the vendor) of the endpoint SONET equipment. There is no standard usage, but it is a way for the endpoint customer premises equipment to pass network information.

H4 multiframe pointer: This byte has several uses. For SPEs carrying ATM cells, this was originally planned as on offset (pointer) to the first byte of the first full ATM cell following the H4 pointer in the SPE. The use is now obsolete.

Z3-Z5 growth: These bytes are reserved for future functions.

This may seem like a lot of overhead. It is. The fact remains, however, that the entire T-carrier hierarchy suffered from a severe lack of adequate overhead for even routine error and alarm conditions. This meant that T-carrier bits had to be taken ("robbed") from other functions and used for these much-needed overhead activities (e.g., yellow alarm in T-1 and C-bit parity in T-3). But not even all the overhead bytes in SONET will be supported initially by equipment vendors.

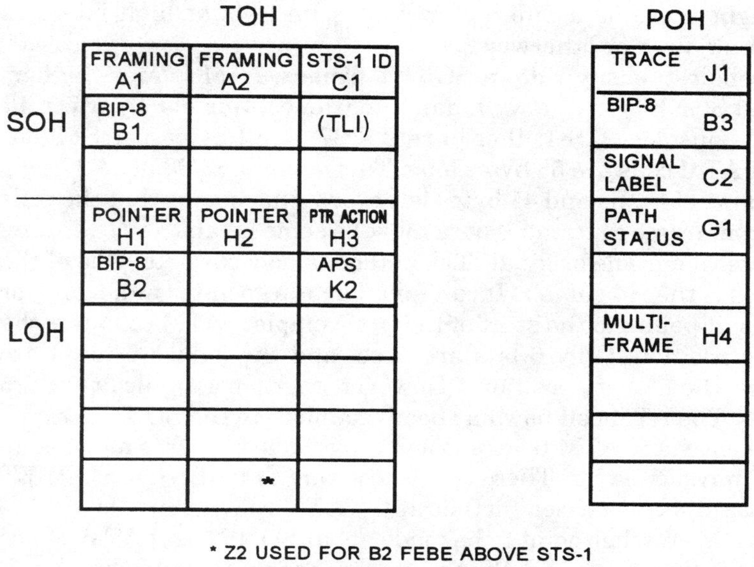

TOH

FRAMING A1	FRAMING A2	STS-1 ID C1
BIP-8 B1		(TLI)
POINTER H1	POINTER H2	PTR ACTION H3
BIP-8 B2		APS K2
	✷	

SOH — top three rows, LOH — bottom rows

POH

TRACE	J1
BIP-8	B3
SIGNAL LABEL	C2
PATH STATUS	G1
MULTI-FRAME	H4

* Z2 USED FOR B2 FEBE ABOVE STS-1

Figure 4.13 Supported SONET overhead.

Figure 4.13 shows the currently supported SONET overhead bytes. Note that the F1 byte is currently used for network management, but of a particular type known as TLI among the carriers. Also note that the current use of the Z2 byte is not for "growth" or future use but is instead employed today for a method whereby a receiver may inform the sender of certain error counts. This field's exact use will be discussed later.

SONET installation and availability in the public network have been steadily growing over the past few years. The manufacturers of fiberoptic cable have been ramping up production for an anticipated rise in the demand for fiber as SONET miles and the rate of installation increase over the next few years.

Remember that SONET terminology differs in SDH, although the structure and purpose of the two are virtually identical. Here are some of the more important SONET terms and their SDH equivalents:

LOH/SOH: There is only SOH in SDH terminology.

SPE: VC (virtual container).

H1/H2 pointers: AU (administrative unit) pointers.

ATM cells and SONET.   The discussion so far has neglected some important issues. Two questions immediately come to mind: How does one fit cells inside an STS frame? And second, given the scarcity of SONET links, might there be a different way to send cells at high bit rates across a link, fiber or otherwise?

ATM cells can easily ride in SONET frames. ATM is at a "higher" layer than SONET, so cells will map into frames. It is not a perfect fit, however. Consider STS-1; there are $9 \times 87 = 783$ bytes per SPE for data. But ATM cells are 53 bytes long. This means $783/53 = 14.77$ cells fit in a frame (14 cells and 41 bytes left over). This means that the cells "creep" from frame to frame. There must be some means for the receiver to locate them. The original ITU method is now obsolete. One of the POH bytes is the H4 *pointer*. It can function as a "pointer indicator" for ATM cells; it points to the start of the first complete ATM cell after the H4 frame position. Only 6 bits are used, and the values 0 to 63 are enough for the 53 byte positions. However, there is a *big* drawback to doing this. The ATM cell now has been "coupled" to the SONET frame. More explicitly, the ATM transmission convergence layer is now tied to the ATM physical layer. There *is* a better way to find cells in SONET frames. It will be discussed further at the ATM convergence layer.

There is one further point to be made about SONET and ATM. Since SONET is *synchronous* and ATM is *asynchronous,* how can they possibly work together?

The answer is twofold. First, the word *synchronous* in SONET refers to the clocking scheme used to align information at different levels of the SONET hierarchy. This is done so that *any* byte can be accessed at *any* level, up and down the hierarchy. The word *asynchronous* in ATM just means that ownership of bits is *not* determined by position in the data stream.

Second, and just as important, ATM exists at a higher layer in the B-ISDN protocol model than SONET. Thus, in the spirit of layer independence, there is no need at all for one layer to be dependent on the techniques used at another. Think of connection-oriented layers in ISO (e.g., TCP) on top of connectionless layers (e.g., IP).

The second issue mentioned above, the scarcity of SONET links for running ATM networks, is dealt with by current ATM Forum agreements. While there has been some talk about running SONET links within a building to provide ATM LANs, most physical layer ATM discussions center around what other media can and should be used for the transmission of ATM cells and just how they should be employed for this purpose. The following sections detail the currently supported transports.

4.4.2   100-Mbps TAXI (FDDI)

Most users are much more likely to encounter fiber transport not as SONET or SDH but rather as fiber distributed data interface (FDDI) architected LANs or MANs. This 100-km version of Token Ring was developed by ANSI as X3T9.5 (now designated X3T12) and adopted by the IEEE as 802.8. FDDI is more properly a series of standards issued by ANSI, but it is common to just speak of FDDI as if it were a single specification or standard. FDDI still runs as a MAC layer protocol under IEEE 802.2 logical link control (LLC) at layer 2a of the OSI-RM. FDDI runs at 100 Mbps, signaled with 4-in-5 (4/5) encoding at 125 Mbps.

In ATM Forum documents, 100-Mbps ATM is commonly known as TAXI, because the chipset originally used was the AMD (Advanced Micro Devices) TAXI chip. FDDI chips are modified for use in ATM-based LANs. Several vendors use this approach, which is attractive because the FDDI rings may be in place already.

This 100-Mbps TAXI transport uses the FDDI 4B/5B encoding. However, it does not use the full FDDI ring architecture and protocols. It is *physically* the same, but it runs standard compliant ATM protocols (and generates cells) over the (former) FDDI network. In other words, ATM cells cannot be mixed with FDDI traffic on a 100-Mbps TAXI network.

As originally conceived in the 1980s, FDDI was developed by computer manufacturers as a way to share peripherals and back up data between processing centers with fiberoptic cable. Adapted by ANSI in the late 1980s, and by ISO as well, it is related to both 802.2 LLC and Token Ring LAN concepts. With FDDI, a satellite processing center did not have to have all the disk or tape capacity as the main center. FDDI, acting as a computer backplane connectivity network, could quickly backup to disk or tape. One problem with this intended use was the fact that FDDI required right-of-way between sites to be employed on a private network, which has limited its deployment for this strategy.

However, the whole philosophy of corporate computing has changed in the last few years, propelled mainly by the rise of the PC as the platform of choice for applications and the rise of LANs as the networks of choice for connecting these PCs. FDDI has renewed importance as a provider of "backbone" LAN internetworking. Its reliable medium and high speeds make it an excellent choice for LAN connectivity, be it 802.3 Ethernets, 802.5 Token Rings, or any IEEE LAN protocol.

It is not unusual today to find a separate Token Ring or Ethernet (802.3) on each floor of a building connected by an FDDI "riser" cable system. Of course, the device used to connect the LANs to the FDDI fiber should more accurately be called a *router* or *brouter*.

Figure 4.14 is an overview of how FDDI and the IEEE 802.X protocols relate to one another at the lower two layers of the ISO model. Keep in mind that FDDI is the "odd man out" in some respects, being ANSI and not IEEE. But it is still ISO, and it is still in a lot more places than 802.6, for instance. FDDI is a logical extension of 802.5 Token Ring technology, and although not aligned with the IEEE, it uses 802.2 LLC as its upper layer 2. It offers speeds of 100 Mbps for up to about 100 km (about 63 miles) and runs (initially) on multimode fiber configured as dual counterrotating rings.

LAYER 2	802.2 LLC				
	FDDI MAC (TOKEN RING)	802.3 MAC (CSMA/ CD)	802.4 MAC (TOKEN BUS)	802.5 MAC (TOKEN RING)	802.6 MAC (DQDB)
LAYER 1	FDDI PHY	802.3 PHY	802.4 PHY	802.5 PHY	802.6 PHY
	FDDI PMD	802.3 PMD	802.4 PMD	802.5 PMD	802.6 PMD

Figure 4.14   FDDI and 802 protocol stack.

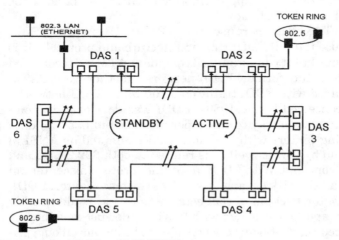

Figure 4.15   100-Mbps TAXI (FDDI).

The data frames are variable length, up to about 4500 bytes, and with one token possession, more than one frame may be sent. With multi-mode fiber, nodes may be up to about 2 km apart without repeaters. Single-mode fiber will increase this to about 60 km, but other changes to parameters and utilization are necessary. FDDI is an ANSI (X3T9) (1989) *and* ISO (1990) standard.

Figure 4.15 shows the architecture of an FDDI backbone connecting LANs. The nodes are known as *dual attached stations* (DASs) because all nodes of this type have two sets of ports. One set is for the *active* ring in-out, and the other is for the *standby* ring in-out. All traffic normally is sent on the active ring. However, if the ring is broken, the standby ring is used to ensure continued operation of the FDDI network. The adjacent DAS will "wrap" at the dual ports to provide this function.

In addition to DAS nodes, there are also dual attached concentrators (DACs), which allow more than one FDDI device or LAN to connect to it. A DAC will be connected to a single attach station (SAS), which may be a bridge or router on the LAN. SASs had only one set of ports: active in and active out.

4B/5B encoding. Does FDDI run at 100 Mbps or 125 Mbps? The data rate is 100 Mbps. But the answer is not this simple. 100 Mbps is the *data* rate, but the ring runs at a 125-Mbps *signal* rate. Why the difference? Because FDDI uses something called *4B/5B group encoding,* which means that data bits are taken 4 at a time (a "nibble") and sent on the ring as 5 bits. So 5 *code bits* represent 4 *data bits.*

There are good reasons to do this. This scheme is much more efficient than other LAN encodings such as Manchester or differential Manchester. These use 2 code bits to represent 1 data bit, for a 50 percent efficiency. This ensures enough data transitions from 0 to 1 that the receivers do not have to worry about consecutive 0s (as T-1 networks did). However, 4B/5B encoding uses only 5 code bits for 4 data bits, which is 80 percent efficient. Also, receivers can now derive the clock from the data stream, saving the trouble of sending a separate clock pulse and building special clocking circuitry into each DAS.

ATM cells on 100-Mbps 4B/5B TAXI. For transporting ATM cells, TAXI networks will use the FDDI code group. Five bits will represent 32 distinct values. Sixteen values were chosen in FDDI to represent the 16 possible 4-bit data input combinations, and the remaining 16 values were used for line-state and control symbols. These are shown in Fig. 4.16.

The ATM Forum has taken some of these FDDI 4B/5B "command" codes and used them as ATM control codes. These are made up of pairs of the various FDDI command codes. For example, the JK control code

- 00000   Q   Quiet Line State
  00001   H   Halt Line State
  00010   H   Halt Line State
  00100   H   Halt Line State
  01000   H   Halt Line State
  11111   I   Idle Line State

- 11000   J   First Start Delimiter
  10001   K   Second Start Delimiter

- 11110   0   Binary 0000
  01001   1   Binary 0001
  10100   2   Binary 0010
  10101   3   Binary 0011
  01010   4   Binary 0100
  01011   5   Binary 0101
  01110   6   Binary 0110
  01111   7   Binary 0111
  10010   8   Binary 1000
  10011   9   Binary 1001
  10110   A   Binary 1010
  10111   B   Binary 1011
  11010   C   Binary 1100
  11011   D   Binary 1101
  11100   E   Binary 1110
  11101   F   Binary 1111

- 01101   T   End Delimiter
  00111   R   Reset Control Indicator
  11001   S   Set Control Indiator

Figure 4.16   4B/5B symbol encoding.

- JK (Synch) Idle
  II   Reserved
  TT   Start of Cell
  TS   Reserved
  IH   Not Recommended
  TR   Reserved
  SR   Reserved
  SS   Unused
  HH   Not Recommended
  HI   Not Recommended
  HQ   Not Recommended
  RR   Unused
  RS   Reserved
  QH   Not Recommended   **Figure 4.17**   100-Mbps symbol encoding.
  QI   Not Recommended
  QQ   Not Recommended

is made up of the FDDI J and K symbols. The full table of defined ATM Forum TAXI control codes is shown in Fig. 4.17.

These control codes are used to transmit cells. Most of the combinations are "reserved," "not recommended," or "unused." If generated by a transmitter, they are to be ignored by the receiver. "Reserved" codes will be used for future functions.

The ATM Forum further notes that because of the limitations of 4B/5B error checking and handling, performance and services on 100-Mbps TAXI ATM networks may be limited. No further specifics are mentioned.

4.4.3   155-Mbps 8B/10B encoding (Fibre Channel)

Another interesting possibility for ATM cell transport is Fibre Channel, a product of the ANSI X3T9 task group, who did FDDI. (The British "fibre" spelling was intentional, the better for international acceptance. In early drafts, it *is* "fiber channel.") Fibre Channel, work on which began in 1988, runs IBM's "8-in-10 encoding" (similar, of course, to FDDI's 4B/5B encoding). Defined on fiber, coaxial cable, and STP, Fibre Channel has wide support, especially from IBM, HP, and SUN.

Because there are no cells, Fibre Channel is sometimes positioned as a rival or alternative technology to ATM. There are certainly differences. ATM is positioned as an architecture, not just a transport. It turns out that ATM can use Fibre Channel as well as FDDI or other physical layer media for cell transport. Thus straightforward comparisons are not really possible.

A Fibre Channel network is literally designed to be a channel. That is, it is a conscious recreation of internal, channel-based computer system communications. There is really no protocol overhead at all. Fibre Channel networks just transfer data from one device buffer to another. The channel does not care about the format or meaning of the bits. It only controls the transfer of the data and provides a simple means of detecting errors.

Yet its very simplicity is its strength. The speed of channel communication and flexible interconnection of protocol-independent devices make it very attractive as an alternative to software-intensive network protocols. While there are "switches" in Fibre Channel, at its simplest, a Fibre Channel "network" consists of a series of point-to-point links between "N-ports." A "fabric" configuration does exist, with switching between "F-ports" possible. These are shown is Fig. 4.18.

Fibre Channel architecture.   Figure 4.19 shows the layered architecture of Fibre Channel. Of course, when used for the transport of ATM cells, the network may still be physically a Fibre Channel, but it is not the Fibre Channel layered architecture. This is somewhat confusing, especially since the ATM Forum UNI 3.0 specification never specifically called this "155-Mbps interface" Fibre Channel, although this is in fact what it is.

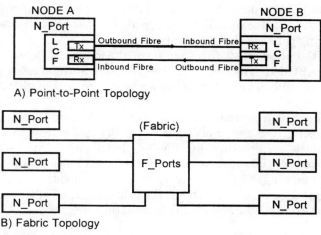

A) Point-to-Point Topology

B) Fabric Topology

Figure 4.18 Fibre Channel network.

ULPs	IPI-3	SCSI	HIPPI	IP	Other
FC-4	IPI-3 Mapping	SCSI Mapping	HIPPI Mapping	IP Mapping	Other Mappings
FC-3	Common Services				
FC-2	Signalling Protocol				
FC-1	Transmission Protocol				
FC-0	Interface / Media				

FC-PHY (spanning FC-2, FC-1, FC-0)

Figure 4.19 Fibre Channel architecture.

There are five layers to the Fibre Channel (FC) architecture. The bottom layer, FC-0, defines the physical link itself, both interface (connector and more) and media (STP, coax, or fiber). The media are distinguished by type, speed, transmitter type, and distance. For ATM cell transport on Fibre Channel, both multimode fiber and STP are supported by the ATM Forum, but in practice, Fibre Channel will be used when STP building cabling over distances of 100 m or less is necessary.

Above the FC-0 layer is the FC-1 layer, which defines the electrical signaling (transmission protocol) used on the link. This is where ATM cells will use Fibre Channel's 8B/10B encoding, first used for IBM's ESCON (Enterprise Systems Connection) channels.

The FC-2 layer defines rules for the sending and receiving of various types of messages and their formats between Fibre Channel nodes. This layer is very similar in function to the MAC sublayers in IEEE LANs. FC-2 also includes definitions of several services, as does the logical link control (LLC) sublayer in IEEE LANs. There are several frame formats at the FC-2 layer. ATM cells will use their own frame format for packaging cells inside an FC-2 frame.

Layers FC-0, FC-1, and FC-2 together form the physical layer of Fibre Channel, the FC-PH. The current Fibre Channel standards stop at this point, but other layers are part of the architecture, although not fully specified.

Layer FC-3 will define a common set of services that Fibre Channel networks will support. It is a way of "hiding" FC-PH differences from the upper layers of the architecture. FC-4 will define a way to interface various existing protocols (up to 255 will be allowed) with Fibre Channel networks. These "mappings" form a convergence service for these protocols, ensuring that they will function over the Fibre Channel network. The upper layer protocols (ULPs) will stay just as they are.

Fibre Channel and ATM. If the functions of the whole Fibre Channel architecture look vaguely familiar, they should. It is no stretch of the imagination to see in Fibre Channel a very similar form to the layers of the ATM architecture. Fibre Channel FC-2 even defines video frame formats. The main difference is the variable size of FC-2 data units, up to about 2000 bytes, as opposed to ATM's fixed-length cells.

Figure 4.20 shows a possible relationship between ATM layers and Fibre Channel layers. For the transport of ATM cells, the FC-1 and FC-0 layers will be used to transport ATM cells rather than FC-2 data units.

4.4.4   45-Mbps DS-3

Even more common than the fiber-based transports (except for Fibre Channel on STP) examined above will be ATM network transports

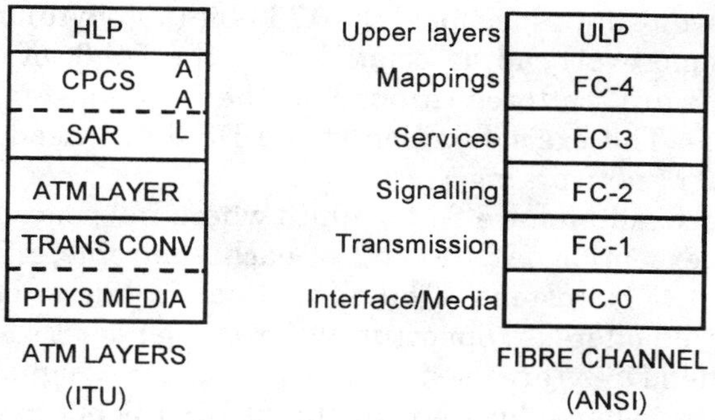

	ATM LAYERS (ITU)			FIBRE CHANNEL (ANSI)	
HLP			Upper layers	ULP	
CPCS	A		Mappings	FC-4	
SAR	A L		Services	FC-3	
ATM LAYER			Signalling	FC-2	
TRANS CONV			Transmission	FC-1	
PHYS MEDIA			Interface/Media	FC-0	

HLP: HIGHER LAYERS PROTOCOLS
CPCS: COMMON PART CONVERGENCE SUBLAYER
SAR: SEGMENTATION AND REASSEMBLY
AAL: ATM ADAPTATION LAYER
SIP: SMDS INTERFACE PROTOCOL

Figure 4.20 ATM layers and Fibre Channel layers.

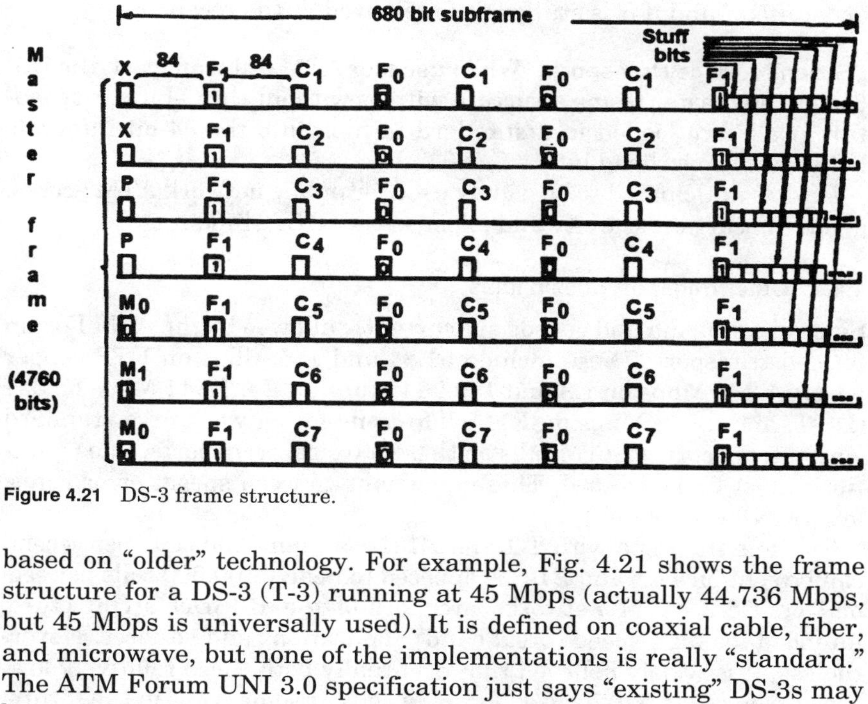

Figure 4.21 DS-3 frame structure.

based on "older" technology. For example, Fig. 4.21 shows the frame structure for a DS-3 (T-3) running at 45 Mbps (actually 44.736 Mbps, but 45 Mbps is universally used). It is defined on coaxial cable, fiber, and microwave, but none of the implementations is really "standard." The ATM Forum UNI 3.0 specification just says "existing" DS-3s may be used for cell transport, but other ATM documents specifically mention DS-3 on coaxial cable.

DS-3 frame structure. The structure of a DS-3 frame, known as a *master frame,* consists of seven *subframes,* each of which is 680 bits (not bytes) long. The seven subframes form the 4760-bit (595-byte) master-frame. There is some overhead associated with the DS-3, of course. These overhead bits are scattered throughout the DS-3 master frame, 8 in each subframe. The exact function of the DS-3 overhead bits is unimportant for ATM networking.

Between the overhead bits are 84-bit units where information may be sent, with one exception. At the end of each subframe, after the eighth overhead bit (F1), instead of having a final 84-bit set of information, the subframe offers an opportunity for the sender to "stuff" a bit. This is used when DS-3s are used to multiplex 28 DS-1 signals. Due to timing differences, when a bit from one input DS-1 is not available, it is necessary to invent ("stuff") a bit somewhere in the output stream. These stuff bits may be placed in the first bit position after the last F1 bit in subframe 1, the second bit position after the last F1 bit in subframe 2, and so on to the seventh bit position after the last F1 bit in subframe 7. The other overhead bits indicate whether this bit is "live" or "stuffed," and if it is stuffed, it is removed at the receiver.

DS-3 and ATM cell transport. When used for ATM cell transport, the DS-3 uses the master frame structure with or without the C-bit parity feature. Cells are loaded in a standard fashion into the 84-bit intervals between the overhead bits.

DS-3 is anticipated to be widely used for public network ATM access, given the current scarcity and expense of SONET links.

4.4.5   Other transport possibilities

Some other media and speeds are currently allowed by the ATM Forum for cell transport. These include 51.84 and 155 Mbps on UTP copper wire, 34.368 Mbps on E3 and 139.264 Mbps on E4, 1.544 Mbps on T-1 (DS-1) and 2.048 Mbps on E1. Before completing work on a standard way of transporting ATM cells on these physical transports, some questions must be addressed. These questions concern speed, error rates, and SONET availability.

Speed is the issue with T-1 and E1. Less than 4000 cells per second can be sent on T-1s and E1s, as opposed to nearly 100,000 cells per second on DS-3. ATM networks are part of the B-ISDN architecture, intended for high-speed (broadband) applications and services. Nevertheless, it is widely believed that eventually both these relatively low-speed transports will be used for ATM cells at some point in the future, but probably only to transport ATM cells from a remote location to a large ATM node. This "aggregation" of traffic will not be necessary immediately, however.

Bit error rates (BERs) are the issue with the UTP rates. Even on highly reliable category 3 UTP (for 16 Mbps or so) and category 5 UTP (for 100 Mbps), the question is whether UTP copper wire can sustain the low BERs ATM networks expect over even modest (100 m or less) distances. This is due to the initial expectations that ATM networks would run only on very low BER fiber networks. Preliminary studies have shown acceptable BERs for the wire itself, but BERs "in the field" on installed cable systems (with loose connectors and electrical noise) remain largely unknown. Current ATM Forum thinking is that cells should not be transported on transports with BERs in excess of 10^{-10}. This is only a guideline, however, not a rule or documented agreement.

The last two transports mentioned, E3 and E4, are widely used in Europe and elsewhere in the world. The issue here is whether to bother standardizing a cell transport if SDH (the international standard on which SONET is based) becomes widely available. There are European companies participating in the ATM Forum working groups, and the approval of ATM cell transport on E3s and E4s will largely be driven by them, if at all.

4.4.6   ATM raw cell transport

Although not expected to be widely used in North America, it *is* permitted to put "raw cells" over a fiber link running at SONET or SDH speeds (starting at 155 Mbps). The raw cells flow end to end through the network, transparent to each physical layer. They form a synchronous (it is still SONET/SDH), constant cell stream (special idle cells must be sent if there are not live data).

However, raw cell transport does away with the extensive framing system of SONET and SDH, which some claim benefits mainly the carrier, not the user. However, now some kind of "framing" must be provided by the cells themselves (where does a group of cells begin?). This framing information is provided by more specialized cells that repeat at known intervals.

A more serious drawback is the need to prevent user data from masquerading as framing or header information. There is a method of "scrambling" the data bits in an ATM cell for this purpose, much as SDLC did bit stuffing to "mask out" 7E from data. Of course, this procedure adds processing overhead in place of the framing overhead done away with.

4.5   ATM Transmission Convergence Sublayer

The next sublayer in the ATM protocol reference model is the ATM transmission convergence (TC) sublayer. This forms the upper part of the ATM physical layer itself. The task of transmission convergence is to properly load the ATM cells into the physical transport transmission frame (SONET, DS-3) on the sending side of the network and remove them at the receiving side. Alternatively, for some physical transports, cells must be associated into "blocks" (4B/5B, 8B/10B) for transmission purposes.

The five functions defined at the TC sublayer are

1. *Cell rate decoupling.* Since many framed transports must generate a fixed number of bits every second, the TC sublayer must insert special idle cells that are removed by the receiver in order to satisfy this bit-rate requirement.

2. *HEC sequence generation and verification.* The header error code (HEC) is generated on the ATM cell header fields by the sender and verified by the receiver. That is, the HEC is regenerated and compared with the received value. If possible, the cell header errors are corrected and the cell processed. If the error is not correctable, the entire cell is discarded.

3. *Cell delineation.* Receivers must be able to detect the cell boundaries from a continuous stream of bits. To prevent false delineation, the information payload of a cell is scrambled (rearranged, not encrypted) under normal conditions by the sender and descrambled by the receiver.

4. *Transmission frame adaptation.* Depending on the type of physical transport, it may be necessary for the sender to package the ATM cells into a transmission frame and unpack the cells at the receiving side.

5. *Transmission frame generation and recovery.* Generally, transmission frame usage will involve more than just packing ATM cells bit by bit into a transmission frame and sending it out. This function defines this additional process.

Before getting into the details of the various functions of the ATM convergence layer, an important distinction must be made. That is, cells in ATM fall into two main categories in the overall ATM architecture: at the physical layer and at the ATM layer itself. There are not frames at one layer and packets at another layer, as in the OSI-RM. This is so because there are only cells to work with and nothing else. However, it makes little sense to send idle (empty) cells up to the ATM layer itself when they have meaning only to the ATM physical layer.

Therefore, some cell structures and header values make sense *only* to the transmission convergence sublayer as part of the physical layer. These cells are generated and used by the physical layers *only* and are *never* passed to the ATM layer, where the values would be very confusing to the ATM layer itself.

Figure 4.22 shows the structure of the headers of these two types of ATM cells. In the figure, bit positions marked P are used for special functions by the transmission convergence sublayer, and those marked A are used by the ATM layer. The fifth byte is still a valid HEC sequence over the entire header.

	OCTET 1	OCTET 2	OCTET 3	OCTET 4
RESERVED FOR PHYSICAL LAYER	PPPP0000	O0000000	O0000000	0000PPP1
UNASSIGNED CELLS (ATM)	AAAA0000	O0000000	O0000000	0000AAA0

Figure 4.22 Physical cells and ATM cells.

At first glance, it may seem that this cannot possibly be correct. The ATM UNI header defines the first 4 bits of the ATM cell header as generic flow control (GFC). The last bit in the last header byte is the cell loss priority bit (CLP), and the 3 bits before that form the payload type indicator (PTI) field. If cells generated by a sending physical layer are removed by the receiving physical layer, how are they distinguished from other types of cells? The answer is in the use of other fields—the VPI and VCI header bits. They are all set to zero in physical layer cells and unassigned cells destined for the ATM layer itself. This use of VPI = 0 and VCI = 0 is a first look at ATM VPI and VCI values reserved for special functions.

A receiving TC sublayer getting a valid cell header with VPI = 0 and VCI = 0 will check the value of the last bit in the fourth byte. If the bit is 1, then the cell has been sent by the physical layer at the sending side and contains information for the receiving physical layer itself. This cell is not sent to the ATM layer. A cell with the last bit in the fourth header byte set to 0, however, is passed up to the ATM layer.

4.5.1 Cell rate decoupling

The first TC sublayer function to consider is the idea of cell rate decoupling. Over any framed physical transmission path, a fixed number of bits must be sent in a given time interval (i.e., so many frames per second). This is especially true of synchronous schemes such as SONET but is also true of others as well. Consider a customer site connected to an ATM network node with a SONET link running at 155 Mbps (STS-3c). Clearly, if a sender on this ATM network link is only generating data bits to be packed into cells at 100 Mbps (for example), the ATM equipment must adjust this rate to the line rate of 155 Mbps (actually less, given the SONET overhead).

The "extra" 55 Mbps of cells is inserted by the sender with a special physical layer cell bit pattern and removed by the receiver based on that

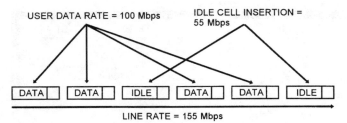

Figure 4.23   Cell rate decoupling.

OCTET 1	OCTET 2	OCTET 3	OCTET 4	OCTET 5
00000000	00000000	00000000	00000001	VALID HEC CODE

INFORMATION FIELD = 01 10 10 10
(REPEATING)

Figure 4.24   TC layer idle cell.

bit pattern. This feature gives ATM networks great flexibility in connection speeds over the same physical line rate and delivers "bandwidth on demand" in some services. This process is illustrated in Fig. 4.23.

Figure 4.24 shows the format of the TC sublayer idle cell. This is a first look at a cell that has a special meaning in ATM networks. Others are used for ATM signaling and other functions and will be examined later. For now, notice that an idle cell header consists of all zeros except for the last bit of the fourth byte in the cell header. The information field is present as well but contains a pattern of 01 10 10 10 (6C in hex) repeated throughout the cell. The receiver will discard any idle cells and examine any other cells with the last bit in the fourth header byte set to 1 for physical layer information. Only cells with the last bit in the fourth header byte set to 0 will be passed on to the ATM layer.

4.5.2   Header error control (HEC)

The last field (byte) in the ATM header is the header error control (HEC) field. It is detailed in CCITT I.432 and is used for error detection and correction on the ATM cell header only, not the actual data or information in the cell itself. The HEC's main purpose is to supply robust error correction and detection for addressing errors. Since the UNI cell header has 20 of the 32 bits in the first 4 bytes set aside for connection identifiers (8 bits for VPI, 16 bits for VCI), most bit errors in cell headers will affect these fields. In ATM networks, these VPI and VCI errors will show up as invalid VPI/VCI values in those fields. There is no sense in switching a cell all the way across the network to find out it has ended up in the wrong place, if for no other reason than a lot of effort has been expended to get the cell there. And users will be reluctant to pay for the delivery of many cells to the wrong places. At the same time, if only 1 bit is wrong, it would be helpful to be able to correct it instead of discarding the whole cell.

To allow this correction to happen, the HEC sequence uses a much more complex algorithm than simpler parity checks do. HEC offers SECDED (single error correction, double error detection) forward (i.e., no retransmission needed) error correction. Since most fiber errors are single-bit errors, this is an optimal solution, but it may lose effectiveness on other media, especially copper-based media with burst error characteristics.

Perhaps surprisingly, current ATM Forum documentation recommends that *any* cell received with detected errors be discarded on the 4B/5B (FDDI) and 8B/10B (Fibre Channel) transports. Even ATM Forum support for single-bit error correction on the DS-3 and SONET transports is optional.

Since the HEC algorithm is adapted for single-bit error correction, rather than merely to indicate errors and request retransmissions, as have other error-correction schemes in the past, some further exploration of HEC operation is in order. Explanations of how SECDED actually works (especially the SEC part) have been scarce and cloaked in mathematical terminology that not many networking specialists are familiar with. Thus several examples of HEC use are included.

HEC receiver actions.   Figure 4.25 shows the actions that a receiver follows to implement the HEC verification processing. The SECDED algorithm has two modes: It can correct single-bit errors, or it can detect double-bit errors. Normally, it is in correction mode. If no HEC error is detected when the receiver's calculated HEC value on the received cell

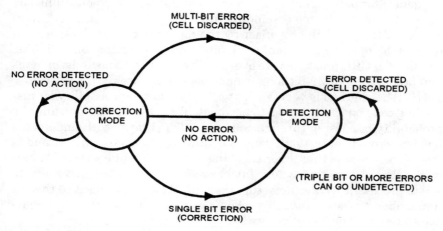

Figure 4.25   HEC receiver actions.

header is compared with the value received with the cell, no action is taken. Even after the receiver has corrected a single-bit error and recalculated the proper HEC, the receiver will transition to detection mode. Of course, the receiver will always transition there after a multiple-bit error is detected, after discarding the uncorrectable cell.

In detection mode, *no* errors are corrected, and all errored cells are discarded. This means that all sequences (consecutive runs of cells of *any* number) of cells containing errors are not propagated through the network. Once a cell with a valid HEC is found in detection mode, the receiver will transition back to correction mode again. Thus the receiver will in practice correct only every other cell in a sequence of cells with invalid HEC values. The philosophy behind this is that on a fiber-based network, single-bit errors occurring twice within a 53-byte or so span (in consecutive cell headers) should not happen with any regularity, and even if they did, the TC sublayer has more to do at the receiving side than to spend processing time correcting bit errors in runs of consecutive cell headers.

It is important to realize that errors that affect more than 2 bits in the 40-bit header *may* go undetected. In this case, although the receiver thinks that the cell header is valid, it will most likely be switched to the wrong link and ultimately the wrong destination. This is the primary source of inserted cells in ATM networks.

HEC performance.   HEC receiver operation is based on the characteristics of fiber transmission systems. Most errors are single-bit errors, and the rest are truly huge error bursts (wiping out more than a whole cell header). One method cannot handle both adequately. Therefore, HEC is designed to correct the single-bit errors and throw everything else away.

The actual algorithm is "the remainder of the division (modulo 2) by the generator polynomial $x^8 + x^2 + x + 1$ of the product x^8 multiplied by the content of the header excluding the HEC field." The inherent complexity of the algorithm is offset by the fact that the HEC generation process is operating on only 40 bits and generating only 8 bits. Traditional CRC must operate over hundreds, even thousands, of bytes and produce 16- or 32-bit-long frame-check sequences.

The HEC method is very good; at a 10^{-8} BER, the probability for discarding cells has been shown to be about 10^{-13} (1 in 10 trillion), and the probability of passing through cells to the ATM layer with undetected header errors is only 10^{-20}. This is a vanishingly small amount and is one of the reasons that error checking is so rudimentary on ATM networks. Errors are so few and far between that it is not necessary to waste processing power detecting them all the time, at least in theory. Remember, however, that this scheme was intended for the error characteristics of fiber-based networks.

How the HEC works.   The HEC check on single-bit errors in the ATM header is a distinguishing feature of the ATM protocol architecture. While many other communications protocols include a check sequence on data for error-control purposes, ATM error control is virtually unique in two respects. First, the HEC error-control check only covers the first 4 bytes (32 bits) of the ATM header (the 8-bit HEC field itself forms the fifth byte of the header). None of the ATM cell payload bytes are protected by the HEC field. Second, the HEC field is capable of providing for SECDED protection on the cell header bytes rather than just using the error-control field for requesting retransmission of traffic received with errors, as in most other data protocols.

SECDED is *single error correction, double error detection* and refers to the capability of the HEC check to enable a receiver of an ATM cell to correct any single-bit error in the cell header and detect any double-bit errors in the cell header. This first property is especially useful in ATM networks using fiberoptic-based transports, since the vast majority of bit errors in these fiber networks are indeed single-bit errors.

The single-bit error-correction capability of ATM networks means that receiving network nodes and end nodes on an ATM network can correct these single-bit errors in the cell header without having to request that the cell be resent from the originator. This is important in ATM networks because many of the time-sensitive applications using the ATM network will not tolerate the delays that may be imposed waiting for this retransmission of traffic.

Thus what is it about the HEC check in ATM that allows the receiver to correct these single-bit errors? Since explanations of this capability, especially in nonmathematical language, are few and far between, this section will detail the operation of ATM's HEC check single error correction. The double error detection, while necessary, does not vary much from traditional error-detection techniques in other protocols such as X.25 or SDLC and so will not be dealt with in any detail. Of course, it should not be overlooked that multiple-bit errors in excess of 2 in a 40-bit cell header sequence may be interpreted by the receiver as a single-bit error. Then the correction procedure will not work and may result in a misdelivered cell. However, multiple-bit errors on modern telecommunications networks should be so few and far between that 3 or more bit errors in a 40-bit sequence should almost never occur.

The sender in an ATM network generates the HEC sequence and appends it to the first 4 bytes of the cell header, forming the full 5-byte (40-bit) header sent across the network. Exactly how the sender does this is detailed in ITU-T Recommendation I.432, Sec. 4.3.2, "Header Error Control (HEC) Sequence Generation." The relevant portion of the section reads:

The HEC field shall be an 8-bit sequence. It shall be the remainder of the division (modulo 2) by the generator polynomial $x^8 + x^2 + x + 1$ of the product x^8 multiplied by the content of the header excluding the HEC field.

A *generator polynomial* is just a mathematical way of representing a string of 0s and 1s. In this notation, the string 10001001 can be represented as $x^7 + x^3 + 1$. To find the proper values of x, the bit positions are numbered from right to left starting with 0. In the example, a 1 bit appears in positions 7, 3, and 0 in the string. Therefore, the polynomial representing 10001001 is expressed as x^7 (a 1 in the seventh position) plus x^3 (a 1 in the third position) plus 1 (a 1 in the initial zeroth position). For the ATM HEC sequence, the polynomial used to generate the HEC sequence, hence the *generator polynomial,* is the bit string 100000111.

This 9-bit-long bit string is used by the sender as a divisor of the 32 bits from the first 4 header bytes of the ATM cell. But not ordinary division. This division is *modulo 2,* a type of division for 0s and 1s that is easy and quick to do. It can be done easily with a series of shift registers and a number of XOR operations. The XOR binary operation results in a 0 if both bits are 0 or both bits are 1 or results in a 0 if the two bits are different. Thus 101010 XOR'd with 111000 equals 010010.

Before this XOR division takes place, eight 0 bits are appended to the 32 bits of the first 4 bytes of the ATM cell header, making 40 bits in all. This is "the product x^8."

Now all the pieces are in place to understand how the 8-bit HEC check sequence is generated. In this example, consider an ATM cell with VPI = 7, VCI = 11, PTI = 0, and CLP = 1. Since the GFC field is set to 0000, the first 4 bytes of this cell header would be

$$0000\ 0000 \quad (GFC = 0000)$$

$$0111\ 0000 \quad (VPI = 7)$$

$$0000\ 0000$$

$$1011\ 0001 \quad (VCI = 11, PTI = 0, CLP = 1)$$

The first thing the sender must do is append eight 0 bits to this sequence, which now becomes

00000000 01110000 00000000 10110001 00000000

Next, the whole thing is "divided" by 10000111:

$$100000111\ \overline{)00000000\ 01110000\ 00000000\ 10110001\ 00000000}$$

In this operation, the sender is not interested in the result of the division per se, but rather in the "remainder," that is, the bit pattern left over at the end of the entire XOR division operation. Since the divisor is 9 bits long, the remainder must be 8 bits long, the 8 bits that will form the HEC check sequence.

The rules of XOR binary division are simple: The entire string is scanned left to right. If a 1 bit is encountered, the divisor is XOR'd with the next 9 bits and the remainder examined anew. The whole process is easier to illustrate than describe:

```
100000111 )00000000 01110000 00000000 10110001 00000000
                1000001 11
                110001 110
                100000 111
                 10001 0010
                 10000 0111
                  0001 01010000
                     1 00000111
                       01010111 10
                       1000001 11
                        010110 0111
                        10000 0111
                         0110 000000
                          100 000111
                           10 0001110
                           10 0000111
                            0 00010011 0000
                              10000 0111
                               0011 0111000
                                 10 0000111
                                  1 01111110
                                  1 00000111
                                    01111001
```

This remainder, the 0111 1001 string, is the HEC sequence. The sequence is appended to the 4-byte ATM cell header when sent across the link to the receiver.

Now, in practice, the ATM sending nodes do not do this division operation at all. The entire operation can be implemented easily as a series of shift registers with XOR gates in the proper positions. The "long division" method above is easier to visualize, however.

None of this explains how the HEC check is used by the receiver to correct errors. The documentation is not very helpful. All I.432 says is that the receiver recomputes the HEC sequence on the first 4 bytes received and compares the result with the received value. If they match, there is no error. If they do not match and the receiver considers the comparison to indicate a single-bit error, the single-bit error may be corrected and the cell processed as normal. However, just how does the receiver determine exactly which bit is in error? The receiver actions are considered next.

The receiver in the ATM network, be it an ATM network node (switch) or end node (customer premises equipment), will recompute the HEC check (known as the *syndrome*) based on the received value of the first 4 header bytes. This computed value is compared with the received value of the HEC field. At this point, a couple of different things can happen.

The comparison of the two HEC fields, the received value and the computed value, is done via another XOR operation on the two 8-bit values. If they are identical, the result is zero, and the received header is accepted as valid and passed up to the ATM layer for switching or further processing. Keep in mind, however, that the HEC check is not perfect. There may have been multiple-bit errors in the header fields, including the HEC field itself, that caused the header to be accepted as valid and innocently switched to an improper connection. This is the origin of misdirected or inserted cells on ATM network connections.

The other thing that may happen is that the result of the XOR operation is nonzero. In this case, there has been at least one, and possibly more, detected bit errors in the cell header. If there are two bit errors in the 40-bit header, the receiver is guaranteed to detect it, and the cell header cannot be corrected. The receiver discards the entire cell. No further action is taken (i.e., no notification message is sent to the sender). This is the double error detection (DED) feature of the HEC check algorithm.

But how does the receiver know, based on the result of the XOR operation on the received and computed HEC check, whether the error is a single-bit error and therefore correctable or whether the error is a double-bit error and therefore uncorrectable? The answer is simple: The result of the XOR operation is looked up in a table. If the result is in the table, the table entry tells the receiver exactly which bit is in error in the cell header. This error indication includes the HEC field itself. The table entry merely indicates error position. If the received bit in the indicated position was a 0, it should have been a 1 bit, and if the received bit in the indicated position was a 1, it should have been a 0 bit.

Now there is only one further question to answer. Where did the table come from? The table is computed once (and included in the receiver equipment) by setting a 40-bit sequence to all 0 bits except for a single 1 bit and "dividing" by the generator polynomial of 100000111. This still enables the receiver to correct single bits "flipped" from 0 to 1 or 1 to 0. Only the position is significant. For example, the computation for position 30 is as follows:

$$100000111\ \overline{)000000000\ 00000000\ 00000000\ 00000100\ 00000000}$$

$$\underline{100\ 000111}$$

$$00\ 00011100$$

As a result of this operation, the table entry of 0001 1100 will indicate a single-bit error in position 30. These table entries may be computed once and used in receiver hardware or software implementing the HEC check.

Here is an example of the whole process, illustrating both a single-bit error from a 0 to a 1 and from a 1 to a 0.

Suppose the received cell header in fact did have a single-bit error in position 30. In this case, the received cell header would appear to have a PTI field of 2 (binary 010) instead of 0 (binary 000):

        0000 0000   (GFC = 0000)

        0111 0000   (VPI = 7)

        0000 0000

        1011 0101   (VCI = 11, PTI = 2, CLP = 1)

        0111 1001   (Received HEC value)

The receiver, of course, will reapply the HEC check on the received header fields, with the HEC field set to all 0:

```
100000111 )00000000 01110000 00000000 10110101 00000000
                                                ↑
                    1000001 11                  Bit error
                    ─────────
                    110001 110
                    100000 111
                    ─────────
                     10001 0010
                     10000 0111
                     ─────────
                      0001 01010000
                         1 00000111
                         ─────────
                          01010111 10
                          1000001 11
                          ─────────
                           010110 0111
                           10000 0111
                           ─────────
                            0110 000001 ←Bit error
                             100 000111
                             ─────────
                              10 0001100
                              10 0000111
                              ─────────
                               0 00010111
                                 10000 0111
                                 ─────────
                                 0111 011100
                                  100 000111
                                  ─────────
                                   11 0110110
                                   10 0000111
                                   ─────────
                                    1 01100010
                                    1 00000111
                                    ─────────
                                      01100101
```

This computed result, 0110 0101, is now XOR'd with the received HEC value, 0111 1001:

$$0111\ 1001$$

$$\text{XOR} \quad \underline{0110\ 0101}$$

$$0001\ 1100$$

This value is used as an index into the table. And, as calculated above, there is indeed an entry for 0001 1100. It indicates a single-bit error in position 30. The receiver can now correct the thirtieth bit from a 1 back to a 0, restoring the PTI field to 0 (binary 000) and processing the cell correctly.

The same process still works for bit errors that flip a 1 bit to a 0 bit. The calculation is still based on a field of forty 0 bits with the error represented as a single 1 bit in position 28:

$$100000111\ \overline{)000000000\ 00000000\ 00000000\ 00010000\ 00000000}$$

$$\underline{10000\ 0111}$$

$$0000\ 01110000$$

The table index value for a bit error in position 28 of the ATM cell header is therefore 01110000.

To illustrate this case, suppose the received header has a single-bit error in position 28, changing the VCI from 11 to 10 (decimal). Now the received header is

0000 0000	(GFC = 0000)
0111 0000	(VPI = 7)
0000 0000	
1010 0001	(VCI = 10, PTI = 0, CLP = 1)
0111 1001	(Received HEC value)

And the calculated HEC field is

```
100000111 )00000000 01110000 00000000 10100001 00000000
                                               ↑
                     1000001 11               Bit error
                     ─────────
                     110001 110
                     100000 111
                     ─────────
                      10001 0010
                      10000 0111
                      ─────────
                       0001 01010000
                          1 00000111
                          ──────────
                            01010111 10
                            1000001 11
                            ──────────
                             010110 0110 ← Bit error
                             10000 0111
                             ──────────
                              0110 000100
                               100 000111
                               ──────────
                                10 0000110
                                10 0000111
                                ──────────
                                 0 00000011 0000000
                                            10 0000111
                                            ──────────
                                             1 00001110
                                             1 00000111
                                             ──────────
                                               00001001
```

This calculated value, 0000 1001, is XOR'd with the received HEC value of 0111 1001:

$$
\begin{array}{rr}
 & 0111\ 1001 \\
\text{XOR} & 0000\ 1001 \\
\hline
 & 0111\ 0000
\end{array}
$$

This time the table entry indicates a single-bit error in position 28. The cell header VCI field is corrected and processed.

Here is the entire table, showing the bit configurations and hex values used to correct single-bit errors in header bit positions 1 through 40:

Pos	Binary	Hex
1	0011 0001	31
2	1001 1011	9B
3	1100 1110	CE
4	0110 0111	67
5	1011 0000	B0
6	0101 1000	58
7	0010 1100	2C
8	0001 0110	16
9	0000 1011	0B
10	1000 0110	86
11	0100 0011	43
12	1010 0010	C2
13	0101 0001	51
14	1010 1011	CD
15	1101 0110	D6
16	0110 1011	6B
17	1011 0110	B6
18	0101 1011	5B
19	1010 1110	AE
20	0101 0111	57
21	1010 1000	A8
22	0101 0111	54
23	0010 1010	2A
24	0001 0101	15
25	1000 1001	89
26	1100 0111	C3
27	1110 0000	E0
28	0111 0000	70
29	0011 1000	38
30	0001 1100	1C
31	0000 1110	0E
32	0000 0111	07
33	1000 0000	80
34	0100 0000	40
35	0010 0000	20
36	0001 0000	10
37	0000 1000	08
38	0000 0100	04
39	0000 0010	02
40	0000 0001	01

Note that the HEC field itself, bit positions 33 through 40, are protected from single-bit errors as well. The great benefit of the HEC algorithm is to eliminate the need for a receiver to request that a duplicate of an errored cell be sent across the network all over again, as in virtually all other networking error-correction procedures. And even in protocols that provide error correction as well as detection on the part of the receiver, the price is usually high overhead in terms of bandwidth and/or nodal processing delay.

In ATM, the process is nearly painless. The long division method used above is merely a visualization technique for illustrative purposes. In practice, the HEC is done in hardware with shift registers and XOR operations as the bits leave or arrive serially. Since this is what the bits must do anyway, there is essentially no additional overhead or delay to consider. All in all, the single-bit error-correction (SEC) aspect of the HEC is an important feature of ATM networks.

4.5.3 Cell delineation

Cell delineation is the process of determining, at the receiver, where the cell boundaries are. Cells are sent "head to tail" by the sender, with no special delimiter or preamble or length field (they are all the exact same size). Thus, once one cell is found, it is relatively easy for the receiver to find subsequent cells; they are always 53 bytes away. The trick is to pick out the first cell from the constant stream of bits arriving at the TC sublayer from the physical media sublayer.

At least one possibility exists for determining cell boundaries: They can be found via the H4 pointer available in the path overhead (POH) of a SONET/SDH frame. However, this method presumes the use of SONET/SDH as the physical cell transport. Clearly, a preferred method would be to find cell boundaries independent of the physical cell transport.

Fortunately, the current standard method of cell delineation, used by the ITU-T and the ATM Forum, is to use the HEC verification process at the receiver for cell delineation. That is, if the HEC syndrome is zero (i.e., no error), then the receiver assumes it has found a valid header and, by extension, the rest of the cell. Other cells are 53 bytes away in either direction in the receiver memory buffer.

However, the HEC method is not easy to do. If the data "mimic" a valid header and HEC sequence, cell misalignment is possible. Thus the HEC method requires the information field in the cell to be "scrambled." This is the ATM equivalent of bit stuffing in SDLC. Also, this introduces considerable processing into the ATM TC sublayer. Despite the added complexity, the benefits of HEC-based cell delineation make it the method used today.

HEC cell delineation. The HEC method requires an elaborate mechanism to ensure proper functioning. There are three major states and four transitions. Initially in HUNT state, the receiver checks bit by bit for a valid HEC sequence. (If the H4 pointer is available, it *may* be used.) Once a valid HEC is found, it goes into the PRESYNCH state. If it was just a fluke, the next invalid HEC sends it back to HUNT. However, after δ consecutive correct HECs, it is now in the SYNCH state, which is where it should always be. If α consecutive incorrect HECs are encountered, not only will the cells be discarded, but the receiver goes back to the HUNT state. Clearly, the performance of the receiver is heavily dependent on the values of α and δ. Probably their values will be set at a default of α = 6 and δ = 7, but lower values will be optional for equipment manufacturers and vendors.

HEC scrambling.   HEC scrambling is done to enhance the performance of the HEC delineation process. A valid header and HEC sequence could be mimicked in the data field in the same way a 7E flag can appear in an SLDC frame. Also in the same way, this may appear innocently as a by-product of the user data content (software bug), or it may be done maliciously by a discontented user. In any case, it is to be prevented.

The header fields themselves (first 5 bytes) are not scrambled by the sender, but the payload information is subjected to a "self-synchronizing" scrambler of the polynomial form $x^{43} + 1$. At least this is recommended for SONET and SDH transports. Other cell transports may use something else, but it will most likely be virtually identical in the result.

Figure 4.26 shows the HEC cell delineation process at the receiver TC sublayer. There are three major states and four transitions. The receiver is in one of three modes: HUNT, PRESYNCH, or SYNCH. Initially, the receiver is in HUNT mode and views the input from the physical cell transport as a continuous stream of bits. In HUNT mode, no descrambling is attempted, and the receiver does a bit-by-bit check on the received bit stream. In other words, the receiver looks at a sequence of

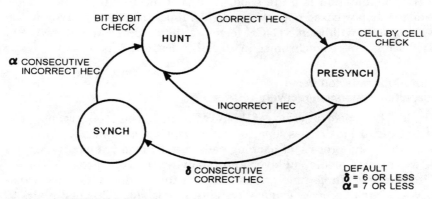

Figure 4.26   HEC cell delineation.

40 bits and presumes that this sequence is potentially a valid cell header. If that is so, then the last byte (8 bits) must be the HEC field and the first 4 bytes (32 bits) must be the rest of the header. The receiver then recalculates the HEC field and compares it with the last 8 bits. If the HEC is incorrect, the receiver essentially slides over one bit and tries again. Eventually, a valid sequence is found. But it may be due to chance, even with scrambling (there is a small but real possibility that payload information may be scrambled *into* a valid header 5-byte sequence). Thus the receiver transitions into the PRESYNCH state (maybe this is really the cell boundary).

In the PRESYNCH state, the receiver "looks" 53 bytes downstream in the receive memory buffer. If the valid header sequence was in fact a false delineation, there is only a small chance that it will be repeated exactly every 53 bytes. If the subsequent HEC check fails, the receiver transitions back to the HUNT mode and continues the bit-by-bit check. However, if the valid header sequence is really the cell boundary, there will be repeated valid sequences exactly 53 bytes apart. This is the cell-by-cell checking done in PRESYNCH mode.

How many valid HEC checks in a row are enough? Current ATM standards say that the δ value for consecutive correct HECs must be 6 or less. Most implementers will choose exactly 6. After δ consecutive correct HECs, the receiver transitions into the SYNCH mode, which is the normal operating mode for a receiver in an ATM network.

In the SYNCH mode, the receiver descrambles the payload information. Errors, of course, may still occur. If the receiver calculates α consecutive headers with invalid HEC sequences (which should happen only rarely on fiber-based networks), the receiver must assume it has lost the cell boundaries altogether. The receiver must transition back to the HUNT state and begin all over again. The value of α must be 7 or less. Most implementers will choose exactly 7.

HEC delineation is quite good. At a BER of 10^{-4} (extremely poor, even for copper-based networks), at 155 Mbps with $\alpha = 7$ and $\delta = 6$, the ATM system will be in SYNCH for more than *1 year!* And after loss of SYNCH, it can resynchronize in 10 cell-times, or 28 µs.

4.5.4   Transmission frame adaptation/generation/recovery

The last two basic functions of the ATM transmission convergence sublayer are hard to discuss separately. *Transmission frame adaptation or framing* is the process of packing cells into framed transports for the ATM physical media sublayer and removing the cells at the receiver. *Transmission frame generation* is done at the sending side, and *transmission frame recovery* is done at the receiving side. This just refers to the sender producing frames acceptable to any intermediate transport equipment. Since these two processes are intimately connected, they will be discussed together.

There are two main ways to package ATM cells at the TC sublayer for transport at the physical media sublayer. The first method is used with framed transports (i.e., SONET, DS-3), and the second is used with the TAXI and Fibre Channel transports. For framed transports, the ATM cells are packaged into a data unit known as the *physical layer convergence protocol* (PLCP). For the other two, ATM cells are *block-encoded*, i.e., associated in groups of one or more and sent as a unit.

The following subsections also will investigate methods for putting ATM cells into transports such as DS-1s (T-1s) and over UTP copper wire. The last subsection will look at putting "raw cells" on the line with no frame or block structure surrounding them at all.

4.5.5   SONET PLCP

ATM cells ride easily inside SONET frames. The H4 pointer method is not the best solution for finding the cells because of the coupling between the ATM TC sublayer and the SONET transport. The cell alignment technique using the H4 pointer is obsolete. Current standards call for cell delineation via the HEC field, as outlined above. SONET framing is not expected to be a common mode for ATM cell transport for a few years yet, due to the need for wider SONET availability. However, proposals for running STS-1 and STS-3 over coaxial cable for short distances (called STSX-1 and STSX-3) have been made.

It is important to note that ATM cells are sent in a special type of SONET STS-3. All SONET STS-3s run at 155.52 Mbps, but these are still *channelized* transports. This means that an STS-3 is divided into three separate STS-1s, each with its own set of transport overhead bytes (three sets of three columns). Each set of H1 and H2 pointers points to a separate STS-1 SPE with the STS-3 frame. This is clearly not acceptable for sending cells at a full 155.52 Mbps. What is needed is *one* SPE just for cells packed head to tail in the SPE itself. Fortunately, such an unchannelized version of STS-3s exists, which is known as STS-3c (the *c* meaning the three STS-1s have been *concatenated* into one SPE). Thus ATM cells must be sent in an STS-3c frame consisting of 9 rows and 270 columns of bytes. The first 9 columns are the STS-3c TOH, and the remaining 261 columns form the STS-3c information payload. The SPE within the STS-3c information payload forms the PLCP for ATM cells on the SONET transport.

Not all the 81 TOH bytes are active when ATM cells are sent on an STS-3c. Some are not active by definition (they are valid only for the first STS-1 in an STS-3 anyway), and some are unused for ATM cell transport.

Figure 4.27 shows the TOH bytes defined for ATM cell transport over an STS-3c. Their coding and function are as follows:

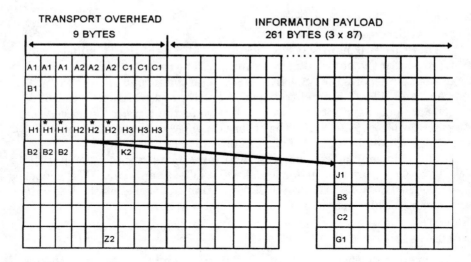

NOTE:
All other overhead bytes undefined at UNI
Second sets of H1, H2 bytes are concatenation indications

Figure 4.27   STS-3 overhead.

A1, A2 framing bytes: Used for the regular F6 28 SONET framing pattern in each STS-1.

C1 identifier byte: Coded for each concatenated STS-1 TOH.

B1 BIP-8: BIP check on the previous STS-3c frame (only present in first STS-1 TOH).

B2 BIP-24: BIP-24 for previous STS-3c frame payload minus the SOH bytes.

H1 pointer byte (initial 4 bits): 0110 indicates normal operation; 1001 indicates change in pointer value. Valid in first STS-1 TOH only.

H1, H2 pointer bytes (last 10 bits): The pointer to the first POH byte of the SPE. Valid in first STS-1 TOH only.

H1, H2 pointer bytes in last two STS-1s: Set to 93 FF in last two STS-1's TOH, forming the concatenation indicator. Further, setting these bytes to FF indicates an alarm indication signal (AIS), which is equivalent to the T-carrier blue alarm condition (a lower-level input signal has been lost).

H3 pointer action byte: Used to indicate changes in SPE position. Valid in all STS-1 TOHs.

K2 automatic protection switching byte (last 3 bits): All 1s indicate SONET line level AIS; 110 indicates SONET line level remote defect indicator (to signal sender of loss of frame, signal, or pointer and signal label mismatch). Any non-110 values indicate removal of SONET line level RDI condition.

Z2 growth byte in third STS-1 only (last 6 bits): Used to indicate the B2 error count (BIP-24 check). SONET line level far end block error (FEBE), which is the number of bit positions the received STS-3c B2 field differs from the value calculated at the receiver. Because this is a bit-by-bit check, values up to 25 are valid.

Figure 4.27 also shows the POH (end-to-end) bytes that are used with ATM cell transport. These each appear only once in the concatenated STS-3c SPE. Their coding and function are as follows:

J1 path trace byte: Used as recommended to indicate the source of the cells. Contains ATM network address of source.

B3 BIP-8 byte: BIP check on previous STS-3c SPE.

C2 path signal level indicator: Coding as 00010011.

G1 path status byte: The first 4 bits indicate the B3 error count (path FEBE). Values up to 9 are valid. The fifth bit is 0 or 1, depending on the SONET path RAI. A 1 bit indicates loss of cell delineation at the receiver end.

4.5.6 DS-3 PLCP

It is widely expected that the most common transport on the UNI for attaching customer premises equipment (CPE) to transport cells into a public ATM network node will be DS-3. Many more DS-3 miles exist in the national networks than SONET miles, and they are more affordable for many organizations.

ATM cells will be loaded into DS-3 frames in the 84-bit spaces between the DS-3 frame overhead bits in each subframe. They will not be loaded directly but rather will first be loaded into a DS-3 PLCP unit and then mapped into the DS-3 frame. It should be noted that DS-3s supporting a feature called *C-bit parity* can be used, as well as those which do not support this feature.

Figure 4.28 shows the structure of the DS-3 PLCP. Twelve ATM cells are packaged with a 4-byte field in front of each cell. The first 2 bytes repeat the SONET A1 and A2 framing pattern, F6 28. The path overhead indicator (POI) byte is essentially a counter that cycles from a high value to a low value and lets the receiver know what the function of the following byte is.

Six of these path overhead (POH) bytes are for future use (the Z1 through Z6 growth bytes) and are set to all 0s. Three other bytes (the X bytes) are unassigned and ignored by receivers (these have been defined for SMDS transport over DS-3s).

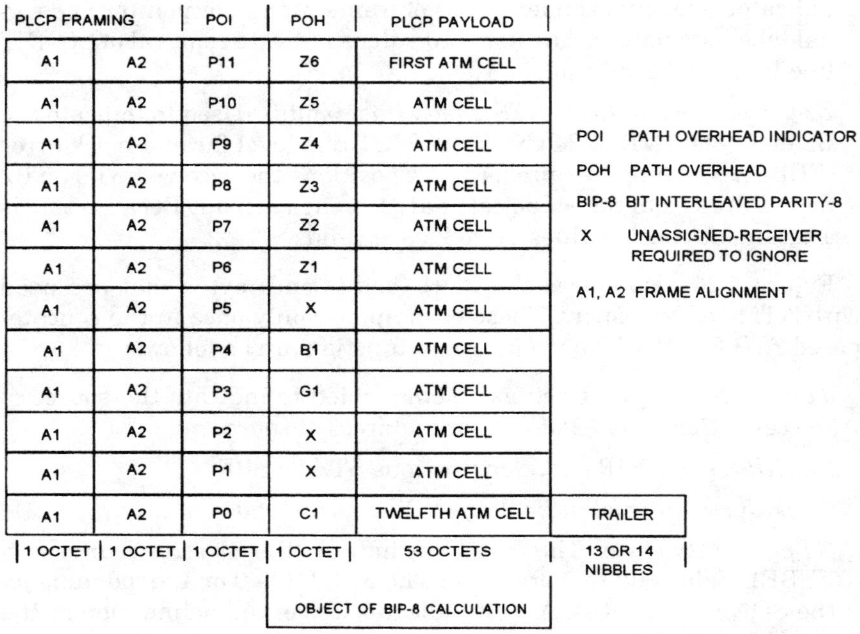

PLCP FRAMING		POI	POH	PLCP PAYLOAD	
A1	A2	P11	Z6	FIRST ATM CELL	
A1	A2	P10	Z5	ATM CELL	
A1	A2	P9	Z4	ATM CELL	
A1	A2	P8	Z3	ATM CELL	
A1	A2	P7	Z2	ATM CELL	
A1	A2	P6	Z1	ATM CELL	
A1	A2	P5	X	ATM CELL	
A1	A2	P4	B1	ATM CELL	
A1	A2	P3	G1	ATM CELL	
A1	A2	P2	X	ATM CELL	
A1	A2	P1	X	ATM CELL	
A1	A2	P0	C1	TWELFTH ATM CELL	TRAILER
1 OCTET	1 OCTET	1 OCTET	1 OCTET	53 OCTETS	13 OR 14 NIBBLES

POI   PATH OVERHEAD INDICATOR

POH   PATH OVERHEAD

BIP-8 BIT INTERLEAVED PARITY-8

X   UNASSIGNED-RECEIVER REQUIRED TO IGNORE

A1, A2 FRAME ALIGNMENT

OBJECT OF BIP-8 CALCULATION

Figure 4.28 DS-3 PLCP frame.

The three remaining bytes are used as follows:

B1 byte: BIP-8 check on the 12 ATM cells and associated POH bytes of the previous PLCP frame.

G1 path status byte: The first 4 bits form an FEBE count of BIP-8 errors. Valid values are from 0 to 8. If not implemented, this field is set to all 1s. Any other value not defined is interpreted as 0 errors. The next bit indicates a remote alarm indication (RAI), which is equivalent to the T-carrier yellow alarm signal (this indicates loss of the incoming signal at the receiver). A value of 1 for 10 consecutive frames indicates RAI. A value of 0 for 10 consecutive frame removes the RAI. The last 3 bits are ignored.

C1 cycle / stuff counter byte: The DS-3 PLCP will end with 13 or 14 nibbles (4 bits) coded as 1100. Stuffing is used to align the PLCP frame with the physical DS-3 frame. A stuffing opportunity occurs every third frame (375 μs) of a three-frame stuffing cycle. The C1 byte is coded as all 1s in the first frame of the cycle, and the trailer is 13 nibbles. The C1 byte is coded as all 0s in the second frame of the cycle, and the trailer is 14 nibbles. If the C1 byte is coded in the third frame of the cycle as 01100110, there is no stuff, and the trailer is 13 nibbles. If it is coded as 10011001, then a stuff has occurred, and the trailer is 14 nibbles.

Cell delineation with the DS-3 PLCP is relatively easy, since the ATM cells occur in predetermined locations. The detection of the A1 and A2 framing bytes determines the position of the ATM cells in the PLCP.

Cell payload scrambling is disabled by default on the DS-3. Optionally, it may be enabled as a configurable parameter.

4.5.7 100-Mbps 4B/5B block encoded (FDDI/TAXI)

Framed transport for ATM cells is one of the most complex schemes. Transporting ATM cells over 4B/5B transports at 100 Mbps (FDDI/TAXI) is one of the simplest. This uses a technique known as *block encoding* because the cells are sent as a "block" of bytes that includes some additional overhead bytes.

On the 100-Mbps 4B/5B transport, ATM cells will be sent totally asynchronously, i.e., as they arrive, without the need for cell-rate decoupling. When idle, the sender will generate idle codes (JK sync code). This bit sequence is normally used in FDDI as a start frame delimiter (coded 11000 10001). One JK symbol must be sent every 1/2 second. This "keep alive" signal lets the receivers know that the link is not down, just idle.

When ATM cells containing live data are to be sent, they will be preceded by a TT (start of cell) line code, which is normally used in FDDI as a frame ending delimiter (coded in FDDI as 01101 01101 using 4B/5B encoding). Therefore, the block-encoded ATM cell is 54 bytes (really symbols) in length—the TT code and the rest of the cell.

The HEC sequence is generated but used only to detect header errors, not correct them. Cells with detected errored headers are discarded by the receiver. That is all there is to it.

4.5.8 155-Mbps Fibre Channel block encoded

The Fibre Channel transport is also capable of transporting ATM cells. In this case, however, the ATM cells are grouped into blocks of 26 cells with a special cell at the front—a physical layer overhead unit (PL-OU).

This block is therefore 27 cells long: 26 "data" cells and one "overhead" cell, which is in turn broken down into two fields. The first is the frame delimiter field, which takes the place of the ATM cell header itself. The second is the physical layer operations and maintenance (PLOAM) field, which contains a subset of the SONET overhead fields detailed above.

The structure of the Fibre Channel block is shown in Fig. 4.29. The physical layer overhead cell is just a special ATM cell for Fibre Channel.

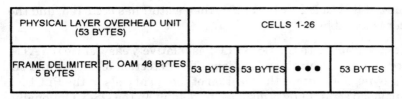

Figure 4.29 Fibre Channel block encoded.

Instead of a normal header, the first 5 bytes are used for framing (synchronization) symbols. Only three of the total 8B/10B encoding symbols are used for ATM cell transport: the K28.2 symbol, the K28.5 symbol, and the K28.7 symbol. The K28.2 symbol is used for special purposes. The PL-OU begins with four consecutive K28.5 symbols and a single K28.7 symbol. The next 48 bytes, normally used for payload information, is used in the PL-OU for the PLOAM field.

Only the first byte of the PLOAM (byte 6 of the PL-OU) has a defined function. The other 47 bytes must be set to all 0s. In the first PLOAM byte itself, the first 5 bits are set to 0, and the last 3 bits are set aside for alarm indications. The alarm indication signal (AIS), when set to 1, indicates to the sender the loss of signal or loss of frame synchronization by the receiver. The errored frame indicator (EFI), when set to 1, indicates to the sender the presence of a coding violation (e.g., bad 8B/10B symbol). The far end receive failure (FERF), when set to 1, indicates to the sender that the receiver is not seeing any bits from the sender. These bits are all used to indicate status of cells on the receiver's part. That is, the receiver sends them to the sender for error signals. The rest of the content of the PLOAM is "under study."

The remaining ATM cells in the block are sent in the standard format. The HEC sequence is used, but detected single-bit errors are not corrected. Received ATM cells with detected header errors are discarded. Scrambling of the cell payload bytes is undefined.

4.5.9 PLCP for 1.544-Mbps DS-1

Transporting ATM cells on existing DS-1 is now accepted by the ATM Forum. The PLCP for placing ATM cells inside an existing DS-1 frame is similar to the PLCP used for placing ATM cells on a DS-3. Regarding the DS-1 transport of ATM cells, Fig. 4.30 details the structure of the DS-1 PLCP. In the latest ATM Forum documents, this PLCP is not needed, however.

Only 10 cells are put into the PLCP, and 2 of the Z overhead bytes are not used. The padding trailer is fixed at 6 bytes. The whole frame takes 3 ms to transmit, much longer than a 125-µs DS-1 frame of 193 bits. The whole obviously must span many consecutive DS-1 frames.

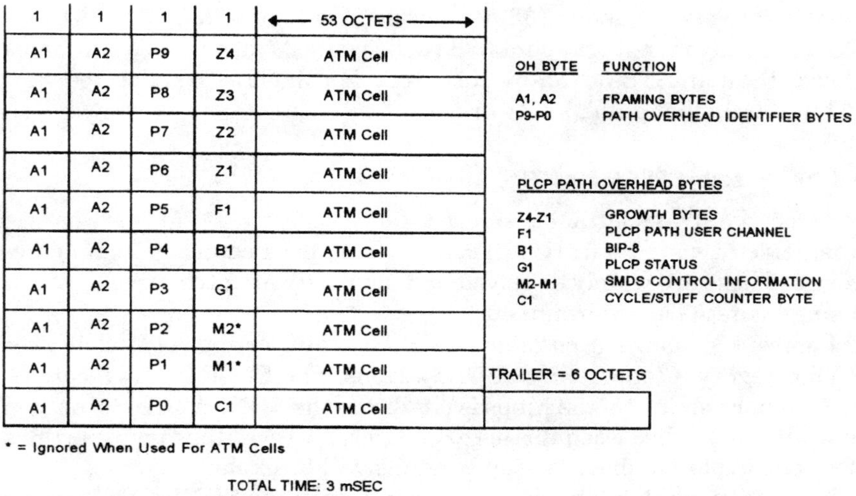

1	1	1	1	◄─── 53 OCTETS ───►
A1	A2	P9	Z4	ATM Cell
A1	A2	P8	Z3	ATM Cell
A1	A2	P7	Z2	ATM Cell
A1	A2	P6	Z1	ATM Cell
A1	A2	P5	F1	ATM Cell
A1	A2	P4	B1	ATM Cell
A1	A2	P3	G1	ATM Cell
A1	A2	P2	M2*	ATM Cell
A1	A2	P1	M1*	ATM Cell
A1	A2	P0	C1	ATM Cell

OH BYTE	FUNCTION
A1, A2	FRAMING BYTES
P9-P0	PATH OVERHEAD IDENTIFIER BYTES

PLCP PATH OVERHEAD BYTES

Z4-Z1	GROWTH BYTES
F1	PLCP PATH USER CHANNEL
B1	BIP-8
G1	PLCP STATUS
M2-M1	SMDS CONTROL INFORMATION
C1	CYCLE/STUFF COUNTER BYTE

TRAILER = 6 OCTETS

* = Ignored When Used For ATM Cells

TOTAL TIME: 3 mSEC

Figure 4.30   DS-1 PLCP frame.

It is instructive to explore some of the implications of transporting ATM cells on existing DS-1s, which point out some of the reservations expressed concerning DS-1 cell transport approval. The ATM Forum PLCP frame used for DS-1 transport is essentially identical to the DQDB PCLP used by IEEE 802.6.

A DS-1 frame is only 24 bytes long (plus the 193rd framing bit, which is transparent when used for ATM cell transport), much shorter than a full 53-byte cell. A common but older grouping of DS-1 frames is known as *D3/D4 superframing*. This groups 12 consecutive DS-1 frames into a unit, called the *D3/D4 superframe*. This unit is $12 \times 24 = 288$ bytes long. Another common, but newer, grouping of DS-1 frames is known as *extended super frame* (ESF). ESF groups 24 consecutive DS-1 frames together. ESF units are therefore $24 \times 24 = 576$ bytes long.

A look at the DS-1 PLCP shows that there are 10 ATM cells with 4 bytes of additional overhead in front of each. The function of the overhead bytes is identical to that of the DS-3 PLCP overhead bytes. Thus the entire unit is $57 \times 10 = 570 + 6$ trailer bytes = 576 bytes long. This is exactly equal to an ESF unit. Therefore, ATM cell PLCPs must be aligned with ESF and require ESF. However, many older DS-1s still do not have ESF, which now becomes a prerequisite for ATM cell transport.

In addition, the entire PLCP unit is sent in 3 ms. The other framed transports, SONET STS-3c and DS-3, generate frames 8000 times per second. The cell capacities are therefore about $42 \times 8000 = 33,600$ cells per second for STS-3c and about $12 \times 8000 = 96,000$ cells per second for DS-3. However, DS-1 PLCPs contain only 10 cells and are generated at a rate of only about 333 per second (1 s/3 ms = 333.33...). Thus a DS-1 can only transport about 3333 cells per second, or about 100 times slower than an STS-3c. Many observers feel that DS-1 is just too slow to build broadband ATM networks.

4.5.10 Possible PLCP for UTP

One of the transports considered for a private ATM network is unshielded twisted-pair (UTP) copper wire, both category 3 and category 5. These are widely deployed and obviously are attractive to use in a single-site ATM environment.

Figure 4.31 shows a possible PLCP for transporting ATM cells over UTP category 3 copper wire at 51.84 Mbps. The PLCP for UTP category 5 copper wire at 155.52 Mbps is similar to the SONET STS-3c method and will not be discussed further. However, a 51.84-Mbps transport has not been explored above, so some details will be explained here.

The active overhead bytes are the same as in the SONET STS-3c cell transport, with the following exceptions:

C1 identification byte: Always coded as 00000001.

H1, H2, and H3 bytes: The H1 byte is always coded as 0110xx10. The H2 byte is always coded as 00001010. The H3 byte is always coded as all 0s. (There is one exception: all 1s in these bytes means path AIS.)

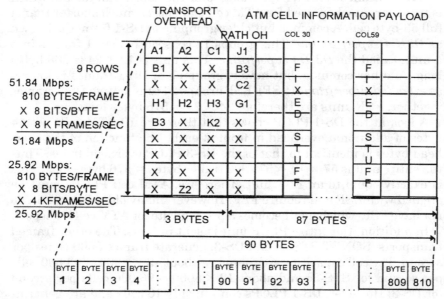

Figure 4.31 ATM cells on UTP PLCP.

What these codings mean is the following: the pointer bytes (H1, H2) always point to offset 20A hex, which is equal to 522 decimal. This forces the location of the "SPE" (this is not really SONET), namely, the first byte of the path overhead (J1) to the byte immediately following the C1 byte. That is, it is aligned with the beginning of the PLCP itself and cannot "float" as a SONET SPE does in the STS-3c transport. Setting the H3 pointer action byte to all 0s forces the SPE to remain there.

C2 path signal byte: Always coded as 00010011.

In addition, although the Z2, K2, and J1 bytes are present, the use of these bytes is optional.

Cells are loaded into the PLCP byte by byte with one exception: Columns 30 and 59 are reserved for fixed stuff bytes and are never loaded with ATM cell bytes. These are coded as all 1s. Since an integer number of ATM cells will not fit into the PLCP, HEC delineation must be used at the receiver.

It has been further proposed that these PLCPs on category 3 UTP be allowed to be generated not only in 125 μs, giving a bit rate of 51.84 Mbps, but in 250 μs (25.92 Mbps) and even in 500 μs (12.96 Mbps). Even rates as low as 6.48 Mbps are possible.

4.5.11 Utopia

Before moving on to the ATM layer itself, the topic of the next chapter, one more topic should be explored. This is the concept of Utopia, a specification proposed by the ATM Forum physical layer group. *Utopia* stands for *universal test and operations PHY interface for ATM.* The whole idea behind Utopia is that although ATM standards do an admirable job at specifying standard interfaces between ATM network devices, little has been done in the way of specifying standard interfaces within the devices themselves. As important as the user-network interface may be, it is probably just as important to an ATM network vendor and/or implementer what the interface is between the ATM physical media layer and the ATM layer itself.

There are several reasons for this. The simple ATM protocol stack of physical-ATM-AAL layer may not be implemented in a one-to-one fashion. What about the need for backup links or multiple types of physical layer sharing one ATM layer? What about the need to support circuits (AAL-1), connectionless data services (AAL-3/4), and connection-oriented data services (AAL-5) on the same ATM layer? Currently, these functions and devices can be implemented in a proprietary or stand-alone fashion, and many are. The whole idea of the ATM Forum, however, is implementation agreements between cooperating vendors, so a standard method of doing anything is the preferred approach.

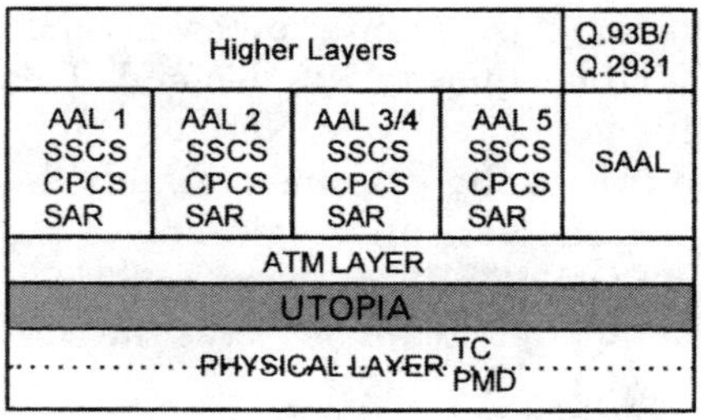

Higher Layers				Q.93B/ Q.2931
AAL 1 SSCS CPCS SAR	AAL 2 SSCS CPCS SAR	AAL 3/4 SSCS CPCS SAR	AAL 5 SSCS CPCS SAR	SAAL
ATM LAYER				
UTOPIA				
PHYSICAL LAYER TC PMD				

Figure 4.32 Utopia level 2 interface.

Accordingly, Utopia was proposed to standardize the interfaces between the various layers of the ATM architecture itself. Four levels of Utopia have been proposed: Level 1 will define a chip-to-chip interface so that boards containing chips from different vendors may use chips from different vendors. Level 2 defines a board-to-board interface for "intrarack communication" among ATM device components. Level 3 is for rack-to-rack communications ("interrack"), and level 4 is for system-to-system communications (i.e., between ATM network nodes). Utopia level 4 therefore parallels the development of standard ATM interfaces such as the UNI and NNI, but the emphasis is on levels 1 through 3 in all proposals, level 4 being included for completeness.

Most proposals address the Utopia level 2 interface. Figure 4.32 shows a possible use of the Utopia level 2 interface to connect a single ATM layer to multiple ATM physical layers. These layers could be implemented in a series of rack-mounted components provided by various vendors and wired together according to a Utopia standard to ensure interoperability. A further advantage is that vendors could concentrate on one aspect of ATM (e.g., AAL-1) and market compatible devices that are only within their specialty area.

The future of Utopia (Utopia was an ideal place, but it did not exist) is promising but uncertain. Just because an idea makes perfect sense does not guarantee its success or even acceptance.

The ATM Protocol Stack:
The ATM Layer

The middle of the ATM protocol architecture is formed by the ATM layer itself. It can be disorienting to have a layer with the same name as the architecture itself, but this is no more than TCP/IP does. In fact, TCP/IP is worse: TCP is part of the name of the architecture, a layer within the architecture, and a protocol that runs at that layer. However, the ATM layer is well-named. Most of the features and functions that come to mind when ATM is discussed (asynchronous multiplexing, cell switching, etc.) are implemented at the ATM layer. It lies at the heart of the ATM protocol model.

This chapter provides an in-depth look at the functions of the ATM layer. This layer consists of a stream of ATM cells which the ATM layer multiplexes and demultiplexes (mostly at the endpoints) and switches (mostly in the network nodes). The physical layer sends and receives cells, but the ATM layer processes them. That is, this layer examines the cell header, and sometimes the cell payload contents, to decide just what should be done with the cell at the node. There are many kinds of cells the ATM layer must deal with, traffic cells (information/data-carrying cells), network management cells, and signaling cells being the most significant. Above the ATM layer, at the AAL, the cell headers are not available for inspection, so any function involving cell headers *must* be done at the ATM layer.

Even if all questions regarding the sending of ATM cells over physical media are answered, it would be too much to expect that every source and destination in an ATM network (or any other kind of network, for that matter) would be connected by a single-hop point-to-point link. There will always be a limited number (in many cases, exactly one) of paths by which an end-user device can send bits into a network. Thus there must exist some method of taking bits off of one path and putting them on another to get these bits a little further on through the network and closer to their destination.

In ATM networks, this network relay device (intermediate system in the ISO-RM) is the switch. The switch must take a cell from an input port and, based on some information the switch has access to, get the cell to an output port. ATM switches also will generally modify the header information as well. There are questions about switches in ATM networks also, such as, What is the best way to build an ATM switch? How fast must it operate? How many cells can accumulate at an output port of the switch? And so on.

ATM is a switch-based, connection-oriented protocol (as opposed to router-based, connectionless protocols such as TCP/IP), and therefore, the performance and operation of these network node switches are of vital importance in an ATM network. Various switch architectures have been proposed for ATM network nodes, and the major categories are examined in this chapter.

Switching is the main topic of this chapter, but it is not the only topic. Network management is critical in any network, but since ATM networks are not "just" voice or video or data networks, the issue of network management for *any* type of connection becomes very important. ATM has a rather unique solution to this problem, which is discussed in detail.

Signaling is the procedure used to establish, maintain, and terminate connections in a switched environment. There are other critical issues as well, such as signaling protocol interoperability and efficiency. All these are treated at the end of this chapter.

5.1   The ATM Layer

The ATM layer consists of a stream of cells. That is all there is to work with. The header of the cell is available for inspection by the ATM layer, but the 48-byte cell information payload is not usually looked at for two reasons. First, the ATM network node must operate very rapidly (at STS-3c speeds, a cell arrives at a switch input port every 2.7 µs or so), and second, the small size of the cell itself makes it extremely unlikely that the contents of any one cell will be meaningful enough to the ATM layer. This means examining many cells, with the associated delays involved.

Therefore, the ATM layer is mostly concerned with the content of the cell headers, not the information fields within the cells. The net result is an important one. At the ATM layer, all cells look the same to the network. Extra work must be done to distinguish them. The situation is similar to the functioning of electronic devices. All electrons look the same to a transistor: point charges. A researcher may determine that these electrons have an up or down spin in some proportion, but only after considerable effort. However, that is okay; the transistor's main function depends on the flow of electrons, not their details. Thus it is with the ATM layer.

At the ATM layer, some cells have a function other than carrying data or information. These cells must be picked out of the cell stream and processed in some further fashion and not just switched by the network node. One important type of "special cell" is the operation and maintenance (OAM) cell, which has a special structure in ATM and is identified by certain cell header values.

Cells are sent across the network, of course. In ATM, the cells are *always* sent from bit 8 (leftmost bit) to bit 1 (rightmost bit). The first bit sent (leftmost bit) is the most significant bit (MSB) of the cell byte. At the ATM physical layer, special "idle" cells are used for cell-rate decoupling. These cells are *never* seen by the ATM layer itself. If somehow they do appear at the ATM layer, the ATM layer must pick out these "illegal cells" and discard them.

Finally, there are signaling cells at the ATM layer. The development of a signaling protocol for ATM networks has proved to be a considerable task. Current methods and standards for ATM network signaling are slowly arriving.

Other functions of the ATM layer are the critical ones for ATM networks; since this is the last layer where the cell header is available, the ATM layer is where generic flow control (GFC) is done. The ATM layer is where the cell headers are built and acted on at the end nodes. The VPIs and VCIs are "interpreted" at the ATM layer so that the cell is sent on its way across the network to the proper destination. Lastly, here is where the cells for voice, video, and data are mixed together on the UNI and separated at the destination.

Figure 5.1 shows the functions of the ATM layer as determined by the ITU. The ATM Forum has recommended adding another function, one that has been defined by the ITU for the physical layer. In the last chapter, one of the functions of the transmission convergence sublayer of the physical layer was cell-rate decoupling. This was the practice of "filling in" a framed transport with enough "idle" cells to match the transport cell capacity to the actual cell capacity. The idle cells are removed by the

- NRM: Network Resource Management

- CAC: Connection Admission Control

- Feedback Controls (OAM)

- UPC/NPC: Usage/network Parameter Control

- Priority Control (CLP bit)

- ATM Forum adds:
  Cell Rate Decoupling (Unassigned Cells)

Figure 5.1 ATM layer functions.

receiving physical layer and never seen by the ATM layer, at least in the ITU model.

However, the ATM Forum allows other transports for ATM cells besides framed transports. Therefore, it was felt that this function was better implemented at the ATM layer than at the physical layer, which under the ATM Forum transports had to be conscious of the physical functioning of the media itself. The ATM Forum recommends cell-rate decoupling be done at the ATM layer. The argument that this must slow down processing at the ATM layer is offset by the fact that the ATM layer must do many different things already, and therefore, the effect would be marginal at best. Special cells exist (even in the ITU model) at the ATM layer that make the cell-rate decoupling function relatively easy to implement at the ATM layer. These are defined as *unassigned cells*. The ATM Forum recommends using unassigned cells to perform cell-rate decoupling at the ATM layer itself. The ATM layer in ATM Forum documentation must perform other generic (general) functions in addition to those outlined above. Namely, it is this layer of the ATM protocol architecture that is responsible for network resource management (NRM), connection admission control (CAC), usage parameter control (UPC), priority control (PC), and traffic shaping (TS). In addition, the ATM Forum uses the term *network parameter control* (NPC) to refer to the equivalent process of UPC, not across the UNI, but rather across the NNI in a public network.

The ATM layer is the obvious place to provide these functions because the physical layer has different implementations based on different media types, and the ATM adaptation layer is, generally, active and present only on the end nodes of the ATM network and does not have access to cell header information in any case. No standard mechanisms have yet been defined to provide for these functions, but some of the issues involved in their use will be explored later.

The whole goal of these further generic functions is to provide the users of the ATM network connections the quality of service (QOS to the ATM Forum) they expect and need. The process of determining and delivering the required QOS parameters for each connection on an ATM network is referred to by the ATM Forum as the *traffic contract specification* and is enforced by the generic functions of the ATM layer.

5.1.1   ATM cell structure details

Asynchronous transfer mode (ATM) was easy to define: It is simply a method of transferring information as it arrives using fixed-length packets called *cells*. This is a detailed look at the ATM cell structure, since the upcoming sections will emphasize various values of the fields.

Figure 5.2 shows the structure of an ATM UNI cell header. It was not emphasized before, but there are *two* cell header formats in ATM: the

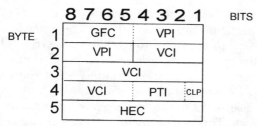

VCI: VIRTUAL CHANNEL ID   PTI: PAYLOAD TYPE INDICATOR
VPI: VIRTUAL PATH ID   CLP: CELL LOSS PRIORITY
UNI: USER NETWORK INTERFACE   RES: RESERVED
GFC: GENERIC FLOW CONTROL

Figure 5.2 ATM UNI cell header.

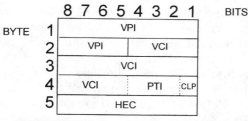

VCI: VIRTUAL CHANNEL ID   PTI: PAYLOAD TYPE INDICATOR
VPI: VIRTUAL PATH ID   CLP: CELL LOSS PRIORITY
NNI: NETWORK NODE INTERFACE   RES: RESERVED
GFC: GENERIC FLOW CONTROL

Figure 5.3 ATM NNI cell header.

B-ISDN user-network interface (UNI) format shown in Fig. 5.2 and another called the *network node interface* (NNI). The NNI is sometimes defined as meaning "network-network interface," but the usage here is more common in the ATM Forum itself. Many sources use the definitions inconsistently, interchangeably, and indistinguishably. Figure 5.3 shows the structure of the ATM NNI cell header. The only difference is the absence of the GFC field, the 4 bits of which have been assigned to the VPI field.

The UNI has a number of fields that are important to the functioning of the ATM layer. Some of the UNI header fields have familiar functions.

HEC field. The HEC has been discussed already. If the HEC detects more than one bit error in a cell header, as a result of a comparison of the recalculated HEC value with the received HEC value, the receiver will discard the entire cell. Nothing else need be done by the ATM node. Remember the whole ATM philosophy: Move error detection and control to the "edges" of the network. The higher layers may need to retransmit the information that was contained in the cell payload (usually a small piece of a larger data unit), but that is not of concern to the ATM layer.

VPI and VCI fields. The ATM cell header has two fields for identifying the cells it sends. These are the virtual path identifier (VPI) field and the virtual channel identifier (VCI) field. Recall the fundamentals of VPIs/VCIs: The VPI is 8 bits long, and the VCI is 16 bits. There are two fields because ATM allows users to group up to 64,000 VCIs (16 bits) into up to 256 VPIs (8 bits). This grouping of *channels* into *paths* is done mainly for "switching" purposes; each cell can be "routed" from source to destination based on the VPI value alone.

The ITU recommends the use of VPIs for "static, semipermanent" connections on the ATM network. This is usually interpreted as site-to-site connectivity. That is, a site on an ATM network is assigned a VPI at service provision time (e.g., when the contract for service is signed between the service provider and customer/subscriber). The user also is given the values of the VPIs for the sites to which the ATM network will provide connectivity. These are used to configure the customer premises equipment (CPE) on the ATM network. Although the VPIs have local significance only and need not match at each end, their values must be known to users (actually, of course, the users' software) both inbound and outbound. Then when user A sends a cell to user B, the CPE places the value VPI = 46 (for instance) in the cell header's VPI field. It may arrive with VPI = 167, but the CPE at user B's site is configured to realize that a cell with VPI = 167 is from user A. VPIs may be changed, but not on a short-term basis. Precise definitions for terms such as *static* or *short term* are lacking at the present time, but the consensus seems to be that the static time frame should be measured in days, not minutes or hours.

On the other hand, the ITU says that VCIs are for "dynamic" connections on the ATM network. They are for the actual connections between applications (not just data applications but voice and/or video applications as well) on the ATM network. There may be several voice, video, or data connections established between user sites all following the same path through the network. There may be hundreds or thousands of connections per VPI connecting site on the ATM network. The whole point is to allow the switching of cells between sites in a fast—very fast—and efficient manner.

The ATM Forum has not extended these basic ITU definitions for the use of VPIs and VCIs. Both VPIs and VCIs are initially to be "semipermanent," usually just referred to as *permanent virtual circuits* (PVCs), until a stable switching mechanism is in place. [Keep in mind that the terms *permanent virtual circuit* (PVC) and *switched virtual circuit* (SVC) are not ATM terms at all and have no definition or meaning in ATM standards. Their use is just common to the whole connection arena.] True switched virtual path connections (SVPCs, or just SVC for switched virtual circuit) and switched virtual channel connections (SVCCs, or just PVC) will come with standardized switching protocols. However, the use of VPIs should still be "semipermanent" despite the capability of changing their values and destinations rapidly with a signaling protocol.

One other point should be made about VPI usage for static ATM network connections. Consider a user of ATM network services. This user has a large corporate network with many company sites within the entire organization, potentially many more sites than 256. However, 256 is the limit on any single UNI (the 8-bit VPI field is the limit). To reach 300 remote sites (i.e., to be able to define more than 256 "static" connections), a *second* UNI must be installed. Clearly, with the present cost of DS-3s or SONET STS-3c (the currently defined UNI speeds for ATM WANs), this approach is just not feasible.

Two possible solutions present themselves: the use of VPIs for dynamic connections and the use of VCIs to divide a VPI into "subnets," much in the way that IP addresses are. The first approach is not forbidden and allows the user to establish VPI = 38 for connectivity to site X in the morning (i.e., cells sent with VPI = 38 end up at site X) and then use the same VPI, VPI = 38, for connectivity to site Y in the afternoon. This requires a full signaling protocol and a network services provider allowing "dynamic" connection VPI usage. The second approach assigns VPI = 38 to *both* site X and site Y at the same time. Now, however, cells with VPI = 38 and VCIs in the range 0 to 32,000 end up at site X, and cells with VPI = 38 and VCIs in the range 32,000 to 64,000 end up at site Y. This requires not only a full signaling protocol but also the use of full ATM switches (those capable of switching on not only the VPI but also the VCI field) in the service provider's ATM network.

Generic flow control.   The term *generic* in GFC refers not to "cheaper than the brand name," as in "generic corn flakes," but to "common" or "nonspecific." This reflects the fact that the GFC used on a UNI in an ATM network must work to control the flow of cells across a connection not only for data connections but also for other kinds of connections as well. It is generic, not specific to traffic type.

No current specification for the standard use of these 4 bits exists. The ATM Forum has circulated some proposals, and others have been made based on GFC as implemented in IEEE 802.6 MAN networks (which is also cell-based but essentially for data-only networks), but none has even been seriously discussed for implementation. For the time being, the 4 bits of the GFC field in a UNI ATM cell header must always be coded to 0000.

This lack of a standard mechanism has an impact on such issues as congestion control in an ATM network. Congestion is a global property of a network, and flow control refers to a specific aspect of the sender-receiver process. *Flow control* just means that a sender should never be able to overwhelm a receiver. *Congestion* refers to the network as a whole; no sender is sending too fast to a receiver, but the network is hopelessly congested. There is just too much traffic. Congestion control may interact with flow control. If there are too many cells present in an ATM network, GFC may be used to slow down senders in heavily used portions of the network. This will eventually alleviate the congestion.

Without a standard GFC to invoke in this case, the ATM network must be more creative in implementing congestion-control mechanisms. The ATM layer will use such mechanisms as network resource management, connection admission control, usage parameter control, and all the others defined to try and prevent congestion from occurring in the first place.

Other ATM UNI fields.   The two other ATM header fields are the payload type indicator (PTI) field and the cell loss priority (CLP) field (bit). The payload type indicator lets the ATM layer know whether the cell contains user or network information (e.g, network management information). The 3 bits in this field limit the possible PTI values to eight (0 to 7).

The cell loss priority bit indicates whether the cell may be discarded under certain network conditions (CLP = 1). CLP = 0 cells are supposed to be discarded only as a last resort. This bit is to be used with the priority control function of the ATM layer.

A lot of misunderstanding of the use of the CLP bit has been propagated by observers of ATM standardization. The concept is hardly unique to ATM networks. Frame relay defines a discard eligibility (DE) bit, and TCP/IP networks have routinely discarded datagrams when the router buffer condition warrants it. It is also true that no one would build an ATM network that discards any cells, CLP bit set to 1 or not, on a consistent basis. This would mean forcing users to constantly retransmit traffic and taking the time and effort to switch a cell part way to its destination (potentially 90 percent of the way) and then ultimately discard it. Both cases are clearly a waste of scarce network resources. Better to delay than to throw away.

A further issue involves control of the CLP bit. If the user does not set it (CLP = 0) and the network needs to discard a cell and there is no CLP = 1 cell to be seen, may the network set the bit to 1 and then discard the cell anyway? If so, then this is really not a mechanism at all. However, if the network is *not* allowed to set the bit to 1 and only CLP = 0 cells are flowing through the network node, what is to be done? No clear answers suggest themselves beyond the obvious tactic of ensuring that there are plenty of CLP = 1 cells flowing through the ATM network.

Because cells, even if discarded, contain relatively little information individually (48 bytes or less), occasional discarding of a cell looks to the end users of the ATM network as a slightly elevated bit error rate (BER) on the connection. It closely mimics the burst errors on copper-based networks. Since the ATM architecture is optimized for the BERs of fiber-based networks, where BERs are extremely low, cell discarding in ATM networks will be effectively unnoticed by end users if kept to a reasonable level.

NNI cell header. The ATM network node interface (NNI) cell header is virtually identical to the UNI cell header, but with one important difference. There is *no* GFC field in the NNI cell header. These bits are assigned for the ATM network for larger VPI identifiers. This is a good idea. There will be more VPIs internal to the ATM network, connecting ATM network nodes, than to any single user interface.

The UNI VPI field is 8 bits, allowing 256 distinct VPIs. The NNI VPI field is 12 bits, allowing 4096 distinct VPIs per interface. In both cases, the VCI field is 16 bits, allowing 65,536 VCIs for *each* VPI on an interface. The whole idea is that an ATM network node may have many UNI interfaces, perhaps one for each customer premises. On the network side, however, where the network nodes themselves connect, this UNI cell traffic will be aggregated onto higher-speed trunks capable of carrying the total traffic of many UNI interfaces to other ATM network nodes on the network. Since each connection needs a distinct VPI/VCI combination, multiple user interfaces require a larger number of VPI/VCI numbers available on the trunk side. With the 12-bit VPI field, up to eight fully configured and connected UNI links (with 256 VPIs each) can be sent across one ATM NNI trunk interface to another ATM switch.

The lack of a GFC field is not a limitation at all. It is defined as controlling the flow of cells *into* the network across the UNI. A cell sent between ATM switches is already in the network and already came from a user controlled by the GFC field on the user's UNI interface. Another mechanism, unspecified to date and obviously not dependent on a NNI cell header field, must be used to control the flow of cells across a trunk between ATM switches. On this trunk NNI interface, the concern is not flow control but really congestion control.

5.1.2   ATM cell types

The ATM layer is where the cells are. There are actually many different kinds of cells, some of which have been detailed before and make sense only to the ATM physical and transmission convergence (TC) sublayer; thus they are never passed up to the ATM layer itself. They are included here for completeness. Idle cells are for use by the ATM physical layer and are never seen by the ATM layer. Unassigned cells are "empty" cells and contain no user information. They are sent when the user has no data to send and *do* appear at the ATM layer (in fact, they are generated by the ATM layer itself). This ATM layer counterpart of the physical layer idle cell is used by ATM Forum implementations to perform cell-rate decoupling not at the TC sublayer but at the ATM layer.

A distinct class of cells is used for virtual path (VP) operations, administration, and maintenance (VP OAM), and these will be examined later. Many different kinds of cells can appear carrying different VPI and VCI identifiers. Some, of course, have user data, but some values of VPI and VCI combinations have special uses also. These have various combinations of VPI and VCI values and form a class known as *VP/VC traffic cells*. Types of cells that fall into this category are metasignaling (signaling to control other signaling connections) cells, signaling cells themselves, virtual channel (VC) OAM cells, SMDS (connectionless ATM) cells, and interim layer management interface (ILMI) cells. There are, of course, cells for user traffic as well, but these have no set, preassigned values. These VPI/VCI values will be looked at in more detail.

Figure 5.4 is a more detailed look at some of these cell types, with what are known as *predefined header field values*. As mentioned above, cells with the last bit of octet 4 set are reserved for use by the ATM physical layer. The detail added is to identify the idle cells (ending in 0001) and the physical layer OAM cells (ending in 1001).

Of course, these cells never make it to the ATM layer. However, the unassigned cells do and have the GFC field (AAAA) available, as well as the payload type indicator (PTI) field (AAA at the end).

Obviously, VP/VC traffic cells cannot use VPI = 0 and VCI = 0 for identifiers. And there are many kinds of VP/VC traffic. So what *do* they use? Figure 5.5 shows the currently defined values for "reserved" VPI/VCI combinations, and the addition of one proposed by the ATM Forum but not standardized. This is the use of VPI = 0 or N, VCI = 15 for SMDS (connectionless ATM) traffic. It may be surprising to find a connection dedicated to connectionless service, but there is really no choice

	OCTET 1	OCTET 2	OCTET 3	OCTET 4
RESERVED FOR PHYSICAL LAYER	PPPP0000	O0000000	O0000000	0000PPP1
PHYSICAL LAYER OAM	O0000000	O0000000	O0000000	O001001
IDLE CELLS	O0000000	O0000000	O0000000	O0000001
UNASSIGNED CELLS (ATM)	AAAA0000	O0000000	O0000000	0000AAA0

Figure 5.4 Physical cells and ATM cells.

CELL TYPE:	VPI =	VCI =
USER DATA	"ANY"	"ANY"
UNASSIGNED CELL	0	0
META-SIGNALING	0	1
Remote:	N	1
BROADCAST SIGNALING	0	2
Remote:	N	2
PT-PT SIGNALING:	0	5
Remote:	N	5
VC OAM	0	3 or 4
SMDS CELL	0 (or N)	15
ILMI CELL	0	16

Figure 5.5 Predefined cell VPI/VCI values.

in the matter. All ATM networks are connections, so the only way to provide connectionless service (which, of course, demands no connection at all) is to use the *same* connection number for all "connectionless" traffic on the UNI. Maybe not an elegant solution, but it is a workable one, with one reservation.

If all connectionless services (and this argument applies not only to SMDS but also to any connectionless ATM service, including the incomplete CLNAP/CLNS of the ITU-T ATM specifications) must send cells to every destination on the same connection with the same VPI/VCI combination, how can the ATM switches tell them apart? How can they possibly be distributed to their proper destinations? This issue will be explored in more detail later, and the resolution will have far-ranging consequences for the future of connectionless networks (router-based networks) in the world of connection-oriented switch-based networks.

All other VPI/VCI combinations are currently used for VP/VC traffic cells; i.e., they have information for the ATM layer itself or for the ATM layer to deliver. User data are allowed to use any VPI/VCI combination not reserved for other purposes (e.g., no VPI = 0, VCI = 0, etc.), but this is not too much of a hardship.

Interim local management interface (ILMI) is used as an ad hoc signaling method until "real" signaling comes along. It also provides a method of managing an ATM network node with industry-standard methods such as use of the simple network management protocol (SNMP) and management information base (MIB).

More details on the current functioning and use of SMDS and ILMI with ATM networks will be explored in later sections.

5.1.3 ATM connection types

The ATM layer must maintain different *kinds* of connections as well as different numbers of connections. Both the VPC and the VCC may be

Point-to-point: For direct connectivity. This type of connection is the fundamental building block of ATM networks, built up of one-way, single-hop connections between adjacent network nodes.

Point-to-multipoint: For multicast/broadcast-type services. These connections will be especially useful for video connections, where one cell into the network on a single connection must result in multiple cells output on many connections. It is too much to expect the user application to establish a point-to-point connection for each destination and then send multiple copies of the same cells on each one.

Multipoint-to-multipoint: For conference arrangements. The idea is similar to the point-to-multipoint connection, but with one important difference. The cells may be sent from *any* endpoint to multiple destinations, not just in the "root to leaf" direction as in the point-to-multipoint connections. For all multipoint connections, the ATM network node is responsible for, and therefore must be capable of, sending out multiple copies of a single cell received on a single input port.

These ATM network connections also may have

Asymmetrical bandwidth: 155 Mbps into the network and 600 Mbps out of the network (connections are unidirectional). This would be helpful in the client-server environment, where servers tend to receive lots of small messages from clients but send out much larger messages to the clients in reply.

These ATM network connections may even be

Specified by class: For example, a connection for "class 57 service." This class 57 service is defined and delivered by the ATM network service provider.

Specified by parameter: For example, a connection with 52-ms end-to-end delay maximum. Again, the ATM network service provider would be responsible for establishing connections with the parameters requested and enforcing their adherence.

The only connection types supported on ATM networks today are point-to-point and point-to-multipoint. However, even point-to-multipoint connections are rarely offered and are still difficult for ATM switches to deliver.

ATM virtual connections, whether VPCs or VCCs, point-to-point or point-to-multipoint, may be set up on a permanent (really "semipermanent") basis or dynamically set up and released as in normal switched circuits today. Usually called *permanent virtual circuits* (PVCs) and *switched virtual circuits* (SVCs), they really should be called *connections* in ATM networks.

Initially, ATM connections, VPCs and VCCs alike, will *all* be PVCs established by ATM network operators and managers at the ATM network service provider's management center. A user will have to call the center to change the connections, and it will not be done at once. Eventually, the signaling methods and protocols will be a standard, and network service providers can implement SVCs with users signaling connections directly. When will this be? Actually, there is a deeper reason for this lack of SVC implementation in initial public (or shared private) ATM networks.

The fundamental reason for using PVCs heavily in ATM networks has to do with the concept of "call setup to holding time ratio." This is a concern in *any* public or "charging" network offering, and the voice network is a perfect example.

When a person dials a phone, there is a time interval during which the network resources are in use to route the call before the phone is answered. Network resources are again used to "free up" the trunks and switching buffers at the conclusion of the call. The phone company makes no money from users during these intervals.

However, if call setup and disconnect take 2 seconds each and the voice phone call averages just under 3 minutes (this is why the rate goes down at 3 minutes) for residential use and about 4 minutes for business use, that ratio is okay: 4 of about 180 to 240 seconds. In an ATM network, however, the "holding time" (connection duration) may be on the order of 1 second at 155 Mbps (during which time, the whole contents of a hard drive may be sent across the network). This ratio of 4:1 is not tolerable. Therefore, until ATM call setup is very fast and efficient, providers of ATM network services will continue to use PVCs and not SVCs.

5.1.4 ATM cell multiplexing

The last function of the ATM layer is cell multiplexing and demultiplexing. Cell streams from various sources are multiplexed on the same ATM link, across both the UNI and the NNI, but the multiplexing and demultiplexing function takes place mainly on the UNI between the CPE device at the users' ends of the network and the ATM network node. These cells may represent voice, video, or data. Although the ATM layer is present on both CPE devices and ATM switches, it is not wrong to say that the main function of the ATM layer in the CPE device is multiplexing and demultiplexing and not switching, and the main function of the ATM layer in ATM network nodes is switching and not multiplexing and demultiplexing. Of course, the ATM layer itself is fully capable of both functions.

The ATM layer must generate a continuous stream of cells. Thus unassigned (empty) cells are inserted in the output stream when no data cells are available. This is the process of cell-rate decoupling applied to the ATM layer and not the physical layer of the ATM. These cells are distinct from the special idle cells used by the ATM transmission convergence sublayer for cell-rate decoupling, which have to do with framed transports such as SONET. Idle cells are never passed to the ATM layer.

The process of multiplexing in particular is especially complex in an ATM UNI device. Not only must the sending ATM layer deal with the asynchronous arrival of cell information payloads from the various and varied ATM adaptation layers (AALs) above, but the sending ATM layer must make sure the resulting "pattern" of interleaved cells from multiple connections being sent on the UNI gives each AAL the proper QOS parameters it needs to function properly. It is not only the different kinds of AALs and classes of service (A, B, C, D) that complicate the task but also the fact that each AAL type may have multiple instances running at the same time. For example, the accounting department voice connections in a company may be handled in a separate AAL from the voice connections for the executive offices, even though they are delivered the same class of service (probably class A or B) by the ATM CPE device.

Demultiplexing remains the relatively simple process of reading the cell headers as they arrive off the UNI from the network node and distributing them to the proper AALs as mapped by the connections established by VPI/VCI value. Now this task may be somewhat complicated by some recovery process at the receiver (e.g., a receiving video connection may compensate for absent cells by "inventing" special "predictive" cells to mimic the expected cell content now missing). Generally, however, this will be the responsibility of the AAL itself rather than the ATM layer.

The multiplexing function will have some help in the form of guidelines to provide adequate multiplexing service on the ATM network connections. These are in the form of special traffic management functions. Since these form an important class of functions in the current ATM Forum implementation agreements, they will be dealt with in some detail.

5.1.5 ATM traffic management

A relatively trivial task in channelized networks, the process of controlling traffic on a UNI in an ATM network becomes quite complex. When there is a fixed bandwidth available, as in channelized networks, the network need not be concerned by questions of usage on these channels. If the usage in terms of bandwidth demand for information transfer is below the fixed bandwidth assigned, idle patterns must be generated and sent. If the usage demand is above the bandwidth design, it is up to the user to either buffer or discard the excess information (in which case, the *user* may be sensitive to channel utilization but not necessarily the network service provider).

In ATM, things are different. There is no fixed bandwidth allocated to an individual connection, and a connection's instantaneously perceived bandwidth may vary considerably over very short time intervals based on the bandwidth needed at a particular moment. Since ATM multiplexing is a very sophisticated form of statistical multiplexing, many more connections than add up to the UNI bit rate may be active at the same time, as long as the connections do not all demand the maximum service level at the same time. Any ATM connection's bandwidth profile over time will exhibit a peak bit rate, an average bit rate, a sustainable bit rate (which all may be the same for applications such as class A), and a maximum string size of contiguous bits that can be generated without pausing (e.g., the maximum frame size of 1518 bytes in Ethernet-based LANs). ATM traffic management exists to prevent one user connection from continually hogging the available bandwidth on the UNI.

There will be times when all connections on the UNI taken together are presenting more active cells than can be sent across the UNI into the ATM network. What the ATM layer does to still multiplex these connections depends on the QOS parameters established for the connection when the connection was admitted onto the ATM network.

ATM traffic parameters and descriptors. The ATM Forum has defined several parameters and descriptors to characterize the behavior of a connection on the UNI. These may be used to help the ATM layer provide adequate service to all the connections that are being multiplexed into the ATM network across the UNI. These are much more complex than the usual BER and delay (including jitter—delay variation) parameters specified for channelized networks. Many of the parameters are being implemented today, but some do not yet have standard definitions finalized. The ATM Forum parameters are

Cell loss ratio (CLR): The ratio between the errored cells and the sum of the errored cells and good cells sent on a connection. This reduces to the ratio of the number of cells lost to the number of cells sent. Although no absolute values have been specified for various QOS classes, the lower the CLR, the better the service on the connection.

Cell misinsertion ratio (CMR): The ratio between the inserted cells and the sum of the inserted cells and the total cells sent on a connection. This reduces to the ratio of the number of cells received minus the number of cells sent divided by the number of cells sent. No absolute value has been established. *Note:* This parameter was defined previously as a rate over time, but the ATM Forum recommends a ratio as being easier to calculate and compare, given the differing bit rates available.

Severely errored cell block ratio: The ratio between the number of severely errored cell blocks and the total number of blocks sent over time. A *severely errored cell* is currently defined by the ATM Forum as a lost or misinserted cell, although this varies from the ITU-T definition, which is based on bit errors in the cell headers. If the number of lost or misinserted cells in a given block exceeds M (unspecified to date), that block is counted as a severely errored cell block. A *block* is currently defined by the ATM Forum as the number of cells sent between consecutive OAM cells, which are supposed to be generated once per second.

Cell error ratio (CER): A test measurement (i.e., an out-of-service procedure) of the ratio of errored cells (undefined precisely) to the total cells sent. The CER cannot be used directly for traffic management.

Mean cell transfer delay (MCTD): The arithmetic average (mean) time it takes from the insertion of the first bit of a cell sent across the UNI until the exiting of the last bit of the cell sent across the UNI at the destination. There are two components to this delay: *propagation delay* (delay effects due to the finite speed of light or electricity) and *processing delay* (due to the time it takes an ATM network node to process and switch a cell). Generally, the connection will have a fixed propagation delay (due to the consistent and persistent connection path) and a variable processing delay (due to switch and network congestion). This processing delay is introduced and variable on *each* network node on the ATM network.

Cell delay variation (CDV): Since the processing delay will vary over time, the end-to-end cell transfer delay will vary over time as well. For some QOS classes (e.g., class A constant-bit-rate voice), however, a CDV of more than a few milliseconds could be noticeable to the end equipment. No absolute values have been specified, although a value of ±5 percent of the raw cell transfer delay has been mentioned frequently as a guideline.

Two variations on CDV measurements have been proposed, one seemingly aimed at class A (delay-variation-sensitive, constant-bit-rate) connections and one more geared for class B (delay-variation-sensitive, variable-bit-rate) connections. CDV-1 ("one-point CDV") is based on the peak cell rate (which should match the sustainable cell rate on CBR connections). It is measured as the difference between the expected arrival time (really cell arrival interval) and the actual arrival time (interval) of the next cell. It should, of course, always be exactly equal to 0. In practice, a value greater than 0 indicates a phenomena known as *clumping* (cell arrivals closer and closer together), and a value less than 0 indicates *dispersion* (cell arrivals further and further apart).

CDV-2 ("two-point CDV") compares the actual delay (not cell arrival interval) between two points in the ATM network (most likely, but not necessarily, the endpoints) with the delay value of a "reference cell" (most likely, but not necessarily, the previous cell). Use of the terms *one-point* and *two-point* in CDV measurements indicates the use of synchronized and accurate clocking and either one or two points on the ATM networks. CDV-2 is more suited to VBR classes because cell arrivals will generally not be predictable in any real sense.

Toleration to CDV on a connection will be an important part of the service contract.

Cell nonconformance ratio: The CLP bit in the ATM cell header on the UNI is used for cell priorities. All traffic on a connection either has this bit set or not, so CLP = 0 + 1 equals all cells sent. The user, at connection setup time, may agree to set the CLP bit on some cells to 1 and on others to 0. The cell nonconformance ratio is the ratio between the observed number of cells with CLP = 1 and the agreed-on number of cells with CLP = 1.

ATM connection traffic parameters. The whole concept of guaranteeing a contracted QOS on an ATM network connection revolves around two processes: deciding if a connection should be granted on the ATM network, based on some initial traffic parameters, and then ensuring that the connection stays within these parameters. It is critical not only that a new connection have the resources it needs in terms of cell handling, but also that the new connection does not detract from the cell-carrying capabilities of the older, already established connections.

For early ATM networks based only on PVCs, this specifying of traffic parameters for a connection should be easy. If two people sit down to hammer out the traffic pattern a connection will generate on the ATM network, they should be able to ask each other any question about the traffic at all and potentially find an answer. If the answer is important enough, even such sticky questions as "How much data has this application generated in the last week?" may be uncovered in a variety of ways. The PVC will not be granted until some agreement between the two parties is reached.

With signaling protocols to set up SVCs, however, the situation is different. The protocol will only be able to deal with parameters that have been defined ahead of time, and the values of the parameters must be known ahead of time. For the signaling protocols in use by the ATM Forum, only three traffic load parameters will be used: the peak cell rate, the sustained cell rate (the relationship of this "sustained" cell rate to other concepts such as the "average" cell rate is not precisely defined), and the maximum burst size. Most implementers will interpret these parameters as follows: Peak cell rate would be the absolute maximum number of 53-byte cells that could be generated by the end user (e.g., a 4-Mbps Token Ring LAN) or sent across the UNI (e.g., 45-

Mbps DS-3). The sustained cell rate would be the average cell rate over a long time period (e.g., hours), and the maximum burst size would be calculated from the maximum data unit the end user could generate (e.g., a 4500-byte-long 4-Mbps Token Ring frame) divided by the physical bit rate of the UNI.

5.1.6   ATM quality of service and traffic management

The ATM layer provides the multiplexing and switching function in the ATM network. It must provide an adequate QOS to each connection established on the network. To do so, the ATM layer has access to a number of traffic parameters, described above. But how do the traffic parameters translate into delivery of the proper QOS class for a given connection? The two main methods are *connection admission control (CAC)* and *usage parameter control (UPC)*. The term *UPC* is used by the ATM Forum. The ITU-T refers to this same process as *usage parameter control/network parameter control (UPC/NPC)*. The ATM Forum reserves the term *NPC* for the UPC process performed on the public NNI rather than across the UNI.

Connection admission control.   When a local ATM node (defined as the ATM network node with the direct UNI connection to the user's CPE) receives a request for a connection (*call setup* request) from a user, several things must happen very quickly. The ATM switch must decide whether the resources currently available at the node will be able to support the QOS needed by the user on the new connection. This is not just a question of switching capacity but of delay variation as well. And complicating the matter is the fact that each new connection granted will incrementally affect all the other connections on the network.

A very quick method of performing this connection admission control (CAC) is needed. The parameters furnished by the user according to the ATM Forum are few: the service class (A, B, C, D), the peak cell rate (PCR), the sustainable cell rate (SCR), the maximum burst size (MBS), and the cell delay variation (CDV). Of these, only the PCR and CDV are actually mandatory. SCR and MBS (or burst tolerance) are optional parameters, although if one is specified by the user, so must the other.

The switch must quickly find an answer to the most essential question about the new connection: Just exactly how much bandwidth and resources (in terms of cells per second and delay variation tolerance) will the new connection need? Once this question is answered, it is a relatively simple matter to see if the needed resources (cell capacity and delay) are available.

The reason that cell delay variation sensitivity enters the equation is due to the definition of the two time delay variation–sensitive classes of service, A and B, for the temptation is for a network to admit as many connections as users want (no one makes money from denying service) and then dealing with excess traffic by delaying (buffering) cells all over the network. This will not work well in ATM networks anyway; there are just too many cells arriving too fast (96,000 per second on a DS-3) to buffer substantial quantities of them for more than the merest fraction of a second.

Thus the CAC process should be handled very quickly by the local ATM node itself. There is probably not enough time to send a message across the network to a central resource manager. It would be a real stretch of the switch's computing power (considering the other tasks the switch must do) to crank the traffic parameters through a complex mathematical formula that would find the "equivalent capacity" of an ATM connection request. The "average" cannot be used for this purpose, since, on average, connection traffic will be above this value fully half the time. Such equivalent capacity formulas do exist, but only a few of them are simple enough to implement effectively. One even measures the impact of a new connection on the other, established connections.

Once the decision to admit a connection is made, the local ATM switch can set a up a path for the connection through the network. Delay variation sensitivity will be handled by limiting buffer sizes on the switches involved in handling the connection and having all cells follow identical paths on a connection. No work has been done on standardizing this process.

Usage parameter control.   The whole process of usage parameter control (UPC) starts when the CAC process has admitted and established a new connection on the ATM network. This is called the *traffic contract,* and it binds the ATM network service provider to provide the QOS needed by the user. However, it also binds the user to observe the connection parameters supplied to the network. Any "nonconforming" traffic will not be guaranteed the QOS, and the traffic may be discarded by the network. Since ATM networks currently lack an adequate generic flow control (GFC) mechanism, the UPC function must discard cells to prevent congestion on the ATM network from denying adequate service on other connections. (Congestion is much easier to prevent than alleviate in any case.)

The ATM Forum recommends that ATM network service providers, whether public or private carriers or even the network service department of a private corporation, set specific values for the traffic parameters and descriptors defined above. These values should provide adequate QOS for the ATM class A to D connection types. Then all a user need do is specify a "class A connection" without needing to supply cell loss, delay, and delay variation information with every connection.

In point of fact, only class A and C services are currently supported on ATM Forum networks, with the addition of a "class X" service that fits none of the class descriptions at all (the "null" service class).

However, traffic load information will always be needed, especially for data connections (presumably voice and video will require a smaller range of standard cell rates and perhaps even only one for each). The UPC process must make sure that the cell traffic on each connection stays with the parameters established by the CAC process. This is to prevent users from degrading the service on other connections and getting more service than their traffic contract implies (and, presumably, more service than the user is paying for); UPC will test each cell for conformance to the QOS established for the connection.

To enforce this conformance, UPC can do one of three things to each cell as it arrives across the UNI on each connection:

1. Pass the cell into the network without changing the CLP bit in the cell header.

2. Change the CLP bit in the cell header to 1 (a procedure known as *tagging,* which is an optional function).

3. Discard the cell.

Generally, if the CLP bit in the cell header is set to 0 and the cell does not conform to the cell rate agreed on for that connection in the traffic contract, UPC sets the CLP bit to 1. Since there are different sets of rules for the handling of CLP = 1 cells, a new set of traffic parameters is applied to the CLP = 1 cell rate. If this cell still does not conform to the traffic contract, it is discarded. Now the only questions are whether to change the CLP bit or not and whether to discard the cell or not. But how are these decisions to be made?

The ATM service provider may, as an option, adjust the sustained cell rate (SCR) and maximum burst size (MBS, also called *burst tolerance*) to reflect the actual flow of user traffic on a connection. Preferably, the ATM Forum recommends the use of the generic cell rate algorithm (GCRA) for this purpose.

Generic cell rate algorithm (GCRA). The GCRA is another example of the use of the term *generic* to mean "general" or "good for all types" rather than "not as good as the real thing." It is referred to by the ATM Forum as a "virtual scheduling algorithm" or "continuous-state leaky bucket" and can be expressed as a very complex series of formulas and diagrams. In most ATM network implementations, it is widely known as the *double leaky bucket algorithm.* The ITU-T has standardized a "peak cell rate algorithm" which the ATM Forum has adapted and generalized somewhat into the GCRA, meaning it applies to other cell rates than peak.

Calling the GCRA a "leaky bucket" is a very good analogy, because GCRA functions exactly as a bucket with a hole in it. The bucket "leaks" at a steady rate, no matter when water is poured, unpredictably, into the bucket. The bucket may be initially empty, partially full, or filled to the brim. The water poured in may be a splash, a torrent, or completely overflow the bucket if poured in from a much larger container. No matter, the water emerges from the hole in the bucket at precisely the same rate at all times. It drains the bucket at a steady rate. Some water may be lost if the bucket overflows, but the goal here is to smooth out the arrival of "water," not necessarily provide a way out for every drop of water presented to the bucket (spilled water is lost).

Of course, there are no buckets in computers or networks (although the term *bit bucket* is heard all the time). There are, however, counters all over the place. The simplest "leaky bucket" implementation (the ATM Forum says nothing about *how* a UPC with GCRA is to be bundled or packaged into an ATM network switch or CPE) is a counter. The counter has a minimum value (usually 0) and a maximum value (the limit). The counter is given some initial value when the connection is accepted (again, usually, but not necessarily, the minimum). As each cell is sent into the ATM network across the UNI, the counter is incremented. If the counter reaches the limit (maximum value), no further incrementing takes place, and subsequent cells are discarded instead of being admitted to the network. The counter decrements over time (usually by 1 per second, but not necessarily). No further decrementing takes place at zero (the minimum). Cells are only accepted by the network if the counter is not at its limit (maximum value). Figure 5.6 shows an example of a "leaky bucket" with a limit of 100 and an increment of 1 (cell) per second.

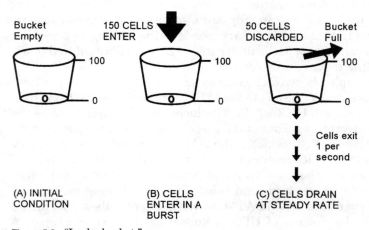

Figure 5.6 "Leaky bucket."

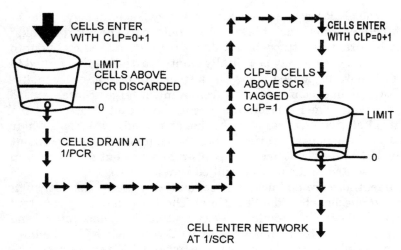

Figure 5.7 "Double leaky bucket" GCRA.

Figure 5.7 shows the concept behind the "double leaky bucket" method of UPC, which most early ATM network implementers will employ, although other, more complex configurations of GCRA are possible. Cells arrive from the user CPE across the UNI at totally uncontrollable (by the network) times. Generally, all cells seeking entry to the ATM network will be sent by the user with CLP = 0. As long as the arriving cells do not exceed some rate, they are all admitted to the network unchanged. If the cell arrival rate exceeds some limit L imposed by the network, namely, the sustained cell rate (SCR) of the connection, then the cells in excess of this limit L have their CLP bits changed to a 1. The cells with CLP = 1 are subjected to another "leaky bucket" with another limit L (not necessarily the same as the first L). Any cells sent by the user with CLP = 1 already are also added to this cell stream. However, this time the limit L corresponds to the maximum burst size (MBS) of the connection. Cells under this MBS are admitted to the network, while the rest are discarded.

GCRA is completely characterized by only two parameters: the limit L and the increment I (T and t to the ITU-T). A particular GCRA is indicated by the notation GCRA(I, L). The increment is expected to be the inverse of the reciprocal of one of the three main traffic rate parameters: the peak cell rate (1/PCR, which is the ITU-T recommendation), the sustained cell rate (1/SCR), or even the maximum burst size (1/MBS).

At the user site, where the CPE equipment must multiplex the cells from many connections and send them into the ATM network across the UNI, or even in a private ATM network where cells are feeding a private UNI, the process of UPC is known as the *virtual shaper*. A GCRA(I, L) is used here also, but mainly to smooth out the flow of cells from these many asynchronous sources and set CLP bits into the network rather than discard cells before they have even started out. Vendors of CPE will have a lot of flexibility with GCRA(I, L) values. For instance, when applied to the peak cell rate, the GCRA(I, L) may be the sum of all the peak cell rates of all VCCs within a VPC and then all VPCs on a UNI, public or private.

When coupled into "double leaky bucket" configurations, there are three allowable variations of the two GCRA(I, L) "buckets" as applied to cell streams:

1. PCR of all CLP = 0 + 1 cells and then PCR of the CLP = 0 cells
2. PCR of the CLP = 0 + 1 cells and then SCR of the CLP = 0 cells
3. PCR of the CLP = 0 + 1 cells and then SCR of the CLP = 0 + 1 cells

Of course, tagging of CLP = 0 cells (changing the CLP = 0 to CLP = 1) and then reapplying a GCRA are always allowed. The nice thing about "double leaky bucket" congestion control methods is that they are simple and they work.

5.2 ATM Switching Principle

There are several kinds of ATM switches, e.g., for switching VPCs or VCCs, but they all follow a general model, known as the *ATM switching principle,* illustrated in Figs. 5.8 and 5.9. A number of incoming links transport ATM cells into the switch. Depending on the value of the header field, this information is switched to an outgoing link, and a *new header* value is provided, based on some information in a "translation table." ATM switches, and indeed switches in general, are usually shown with a series of input ports on one side of the diagram and output ports on the

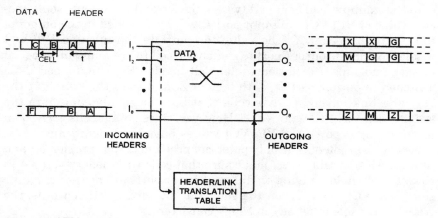

Figure 5.8 ATM switching principle.

INCOMING LINK	HEADER	OUTGOING LINK	HEADER
I_1	A B C	O_1 O_8 O_2	X Z W
⋮			
I_8	A B F	O_1 O_2 O_8	G W M

Figure 5.9 ATM switching principle—transition table.

other. The switch "fabric" connects input ports to output ports in some fashion. However, switch implementations usually incorporate the input and output ports of a digital communication link on the same board in the switch itself. Digital links being inherently unidirectional (i.e., an input twisted-pair/fiber and an output twisted-pair/fiber), it is no real stretch to schematically "unfold" the switch and let all the inputs appear on the left and all the outputs appear on the right.

The ATM switching principle works by examining the header fields of incoming cells on each input port. Special-purpose cells (e.g., those with preassigned VPI/VCI values defined above) are processed according to their own special procedures. The rest of the cells, generally user traffic cells, are to be switched to an output port on the ATM switch. A table is used (the header and link translation table) to determine which output port to transfer the cell to and what VPI/VCI value should be in the cell header when it emerges from the switch. The table is organized by input port and then is further broken down by VPI/VCI value.

In the example, cell header A (where the letter A represents some specific value of VPI/VCI) on input port I_1 will be switched to the outgoing link O_1 with header X. The value to translate the inbound VPI/VCI header to and the output port to switch the cell to are found in a special header and link translation table. Cell header B on input port I_1 is switched to output port O_8 with header Z, and so forth. Note that the outgoing link labeled O_1 has cells that both originally came into the switch with VPI/VCI values of A. However, since both A cells arrived on separate input ports and VPI/VCI values have local significance only, this is not a problem. The only potential problem is that the header and link translation table *must* make sure that cells with header value A in the VPI/VCI field arriving on different input ports are not assigned the same VPI/VCI value (X) on the same output port. In other words, the translation table must be internally consistent.

This diagram says *nothing* about switch implementation. It does not say exactly how cells find their way from input port to output port. It does not say how the header and link translation table is organized, built, and changed or even where it is located. Various schemes have been suggested. It does not even say if the VPI only is changed, the VPI and VCI both, or only the VCI. Note the similarity with "label swapping" routing in TCP/IP networks, where the data link layer address in an incoming frame is "swapped" with a new address on the output link of the router.

5.2.1   ATM switching issues

There are several crucial issues that will affect the performance, reliability, and even price of ATM switches. These issues lie beyond considerations such as whether the switch changes only VPI values, or VPI/VCI, or the like. It involves essential issues that reflect the structure and operation of the ATM switches themselves. They also form a useful criteria for comparing ATM switches from different vendors. The four most important are

What is the structure of the cell translation table?

Where is the cell translation table located?

How is the cell translation table maintained?

What is the switching fabric?

Some of these ATM switch questions have multiple, equally valid answers, and some have strict alternatives that will have profound implications for ATM network service providers.

The structure of the switch tables is a multiple-right-answer situation: a flat, two-dimensional table is the simplest (as in Fig. 5.9), but more complex tables (such as full relational databases) are not a problem. There may even be structures like linked lists used instead of tables for efficiency. Since the tables are never used by any other piece of equipment but the switch in which they dwell (the information may be shared across the network but not the table itself), any structure at all will do, as long as it works.

Table location and maintenance are more crucial. The table may be in the switch (most likely), in a separate box (for speed), or central to the entire ATM network (if one site has all the switching information, this could be a major task over a wide area, but not so bad in a single building).

Maintenance may be done by hand [exactly like an old network control program (NCP) generation on an SNA network] or by a special protocol (the signaling protocol). It can be a difficult task to make all the rows and columns of a switch table in an internally and externally consistent manner on even the smallest ATM network. And maintaining a table by hand when all other switches do it by a signaling protocol (which can easily happen in a multivendor environment) can become an issue also.

The most important issue regarding ATM switch construction and function, however, is the last item on the list: How do cells, once their output link has been determined and the cell VPI/VCI translation done, find their way to the output port? In other words, just what is the switch fabric?

5.2.2   ATM switching fabrics

Telephones can be made out of molded plastic and processor chips. They also can be made out of electromechanical parts with real bells and rotary dials. They also can be made out of two tin cans and a string (which, by the way, usually has much less noise than many modern digital circuits, and the voice quality is remarkably good). They are all telephones and can be used for voice transmission. None is really "better" than the other, although they are better suited to different tasks and different situations (tin cans look lousy on an executive's desk).

The same holds true for ATM switch fabrics. They come in all shapes and sizes, faster and slower, bigger and smaller, but they all switch cells. And if the feature that distinguishes one vendor's switch from another vendor's switch is not important to the customer, then that feature is not an advantage at all. Someone may actually like tin cans on a desk.

Many writers on ATM matters have an uncommon fascination with the internal structure of an ATM switch. These are the same kind of people who will immediately open the hood of a car to inspect the engine, as if the horsepower or top speed were on a sticker somewhere inside. All that this presumes, though, is that the internal structure matters. In fact, it matters very little, as long as the device, be it an engine or a switch, delivers the service promised or required (which is transportation in both cases).

This is not to say that ATM switch fabrics are all the same or that they cannot be compared with each other. They surely are not and surely can. All it means is that the different characteristics of one architecture may be important to one user or network service provider but not to another. Therefore, rather than speak of advantages or disadvantages of one method over another, it is better to speak in terms of pluses and minuses. A *plus* in this context is a potential advantage, but only if the characteristic is important to the user.

There are currently three main architectures in use for ATM switching fabrics:

1. Multiple high-speed backplane switching
2. Distributed matrix switching
3. Optical switching

Each architecture is detailed here. It may not be clear why the ATM network node must be a switch and not a router. There are several reasons. First, the ATM switch must handle delay-sensitive connections. Second, the cells on these connections arrive very quickly, up to 96,000 per second on a DS-3, which is just about the slowest of the currently supported interfaces.

Representative speeds of routers, older switches, and ATM switches are shown in Fig. 5.10. If ATM connections will carry traffic for "circuit emulation" services (and they will via AAL-1 class A service connections), then it is necessary for the ATM network node to operate as fast as a traditional circuit switch (e.g., a T-1 through a telco central office). But routers and other variable-length frame switches (e.g., frame relay) are still too slow. It is not just a question of architecture but also of how the variable-length frame can "block" time-sensitive frames on an output port (a full frame must be sent, once the first bit is out). Even older cell-relay switches such as those used with IEEE 802.6 MANs were a little slow for true voice connections.

NODE TYPE	PROCESSING TIME
Router (1980s)	10 ms
X.25 Switch (1980s)	10 ms
Router (1990s)	5 ms
Switch (1990s)	5 ms
Frame Relay	1 ms
Cell Relay (1980s)	500 usec
Circuit Switch	450 usec
Cell Relay (1990s)	1 usec
Fore Switch	10 usec
PARIS Switch	.5 usec
B-ISDN "goal"	50 nsec

Figure 5.10 Typical nodal processing delays.

With the rise of new ATM switch architectures such as distributed matrix switches, however, the "magical" 450-µs barrier was broken, indeed shattered, until today researchers speak of "nanosecond" switching of ATM cells. One nanosecond is one-thousandth of a microsecond, or one-millionth of a millisecond, or one-billionth of a second. What this means is that the nodal processing delay is a vanishingly small fraction of the propagation delay through the network, which is generally figured at 1 ms per 100 mi (the United States is usually considered to be between 20 and 25 ms wide). This means that information can be pulled across a wide area network using ATM switches about as fast as off the hard drive on a PC today (12- to 20-ms access time).

Multiple high-speed backplane. The architecture for an ATM switch (or network node) is not part of any standard, of course. All that matters is that cells go in and cells go out, and the delay inside the box is kept to an absolute minimum. It seems clear that ATM switches will have to perform all cell functions in hardware (i.e., embedded code on a chipset, not with a traditional stored-program processor).

One possibility is to use the traditional router/hub architecture employing interface cards and a main control CPU. This is shown in Fig. 5.11. For ATM speeds, these chipsets will be reduced instruction set computing (RISC) chips with the main CPU for control. The ATM input translation tables are usually on the boards themselves, which saves accessing the main CPU and adding delay to the switch. The result is variously known as a *shared-bus ATM switch* or a *multiple high-speed backplane switch*. The backplanes will run at up to 2 Gbps. Due to the backplane nature of the switch, however, the aggregate inputs can *never* exceed the backplane bus speed. If more inputs must be added, multiple backplanes are needed. In fact, the input and output cards usually are capable of putting a cell on either backplane bus.

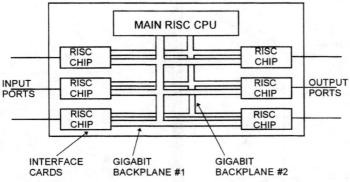

Figure 5.11 Multiple high-speed backplane.

This is sometimes necessary due to the shared nature of the backplane buses. If there is contention on the part of cells being switched from multiple input ports, the main CPU must employ a bus arbitration scheme to resolve the conflict.

Because the technology of backplanes is so well understood, these switches are popular and inexpensive. However, as input line speeds go up, the processor speeds must increase, regardless of backplane number. Also, since the bus itself contains no timing information from board to board, the total length of the bus must be measured in inches. Any increase in length to accommodate more boards will introduce severe timing difficulties into the switch fabric itself. It is said that shared-bus switches do not *scale* well, i.e., grow larger and larger just by extending the bus in a new chassis. Usually, a new "box" must be installed.

Several switch architectures using multiple high-speed backplanes have been built and used in pilot ATM networks. Some vary the backplane scheme by sharing memory access between input and output sides of the switch. That is, a cell is written to memory on the input side, while the output side is busily reading cells from the same shared memory. Some observers even create a separate category for shared-memory switches, but since the basic technology is not radically different from what has gone before, that distinction is not made here.

The most prominent shared-bus/memory switch is the PARIS switch built for the AURORA project pilot "gigabit" network at IBM. PARIS stands for *packetized automatic routing integrated system*. It moves *variable*-sized "cells" (really frames) through the switch. The PARIS switch is capable of handling ATM cells as a special case of normal variable-length traffic. The PlaNet switch is an extension of this same architecture. Both switches perform all functions in hardware. GTE has its broadband (very fast) circuit switch, and AT&T has designed something called a *knockout switch* along the same lines.

Backplane switches have been criticized on several grounds. The first is the obvious limit of input speed versus backplane speed. There is also the need to shunt traffic from backplane to backplane as needed. They also do not scale well. Perhaps there is a better way to switch ATM cells.

Distributed-matrix switch.   Distributed-matrix switches have a variety of alternate names such as the Banyan switch (a preferred Bellcore term) or the delta switch (all deltas are Banyans at heart) or even a parallel switch. They all have a number of characteristics that make them well suited for ATM network switches. In fact, some think they are so well suited that distributed-matrix switching is considered to be a sign of vendor commitment to ATM concepts and technology.

In any case, they are made of a number of identical switching elements, which makes these switches good candidates for large-scale

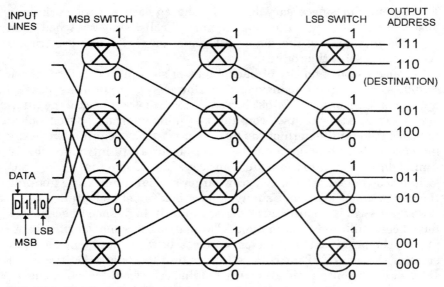

Figure 5.12   Distributed-matrix switch.

chip integration, which should mean falling prices. They have a *self-routing* property, which means that there is no software or control program that tells a cell where to go; it's all essentially automatic.

Banyans and deltas are easily scaled up in stages. Because of the identical switching elements, other modules are quickly added. And there is no need for the matrix to run as fast as the sum of the inputs; since there are multiple paths through the switch fabric, the fabric itself needs to run only as fast as the highest-speed input port.

Figure 5.12 shows the basic architecture of a distributed-matrix switch. It is important to realize that the "data" (D) portion of the input in the distributed-matrix switch represents the *entire* ATM cell, all 53 bytes of header and payload. The 3 bits prepended onto the cell is the output port destination. The table lookups have been done and the VPI/VCIs translated (again, usually embedded on the input board itself), and all that remains is to switch the cells through the fabric to the proper output port. The input cells are gated into an array of simple switch elements. Each makes only a single decision on 1 bit of the prepended destination port. And the decision need only be made on the first bit of the prepended header, which is then stripped off as the remainder is gated to the next set of switch elements. The only decision needed is whether the initial bit is a 0 or a 1, which is about the fastest thing that a microchip can do.

Thus the cell in Fig. 5.12 has arrived at a distributed-matrix switch. The cell will have a 3-bit destination port prepended onto the cell header and payload field. (This simple 8×8 matrix will only switch addresses 0 through 7, but the principle is the same for much larger switches.) The cell is switched—or rather the cell will switch itself—through the distributed-matrix switch to output address 110 (decimal 6). Three stages are necessary, one for each address bit. It follows that more levels are needed for more complex address schemes. Notice that a cell can be input simultaneously on *each* of the input ports, which is why distributed-matrix switches are often called *parallel switches*. However, this simultaneous switching can cause problems.

Distributed-matrix switches suffer from a phenomenon known as *collisions,* in which cells arrive internally or externally at the same element of the switch. Figure 5.13 shows the two types of collisions that are possible in distributed-matrix switches. The figure also shows examples of input conditions leading to the two types of collisions. In an *external* collision, two cells input in the same switching cycle arrive at the same output port simultaneously. It is a totally innocent condition; both cells' translation tables are probably on the input board, so the switch has no way of knowing that these two cells arriving at the same time from two separate input ports will both need to be switched to the same port. Obviously, both cannot be sent out at the same time. In an *internal* collision, also illustrated in Fig. 5.13, the two cells colliding have separate output ports, but they collide internally on the switching fabric, since both initial elements switch the cells. Again, the switch has no control software in the fabric to detect or prevent these kinds of conditions.

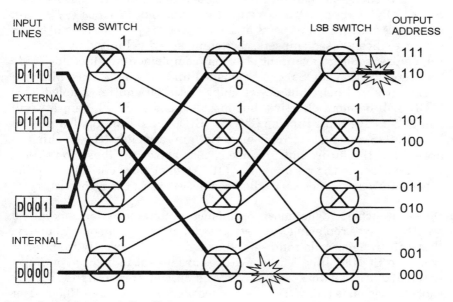

Figure 5.13 Matrix switch: collisions.

There are a couple of ways to deal with both kinds of collisions. For external collisions, a switch could buffer at the output side, but this just introduces nodal processing delay, which the whole switch architecture was designed to keep to a bare minimum. External collisions also could be eliminated by scanning the input cell stream cycle by cycle and preventing repeated destinations from entering the switch at the same time. All these solutions add delay.

Internal collisions could require buffers at each switching element, but this is again adding an additional delay. It is also possible to scan the input cells in a cycle (*very* quickly) and presort the inputs available by destination address. This prevents internal collisions entirely (and it is a proven mathematical theorem) but requires batching the inputs. A cell held back due to a switching conflict gets preference in the next switching cycle, preventing the cell from constantly being rescheduled for later switching cycles.

Distributed-matrix switches that eliminate both internal and external collisions in this fashion are known as *Batcher network switches* (not for the "batching" of input cells but for developer Ken Batcher). Bellcore has the Batcher/Banyan ATM switch. Most vendors of newer ATM switches, including Synoptics (now Bay Networks) and IBM, use distributed-matrix switches as the heart of their ATM network nodes.

However, there is a glaring flaw to building SONET-based ATM networks with the kinds of switches discussed above, both backplane and matrix: They all need to take the light signal and convert it to electricity to switch it and then reconvert it back to light on the output side. Since SONET (and SDH) is defined up to about 13 Gbps (STS-256), switching multiple input ports at these speeds is just not possible with existing silicon-based chipsets. Switching speed is limited by how fast the chipset's clock is running. Normal complementary metallic-oxide semiconductors (CMOSs) can be pushed up to about 2 Gbps. Multiple backplanes will help, but newer chips based on emitter-coupled logic (ECL) will be more effective (but more expensive). ECL chipsets will run at 5 to 10 Gbps. Bipolar CMOSs (BICMOSs) combine features of both CMOS and ECL technologies. Gallium arsenide (GaAs) chipsets are still in the future but promise speeds above 10 Gbps. For optical transmissions in the terabit range (1000 Gbps), pure optical switching is the only way to offer very advanced networks in the next century.

Optical switching. The most promising architecture for an optical switch involves replacing the distributed matrix with an optical matrix that will transfer cells represented as light waves directly from input to output SONET link. These switches are meant to be used on huge, national ATM networks, when ATM is as widespread as POTS and cable television is today. These switches must handle up to 10,000 user interfaces all running at 150 Mbps, 622 Mbps, or above.

Because of the elimination of the need to convert light to current and back again, these switches should easily operate at terabit speeds (1000 Gbps or 1,000,000 Mbps). Until now, optical switches have been built to "split off" the header portion of cell, convert *it* to electricity, delay the cell body, and then use the header information to control the optical cell through the switch. This has turned out to be very tricky to do at high speeds, which is the whole point.

Newer optical switches have already been prototyped at 8×8 arrays. This is an optical equivalent of the distributed-matrix switch, with the "electrified" VPI/VCI cell header fields controlling an array of optical switching elements. Once the indices have been set up by destination port on the array of optical switching elements, a group of optical cells is "switched" to the proper output fibers.

The magic of optical switches is that the layered substrates of silicon, aluminum-gallium-arsenide (AlGaAs), and gallium arsenide (GaAs) will vary their index-of-refraction (light-bending) capabilities depending on the voltage applied. (This is not an *all optical* switch; that will have to wait for optical computers and CPUs.) A cell with header pulse pattern 010 will be fed into a 3×3 array of optical switching elements. The 010 light pulses will be sensed by the control logic of the optical switch and change the index of refraction just enough to direct the cell to the proper output fiber. A control signal is then applied to the array to "desensitize" the matrix until the data portion of the cell has passed. It is *crucial* to optical switches that cell lengths be uniform. Otherwise, the timing must be controlled as well. This has doomed older methods of optical switching based on variable-length data units.

5.2.3   ATM switch comparison

The multiple-backplane ATM switch has many nice features. It uses very well-established CMOS technology and dense chipset designs that are inexpensive. The routing is done on the individual adapter cards, with the backplane or shared memory used for data transfer between cards. The backplane structure is just a simple bus, but very fast.

However, there are some drawbacks to attempting to construct large ATM networks out of these switches. The total throughput will obviously be limited to the total throughput of the backplane(s). Each adapter card must use the backplane to shuttle data through the switch. This may produce collisions (i.e., which adapter uses the backplane next?) that must be resolved by a fair arbitration method (as CSMA/CD solved it for Ethernet).

These are technology limitations. The limitation customers will care about more is the lack of scalability; as the bus gets longer and longer (more cards), it gets slower and slower quickly. Multiple rack-mounted units can extend the number of boards supported, but only so far. Eventually, the bus can be extended no further, and a total "box swap" upgrade is necessary. No one will attempt to make an "ATM toll office" from these.

Distributed-matrix (delta/Banyan) ATM switches are so widely respected that they have become the "standard" in many circles. They do have real advantages: They offer simple, identical switch elements, which should bring their price down rapidly. They need to run only at the input link speed (e.g., 150 Mbps) rather than at gigabit speeds, because there are multiple paths through the switch as opposed to jamming everything onto a high-speed backplane bus or shared memory, as quick as that may be.

Distributed-matrix switches offer the promise of very high throughput and scalability. On the other hand, they are still expensive. They do still have internal and external collisions, which only disappear when source and destination addresses are totally random. This is not a very realistic assumption on any network. Compensating for these collisions adds delay, but no one knows if the delay will turn out to make backplane "just as good." The consensus is that scalability will be the deciding factor.

Today it is hard to conceive of a digital telephone network using an analog switch. Why then should an optical transport ATM network use an electronic switch? The only viable long-term solution will be optical switching. It will require no wholesale light-to-electric-current signal conversion and back again. Once it is developed, the job is done; there is no other transport beyond fiber. This will be the only way national ATM networks can be built.

Of course, this is state-of-the-art stuff. There are many different competing schemes and architectures. The use of GaAs in current prototype optical switches automatically ensures an expensive—*very* expensive—solution. And the technology will not mature for several years (maybe decades) yet. All in all, optical switch fabrics are a future direction, not yet a real solution.

5.2.4   The ForeRunner ASX-100 ATM switch

After discussing various ATM switch architectures and fabrics from a general point of view, it may be instructive to examine a real-world ATM switch is some detail. Many ATM switches are available today for private ATM networks. One of the most respected is the Fore Systems ForeRunner ASX-100 ATM switch.

The ASX-100 is a 16-port backplane ATM switch. The backplane runs at 2.5 Gbps and uses output queuing for a buffering strategy. It supports SPANS, Fore's proprietary signaling protocol to set up both PVC and SVC UNI connections. It supports many interfaces, including TAXI,

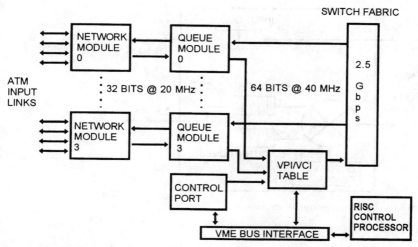

Figure 5.14 ForeRunner switch architecture.

Fibre Channel, DS-3, and STS-3c (all the standard ATM Forum transports). The switch is fast, with about a 10-µs cell processing delay. It also includes multicast and broadcast support.

Fore switch architecture. Figure 5.14 shows the architecture of the ASX-100 switch. The ForeRunner ATM switch has four input modules each supporting four links. They attach to the queuing modules with 32-bit-wide buses running at 20 MHz. The backplane itself runs 64 bits wide at 40 MHz. The control port interprets and generates the signaling protocol to set up the VPI/VCI translation table. The whole runs on a SPARC architecture and uses an Ethernet port for an additional, non-ATM interface.

Although there is an input queue in the queuing module, its function is essentially to implement "leaky bucket" rate control. The switch queuing itself is all done on the output side.

The ForeRunner queue module is an essential part of the switch and is illustrated in Fig. 5.15. The module does queue on both input and output, but the input queue is basically a "leaky bucket" type of rate control. That is, the queue is filled and drained at the input link speed. The backplane outputs at 2.5 Gbps, which means that cells must be queued (buffered) at the output ports if the cells arriving cannot be drained in one "frame time." Interestingly, the queues are divided into type 0 and type 1 cells, which can give preferential treatment to some connections. But this is *not* based on the ATM CLP bit. This requires some extra work to service the queues as compared with some other single-queue methods.

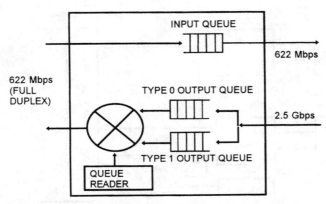

Figure 5.15   ForeRunner queue module.

Each queue on the output port has a tunable logical queue-size parameter set by software. This queue length is set to a multiple of 64 ATM
cells, up to a maximum of 512 (64×8). Each queue module has a *threshold register* set up in software to determine which queue the output
board is to read from. Initially, the type 0 queue is set to 0 (true) and the
type 1 queue is set to 1 (false). The queue reader will count dropped (discarded) cells per queue by port and also measure each queue's depth.

The queue reader chooses a queue to read according to the following
algorithm: If only one queue has cells, read it. Else if the threshold
depth has been reached on one queue, read that one. Else read the type
1 queue and repeat the whole process.

A threshold of 0 means that the queue is never given priority over the
other queue. A threshold set equal to the queue size means that the queue
is always given priority over the other queue. In the switch, cells are
queued until sent out in a first in, first out (FIFO) fashion. They are never
"aged out" of a queue, no matter how long they may have been delayed.

Fore switch VPI/VCI tables.   The ForeRunner is a full VPI/VCI switch.
Both values may change inside the switch. The ports number 0 to 15,
and the VPIs form an index into a path table. This entry is a further
index into a routing table. The routing table is a 64-bit entry that gives
the new VPI/VCI combination, the output port number, and the output
queue type for that connection. Only 10 bits of the VPI are supported
on the NNI, giving "only" 1024 VPIs between switches instead of 4096
(this is a valid option in both ATM Forum and ITU-T standards). The
routing table for the entire switch is limited to 128,000 entries initially. This means that not all 64,000 VCIs may be used on all ports, since
there are potentially many times more VPI/VCI combinations than
"just" 128,000. The two table structures are shown in Fig. 5.16.

PATH TABLE:

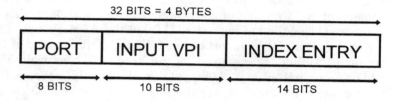

ROUTE TABLE:

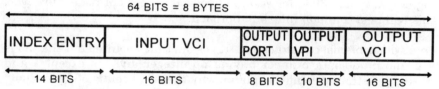

Figure 5.16 VPI/VCI translation tables.

If the VPI only is changed, that information is a single entry in the routing table. There are also cell counters that are incremented based on the number of lookups into the routing table and are indexed by the path table value. The control port has its own table of 4000 entries for signaling.

It may be instructive (and crucial to understanding the potential task of setting up translation tables in ATM networks) to perform a simple exercise that will point out just how large these tables may grow in large ATM networks. A full VPI/VCI entry will take up 12 bytes of memory (32 bits for the path table and 64 bits for the routing table entries). The table *must* be in memory; there is no way that the switch could access a hard disk drive or other device quickly enough to perform the task. There can be up to 64,000 or so VCIs (16 bits) on *each* of up to 1024 VPIs (8 bits on the UNI; the 12-bit NNI VPI tables will be even larger). And even a modest ATM switch may have 16 input ports.

These 64,000 VCI entries for each of 1000 VPIs makes 64 *million* (64,000 × 1000 = 64 million) entries alone. And 16 ports means 16 × 64 million = 1000 million = 1 billion entries. But these are just entries; the actual data in the entry, 12 bytes, means that a fully configured ATM switch with only 16 input and output ports may have to support translation table sizes of up to 12 gigabytes of memory. This is clearly impossible with any currently available switch architecture.

There are two ways to prevent the translation table from growing beyond control: not supporting all bits of the VPI/VCI field and limiting the total table size. For example, instead of supporting 8-bit VPIs and 16 bit-VCIs on a UNI, the switch vendor may support only 6-bit VPIs

(64 total) and 10-bit VCIs (1024 total). Now the total possible entries per port is only $64 \times 1000 = 64,000$ total, a thousandfold decrease from the complement of 64 million entries computed above. In fact, this is the recommended method of both the ITU and the ATM Forum. The Fore switch does limit VPI support on the NNI to 10 bits instead of 12.

The other possibility is employed by the Fore switch as well. The total table size is limited to 128,000 entries. While this prevents the table from growing too large, it introduces another problem. Since the table is not partitioned by port or user, it is possible for a large ATM network user to be using 120,000 entries of the connection table, leaving only a paltry 8000 for *everybody* else on the ATM node. However, this will be a common interim approach.

Fore switch internal cell structure.   It is sometimes pointed out that 53 is a prime number (a number having no integer divisors except 1 and itself), as if that somehow explains why the ATM cell is 53 bytes long. In fact, the odd size of the ATM cell does not map easily into the common 32- and 64-bit-wide architectures of most processors today. Thus, within the ForeRunner switch, a 53-byte ATM cell is handled internally as 14 consecutive 32-bit words. Two additional fields round out the difference (since $14 \times 4 = 56$). The extra 3 bytes are divided into PAD 1 of 8 bits and PAD 2 of 16 bits. This internal cell structure is shown in Fig. 5.17.

Cells move around the switch in this format, which has the advantage of being a multiple of 32 bits and adding some functions for error control. The PAD 1 byte is a CRC check on the first 5 header bytes. It provides further error control on the header exclusive of the HEC. If the header is correct, PAD 1 is 0. The PAD 2 field has a more complex structure.

The PAD 2 field is used by the control port to check for various errors in the ATM cells. The functions of the fields are

Bit 0: Set to 1 if there is a "framing error." That is, the 32-bit word read was not the expected value off the queue.

Bit 1: If the header CRC (PAD 1) is correct, this bit is set to 0.

Bit 2: If the AAL-3/4 CRC on the payload is correct, then this bit is set to 0. Otherwise, it is 1 to indicate an error.

Bits 3 to 5: Currently unused; they are always set to 0.

Bits 6 to 15: The switch computes its own CRC-10 on the cell payload field, including any ATM cell payload (such as in AAL-3/4) CRC check fields. It is always all 0s if there are no errors in the payload. It also can be used for single-bit error correct *if desired.* This is a configuration parameter. On the output side, the PAD 2 field is unused, and PAD 1 is modified.

32-BIT WORD				
0	BYTE 0	BYTE 1	BYTE 2	BYTE 3
1	BYTE 4	PAD 1	BYTE 5	BYTE 6
2	BYTE 7	BYTE 8	BYTE 9	BYTE 10
3	BYTE 11	BYTE 12	BYTE 13	BYTE 14
4	BYTE 15	BYTE 16	BYTE 17	BYTE 18
5	BYTE 19	BYTE 20	BYTE 21	BYTE 22
6	BYTE 23	BYTE 24	BYTE 25	BYTE 26
7	BYTE 27	BYTE 28	BYTE 29	BYTE 30
8	BYTE 31	BYTE 32	BYTE 33	BYTE 34
9	BYTE 35	BYTE 36	BYTE 37	BYTE 38
10	BYTE 39	BYTE 40	BYTE 41	BYTE 42
11	BYTE 43	BYTE 44	BYTE 45	BYTE 46
12	BYTE 47	BYTE 48	BYTE 49	BYTE 50
13	BYTE 51	BYTE 52	PAD 2	

Figure 5.17 Internal cell structure.

Fore switch interfaces. Fore supports a number of different physical interfaces on the network modules. All ATM Forum transports are supported. The NM-4MM/155 has four 155-Mbps SONET STS-3c ports. The NM-4MM/125 has four 100-Mbps FDDI (TAXI) ports. The NM-4MM/175 has four 140-Mbps Fibre Channel ports. There is little difference between these two except for speed. The NM-4DS3 has four 45-Mbps DS-3 ports. The NM-2DS3 has two 45-Mbps DS-3 ports. The only difference between the two DS-3 network modules is the number of physical ports.

5.3   ATM OAM Functions

To be effective, networks must be operated and managed as well as built. This process is variously known as *operations and maintenance (OAM,* the official ITU term), *operations, administration, and maintenance (OA&M,* a newer ATM Forum term), or even *operations, administration, maintenance, and provisioning (OAM&P,* an older term mostly used by Bellcore). Whatever it is called, the ATM layer provides mechanisms for OAM. These special OAM cells provide a means for detecting performance degradation on the ATM network. OAM cells are generated by all compliant ATM equipment, and they perform error monitoring, error detection, and error reporting, also by means of cells.

The network operations center must have access to and use the information in these cells to isolate causes of faults when they occur. For this reason, the standardization of format and use of these cells are crucial. This definition process will be especially challenging because some of these OAM cells may flow on public and/or private interfaces, among several ATM equipment vendors, between different ATM service providers, and across framed and unframed transports.

5.3.1   ATM OAM flows

There are two main flows of OAM cells in an ATM network. Type A flows are for F4 (VP) functions, and type B flows are for F5 (VC) flows. These levels concern ATM itself, rather than the cell transport.

Type A (F4 VP level) flows use a separate VCI set up on the same path as the virtual path connection (VPC). This virtual channel connection (VCC) logically links the ATM end-user devices that terminate connections on the ATM network. Thus, for each distinct VPI established on an ATM interface (e.g., UNI), there will be a standard VCI value set aside for F4 OAM cell flows. These may flow between the cell "entry" and "exit" points and an intermediate ATM network (paths being unidirectional, another VPI/VCI is needed for reverse cell flow). They also could be the "gateway" nodes between a public and private ATM network or even two networks operated by separate ATM network service providers. Type B (F5 VC level) flows are used on each VCC itself. Since a VCC is determined by a locally unique VPI/VCI combination, a separate VPI/VCI combination cannot be used for F5 OAM cell flows. In other words, the F5 OAM cells for VPI = 143, VCI = 1596 cannot be distinguished from user data cells by a different VPI/VCI value. And even if this were possible, it would defeat the whole purpose of F5 OAM flows, which is to follow each connection through the network. Something else must be used.

Actually, there are two types of F4 and F5 flows: one that checks a particular ATM network hop and one that checks an end-to-end path. These are known as *segment* and *end-to-end flows*. They are distinguished by making use of special ATM cell header values. F4 VP OAM segment cells use VCI = 3, and F4 VP OAM end-to-end cells use VCI = 4. The VPI will be different in the OAM cell header, one for each VPC established. The F5 VC OAM segment cells use the payload type indicator in the ATM header (PTI) = 4 (100 binary) to distinguish the OAM cells from user data cells. The F5 VC OAM end-to-end cells use PTI = 5 (101 binary).

The segment F4 VP OAM cell flows are generated wherever a new VPI is assigned to a cell. They are "looped back" at the end of the segment, where the VPI changes again. End-to-end F4 VP OAM cell flows follow the VPI translations all the way across the network. Segment F5

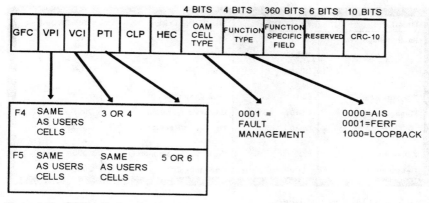

Figure 5.18   OAM cell structure.

VC OAM cell flows are generated wherever a new VCI is assigned to a cell. They are also looped back at the end of the segment, where the VCI changes again. And, of course, end-to-end F5 VC OAM cell flows follow the VPI/VCI translations all the way across the ATM network. The general format of these OAM cells is shown in Fig. 5.18.

However, just what are these OAM cells and flows looking for? Here are just *some* of the things that can be checked using OAM cell flows. When using a framed transport for cells, such as SONET/SDH, the F1 and F2 flows can detect such things as loss of framing or high bit error rates on the link. F3 is used for cell loss, bad HECs, cell errors, and the like. When used with a raw cell transport, F1 and F2 can only report the absence of the expected periodic OAM cells. F3 will still work as above.

At the ATM layer itself, F4 will tell senders and managers that a path is not available, and a combination of F4 and F5 OAM cells will detect and report "unacceptable performance," such as cell loss, cell insertion (misrouted cells), BERs, and so on.

5.3.2   OAM function types

Periodically, ATM equipment will generate these OAM cells. The most common interval is once per second. In the OAM cell payload, the first 4 bits indicate the OAM cell type: fault management (coded 0001), performance management (0010), or activation/deactivation (1000). Another 4 bits indicate function type: alarm indication signal (AIS, coded 0000), far end receive failure (FERF, 0001), or continuity check (0100) for fault management; forward monitoring (0000) or backward reporting (0001) for performance monitoring; and so forth. A complete list of the current OAM function type identifiers is shown in Fig. 5.19.

On an ATM network, any node using OAM flows to detect a failure may generate an alarm. The AIS is sent along the same direction as the

OAM TYPE	4 BIT CODING	FUNCTION TYPE	4 BIT CODING
Fault Management	O001	AIS	O000
	O001	FERF	O001
	O001	Continuity	O100
Performance	O010	Foward Monitoring	O000
Management	O010	Backward Reporting	O001
	O010	Monitoring/Reporting	O010
Activation/	I000	Performance Monitoring	O000
Deactivation		Continuity Check	O001

Figure 5.19   OAM type identifiers.

cell flow (downstream) on all affected VPCs and VCCs to indicate to all other nodes the connection passes through that there has been a failure along the opposite direction from where the nodes have received the cell (upstream). These alarm conditions may be triggered by loss of signal, loss of framing, and even loss of cell delineation.

The FERF is exactly the opposite, being generated upstream *back* along the path from which the cell was received. This indicates the presence of a problem downstream to the receiving node. To avoid a flood of alarm cells being distributed all over, the ATM Forum limits them to 1 percent of all cells generated by an ATM network node. In simpler terms, nodes send AISs out and look for FERFs coming in. They always pass along AISs and FERFs in either direction, of course.

ATM network nodes use the alarms to transition from a normal operating state to an alarm state. A node will return to normal if it receives no alarm OAM cells for 3 seconds or receives a "clear" OAM cell.

5.3.3   OAM cell type formats

Each of the major types of OAM cells has a specific format embedded in the 360-bit-long (45-byte) function-specific field of the OAM cell payload. Three major cell type formats for this field have been defined: fault management OAM cells, performance management (monitoring and reporting to the ATM Forum) OAM cells, and activation/deactivation OAM cells. The format of each is shown in Fig. 5.20.

Fault management OAM cells.   The proposed fields of the fault management OAM cell are

Failure type: An optional 8-bit field indicating the nature of the failure. No codings are recommended yet by the ATM Forum beyond the coding of all 0s or 00000001 for a special loopback indicator.

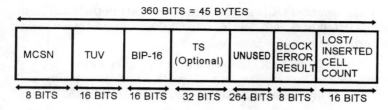

FUNCTION SPECIFIC OAM CELL PAYLOAD

MCSN = MONITORING CELL SEQUENCE NUMBER
TUC = TOTAL USER CELL COUNT
BIP-16 = 16 BIT BIP CHECK
TS = TIME STAMP

Figure 5.20   Performance management: OAM cell fields.

Failure location: An optional 9-byte field for the ATM network address of the equipment that has failed.

For fault management, the other 35 bytes are still undefined. However, when the failure type field begins with seven 0s, this is a special loopback indicator, and several other fields are then defined:

Loopback indication (LBI): A 1-bit field that is set to 0 when the loopback is sent and set to 1 when it is returned.

Correlation tag: A 4-byte field that gives the sender a way to distinguish its own loopback cells from others. If a cell with LBI = 1 is received and the tag does not match a cell "recently" sent (the field cycles in 64,000 cells) by this node, then the loopback cell originated elsewhere. (Many end-to-end loopbacks will be sent on the same connection with the same VPI/VCI/PTI values.) For LBI = 1 and no tag match, the node sends the cell back with LBI = 0. If the LBI = 0 and the tag matches, the loopback has succeeded.

Loopback location ID: A 12-byte field containing the ATM network address of the device that must loopback the cell. A coding of all 1s in this field indicates an end-to-end loopback.

Source ID: A 12-byte field containing the source ATM network address.

All other fields (16 bytes) are undefined and set to 6A in hexadecimal notation.

Performance management OAM cells.   The fields of the performance management OAM cell are

Monitoring cell sequence number (MCSN): An 8-bit field that cycles between 0 to 255 over and over.

Total user cell count (TUC): A 16-bit field indicating the total number of transmitted user cells (cycles 0 to 64,000 over and over) before the monitoring cell itself is inserted.

BIP-16: A 16-bit BIP check computed over the information fields of the entire block of user cells sent since the last monitoring cell. Blocks may be from 128 to 1024 cells long, in groups of 128.

Time stamp (TS): An optional 32-bit time stamp. The default value is all 1s.

Block error result: An 8-bit field at the end of the monitoring cell that carries the number of BIP-16 errors of the last incoming monitoring cell. This is used for backward BIP error reporting.

Lost/misinserted cell count: A 16-bit field that carries the count of lost or misinserted cells noted over the last incoming monitored block. This is also used for backward reporting.

Activation/deactivation OAM cells.   The fields of the activation/deactivation OAM cell are

Message ID: A 6-bit field with one of six possible values to indicate the specific function. The codings are shown in Fig. 5.21.

Direction(s) of action: A 2-bit field that forms a way of telling just which direction the message is traveling in: toward the activator (A) or toward the deactivator (B). When coded 01, the direction is B to A, and when coded 10, the direction is A to B. A coding of 11 is for two-way action, and the coding of 00 (default) is used when not applicable.

Correlation tag: An 8-bit field used for matching requests with responses at a particular node. A number is picked to be sent in this field. The next OAM cell received with this same number is the reply, by definition.

PM block sizes: These two 4-bit fields are used by the activator to supply performance management block sizes (the number of user cells between OAM cells) in both the activator/deactivator (A–B) and the B–A directions. Each bit indicates a block size of 128, 256, 512, or

MESSAGE	6 BIT VALUE
Activate	O00001
Activation Confirmed	O00010
Activation Request Denied	O00011
Deactivate	O00101
Deactivation Confirmed	O00110
Deactivation Request Denied	O00111

Figure 5.21 Activation/deactivation: message ID values.

1024 (e.g., a value of 1010 means blocks of 128 or 512 may be used). This field is active only in the activate and activation confirmed messages. The default value is 0000.

The rest of the bits (336 bits, or 42 bytes) are used and set to 6A in hexadecimal.

5.4 Signaling

The last major topic to be explored at the ATM layer is the whole idea of signaling. This is how the translation tables in the ATM switches will remain consistent across the network and insert, maintain, and delete entries. The whole idea of setting up a connection on a ATM network for an SVC service, rather than a pure PVC service, would be unthinkable without a reliable and standard way of doing ATM network signaling.

Since an ATM network is really several kinds of networks (voice, video, data), the signaling needed must satisfy all the diverse connection speeds, delays, and types users require on the ATM network. To deal with these issues, ATM has introduced a whole new signaling concept: *metasignaling*.

5.4.1 Metasignaling

A very important function of the ATM layer itself involves the concept of *meta* ("beyond") signaling. It is "beyond" the normal signaling of connections in most network types because it involves the setting up of the signaling channels themselves. ATM switched virtual connection (SVC) networks will be set up via a call setup and disconnect protocol, exactly as other networks. But ATM networks need to work not only with point-to-point connections for data but also with broadcast connections for video/audio and multipoint-to-multipoint connections for conferencing.

Metasignaling at the ATM layer is a simple protocol to establish and take down signaling channels themselves. All information in metasignaling is done with one-cell messages.

Only three functions are required for ATM metasignaling. These are shown in Fig. 5.22. First, the metasignaling channel can establish a new signaling channel with the VC assignment operation, a two-phase exchange of cells between user and network. Second, the metasignaling channel can take down an existing signaling channel with the VC removal operation, a three-phase exchange of cells. Finally, the network can check on the status of signaling channels (which may exist for long periods without being used) with the VC checking operation. The VC checking messages perform a "heartbeat polling" function similar

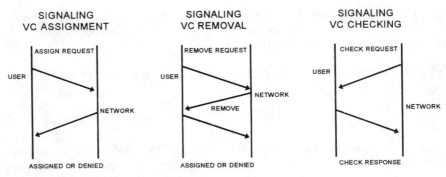

Figure 5.22 Metasignaling messages.

to the status enquiry requests on frame relay networks. Just what the metasignaling cells will look like is not finalized.

5.4.2 ATM signaling

In addition to metasignaling, ATM networks must implement the signaling used in other connection-oriented networks (such as voice) to establish and release connections. This protocol is essentially a formal user request for network resources. It is a user-to-network negotiation process whereby such parameters as connection type (PVC versus SVC, point versus multipoint), call endpoints (ATM network addresses), traffic contract (quality-of-service parameters, bandwidth), and service parameters (which ATM adaptation layer to use). VPI and VCI number allocation is handled here as well.

Three standards have been proposed for ATM user/network signaling. The first is Q.93B from ITU-T, an adaptation of Q.931, standardized as Q.2931. The second is just known as ATM Forum signaling, which is also called "skinny Q.93B" and is a subset of Q.93B. The ATM Forum is committed to ultimately making its own signaling standard compliant with Q.2931. The last is B-ISUP, which is essentially SS7 (signaling System 7, the international standard signaling protocol for voice networks) for ATM networks. B-ISUP stands for *broadband-interim signaling user protocol,* also from ITU-T.

5.4.3 ATM Forum signaling and network addresses

Several of the parameters that must be used with ATM Forum signaling are familiar concepts from previous discussions. The fact that ATM network connections may be static (PVCs) or dynamic (SVCs) has been explored before. The topics of traffic contract, QOS, and service parameters were all treated adequately earlier. The signaling protocol just gives a standard way of expressing these to a local ATM network node across a UNI. The signaling protocol is just another variable-length frame following its own set of protocol rules. Signaling protocols are not exciting or innovative in themselves.

However, there are some concepts that are especially important in ATM signaling that have not been mentioned before. The connection that the signaling protocol is setting up must use some form of network address. This is true of telephone networks, where the network address is the telephone number, as well as data networks. There are four forms of network address supported by the ATM Forum for ATM networks, all based on the ISO NSAP format. The private UNI must support three, while the public UNI must support either the three private formats or just the E.164 public network address format.

The four forms of the 20-byte ATM Forum network addresses are

1. DCC ATM format

2. IDC ATM format

3. E.164 ATM private format

4. E.164 ATM public format

These four forms are shown in Fig. 5.23. Support for the first three is mandatory for private ATM networks.

In more detail, the four formats are

1. *The data country code (DCC) ATM format.*   The first field is the authority and format identifier (AFI) field, which is a value of 39 for this format. The DCC field itself (2 bytes) specifies the country where the

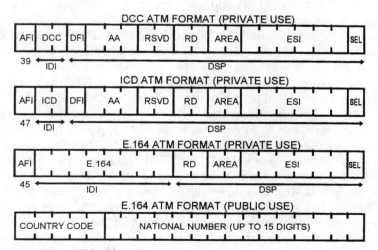

Figure 5.23 ATM address formats.

address is registered. The domain-specific part identifier (DFI) field (1 byte) specifies the structure of the remaining fields. The administrative authority (AA) field (3 bytes) indicates the authority responsible for the rest of the address. There follows a reserved (RSRVD) field (2 bytes) for future use. The routing domain (RD) field (2 bytes) is used to specify a unique routing domain (i.e., just where the address is unique). The area field (2 bytes) identifies a unique area within an RD. The end system identifier (ESI) field (6 bytes) identifies an end system within the area, and the selector (SEL) field (1 byte) is used by the end system for "selecting" an endpoint.

2. *The international code designator (ICD) ATM format.* The first field is an AFI value of 47. The next field is the ICD field itself (2 bytes), which identifies an international organization. The codings are administered by the British Standards Institute, and the rest of the fields are identical to the DCC ATM format.

3. *The E.164 ATM private format.* Both E.164 formats are specified by the ITU-T in Recommendation E.164 originally planned for ISDN networks. The first field is an AFI value of 45. The next field is the E.164 address itself (8 bytes), which may contain up to 15 binary-coded decimal (i.e., the digits 0 to 9) values. The initial 4-bit nibble is set to 0000, and any trailing nibbles, if the address is less than 15 digits, are set to 1111. The rest of the fields are the same as in the DCC or ICD ATM format.

4. *The E.164 ATM public format.* Essentially identical to the E.164 ATM private format but administered and assigned publicly and conforming to the E.164 international format.

Before any ATM connection can be established across a UNI, both the CPE and the local ATM network node must be aware of the address formats in effect. For private UNI address formats, the user side of the UNI supplies the ESI and SEL fields, which form the "user part" of the ATM address. The network adds the "network part" (all the rest of the fields). However, when the E.164 address formats are used, the network supplies the whole 8-byte address field. After the addresses have been "registered" (stored in tables at each side of the UNI), they are used in the calling and called party number information elements that are sent in various signaling messages.

Generally, therefore, the ATM network node will supply all information for the network address fields except the end system ID and selector. These fields come from the user side of the UNI. And, of these two fields, the selector field is not used for routing the signaling message through the network at all. It is strictly used by the endpoints of the connection.

The selector field is supported in the private address formats only and is used optionally within an endpoint on the ATM network to provide the other side of a connection with additional information, such as the type of application (ISO, user-specific, etc.) and layer 2 and 3 protocols (X.25, LAP-B, etc.).

5.4.4   ATM signaling message flows

The ATM signaling systems currently being looked at are all based on Q.931 signaling for ISDN and Q.933 signaling for frame relay. It was given a placeholder number of Q.93B until it is ready for publication and is now Q.2931.

The Q.2931 protocol works by exchanging variable-length messages. Each has a message type and message length field and a number of information elements (IEs). Each IE has parameter values for the circuit attributes being negotiated. Some IEs are mandatory in some messages, and some are optional.

The Q.2931 messages are the familiar ones from ISDN—things like ALERTING, DISCONNECT, CALL PROCEEDING, and the like. The initial standard will be point-to-point and "root to leaf" point-to-multipoint. Multipoint-to-multipoint and video connection signaling will come later. There are also some IE add-ons for ATM-specific functions. Things such as ATM cell user rate and VPI/VPI identifier have been added.

The ATM Forum has decided to standardize on a subset of the full Q.93B/Q.2931, known as "skinny Q.93B." Having a stable subset to build on will allow rapid deployment and acceptance of equipment. It uses no metasignaling at all. This was considered too difficult to implement initially. The ATM Forum just uses the signaling default VPI = 0, VCI = 5 for everything. It is expected to be widely used and accepted. It drops most of the "status" and "information" messages from Q.2931, instead concentrating on the most common set of features for all vendor equipment.

In one important fashion the ATM Forum actually *extended* Q.2931. Considering the importance of conferencing to ATM network implementation, it was decided to add point-to-multipoint signaling capabilities. Initially, this will be "root to leaf" unidirectional. That is, the originator (root) may add parties ("leaves") or drop them, but the "leaves" may not generate signals at all. Additional messages such as ADD PARTY, ADD PARTY ACK, ADD PARTY NACK, DROP PARTY, DROP PARTY ACK, and DROP PARTY NACK have been added for this purpose. True multipoint-to-multipoint and bidirectional point-to-multipoint signaling will follow.

Figure 5.24 shows a sample signaling message flow across an ATM network UNI and NNI to establish a connection. This call setup procedure is virtually identical to any number of similar signaling protocols that have been invented for voice with X.25 packet switching.

Figure 5.25 shows the reverse procedure, namely, the release of a connection. Notice that this process may be initiated by either party, not just the call originator.

Finally, Fig. 5.26 shows that the ATM network itself may clear a call. This will typically happen when the link on the network across the NNI has failed. Instead of seeking an alternate path through the network

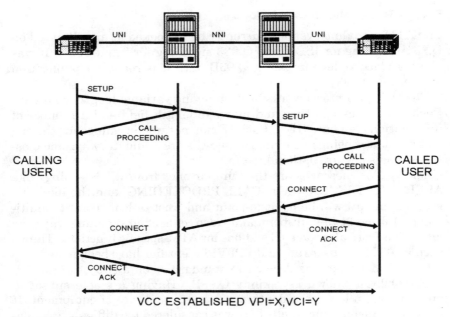

Figure 5.24 VCC connection setup.

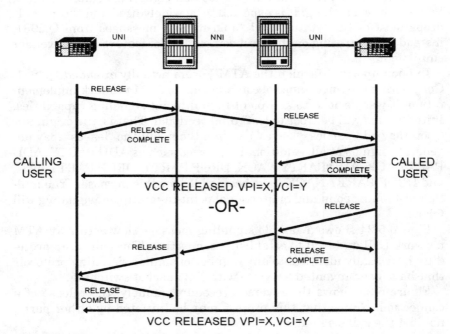

Figure 5.25 VCC connection release.

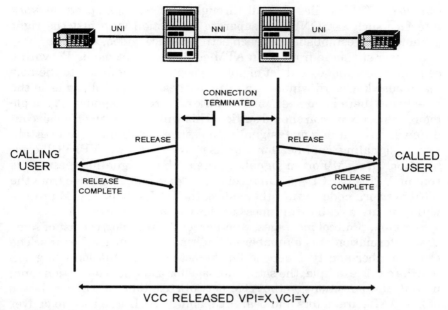

Figure 5.26   Network connection release.

(although SONET is capable of this), the ATM network will just notify the end users that the connections are cleared or released. Usually, the end users will immediately try to reestablish connections and will be given new paths around the failure for their new connections.

5.4.5   ATM signaling example

It might be instructive at this point to consider an actual situation in which ATM signaling would be used to establish multiple connections of different types. Remember that there are no channels in ATM networks; all traffic must be handled via a connection, be it voice or video or data. This means that there will be a lot of connections on an ATM network, even for the simplest activities. This example considers what happens when a user initiates a "multimedia call" on an ATM network.

Keep in mind that what is being described is very difficult to do with existing networks. Multimedia combines voice, video, and data sessions on a single PC or workstation. There are PCs and workstations today that have some voice and video capabilities, but to do the voice and video in "real-time," a separate network connection and communications card are needed. If not, then the voice and video must be downloaded over the data network in its entirety to the hard disk on the PC and then displayed or listened to. All in all, not a clean or sophisticated operation. In contrast, ATM handles this all through a single high-speed network interface such as SONET. A separate connection with just the right parameters is established for each activity: voice, video, and data.

If a user sitting in front of an ATM-equipped, multimedia PC with a camera, microphone, and set of stereo speakers in addition to the normal mouse/keyboard/windowing setup wishes to call a colleague on the telephone, there is no need to even pick up a real telephone: A simple mouse-click on an icon should suffice. This will initiate an off-hook condition and result in a metasignaling message to be generated to establish a signaling channel for the user with its own VPI/VCI combination. In ATM Forum signaling, the off-hook signaling message is sent on VPI = 0, VCI = 5. On receiving a "dial-tone" message from the ATM network node on the other side of the UNI, the user ATM process will generate a "call setup" message for the voice connection.

Signaling protocol messages, whether for ATM or not, consist of some basic information plus a number of "information elements," or IEs. The exact number and type depend on the action and situation being signaled. In this example, the setup message for the voice connection (and, indeed, all connections on the ATM network) contains two major classes of IEs: AAL parameters and bearer capability. AALs are used to deliver classes of service in ATM networks and are discussed in the next chapter. For now, it is enough to recall, as mentioned in Chap. 3, that AALs are defined for class A, B, C, and D services. In this example, the ATM software will request an AAL type 1 for a class A voice connection.

The setup message AAL parameters include codings to request characteristics such as "voice band based on 64 kbps," "circuit emulation" (AAL-1), "clock recovery type," and so on. The bearer capability parameters include codings for characteristics such as "ATM user cell rate" and "called party number," "calling party number," and so on. Notice that this signaling message format is used to set up *all* ATM connections on the network, exactly as in Fig. 5.24.

The network node has a lot of work to do on the call setup request signaling message. It must determine if the network can handle the additional traffic in terms of cells specified by the user signaling message. It also must determine just where in the world the destination is, which may be a difficult task, since the ATM network must not only keep track of all the world's telephones but potentially literally anything that can generate 0s and 1s! The network node must not only locate the destination but also determine the best path through the network for the connection to be routed. These routing decisions may be based on traffic patterns, user requests, administrative policies, or varying combinations of all three. For now, the ATM Forum has no standard method for ATM network route selection, but several proposals are being considered.

If the network can accept the requested voice connection and the receiver "answers" the phone, presumably at an ATM-equipped multimedia PC or workstation of his or her own, voice communications are initiated. The two users converse the same as they ordinarily would. Voice samples generate 64 kbps in each direction, at a constant bit rate with a consistent delay over the ATM network connection. The "circuit" may have a VPI = 30, VCI = 1567, where the VPI may be the "site code" for the other end of the voice connection (but other interpretations, including "no significance," are possible for the VPI field).

Now the users decide to activate the video camera on the PC/workstation. This will activate a video link between the two as well as a voice link. Again, a simple point and click should do. But this time the connection setup signaling message will request a class B, AAL-2 video connection. Again, a number of IEs are included for the AAL and bearer capabilities. Because the ATM network node has a previous connection to the other user for voice, the video connection should be established very quickly, probably over the same path as the voice connection (although video generates more bits and may therefore require a less congested path—if there is one). Once the connection is established, call it VPI = 30, VCI = 4539, the users can now see each other as well as speak to each other.

An interesting addition to standard signaling protocols is provided by ATM network signaling. This is the possibility of point-to-multipoint calls, as mentioned above. Suppose the two users decide to both simultaneously view a video clip stored on the ATM network at a video server site. This not only requires another connection for each user, it also requires that the video server send bits to two endpoints simultaneously so that the video appears the same at both sites. This would generate a series of AAL-2, class B, point-to-multipoint signaling messages, again with a more or less lengthy delay for resource location and route determination. But again, once done, the user has yet another connection active.

This video server connection may appear as VPI = 56, VCI = 3348 to one user and as VPI = 56, VCI = 1986 to the other. It is only the result that is significant. Actually, under current ATM Forum plans, the video connection between the two users and the video server connection as well would probably be requested as AAL-1, class A, or even AAL-5, class C. However, this does not change the scenario for the signaling procedures in any way.

Now, if the users decide to exchange data between each other, this requires yet another connection (four for the two users in this example). If this number seems excessive, remember that the alternative is four *networks:* voice, video, video server, and data. And the data connection is not just for "file transfer" interactions, although this is likely. As long as the connection exists, the two users may view the data, even store the data, and have it updated by the network as it changes due to actions by the two users viewing it or even other users on the network. Of course, this is not a function of the ATM network; this "real-time data update" is a feature of the application software written for the network.

The signaling protocol for ATM networks is much more complex in many regards than other signaling protocols for data or voice only networks.

5.4.6 ATM signaling issues

Experience has shown that signaling is the hardest part of any networking architecture to standardize. National, regional, and vendor variations called *personalities* all exist. ATM will probably be no exception.

In addition, the assignment of private versus public network addresses must be explored. Where routing and path lookup for signaling messages will be done is still an open issue. Multipoint implementations will be particularly resistant to standardization, because vendors will see this as an important method of vendor differentiation in a commodity marketplace. Performance *must* improve. Serious proposals have been made to carry Q.93B messages on the existing 56-kbps signaling links. Of course, to be efficient, the call setup time must be a mere fraction of the holding time or else revenue might be lost. And as for SS7 and B-ISUP, no one knows where that all fits in. All in all, another reason for PVC ATM networks initially.

6

ATM Technology Components: Upper Layers

So far a little time has been spent describing the transport and switching of cells, but just where are all these cells coming from, and where are they all rushing to? It is easy to say that ATM cells flow from the source to the destination, but this is not very helpful. There are user data in most of these cells, but the computer equipment that generates the user data is not necessarily creating or generating ATM cells directly. Rather, an application's data needing to be sent across an ATM network typically will have to be *adapted* to the ATM network. This means, for the most part, making cells from a variable-length data unit at the sender's side of the ATM network and pasting the cells back together into the original variable-length data unit at the destination's side of the ATM network. (Actually, it is only the cell *payloads* that get broken up and put back together; the ATM cell header is *never* seen above the ATM layer itself.)

This whole process of *segmentation and reassembly,* which is the ATM name for this breaking up and pasting back together of user data units, is needed because the vast majority of current network applications and protocols generate data units that are much longer than 48 bytes. What is more, a wide variety of formats and information types (voice, video, etc.) is used in applications for which ATM networks must provide transport services. The whole preparation procedure can be rather complex. The entire preparation process in the ATM protocol architecture is performed by the highest layer of the ATM protocol stack: the ATM adaptation layer (AAL). (It seems ATM acronyms must come in three-letter forms: ATM layer, not AL; AAL, not AA layer. Even a seeming exception such as the TC sublayer is sometimes seen as TCS. There are even instances in writing of the "AAL layer," which boggles the mind.)

There are no cells at the AAL. This is not really surprising. Cells consist of 5-byte headers and 48-byte payloads. It is the payload that is the major concern of the AAL, so obviously the AAL deals with them. But the cell headers are different. ATM cell headers serve two purposes: multiplexing and demultiplexing, and switching based on the VPI/VCI field values. Neither function is needed by the AAL itself, so the cell header is generated by the ATM layer on the sending side and stripped off by the ATM layer at the receiving side of the network. It is sometimes said that the AAL exists only at the endpoints or "end systems" of an ATM network, but this is not always true. Any ATM network node that needs to look inside the payload field of an ATM user data traffic cell (as opposed to an OAM cell, as one example) *must* have an AAL in some form implemented on top of the ATM layer. For instance, a video server on an ATM network must have an AAL to break up the digitized video into cells, even though it is not an "end system" but a network node in its own right.

Not only are there no cells at the AAL, it is really not even a layer. It is really a series of compartments, each of which contains some functions specific to the type of ATM application service the network is providing and some functions that are common to all ATM network applications. Since the functions depend on the type of service needed at a network node, each of the compartments is really a stand-alone unit, giving a large degree of modularity to the AAL arrangement. For example, an ATM network providing data services only to a user's premises would not need an AAL for the support of voice or video services at all.

The AAL is so complex that there is a tendency to get lost in the details of its operation. There was only one physical layer and one ATM layer to discuss, with many functions and options, to be sure, but not all at the same time. This is the way it is with the AAL. Just to keep track of what is what, Fig. 6.1 shows a detailed "roadmap" of most of the possible AAL implementations.

Figure 6.1 is quite complex. It shows a lot of information, so some explanation is necessary to point out the notable features of the AAL. First of all, Fig. 6.1 clearly shows the compartmentalized structure of the AAL. There is only one ATM layer and one physical layer in the diagram, but at least seven different types of AALs are capable of existing on top of this single ATM layer and physical layer. The ATM layer must take cells from each active AAL in a fashion that delivers the required service to the user connections in a particular AAL, at least on the sending side. On the receiving side, of course, the cells are demultiplexed to the proper AALs based on connection number (VPI/VCI).

At the top of Fig. 6.1, some "extra" service classes have been added to the A, B, C, and D classes familiar from the ITU-T definition of the

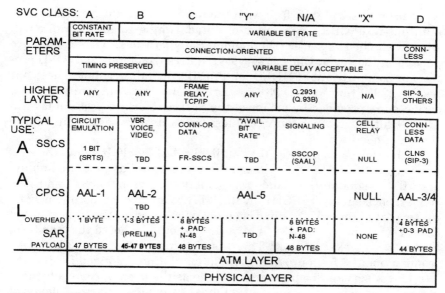

Figure 6.1 ATM adaptation layer structure.

AAL. These are ATM Forum proposals that are being worked on. The two new proposed service classes are known informally as "class X" and "class Y" service. Both are placed under the variable-bit-rate, connection-oriented, timing-insensitive (i.e., time delay variations between subsequent cell arrivals are acceptable to the applications) services, but this is just for information purposes. Both class X and class Y are really beyond the A-B-C-D structure of the ITU. Class X is sometimes defined as an *unassigned-bit-rate* (UBR) service, meaning that cells are transported as presented to the ATM layer. Class Y is defined as *available-bit-rate* (ABR) service, meaning cells are transported across the ATM network if there is capacity available for them. The service class marked "N/A" is the signaling AAL itself, which is not really a service at all. It is included here for completeness.

Below the service classes is the familiar parameter chart from the ITU-T ATM documentation. It is repeated here to supply a convenient way to associate the AAL protocols with the service parameters they represent. ABR (class Y) and UBR (class X) are not included as separate categories because both are still subsets of a variable-bit-rate (VBR), connection-oriented, delay-insensitive service.

The middle section of Fig. 6.1 is taken up by the higher-layer protocols themselves. These are protocols that typically generate the variable-length data units that feed the whole ATM protocol stack. Notice that some of the service classes are very liberal when it comes to just what protocols will interface with them. Anything that generates constant-bit-rate (CBR), connection-oriented, timing-sensitive traffic will work with class A service, and so on. Some of the service classes are particular, however. Class C service requires frame relay's LAP-D protocol or some variant of HDLC for TCP/IP. Signaling is not a class but needs Q.2931 (formerly Q.93B) to perform its task. And connectionless services are provided by means of the SMDS interface protocol layer 3 (SIP-3), although other connectionless protocols may be used, including those defined by the ITU-T.

The bottom section of Fig. 6.1 details the AAL itself. It shows the sublayering of the AAL, which is usually represented as just two sublayers: the segmentation and reassembly (SAR) sublayer and the convergence sublayer (CS) (*C* by itself is not much of an acronym). The upper part of the AAL box has been used to represent the typical use of that service class in an ATM network. It should be noted that the term *typical use* is exactly that: There is nothing to preclude other AAL "compartments" from providing circuit emulation (digitized DS-0s, DS-1s) class A service (for instance), as long as the users receive adequate service. However, this combination makes the most effective means of providing it because this was what the AAL was *designed* to provide. The other typical uses include variable-bit-rate (VBR) voice, audio, and video (usually, but not necessarily, by using compression) with class B, any connection-oriented data service with class C, an available-bit-rate (ABR) service with class Y, raw cell relay with class X, and connectionless data service with class D.

In Fig. 6.1, the CS has been split into two parts itself. The upper part forms the service-specific convergence sublayer (SSCS) and represents a series of particular actions that must be taken to provide each of the respective services the quality-of-service (QOS) parameters needed. Sometimes the SSCS is itself split into two further sublayers: an upper part known as the service-specific coordination function (SSCF) sublayer (sub-sublayer?) and the service-specific connection-oriented protocol (SSCOP). Since these two further divisions are only both nonnull in the case of signaling protocols, Fig. 6.1 groups them together into the SSCS and specifies SSCOP for signaling alone. Figure 6.1 also shows one bit in class A used for SSCS. The SSCS for AAL-2 has been given the name VASSCS by the ATM Forum, which stands for *video/audio SSCS* (never seen as VA-SSCS for some reason). Frame-relay data have their own SSCS as well, the FR-SSCS, and SMDS connectionless service is provided by the connectionless network service (CLNS).

The lower part forms the common-part convergence sublayer (CPCS) and represents a series of common actions that must be taken to provide *any* service with the QOS parameters needed. Although the actions are common, it is common practice for the ITU-T to label each of the CS compartments with an AAL protocol that is designed to take the SSCS data unit and prepare it for segmentation. Again, it is really only by convention that AAL-1 is "for" a class A service like circuit emulation. The ATM Forum avoids all mention of AALs as often as possible, preferring to directly refer to "class A," "class B," and so on. In fact, as has been pointed out, *any* AAL at all can provide any class of service, as long as it works. However, because AAL-3/4, for instance, was designed to deliver class D connectionless data services, it is very common to place AAL-3/4 in the class D "compartment." Some observers have noticed the position of AAL-5 in the AAL structure and have seriously proposed "abolishing" all other forms of AAL except AAL-5. In fact, this makes some sense, as will be explained later.

The lowest part of Fig. 6.1 represents the lower sublayer of the AAL: the segmentation and reassembly (SAR) sublayer. Notice that up to this layer, the user data flowing into the AAL, and therefore the ATM network itself, are still generally a variable-length data unit (with the exception of class X and possibly class A service). There may have been additional headers and trailers put on, depending on the class of service, but what reaches the SAR sublayer looks pretty much like what came in from the higher layer.

But not any more. It is the function of the SAR sublayer to segment cells on the way out (making a series of 48-byte payloads out of the variable-length data units) and reassemble them on the way in (recovering the original variable-length unit in the process). In Fig. 6.1, the SAR level shows two pieces of information that are often obscured by other AAL representations. Namely, the AAL types all have different amounts of *additional* overhead added on a per-cell basis. This limits the amount of user data that actually gets loaded into each cell, sometimes drastically. Notice that this extra payload overhead is in addition to the ATM cell header, which is not even generated until the cell payload reaches the ATM layer.

All the SAR payloads are 48 bytes long, of course. But the figure shows the differing lengths of the overhead (headers and/or trailers) and payloads for all the AAL types (these overhead-payload mixes are tied to the AAL type, *not* the service class). AAL-1 has 1 byte of overhead and 47 bytes of payload, AAL-2 has 1 to 3 bytes of overhead and 45 to 47 bytes of payload (nothing about AAL-2 has been finalized yet), AAL-5 has *none* except for a small trailer (padded to land in the last cell), and AAL-3/4 has the most. In fact, AAL-3/4 has been all but abandoned by many ATM network implementers because it requires an additional 4 bytes of overhead per cell (plus some padding bytes potentially), limiting the usable cell payload to only 44 bytes. Figure 6.1 does have a lot of information, but it gives a good overview of the functions of the AAL.

6.1   ATM Adaptation Layer Functions

The user interface to the ATM protocol stack will be through the ATM adaptation layer (AAL). Different services and applications will require different characteristics of the ATM network. But users do not care for the inner working details of the network itself, as long as what comes out at the destination is the same as what went in at the origin. Just as the captain of a ship who orders "Full speed ahead" does not care about the way this command gets to the engine room or if the ship is diesel or turbine powered as long as the ship gets there, so the AAL will provide the "orders" in terms of user data for the ATM network. Thus the main function of the AAL is to provide a way to hide the workings of the ATM network for the applications using it.

As mentioned earlier, the AAL consists of two sublayers: the segmentation and reassembly (SAR) sublayer and the convergence sublayer (CS). The SAR makes cells of higher-layer data units and remakes the data units at the destination, while the CS makes sure that the cell stream set up and sent is capable of providing the needed service to the application. It will do so with normal service access points (SAPs) to existing (in the vast majority of cases) higher-layer protocols.

The general process of cell generation and recovery is illustrated in Fig. 6.2. This sequence vaguely follows the procedures used with AAL-3/4, but it is used here only for the purposes of illustration. Usually, a variable-length higher-layer protocol data unit (PDU) will

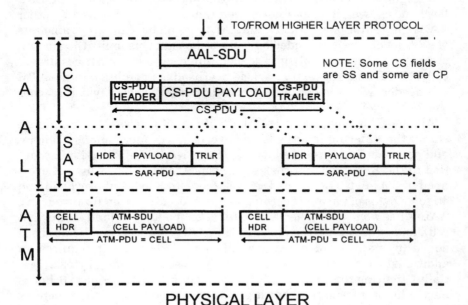

Figure 6.2 General AAL functions and terms.

enter the ATM protocol stack via an SAP to become a service data unit (SDU). After some headers and trailers (generally, structures vary from service to service) that are specific to an application are added, another set of headers and trailers is added no matter which service the SDU came from (again, generally). This whole unit is passed to the SAR sublayer, which breaks the (still) variable-length data unit up into a series of payloads. These payloads, however, are not necessarily ATM cell payloads. They are SAR-PDU payloads, and usually some additional headers and trailers are placed on these "fragments." With the proper header and trailer fields, the payload is now exactly 48 bytes long.

Based on its own service procedure, the ATM layer itself will take cell payloads from *each* of the AALs present and active above it and add a 5-byte cell header. These are multiplexed into the ATM network and switched (based on the header fields) to their proper destinations. The receiving ATM layer will strip off the header and, based on the header field values, distribute the cell *payloads* to the proper AAL above it.

Each sublayer of the AAL will read, process, and strip off the headers and trailers added at the sending side of the network and reassemble the original higher-layer data unit. If all goes well, the original variable-length PDU is delivered to the proper application at the destination side of the ATM network.

Applications and services that generate cells to begin with will need no AAL layer at all; these layers will be *null* [the null AAL is frequently called AAL-0 (zero)]. All the rest will get AAL services based on the concept of "service classes." The AAL service classes will provide a means for dealing with lost or misinserted cells, cell delay variation, error handling, and recovering source timing information (more later on this one) at the receiver.

6.1.1   AAL classes and types

The ITU-T ATM documentation offers four classes of service based on three parameters. These are *bit rate* (i.e., constant or variable), *connection mode* (i.e., connectionless or connection-oriented), and *timing compensation* (technically, "timing relation"). These three can combine in eight ways (three binary states = 2^3 states). However, only four classes have been considered to make "sense" in ATM networks. For example, it is deemed meaningless to preserve timing without a connection (timing compensation = yes; connection-oriented = no). Thus these combinations form the classes that have been established.

The timing compensation parameter is the trickiest to understand. It basically refers to the delay variation that is acceptable for a connection. For digitized voice, 64-kbps PCM samples must be sent so that 8000 bytes arrive per second—a small variation (a few bits one way or the other) is tolerable, but any larger variation in this delay is deadly. Large variations will caused the receiving equipment (the application equipment, not the ATM equipment) to think that something is drastically wrong on the network. This is just the way digital circuits have been set up to run in the past. All circuit emulation on ATM networks must respect this.

Other applications, such as file transfers and other data applications, are more tolerant. Thus the timing compensation parameter can be looked at as "If the cell's not here when expected, does that mean there is something wrong?" If the answer is *yes,* then timing compensation is needed.

The four ITU classes A, B, C, and D are mapped to six AAL *types.* At first this was meant to be a simple relationship: class A = AAL type 1, B = AAL-2, C = AAL-3, and D = AAL-4, but things have turned out to be more complex. As a result, there is now no fixed relationship between AAL classes and AAL types. In other words, connectionless services are just as likely to be delivered with AAL-5 as they are with AAL-3/4, or anything else for that matter. The key is the *service class,* not the AAL type. The relationship between class and type is similar to the relationship between changing a tire on a car and the tire iron and jack. The changing of the tire is a service, and the jack and tire iron are tools designed to deliver that service effectively. However, a tire can still be changed using a large pair of pliers and a lever. The service is still provided, and the customer is happy.

The four ITU classes result in six "types" of AAL services, usually seen as AAL-5, AAL-1, and so forth. A null type of AAL, sometimes called AAL-0 (zero), is used for cell-relay services that are inherently cell-based and need no adaptation.

AAL-1 is typically used for carrying existing E-1 and T-1 circuits, although PCM voice can be put directly on without the framing "package." AAL-2 is designed for variable-bit-rate applications, such as video and audio (or even voice), using compression techniques. Compression techniques will automatically make a constant-bit-rate application into a variable-bit-rate application, depending on the effectiveness of the compression technique, which generally runs anywhere between 10:1 to 50:1 with today's methods.

AAL-3 no longer exists. It is always combined with AAL-4, and it was designed to be used for connection-oriented data transport, mainly frame relay. Other protocols could be used, including TCP/IP, despite the fact that IP itself is a connectionless ISO layer 3c protocol. AAL-4 no longer exists as a separate entity either. It was for connectionless data transport, either CLNS (connectionless network services), SMDS (switched multimegabit data services, a BellCore term), or CBDS (connectionless broadband data services, the ETSI word for SMDS).

What does exist in ITU-T documentation today instead of AAL-3 and AAL-4 is AAL-3/4. The main reason that AAL-3 and AAL-4 were combined was actually very simple. It turns out that the only difference between AAL-3 and AAL-4 was in the use of one single 10-bit field. AAL-3 does not use this field at all, being connection-oriented, but AAL-4 needed to use it because *all* connectionless cells sent over a UNI use VPI = 0, VCI = 15. If there were multiple CPE units all generating connectionless cells at the same time (which is only natural to expect), then the ATM switch needed some method of distinguishing them beyond the fields of the cell header (which are identical in the fields that count).

However, because of the compartmentalized nature of the AAL itself, it would have required a completely separate implementation of all the AAL software and/or hardware to produce both AAL-3 and AAL-4. And the only difference would have been whether this 10-bit field was used or not. (Known as the MID field, this 10-bit field's use will be explored in detail later.) The early implementers balked at this scheme and decided that what really should be done was to merge AAL-3 and AAL-4 into AAL-3/4. Whether the 10-bit field is unused or actually used distinguishes the connection-oriented versions of AAL-3/4 from the connectionless versions.

The implementers also realized that there was enormous overhead associated with AAL-3/4. In addition to the usual 5-byte ATM cell header for each 48-byte payload ($5/48$ = 10.4 percent overhead), AAL-3/4 required an additional 4 bytes per cell payload of overhead. This 9-byte total for each 44-byte data traffic payload gave a total overhead of about 20.5 percent ($9/44 = 0.204545...$). This was unacceptable to data users accustomed to overheads of around 5 percent or less for data applications. Once the merging of AAL-3/4 took place, mainly to preserve the 10-bit connectionless MID field, implementers quickly saw that since this field was not used for connection-oriented data services, there was no longer any need to tie the 20.5 percent overhead of the AAL-3/4 type to delivering class C connection-oriented data services. Thus the exclusive use of AAL-3/4 for connectionless services became a common practice.

However, this essentially left a "hole" in the AAL types for class C services. If AAL-3/4 was to be used for class D connectionless services only, despite its high overhead, what should be used for class C connection-oriented data services? It did not take long for implementers to come up with something that was developed as the simple and efficient adaptation layer (SEAL), mainly for the transport of frame-relay and TCP/IP traffic across an ATM network. Endorsed by the ITU-T as AAL-5 but not finalized as an ITU-T standard, the main attraction of SEAL is restoration of the overhead on the ATM network to around 5 percent, about on a par with other data protocols such as frame relay and TCP/IP.

AAL-5 is for simple (no extra AAL headers, short trailer) and efficient (low-overhead) connection-oriented data transfer services. This "newer" AAL type is how TCP/IP traffic (actually, IP) will be sent over ATM networks.

The remainder of this section describes the details of the functions of AAL-1, AAL-2, AAL-3/4, and AAL-5.

AAL-1 services and functions. AAL-1 is for *synchronous* bit streams. The main use will be for taking T-1 and other pleisiochronous digital hierarchy (PDH) frames across the ATM network. AAL-1 provides for the transfer of SDUs with a constant source bit rate and the delivery of these SDUs at the same bit rate. Therefore, it also transfers some form of timing information between source and destination, as well as information about the data structure. AAL-1 also will check for missequencing due to lost or misinserted cells on the connection.

To deliver these services, AAL-1 must perform a series of functions. These include such things as the following: segmentation and reassembly, handling cell delay variation (CDV), handling lost and misinserted cells, recovering the source clock frequency at the destination, and handling bit errors.

Figure 6.3 shows the structure of the AAL-1 payload at the SAR sublayer of the AAL. This 48-byte cell payload (the cell header is not shown) is known as the SAR-PDU and is divided into two main sections. There is a SAR-PDU header (distinct from the ATM cell header, but following directly behind it as cell bytes are sent in sequence), which is 1 byte long, and a SAR-PDU payload, which consists of the remaining 47 bytes. The SAR-PDU header has two fields: the 4-bit

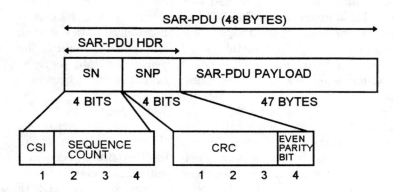

SN   SEQUENCE NUMBER
SNP   SEQUENCE NUMBER PROTECTION
CSI   CONVERGENCE SUBLAYER INDICATOR

Figure 6.3 AAL-1 PDU fields.

sequence number (SN) field and the 4-bit sequence number protection (SNP) field.

The 4-bit SN field also has a structure. The first bit is the convergence sublayer indication (CSI) bit. The default value of this bit is 0. This CSI bit has another use involved with the concept of clock recovery, which will be explored below. The last 3 bits of the SN field form the sequence count field, which cycles between 0 and 7 repeatedly. This results in AAL-1 cells being naturally broken up into 8-cell units, or blocks. The purpose of this field is to detect any lost (if a cell with SN = 3 was last received, only a cell with SN = 4 will be accepted next) or misinserted cells (resulting from undetected cell header errors).

The 4-bit SNP field is also divided into 3-bit and 1-bit fields. The first 3 bits of the SNP field form a CRC field, and the last bit forms an even-parity bit check over the other 7 bits of entire SAR-PDU header.

The use of these fields in the AAL-1 SAR-PDU header means that the receiver is capable of single-bit error correction or multiple-bit error detection. The SAR-PDU header is constructed at the sending side as follows: First, the CSI bit and SN field 3-bit number is set. Then a CRC value across these first 4 bits is computed, and the CRC 3-bit field is set. These 3 bits represent the coefficients of a polynomial of the form $P(x) = x^3 + x + 1$, where the first bit of the SNP field is the highest-order coefficient. Lastly, the sender inserts a bit to yield even parity across the entire SAR-PDU header.

The receiver in AAL-1 has two modes of operation: correction mode and detection mode. These are illustrated in Fig. 6.4. The receiver starts out in correction mode, which is the default mode. In correction mode, the AAL-1 receiver is capable of providing single-bit error correction on the SAR-PDU header (*not* the SAR-PDU payload). If no error is detected in correction mode, meaning that there is a valid SN based on the CRC and parity bit, no action is taken. If a single-bit error is detected

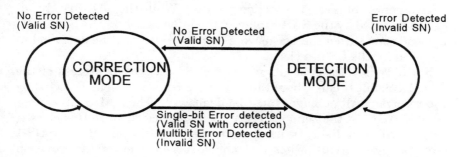

SN = Sequence Number

Figure 6.4   SNP receiver modes.

CRC "Syndrome"	Parity Bit	Action to Take (Current SN+SNP)	Reaction (Next SN+SNP)
Zero	No Violation	No action Declare Valid SN	Stay in Correction Mode
Non-Zero	Violation	Correct single bit Declare Valid SN	Go to Detection Mode
Zero	Violation	Correct Parity Declare SN Valid	Go to Detection Mode
Non-Zero	No Violation	No action* Declare SN Invalid	Go to Detection Mode

* Multibit errors are uncorrectable

SN = Sequence Number
SNP = Sequence Number Protection

Figure 6.5 Correction-mode operations.

and corrected (using the CRC) or a multiple-bit error is detected (same method), the receiver transitions to the detection mode, even if the corrected cell is still accepted and used by the receiver as a now valid cell. In detection mode, all subsequent errored SNs are discarded to prevent "strings" of cells needing constant processing. A valid SN will transition the receiver back to correction mode. The scheme is slightly complicated by the presence of both a CRC and a parity bit. What should happen in each mode when a CRC is good and the parity bit is bad? Or vice versa? A detailed look at receiver actions is shown in Fig. 6.5 (for correction-mode operations) and Fig. 6.6 (for detection-mode operations).

AAL-1, the same as all other AAL compartments, needs a special CS (convergence sublayer) to function properly. While the SAR-PDU header is generated by the SAR sublayer, the information in the SAR-PDU payload comes from the CS above. For class A service, the overwhelming need for the CS is a clock.

Not only is clock generation and recovery a crucial process of the AAL-1 CS, but this is where the lost and misinserted cells detected by the receiver SAR sublayer must be dealt with. The AAL-1 CS cannot possibly request the sender to retransmit lost cells, since this class A service will most likely be used for circuit emulation of DS-0 and DS-1 circuits. These circuit-switching technologies have no defined provision for this retransmission process. And even if it were defined, the delay while cells are resent would be intolerable to the receiver. Instead, the AAL-1 CS must be able to generate "dummy" SAR-PDU payloads. These will obviously not contain the correct data that the receiver

CRC "Syndrome"	Parity Bit	Action to Take (Current SN+SNP)	Reaction (Next SN+SNP)
Zero	No Violation	No action Declare Valid SN	Go to Correction Mode
Non-Zero	Violation	No action Declare Invalid SN	Stay in Detection Mode
Zero	Violation	No action Declare SN Invalid	Stay in Detection Mode
Non-Zero	No Violation	No action Declare SN Invalid	Stay in Detection Mode

SN = Sequence Number
SNP = Sequence Number Protection

Figure 6.6 Detection-mode operations.

expects, but it is better than failing the whole connection. If the dummy payloads are used infrequently enough, they will closely mimic the traditional burst errors seen on DS-1 networks today. The physical transport bit error rate of ATM networks should be low enough to allow this method to be used. Dummy payload bits for DS-1s are to be set to 1, and dummy payload bits for structured video services (i.e., without the DS-1 frame) are currently undefined.

Cell delay variation (CDV) is handled by means of a buffer. In other words, the SAR-PDU payloads at the receiver are kept in a buffer that is always filling with new SAR-PDU payloads that arrive at a slightly variable rate (depending on ATM network node processing delay). The buffer is emptied to the non-ATM equipment at the receiver at a steady rate. It is like a "leaky bucket" in reverse, so to speak. The AAL-1 CS must invent dummy bits in the event of a buffer underflow (empty buffer) and drop an entire buffer's content in the case of a overflow (full buffer).

AAL-1 clock recovery. An important aspect of the AAL-1 CS function is the concept of clock recovery at the receiver. The whole idea of the timing relationship between a source and destination in class A (and class B) services may be interpreted as a fixed number of bits going *into* to the ATM network per unit time at the sending side of the connection and the *same* number of bits coming *out* of the ATM network per unit time at the receiving side of the connection. For a DS-1 circuit emulation service (class A), the number of bits is 1,544,000 bits per second (1.544 Mbps). While some *jitter* (variability of bit arrival times) is permissible at the receiver, ATM networks cannot just be late in sending a couple of bits. The bits are always organized into 47-byte units in AAL-1, which means the jitter at the sender and receiver *must* be in units of $47 \times 8 = 376$ bits. This means that if even one cell is delayed by a sender in a second, the timing jitter is about 24 parts per million (ppm) (calculated as 376/1,544,000). To successfully emulate a circuit in the North American or ITU digital hierarchy, however, timing jitter must be limited to ± 50 ppm. Two cells delayed by a sender in 1 second just about equals this.

Thus the whole concept of circuit emulation across an ATM network is based on establishing a consistent delay across the ATM network characterized by a variable delay (due to the ATM switch nodal processing delay) on the part of the network and variable delay in the sender's generation of bits (due to the pleisiochronous nature of DS-1s and the like). Buffering is part of the solution to this problem, but not the whole answer in any case. It would clearly be better not to rely on a full or empty buffer to detect delay variations, which would only be capable of indicating the presence of delay variation. It would be much more helpful to find a way not merely to indicate that a cell is late (expected arrival time less than actual arrival time) but to indicate just *how late it is*.

Fortunately, AAL-1 provides two methods of providing a receiver with this information. The first is known as the *synchronous residual time stamp (SRTS) method,* and the second is the *adaptive clock method.* The adaptive clock method is CDV detection by means of the receive buffer fill level outlined above and is limited to allowing the receiver a means of compensating for timing differences in a very rough fashion. Only general descriptions of this method exist.

The more promising approach uses the SRTS. It actually provides a way for a sender to time stamp a block of AAL-1 cells (a group of 8) and for the receiver to determine how far off the actual block arrival time is from the expected time, given a totally consistent delay across the ATM network. This lets the receiver know not only that a cell is late (for example), but exactly how late it has arrived, based on the sender's residual time stamp (RTS). Of course, both sender and receiver must have access to a common reference clock signal (stratum 3 or better), or else this method cannot possibly work. (Actually, using this method without synchronized clocks is defined but not fully standardized or even detailed.)

This clock recovery is done by a 4-bit residual time stamp (RTS) field sent over a 3008-bit AAL-1 sequence or block (3008 bits = 8 bits/byte $\times$ 47 bytes/SAR-PDU $\times$ 8 SAR-PDUs/block), which is used with the ATM network clock to duplicate the originator's clock timing at the receiver. In this synchronous residual time stamp (SRTS) method, 4 bits are pulled out of the CS indicator *odd cells* to form the residual time stamp (RTS) field. It is called a *residual* time stamp because the absolute sending time is not actually put into the SAR-PDU. Since the sending clock must "tick" at known intervals and the connection setup parameters convey this frequency of ticking information to the receiver when the connection is first established, both ends of the connection know how often a cell is supposed to arrive. It is the difference (or *residual* part) of this expected sending time from the *actual* sending time that is encoded in the RTS field.

The 4-bit RTS is sent in the CSI bit position (i.e., first bit following the cell header, the initial bit of the SAR-PDU header). The SN field provides 8 potential bits in each block of AAL-1 cells (0 to 7 count). Four of these bits are used for the RTS, and the other 4 are for other uses (only one is standardized; if unused, these bits must be set to 0). The 4 bits used for the RTS are sent in the SAR-PDUs corresponding to SN values of 1, 3, 5, and 7 (i.e., the *odd* SNs). The most significant bit of the RTS is sent in the SAR-PDU header with an SN of 1.

There is more to clock recovery in AAL-1 than variations in when a sender is transmitting cells. Clock recovery must account for an ATM network phenomenon known as the *cell delay variation*. This is handled by a method called ATM *network conditioning*. More details will be covered later, since this is a crucial aspect of providing class A and class B (the timing-sensitive services) services on ATM networks.

AAL-1 structured data transfer (SDT).   There is one other feature of AAL-1 that needs to be detailed. This is known as *structured data transfer* (*SDT*). The use of SDT must be explicitly stipulated when an AAL-1 connection is set up on an ATM network. SDT involves the sending of partially filled cells. It is a general truth about the ATM protocol stack that only full cells are sent. This is the first time there has been an exception to this "rule," and there will be others.

SDT allows the incoming bit stream that the sender places in the SAR-PDU payload to be sent out without waiting for enough input bits to accumulate to fill up a whole cell. This is a method of maintaining the timing relationship between source and destination and cutting down on sender timing jitter. It is also the only really effective way around the problem of "voice packetization delay" discussed earlier.

To employ SDT, a sending AAL-1 uses a special form of the SAR-PDU called the *P format*. The structure and operation of the SAR-PDU that have been described up to now occur in the *non-P format*. This is the only standard use for the even (0, 2, 4, 6) SAR-PDU payloads of the 8-cell AAL-1 block. If SDT is not used, these bits are set to 0000. When SDT is used, a 1 bit in the even SAR-PDU CSI field indicates use of the P format of the SAR-PDU itself. Since SDT use must be stipulated at connection setup time, no data stream indication is necessary. However, the P format is used only when needed in the 0, 2, 4, and 6 cells in the block, and only some CSI bits in the even cells will be set to 1 (P format) and maybe even none. However, if the bits are 0000 when SDT is *not* used, it follows that any non-0000 value (which is not an error) may indicate the use of SDT.

When SDT is employed, the odd cells (1, 3, 5, and 7) of the AAL-1 block still have the non-P format, meaning that the SAR-PDU payload must be a full 47 bytes long. The even cells (0, 2, 4, and 6) in the block may have an extra field in the SAR-PDU payload, depending on whether the CSI bit is set to 1 or not. This is the P format. In the P format, the first byte of the SAR-PDU payload is not user data when the CSI bit is set to 1, but rather a 1-byte pointer field. This 8-bit pointer field consists of a 7-bit offset field and a 1-bit reserved field for future use (the initial bit). The non-P-format and P-format SAR-PDUs are shown in Fig. 6.7.

The 7-bit offset pointer, which can have values between 0 and 128, is set to the value of the offset in bytes between the pointer byte and the *start* of the "live" bytes in the SAR-PDU payload. Valid values are 0 to 93, where 93 indicates that the SAR-PDU is full. The range 0 to 93 does not seem to fit in, but it really does. The non-P format must be used in the odd SAR-PDUs (1, 3, 5, and 7). These SAR-PDUs must be 47 bytes long. The P format *may* be used in the even (0, 2, 4, and 6) SAR-PDUs depending on the value of the CSI bit. These SAR-PDUs may be 46 or 47 bytes long. If they are 47 bytes long and all 47 bytes are filled with user data, the P format need not be used. If less than 47 bytes of data are available to be sent, then the P format is used, and the SAR-PDU payload is only 46 bytes long.

This adds up to 93 bytes (47 + 46 bytes), and the pointer must count the non-P-format bytes (fixed at 47) in the next (odd) SAR-PDU. It must be the next SAR-PDU, because the "0" SAR-PDU starts off a block, but

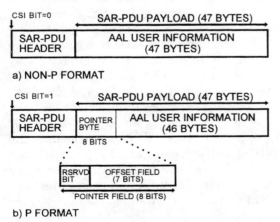

a) NON-P FORMAT

b) P FORMAT

Figure 6.7   Non-P and P AAL-1 formats.

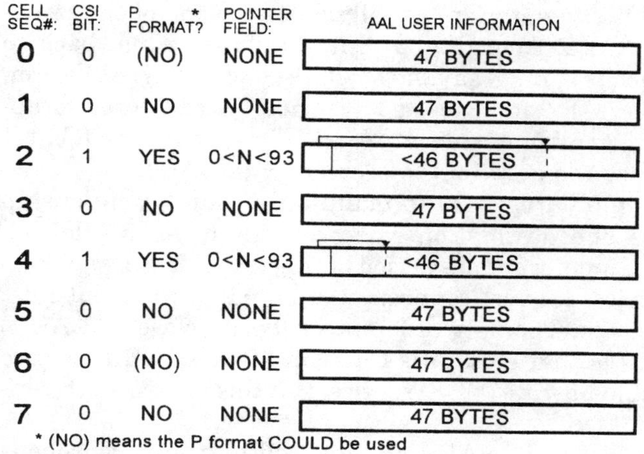

CELL SEQ#:	CSI BIT:	P FORMAT? *	POINTER FIELD:	AAL USER INFORMATION
0	0	(NO)	NONE	47 BYTES
1	0	NO	NONE	47 BYTES
2	1	YES	0<N<93	<46 BYTES
3	0	NO	NONE	47 BYTES
4	1	YES	0<N<93	<46 BYTES
5	0	NO	NONE	47 BYTES
6	0	(NO)	NONE	47 BYTES
7	0	NO	NONE	47 BYTES

* (NO) means the P format COULD be used

Figure 6.8 SDT usage in AAL-1 blocks.

no non-P-format SAR-PDU can be sent until the "1" SAR-PDU. Thus the alternating odd and even cells form units of 93 bytes (with CSI = 1 in the even cells) and 94 bytes (with CSI = 0 in the odd cells). Figure 6.8 shows the possible uses of SDT across an 8-cell AAL-1 block.

An unsolved problem with SDT is the fact that sometimes cells are lost in AAL-1 and special "dummy" payloads are invented to prevent equipment failures at the receiving end. However, if an even SAR-PDU payload is lost with SDT in use, the receiver cannot check the status of the CSI bit and determine just how many live data bytes were lost along with the cell. A possible solution is to employ the P format in some predefined manner, but nothing has been decided.

SDT and SRTS are both allowed to be used at the same time. Since SRTS uses the odd cells and SDT uses the even cells of an 8-cell AAL-1 block, both methods still work with no conflicts. AAL-1 is expected to be widely used for carrying existing DS-1s across ATM networks, especially as time goes by and *only* ATM is available to link remote sites together. The situation is not so optimistic with the next AAL.

AAL-2 services and functions. From the very solid and real world of AAL-1 (most public ATM service providers plan to offer circuit emulation services with AAL-1 early in their implementation plans), this section moves on to the misty and speculative world of AAL-2. This AAL was designed to support class B services (such as compressed audio and video), but one aspect of this intention has proved to be a major obstacle. It is not only a question of standardizing the AAL-2 mechanisms but also of defining just exactly what they should be. In fact, the effort has proved so difficult that two amazing things have happened to AAL-

2. First, the ITU-T documentation actually deleted some of the previous work done on AAL-2 from the current standards. This "back to square one" approach is rare, to say the least. Second, the ATM Forum, after grappling with AAL-2 for over a year, seriously considered scrapping the whole thing in favor of a new "AAL-6." This effort failed, but it illustrates the impact and scope of the problem with AAL-2.

The problem is simply this: how to maintain a timing relationship between the source and destination when no bits at all are flowing between them for an indeterminate period of time. AAL-2 is designed to deliver class B service, that is, connection-oriented, variable-bit-rate, timing-sensitive service. The only difference between class A (AAL-1) and class B (AAL-2) is that class A is constant-bit-rate (CBR) service and class B is variable-bit-rate (VBR) service. But this makes all the difference.

The timing information in AAL-1 is conveyed by the synchronous residual time stamp (SRTS) method and can be combined with structured data transfer (SDT). Both methods can be used with a few other actions at the receiver to ensure that the end-to-end delay across the network remains constant (required for circuits). However, both methods work because of the constant flow of cells from source to destination. There were plenty of bits available for the sender to put timing information into the data stream.

Not with AAL-2, however. The use of compression means that even a constant-bit-rate source (e.g., digitized video scan lines) becomes variable depending on the efficiency of compression. For example, a video camera pointed at a rapidly changing scene may generate, with the most modern compression techniques, about 10 percent of the bits generated without compression (i.e., a 10:1 compression ratio). If the scene is a simple blue backdrop, however, the compression is highly efficient, so less than 2 percent of the uncompressed bits need be sent across the network (i.e., a 60:1 compression ratio).

Thus, where an AAL-1 application could package up 3008 bits in an 8-cell block over and over, consistently, and so use this to convey the SRTS information, an AAL-2 application may only be sending about 300 (10:1 compression) or maybe even only 50 (60:1 compression) bits. These 50 bits (about 6 bytes), or even the 300 bits (about 38 bytes), do not come close to filling up an SAP-PDU payload. Obviously, the cells for AAL-2 must be sent partially filled in this case. But this is not the only complication. Once a video source has sent the compressed equivalent of "showing a blue background," there is no need to send *anything* else until the situation changes. This encoding of *changes* in the video data stream is the essence of newer compression schemes such as the second compression method from the ISO Motion Picture Experts Group (MPEG-2).

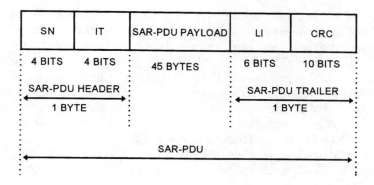

CRC CYCLIC REDUNDANCY CHECK   PDU   PROTOCOL DATA UNIT
IT   INFORMATION TYPE   SAR   SEGMENTATION AND REASSEMBLY
LI   LENGTH INDICATOR   SN   SEQUENCE NUMBER

Figure 6.9   AAL-2 PDU fields.

MPEG-2 will be standardized as N0601. MPEG-2 is so important when discussing possible VBR video (and the audio soundtrack accompanying the video portion) that current proposals concerning AAL-2 are firmly divided along two lines: those which specifically address MPEG-2 as the user of AAL-2 and those for other VBR video and audio techniques. A full discussion of MPEG-2 is beyond the scope of this section.

All this work means that the AAL-2 cell structure still has not been well defined. Figure 6.9 shows an example AAL-2 SAR-PDU structure. It would include a sequence number (SN) field and CRC field with the same functions as the equivalent fields in AAL-1. It would have a length indicator (LI) field for partially filled cells. The information type (IT) would provide a way of distinguishing and processing video, audio, and voice cells. In fact, this field may include an indication of the beginning, continuation, and end of message segments when AAL-2 is used to transfer data units that are larger than an AAL-2 SAR-PDU payload. The need for a length indicator (LI) is less obvious. However, since the timing between source and destination is still critical, the sender may need to send partially filled cells due to the variable bit rate of the source.

Many proposals for AAL-2 structures have recently addressed only MPEG-2 use. Many revolve around the generation and recovery of clock (timing) information at the receiver over the variable-delay ATM network. This *dejittering* function is provided by means of the SSCS in AAL-2, but the problem with doing this is a subtle one. MPEG-2 has plenty of timing information in its own data stream. In fact, the MPEG-2 data stream is made up of a large number of fixed-length blocks (sent at odd intervals) and any number of blocks representing a source time stamp. So far this all sounds good for the ATM network, but it is not. The problem is that the timing information in MPEG-2 expects to be sent on a network with a totally consistent delay, which, of course, ATM cannot provide. The ATM network can *compensate* for these variable delays, but it cannot make them disappear, which is what MPEG-2 expects. Therefore, the problem remains: What should be the relationship between MPEG-2 timing and ATM timing? This issue of MPEG-2 clock recovery remains an open item with no clear solution.

Some proposals have pointed out that MPEG-2 could be sent much more easily over a CBR class A service using AAL-1 than with any VBR class B service AAL-2. This is due to the timing information already present in MPEG-2 and the fixed length of many of the MPEG-2 data units. But this merely brings up new problems. For example, a VBR video application that is *not* based on MPEG-2 still needs to be addressed. And should the situation be allowed to develop to the point that MPEG-2 compressed video is carried as a CBR class A service and yet other compressed video streams are carried as VBR class B?

All in all, AAL-2 remains an area of high activity. When it comes to AAL-2, the term *for future study* is especially apt.

AAL-3/4 services and functions. AAL-1 and AAL-2 are intended for the use of timing-sensitive, connection-oriented services. These services have a host of applications that they may potentially support, from circuit emulation to compressed video, but the vast majority of applications requiring the services of most ATM networks will not fall into these categories. The overwhelming number of applications on ATM networks, especially initially, will be data applications. Data applications will be more forgiving of timing differences than voice or video applications. It is true that data applications may have widely varying delay requirements: shorter delay for real-time or transaction-processing applications, and longer delay for file-transfer or batch-processing applications. However, all these applications will be relatively robust to the effects of delay variation. It does not matter a lot to a file-transfer application if the first record has a network delay of 20 ms and the next record has a network delay of 50 ms, because the file-transfer protocol is not expecting or demanding a fixed delay all the time. All ATM networks will provide response times well within the limits of even the most demanding real-time applications even with delay variations. (This is so because the nodal delays in ATM networks are a much smaller percentage of propagation delays than they ever were in the past.)

AAL-3 and AAL-4 were the AALs meant to deliver data services to ATM network data users in connection-oriented (AAL-3) and connectionless (AAL-4) environments. The days of AAL-3 and AAL-4 as separate entities are over. AAL-3 was originally planned to be a means of providing connection-oriented data services, such as frame relay, over ATM networks, but there are now proposals for doing this much more efficiently than with the whole of AAL-3. There were always many more parts in common between AAL-3 and AAL-4 than significant differences. Both took variable-length frames or data units and broke them into cells.

The original structure of the AAL-3 SAR-PDU is shown in Fig. 6.10. Although AAL-3 has been merged with AAL-4 to form AAL-3/4, the reason this was done is shown in Fig. 6.10. The specific fields and their functions will be discussed more thoroughly below, but in AAL-3, there was a 10-bit field labeled in Fig. 6.10 as "RES." This "reserved" field was unused by AAL-3 but still had to be present to round out the SAR-PDU header to 2 bytes. AAL-4 used this field, as will be detailed below also. It was not considered practical to implement two different versions of AAL hardware and software just based on whether a single 10-bit field was active or not. So AAL-3 was merged into AAL-3/4.

AAL-3/4 is a major AAL for data in ATM. Great efforts have been made to detail the structure of these SAR-PDUs and the CS-PDUs that "feed" them. Because of AAL-3/4's importance, especially in the area of connectionless data services, considerable space will be spent on it.

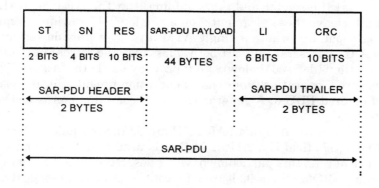

CRC CYCLIC REDUNDANCY CHECK   PDU PROTOCOL DATA UNIT
ST   SEGMENT TYPE   SAR SEGMENTATION AND REASSEMBLY
LI   LENGTH INDICATOR   SN   SEQUENCE NUMBER
RES RESERVED

Figure 6.10 AAL-3 PDU fields.

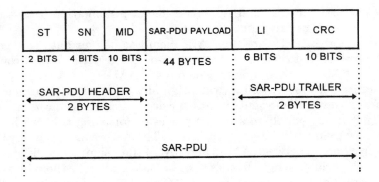

CRC CYCLIC REDUNDANCY CHECK   PDU PROTOCOL DATA UNIT
ST   SEGMENT TYPE   SAR SEGMENTATION AND REASSEMBLY
LI   LENGTH INDICATOR   SN   SEQUENCE NUMBER
MID MULTIPLEXING IDENTIFIER

Figure 6.11   AAL-3/4 PDU fields.

Figure 6.11 shows the structure of the AAL-3/4 SAR-PDU. There is a 2-byte header and trailer, leaving only 44 bytes per cell for the actual SAR-PDU payload itself. This means that AAL-3/4 has the highest overhead of any AAL yet defined. The need for the high overhead is due to the ambitious services and functions that AAL-3/4 must provide, especially concerning connectionless services. In addition to taking a variable-length data unit and dividing it into 44-byte SAR-PDU payloads at the sender and reassembling it at the receiver, AAL-3/4 must interleave these "segments" on a single UNI (providing a multiplexing capability where a single ATM layer can provide services to many AAL-3/4 users), support both "message" and "streaming" modes of operation (defined below), and provide for both "assured" and "nonassured" operation (*nonassured* operation provides for no resending of errored PDUs). A general view of these functions is shown in Fig. 6.12.

The fields of the AAL-3/4 SAR-PDU are defined as follows: The *segment type* (*ST*) field is a 2-bit field that is used to indicate where in a sequence of cells this particular payload lies. ST = 10 is for beginning of message (BOM), ST = 00 is used for continuation of message (COM), ST = 01 is for end of message (EOM), and ST = 11 is for a single-segment message (SSM). An SSM is a message that contains the entire data unit sent inside a single SAR-PDU payload. The ST fields are used to reassemble the cells into the original CS-PDU at the receiving end.

The *sequence number* (*SN*) *field* is a 4-bit field that allows the SAR-PDUs to be numbered in a repeating 0-to-15 cycle. The SN field will

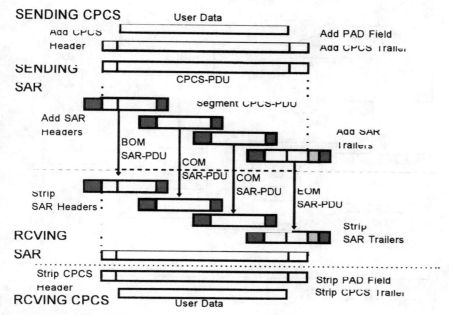

Figure 6.12   AAL-3/4 functions.

increment *only* if the cell belongs to a particular AAL/ATM connection. This gives the receiver a means of detecting lost or misinserted cells. The sender has a choice of starting a SAR-PDU sequence from BOM to EOM with any number from 0 to 15.

However, if the SN field only increments if the cell payload belongs to a particular connection, and many simultaneous connections are allowed to share a single AAL-3/4 (e.g., each router in a user's building having its own AAL-3/4 data stream), how are the sender and receiver to tell them apart? They cannot use the VPI/VCI field values from the cell header, because the ATM cell header does not exist at the AAL. And the problem is not sharing ATM connections but many AAL-3/4 users sharing the AAL itself. The answer is provided by the multiplexing identifier (MID) field.

The *multiplexing identifier (MID) field* is a 10-bit field (giving 1024 possible values) that allows for the multiplexing of many simultaneous segmentations of PDUs by a single AAL-3/4. Each variable-length PDU entering the AAL is assigned a unique MID by the sender. The PDUs are segmented at the same time to avoid unacceptable delays on the part of some AAL users while a sequence of cells is sent from one AAL user. With the use of the MID field, these SAR-PDUs may be interleaved for the more efficient sending of these SAR-PDUs. The whole concept is illustrated in Fig. 6.13.

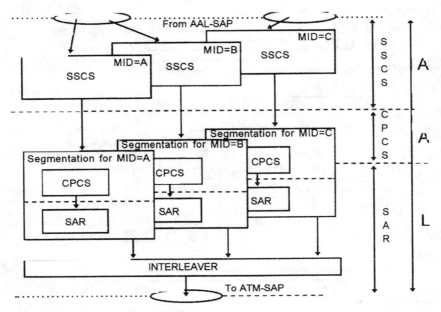

Figure 6.13 AAL-3/4 sender multiplexing.

Note that AAL-3 did not use the MID field. This meant that AAL-3, by itself, was not capable of supporting this whole process, and each AAL user had to be mapped to a unique VPI/VCI connection. This was not much of a handicap for AAL-3, since it was only for connection-oriented data services in the first place. It was *not* good for AAL-4 connectionless services, however. All data had to flow across the UNI with the same connection VPI/VCI number (the connection for connectionless services). Thus the MID method was developed to allow multiplexing of these AAL *users* without separate connections. Of course, this ultimately doomed AAL-3 as a separate AAL. There was no need to provide all the rest of the overhead if the MID field was ignored in AAL-3.

ATM networks multiplex cells from various sources such as voice and video and data. Data traffic *itself* may be multiplexed over ATM, however. Consider a building with four local area networks (LANs), one on each floor of the building. Clearly, the ATM interface must be able to multiplex all four data streams as interspersed cells; otherwise, unacceptable delays may be experienced by some LAN users. The MID field in AAL-3/4 provides for this. Distributed MID assignment algorithms must be standardized to prevent MID number "collisions." Until then, only one MID may be used. It is just a number the receiver uses to associate these AAL-3/4 cells. SMDS-like connectionless service may use only one MID, but 16 will be permitted upon this

Segment Type	Permissible Value
BOM	44
COM	44
EOM	4-44, 63*
SSM	8-44

Figure 6.14   Length-indication values.

* 63 is used in the ABORT-SAR-PDU

standardization of the MID allocation. The ETSI CBDS standard is more optimistic and will allow for 128 simultaneous MIDs as well. An AAL-3/4 implementation is not required to support all values on the entire 1024-value MID range. Current standards do not specify MID limits or any distributed MID assignment algorithm. MID assignment by means of a signaling protocol enhancement or "dynamic negotiation process" is being considered.

Use of the MID field is allowed for connection-oriented services using AAL-3/4. But the use of AAL-3/4 for connection-oriented services just to provide this capability will not be common. If the MID field is not used, it is encoded as all 0s.

The *length indicator (LI) field* is a 6-bit field indicating the length of the active data in the SAR-PDU payload. The LI is present in all segment types (BOM, etc.). However, it only has values other than 44 (indicating a full BOM or COM SAR-PDU payload) in the EOM (ST = 01) and SSM (ST = 11) segment types. The permitted values for the LI field are shown in Fig. 6.14. The reason for the minimum value of 4 for the EOM segment type is that even if there are no user data at all in this SAR-PDU, the CPSC trailer is 4 bytes long. And the reason for the minimum value of 8 in the SSM is that the CPCS header is also 4 bytes long. For these two types, EOM and SSM, the LI field indicates the number of "live" bytes in the SAR-PDU, including any AAL-3/4 CPCS headers and trailers.

The value of 63 in the EOM needs further explanation. This value makes the EOM a special "abort" segment type. Any sequence of SAR-PDUs can be halted before the normal ending by sending an abort SAR-PDU to the receiver (perhaps in response to a "break" indication to the sending application). This is a normal EOM SAR-PDU structure with the payload field ignored (it may be set to all 0s) and the LI field set to 63 (all 1s).

The CRC field is a 10-bit field on all bits of the SAR-PDU, including the header, payload, and LI field bits.

AAL-3/4 convergence sublayer. The "filling" of all the SAR-PDU payload fields is taken from the CPCS-PDU, the layer above the SAR layer in AAL-3/4, just as in all OSI-compliant protocol stacks. Figure 6.15 shows

CPI Encoding	BAsize Field Meaning	Length Field Meaning
All Zeros	Buffer Size is in bytes	Length of CPCS-PDU payload in bytes
All Other Values	For further study	For further study

Figure 6.15   CPI field encoding.

a simple example of this process in which a variable-length frame from a data application is broken up into a BOM, COM, and EOM segment sequence. This CPCS-PDU has its own header and trailer fields.

The *common part indicator (CPI) field* is a 1-byte field that will be used for the receiver to properly interpret the lengths and presence of the other fields in the CPCS-PDU header and trailer. Other uses include the counting units for the header and trailer fields, performance and fault monitoring, MID allocation, and even OAM messages. Nothing has been standardized beyond the use of the value $x00$ to indicate the structure shown and the use of the byte (octet) as a counting unit.

The *beginning tag (Btag) field* is a 1-byte field paired with the *ending tag (Etag)* and used to associate the proper BOM and EOM segments. The receiver checks the value of the reassembled CPSC-PDU to make sure the Btags and Etags, which are chosen by the sender, match. If they do not, this indicates an error condition. Btag and Etag values do not have to be used incrementally but may be chosen at random by a sender.

The *buffer allocation size (BAsize) field* is a 2-byte field used to inform the receiver of the maximum buffer space required to store the reassembled CPCS-PDU in memory (16 bits = 64K = maximum size of an IP datagram). The CPCS-PDU itself must not be larger than the value encoded here, for obvious reasons. This field gives a further check on missing or misinserted SAR-PDUs. If COM segments are lost or misinserted and MID is not supported, then the Btag in the BOM will still match the Etag in the EOM, but the message will still be in error. Rather than waste time processing a message that may be in error (and there is no CRC on the CPCS-PDU itself), the BAsize will not match the reassembled CPCS-PDU, giving the receiver an error indication.

There is a further reason for implementing a BAsize field for data applications. It addresses a real limitation of data protocols such as TCP/IP that also break up PDUs into many smaller units. The only indication available in TCP/IP to tell a receiver that there is "more to come" (i.e., the data are not complete yet and should not be processed as a separate and complete unit) is the "more" bit in the IP header. If the more bit is set, received data is buffered at the receiver until the more bit is turned off. Then the data units are concatenated and presented to the higher layer for further processing. However, use of a single bit for this purpose, although extremely efficient, has some drawbacks. First, there is no way to indicate just how many "pieces" the receiver should expect. It only says "this is the first of many," "this is the next of many," and so on until "this is the last of many." But how many? There is no way to tell a receiver in TCP/IP. A receiver has no way to judge just how big a TCP segment that starts arriving will ultimately be. The second reason the more bit method is a drawback is because these fragments must be reassembled when complete. If they are stored in contiguous memory, this process will be much more efficient than when the fragments are scattered through memory. This happens all the time when memory is allocated as a series of unrelated memory requests. And the memory may be virtual memory, meaning the fragments may even end up on a hard disk at some point. All in all, knowing the size of the total unit as soon as the first unit is received, as in AAL-3/4, is vastly more efficient for the reassembly process, both in terms of time and errors.

The *padding (PAD) field* is from 1 to 3 bytes long, depending on the length of the AAL-SDU field itself. The AAL-SDU will be padded to an integral 32-bit unit length. This ensures that the trailer fields align on 32-bit boundaries for efficient hardware processing. These bytes may be set to all 0, but the receiver will ignore them whatever their value. For transporting the TCP/IP protocol stack (i.e., IP datagrams), this field is never used, since IP datagrams always align on a 32-bit boundary to begin with.

The *alignment (AL) field* is a 1-byte field that forces the CPCS-PDU trailer to be a unit that is exactly 32 bits (4 bytes) long, again for efficiency of processing purposes. This field must be encoded as all 0s.

The *Etag field* is a 1-byte field containing the same value as the Btag field defined above.

The *length field* is a 2-byte field that contains the total length of the CPCS-PDU payload field, which is the length of the AAL-SDU. The only unit supported is the byte (CPI = 0). This field is necessary due to the presence of the variable-length PAD field in the CPCS-PDU payload.

What has been described so far is AAL-3/4 *message mode*. In this mode, before the AAL-PDU can be put inside a CPCS-PDU and the whole thing broken up into SAR-PDUs for sending across the ATM network, the entire PDU must be present in a memory buffer somewhere on the sending side. This is only natural. After all, the sending AAL-3/4 process must put a header and a trailer on the data, and the header includes the BAsize field. In order for this field to be filled in with the correct amount, the AAL on the sending side obviously must know exactly how long the data unit in its entirety is. But these units may be up to 64,000 or more bytes long. Perhaps it would be more efficient to break up a data unit into smaller units as the bytes accumulate (e.g., 200 bytes at a time) and send these bytes right out. The receiving process would use the information in the header of the first unit to arrive (e.g., the IP header "more" bit) to put the whole data unit back together at the receiver. The only possible thing that can go wrong in this scheme is that a partial data unit will start to be sent (e.g., 200 bytes) and then the sender may find that the subsequent units are in error or even missing. In this case, an abort SAR-PDU is used to tell the receiver that the current sequence of already received SAR-PDUs is to be discarded. This "pipelining function" is the main feature of AAL-3/4 *streaming mode*. It is more complex to implement than AAL-3/4 message mode. Not surprisingly, this mode is not seen as being used much, nor has it generated much excitement.

AAL-5 (SEAL) services and functions.   The last AAL type to consider is AAL-5. Sometimes referred to as the *simple and efficient adaptation layer (SEAL)*, especially in older documentation, AAL-5 dispenses with most of the sequencing and integrity checking of AAL-3/4, shifting this burden to the end users of the ATM network. This also strips off the crippling overhead of AAL-3/4, bringing the 20 percent or so overhead of AAL-3/4 more in line with the few percent overhead that data network users (and service providers) are used to. It also aligns better with the 32-bit (4-byte) and 64-bit (8-byte) architectures of current processors. The 44 bytes of AAL-3/4 payload were a forced fit to this architecture, but the 48-byte payloads of AAL-5 fit nicely into either, both 4 and 8 being factors of 48 but not 44. AAL-5 is sometimes considered to be a "subset" of AAL-3/4, in the sense that it has the same service and functions. It is still intended for class C traffic (connection-oriented, VBR, timing-insensitive services), and the low overhead associated with AAL-5 has led to it being considered for many other classes of traffic as well. AAL-5 supports only the message mode of operation, and the lack of an MID field makes it unsuitable for any multiplexing at the AAL layer itself.

Intended for point-to-point ATM networks (e.g., router connectivity over an ATM network), it does away with normal AAL-3/4 overhead and complications. It just adds a short trailer to the data unit itself. AAL-5 then simply puts this AAL-5 CPCS-PDU into cells without any overhead fields in the SAR-PDU at all. All AAL-5 overhead is in the last cell of a sequence. Identified by a special PTI code in the cell header, it contains the AAL-5 trailer. Figure 6.16 shows the structure of the AAL-5 SAR-PDU and CPCS-PDU.

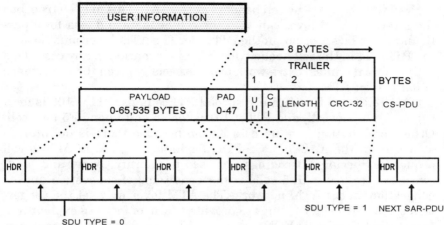

Figure 6.16   AAL-5 PDU fields.

When using AAL-5, the sender must pad the user data (which can be up to 64K long, as in AAL-3/4) with 0 to 47 bytes of padding to force the CPCS-PDU trailer into the last cell of the sequence. That is, the entire AAL-5 trailer *must* be in the last cell of an AAL-5 sequence all by itself. These extra bytes are ignored by the receiver but may be coded as all 0s.

The AAL-5 CPCS-PDU trailer itself has a user-to-user (UU) field [sometimes called the *convergence function (CF) field*] of 1 byte. The UU field can contain information to be transferred transparently to the ATM network between end users of the AAL-5 service. There is a common part indicator (CPI) field of 1 byte that is used to align the entire trailer on a 64-bit boundary (i.e., it is there to make the whole thing 64 bits = 8 bytes long). Further uses are under study. There is a length field of 2 bytes used to indicate the number of bytes in the user information field (excluding the PAD bytes). Finally, there is a CRC-32, a 4-byte error check on the entire CPCS-PDU. The Internet Engineering Task Force (IETF) has stated that the IP protocol from the TCP/IP protocol stack will be sent over ATM networks using AAL-5. This CRC-32 combined with the length field makes the probability of an errored PDU being passed as error-free by a receiver small enough to be ignored in practice.

There is only one stumbling block in the way of using AAL-5 all over the place in ATM networks. Since there is no SAR-PDU overhead at all anymore, just a pure 48-byte payload field, how does the receiver figure out which cell has the CPCS-PDU trailer in it? There are no more BOM-COM indications, and the BAsize is gone from the CPCS-PDU header. AAL-5 gets around this problem by using the ATM cell header itself the provide the receiver with this information.

However, there are no cell headers at the AAL. This may be true, but the receiving ATM layer can scan the cell headers and look for a particular bit to be set or not in the PTI field. The ATM layer must look at the PTI field in the cell headers for OAM information in any case. This is therefore not much extra work to do, especially given the importance of data on an ATM network.

OAM cell flows for ATM use special PTI codings. PTI = 100 is for a segment F5 flow cell, and PTI = 101 is for an end-to-end F5 flow cell. Other combinations are used in AAL-5 because there is no internal structure in the AAL-5 CPCS-PDU for indicating the EOM of a cell sequence. Special PTI codings are used to identify "body" and "end" (with the trailer) AAL-5 cells under conditions of congestion and no congestion on the ATM network. The ATM layer may set the congestion bit in AAL-5 PTI codings to provide a form of forward explicit congestion notification (FECN) over the ATM network. This concept is used in frame-relay networks as well, along with backward explicit congestion notification (BECN), which has no analogous counterpart in ATM networks—yet. The concept of FECN is especially important when ATM networks are used to carry protocols such as TCP/IP. These protocols use a "windowing" method to control the amount of data a sender may send across the network before receiving an acknowledgment. Under congested network conditions, TCP/IP protocols may respond by adjusting window sizes nonsensically. The FECN [known as explicit forward congestion indication (EFCI) in ATM] provided by AAL-5 can be used by the end user TCP/IP applications to prevent this from happening.

Figure 6.17 shows the entire range of codings for the PTI field in the ATM cell header. The main reason that the older 2-bit PT field became a 3-bit PTI field by incorporating the RES bit next to it was to accommodate all these codings for AAL-5.

SAAL: The signaling AAL. Signaling protocols in ATM networks need an adaptation layer as well. This is distinct from the cell-based OAM function seen earlier. These are higher-layer signaling messages similar to SS7 for voice networks and Q.931 for ISDN networks. As designed for special signaling networks, signaling protocols always assume that they will be delivered. Thus they have no robust retransmission, as do many data applications, especially those which run on top of connectionless network layers such as TCP/IP. The signaling AAL, through its own CS known as *service-specific connection-oriented protocol (SSCOP)*, provides connections for this *assured delivery,* which the SAAL requires. AAL-5 will be used as the AAL for signaling protocols.

Each proposed signaling standard for ATM networks will have its own protocol, probably based on LAP-D or LAP-F. For ATM Forum

PTI	MEANING	
000	USER DATA, NO CONGESTION, SDU TYPE = 0	(AAL-5 BODY CELL)
001	USER DATA, NO CONGESTION, SDU TYPE = 1	(AAL-5 END CELL)
010	USER DATA, CONGESTION, SDU TYPE = 0	(AAL-5 BODY CELL)
011	USER DATA, CONGESTION, SDU TYPE = 1	(AAL-5 END CELL)
100	SEGMENT OAM F5 FLOW CELL	
101	END TO END OAM F5 FLOW CELL	
110	RESERVED FOR FUTURE TRAFFIC CONTROL AND RESOURCE MANAGEMENT	
111	RESERVED FOR FUTURE FUNCTIONS	

Figure 6.17   PTI coding.

implementations, the SSCOP will provide support for Q.93B initially and Q.2931 ultimately.

6.2   ATM Services

No one will build an ATM network to provide the services of AAL-3/4 or AAL-5 or any other AAL. Nor will ATM networks be built to provide class A, or class D, or class Y services. Rather, ATM networks will exist to provide services to end users. And end users do not care about classes or AALs or even cells. These are just a means to an end. Users care about end-user services: What can I use the network *for?*

Owing to the ambitious nature of ATM (one unchannelized physical network), the range of services offered by ATM networks will be unprecedented. Data services will be especially well represented. Cell-relay service will just essentially connect "ATM islands" based on private "cell switched" LAN hubs and/or possibly routers. Frame-relay service will offer a cell-based backbone while giving users a familiar variable-length packet interface into the network. Connectionless network access protocol (CLNAP), switched multimegabit network service (SMDS), and connectionless broadband data service (CBDS) are three connectionless protocols for LAN interconnectivity and other connectionless services. Think of SMDS as a U.S. standard, CBDS as the European version, and CLNAP (really CLNS from a service standpoint) as the ITU-T standard to unite them. A new service provided by the ATM Forum definition of ATM is LAN emulation (LANE) service, where the ATM network may connect distant LANs totally transparently to users and applications (as

- CELL RELAY SERVICE (CRS)

- FRAME RELAY BEARER SERVICE (FRBS)

- CONNECTIONLESS NETWORK SERVICE
  (CLNAP/SMDS/CBDS)

- LAN EMULATION SERVICE (LANE)

- AUDIOVISUAL MULTIMEDIA SERVICE (AMS)

- CIRCUIT EMULATION SERVICES (CES)

Figure 6.18   ATM services.

opposed to bridged/routed environments) and even connect separate private ATM networks over an intervening LAN.

Video accompanying audio will be the important "nondata" application for ATM networks, although it will be combined with data in many cases to form multimedia applications. (A concise definition of the term *multimedia* does not exist, but to most observers it means information that is sent over a network not only to be read but also looked at, listened to, and/or both at the same time.) Leased-line "emulation" based on the existing pleisiochronous digital hierarchy (PDH) such as DS-1s and DS-0s will make for more efficient private backbone networks.

Figure 6.18 lists six possible services than an ATM network may need to provide to users. Of course, many more are possible, but even this list may be ambitious at this stage of ATM standardization. Most private ATM networks will be built to provide users with exactly one, or at most two, of these services, with the data services being the most commonly implemented. All are mapped to various classes (A, B C, D, etc.) of service and may be delivered by one (AAL-1 for class A) or more (AAL-3/4 or AAL-5 for class C) AALs. Since these are essentially what people will build ATM networks to deliver and provide, each will be explored in more detail.

6.2.1   Cell-relay service (CRS)

Cell-relay services (CRS to the ATM Forum) will be an important initial offering of public ATM network providers and private ATM network builders. The cells already exist—in the ATM hub or router or multiplexer or even an ATM board in a workstation on the user's premises. The public ATM network service offered would be to connect these local ATM "islands" over larger areas than the private organization may be willing to go or able to afford.

Cell-relay services will not need any of the supporting structures of the AAL itself. Indeed, the whole idea of a "class X" service is to go beyond the definitions of bit rates and so on. CRS will, however, be connection-oriented. All the sender needs to do, however, is to take a 48-byte payload from any higher-layer protocol providing them and add a valid VPI/VCI value in a cell header. Then out it goes. Initially, these CRS connections will be "permanent" (i.e., PVCs, changed with effort and coordination). Sites will be assigned VPIs and perhaps even VCIs, but the VCIs may be changed to provide "mesh" connectivity. These will all be point-to-point connections, at least at the VPI level. True switched virtual circuit (SVC) service for CRS depends on signaling protocol deployments.

While simple in nature, this service will be the easiest for an ATM network provider to implement. The user will be driven by bandwidth-intensive considerations such as multimedia or even heavy client-server database or graphic requirements. The user gets only a very low-delay, high-bandwidth, connection-oriented service, but maybe this is all that is required. The users must make the cell payloads for themselves. No QOS parameters relating to cell delays or timing are supported, since the ATM network is not "doing" anything to the cell payloads except delivering them as they are presented to the ATM layer. Since this involves "only" fixed-length, packetized data, which is well understood on a traffic basis, this offering will expose the ATM network provider to smaller risks than more ambitious service mixes.

6.2.2 Frame-relay bearer services (FRBS)

An important service offered to ATM network users will be the ability to connect frame-relay bearer service (FRBS) networks over the ATM network or even to establish connections that interconnect frame-relay and ATM networks. However, to do this, the FR "core functions" must map into the ATM layers. This is the first example of an *interworking function* [IWF, or sometimes *interworking unit* (IWU)] defined by ATM standards. To support FRBS, the ATM network must provide this IWF at the AAL. For FRBS, the AAL will be AAL-5, with a frame-relay service-specific convergence sublayer (FR-SSCS) placed on top of the CPCS already present in AAL-5. The FR-SSCS will provide a series of validity checks on all frame-relay frames, such as checking that the length of the frame is no more than the maximum negotiated at connection setup time and not less than a minimum length of 5 bytes. The frame also must be an integer number of bytes in length, and the frame-relay data link connection identifier (DLCI) must be assigned and active.

The structure of the frame-relay frame at the FR-SSCS is shown in Fig. 6.19. It resembles the basic core Q.922 frame-relay frame format, but the bits have been reversed for AAL-5 (ATM is "big-endian," MSB first), and there is no CRC-16 (this function is replaced by the AAL-5 CPCS CRC-32). There are no 7E start and end flags or bit stuffing either, as there are in native frame-relay network frames. Two header formats are supported: the mandatory 2-byte frame-relay header and the optional 4 byte-header.

A full discussion of frame-relay frame formats is beyond the scope of this section, but the DLCI is a locally unique connection identifier of 10

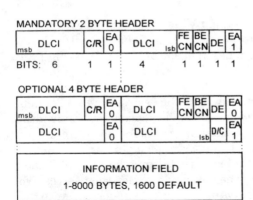

MANDATORY 2 BYTE HEADER

msb DLCI	C/R	EA 0	DLCI lsb	FE CN	BE CN	DE	EA 1

BITS: 6   1   1   4   1   1   1   1

OPTIONAL 4 BYTE HEADER

msb DLCI	C/R	EA 0	DLCI	FE CN	BE CN	DE	EA 0
DLCI		EA 0	DLCI lsb			D/C	EA 1

INFORMATION FIELD
1-8000 BYTES, 1600 DEFAULT

Figure 6.19 Frame-relay SSCS.

(mandatory support) or 23 (optional support) bits. In both cases, the information field is from 1 to 8000 bytes long, with 1600 bytes as the default size. The FR-SSCS first constructs this frame format and then passes it off the AAL-5 CPCS.

The frame-relay header contains a series of "control bits" in addition to the DLCI. A big issue is how these control bits will map to the ATM network equivalents. This is a nontrivial task. The goal of frame-relay–ATM internetworking is to make two frame-relay networks connected by an ATM network in the middle work the same as if the two endpoints were on the same FR network. If there is a function or service mismatch, this may not be the case.

The control bits in the frame-relay frame header are the following:

1. *Discard eligibility (DE) bit.*   If this bit is set to 1, the FR network, under certain conditions, may discard the frame. This is very similar in function and purpose to the CLP bit in the ATM cell header.

2. *Forward explicit congestion notification (FECN) bit.*   If this bit is set to 1, it indicates to all subsequent FR switches on the connection path, and the destination end user CPE as well, that there is congestion on the network along the path that this frame took through the network. The switches and end system may take some action based on this information (e.g., slow down the sender), but nothing has been standardized. This bit is closely related in function and purpose to the PTI field's middle bit in the ATM cell header, which is set for AAL-5 body and end cells depending on congestion.

3. *Backward explicit congestion notification (BECN) bit.*   If this bit is set to 1, it indicates to all previous FR switches and the originating end system that there is congestion on the network along the path that this frame took through the network. Again, the switches and end system may take some action based on this information, but few proposals have even been made. There is no analogous bit in ATM at all, and there is not even any very good place to put it. Thus this bit is ignored

by ATM when set by an FR network and cannot be expressed from the ATM network when traffic is sent onto an FR network.

4. *The command/response (C/R) bit.*   This bit is used for the FR end-points only and is sent transparently through the ATM network.

It would perhaps be nice if *all* the FR control bits could be passed transparently through the ATM network, but this is not a good idea. This is so because there is not just one network between the users anymore, but actually three: the sender's FR network, the ATM network between them, and the receiver FR network. Any of them may be congested or not. Is it really a good idea to tell the sender on the FR network that everything is fine if the ATM network is hopelessly congested? Probably not. Thus some way of mapping an ATM explicit forward congestion indicator (EFCI, the middle bit in the PTI field in AAL-5 values) to the FR FECN is needed, whether the FR networks are actually congested or not.

Current implementation agreements between the ATM Forum and the Frame Relay Forum specify the control bit mapping shown in Fig. 6.20. Transparent transfer of FR control bits by an ATM network is always an option. Generally, from the ATM to FR direction, whatever the FR control bits are in the FR-SSCS frame, that is what they will remain on the receiving FR network.

From FR to an ATM network is more complex. No matter what the FECN was in the original FR frame, it is preserved in the FR-SSCS frame, and the resulting ATM cells always set the EFCI bit in the PTI

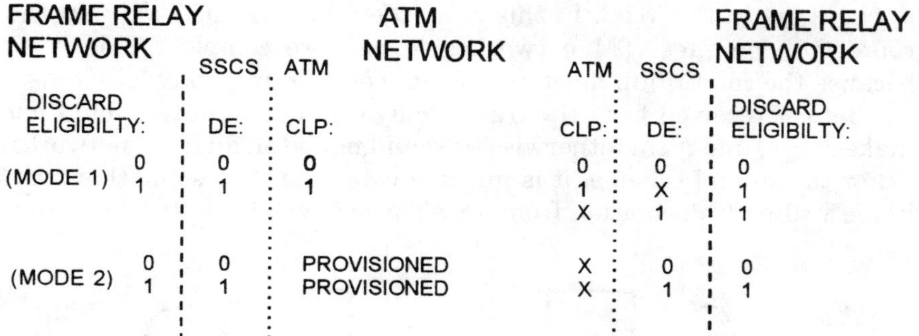

FRAME RELAY NETWORK	SSCS	ATM	ATM NETWORK	ATM	SSCS	FRAME RELAY NETWORK
DISCARD ELIGIBILTY:	DE:	CLP:		CLP:	DE:	DISCARD ELIGIBILTY:
(MODE 1) 0	0	0		0	0	0
1	1	1		1	X	1
				X	1	1
(MODE 2) 0	0	PROVISIONED		X	0	0
1	1	PROVISIONED		X	1	1
FR FECN:	FECN:	EFCI:		EFCI:	FECN:	FR FECN:
0	0	0		0	0	0
1	1	0		1	X	1
				X	1	1
FR BECN:		IGNORED		N/A		

NOTE: "X" MEANS 0 OR 1

Figure 6.20 Mapping FR control bits.

to 0. This use of this bit is for the ATM network only. But note that if an FR frame with FECN = 0 is sent in an ATM cell with EFCI = 0 but an ATM switch sets the EFCI bit to 1, then the receiving FR network will receive an FR frame with the FECN bit set to 1.

For DE to CLP mappings, two modes are defined. In mode 1, the IWF maps the FR DE bit to both the FR SSCS and ATM layer CLP bit as received. On the other side of the network, the CLP bit will "override" the FR-SSCS DE bit setting *if* the CLP bit has been set to 1 by the ATM network. In mode 2, the DE bit is passed transparently in the FR-SSCS frame, regardless of the CLP bit setting.

For connecting frame-relay and ATM networks, two multiplexing schemes [FR data link connection identifiers (DLCIs) to ATM VPI/VCI combinations] exist, as well as two ways to internetwork FR with ATM.

Considering internetworking first, Fig. 6.21 shows one possibility: frame relay to frame relay over an ATM network. One possibility for carrying frame relay over ATM is to just put an ATM network "cloud" between two frame-relay networks. This requires an ATM internetworking unit (IWU), of course. In this case, the two routers with the frame-relay interfaces communicate to other routers on their own FR networks exactly as they did before. However, now traffic between them is sent over the ATM network. Obviously, the IWUs for the FR service must be fully compatible, i.e., either from the same vendor or built to the same (open?) standards.

It is also possible to have a case where an existing frame-relay router network would want to connect to a router (or even a hub) on an ATM network, as in Fig. 6.22. In this case, there is only one IWU, but the router/hub on the ATM network side is more complex. This is so because the router/hub must now handle *both* frame relay (otherwise, the data it received from the frame-relay originator router would not make sense) and ATM (otherwise, it would not be on an ATM network).

For the second scheme, it is important to note that while this technique will get information from an ATM network back and forth to a

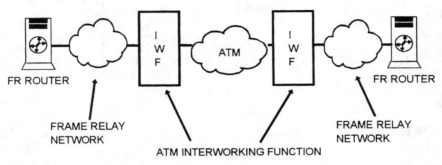

Figure 6.21   Frame relay to frame relay.

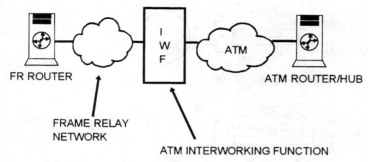

FR ROUTER

ATM ROUTER/HUB

FRAME RELAY
NETWORK

ATM INTERWORKING FUNCTION

Figure 6.22   Frame relay to/from ATM.

frame-relay network, it does not really guarantee that the *services* that use ATM and frame relay will be able to interoperate. What this means is that neither frame relay nor ATM in itself forms a complete protocol stack from user to physical network (i.e., neither forms all seven layers of the OSI-RM). Thus both networks will have other higher layers using them for data transport. However, if the frame relay is putting OSI layer 3 PDUs inside a frame-relay frame (as the Frame Relay Forum proposes) and the ATM network is putting ISO layer 2 logical link control (LLC) frames inside the FR-SSCS frame (as the ATM Forum proposes), users on the two networks will never be able to do something as simple as transfer a file, although bits will flow freely between them. If the IWF is provided by a router using a frame-relay interface, then the IETF allows the higher-layer protocols to be IP, IPX (Novell), or Appletalk.

There are also two ways of mapping FR DLCIs to ATM VPI/VCIs. The first method is to map many FR DCLIs to one VPI (technically, one VCC). There are as many VCIs inside the VPI as there are DLCIs hooked up to it via the IWUs, however. The link identifiers have only local significance and have to be negotiated at call setup time or by subscription for both sides of the IWU. The chief advantage of this approach is that the ATM network functions as a simple crossconnect between the FR networks.

A more complex arrangement is to allow FR DLCIs to map to many VPI/VCI combinations. These mappings are handled by regular ATM switches and must be understood by the IWUs. While much more flexible in approach, this method will not be able to rely on DLCI information to choose a path through the ATM network. Everything is just a VPI/VCI through the network and must be switched like everything else. However, this is an easy way to connect more than two frame-relay networks across an intervening ATM network. The DLCI connections can originate in a frame-relay network and end up in any frame-relay network attached to the ATM network. Link identifier val-

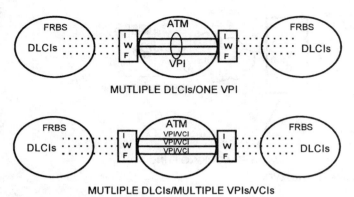

MUTLIPLE DLCIs/ONE VPI

MUTLIPLE DLCIs/MULTIPLE VPIs/VCIs

Figure 6.23   FR DLCI to ATM VPI/VCIs.

ues are still handled as before: local significance, assigned by subscription (PVC), or at call setup time (SVC). Both scenarios are shown in Fig. 6.23.

6.2.3 Connectionless services (CLNS/SMDS/CBDS)

An interesting possibility for ATM network services is transport of the newer LAN interconnectivity services such as SMDS. Switched multi-megabit data services are an early implementation of broadband networking principles from BellCore (Bell Communications Research), the R&D group of the "Baby Bells" carved out of AT&T Bell Labs after the AT&T breakup in 1984. SMDS is sometimes called the "first broadband-ISDN service" or "first ATM service" and is meant to provide connectionless, public LAN internetworking over a metropolitan area (100 km or less). It may be delivered on an ATM network running over SONET. Connectionless broadband data services (CBDS) are the ETSI (European Telecommunications Standards Institute, the "new" CEPT) equivalent, and the ITU-T's connectionless network services (CLNS) with connectionless network access protocol (CLNAP) will supposedly wed them into a standardized whole.

All three are virtually identical and offer customers LAN-like features. *LAN-like* means a fast, connectionless, and non-error-correcting (no retransmissions in the network) service. The philosophy seems to be that since LANs are connectionless networks, the network linking them together should be connectionless also. These will use AAL-3/4 (or maybe even AAL-5 in some instances) for transporting their traffic over an ATM network. The attraction to ATM network providers of SMDS services is that most SMDS offerings will be at the local exchange carrier (LEC) level, leaving it up to a number of players to provide wide-area (>100 km) connectivity for SMDS users.

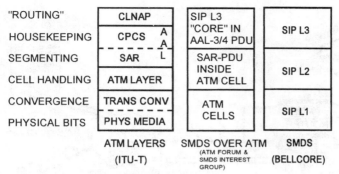

"ROUTING"	CLNAP	SIP L3	
HOUSEKEEPING	CPCS A - - - - - A	"CORE" IN AAL-3/4 PDU	SIP L3
SEGMENTING	SAR L	SAR-PDU INSIDE	SIP L2
CELL HANDLING	ATM LAYER	ATM CELL	SIP L2
CONVERGENCE	TRANS CONV	ATM CELLS	SIP L1
PHYSICAL BITS	PHYS MEDIA	ATM CELLS	SIP L1
	ATM LAYERS (ITU-T)	SMDS OVER ATM (ATM FORUM & SMDS INTEREST GROUP)	SMDS (BELLCORE)

CLNAP: CONN-LESS NETWORK ACCESS PROTOCOL
CPCS: COMMON PART CONVERGENCE SUBLAYER
SAR: SEGMENTATION AND REASSEMBLY
AAL: ATM ADAPTATION LAYER
SIP: SMDS INTERFACE PROTOCOL

Figure 6.24 ATM layers and SMDS layers.

However, SMDS has its own layering system, which is slightly different from ATM layers. This is only natural, since BellCore adapted the SMDS protocol stack from IEEE 802.6 DQDB before the full ATM protocol stack became standardized. Nonetheless, the matchup between BellCore's SMDS layers (SIP, the SMDS interface protocol) and the ITU-T's ATM layers is a good one. They differ slightly only because BellCore began "filling in the gaps" of the existing ATM standards long before they were addressed by the ITU-T. Figure 6.24 shows the relationship of SMDS layers and IEEE 802.6 DQDB layers to ATM layers.

Although SMDS may be an official ATM service offering, there are important issues to consider because of the anticipation of ATM standards on the part of BellCore. These deserve a section of their own. The rest of this section focuses on the provision of connectionless services in general on an ATM network.

Connectionless ATM service.   Since ATM networks are inherently connection-oriented, any connectionless service must still be mapped to a connection, whether the end user sees it as a connection or not. ATM handles this by assigning VPI = 0, VCI = 15 as the default connection for connectionless services over a UNI. This means that *any* user of CLNS on the UNI sends cells with VPI = 0, VCI = 15 in the local ATM network switch and receives cells from the switch on the outbound VPI = 0, VCI = 15 connection. At first glance, it seems that this cannot possibly work. How can *all* cells from two different users (who may be attached to the same CPE, as with a building with routers on two different floors, or who may be different customer sites on the same UNI) send and receive on the same connection? Consider a network arrangement as shown in Fig. 6.25. User *A* and user *B* both have CLNS over

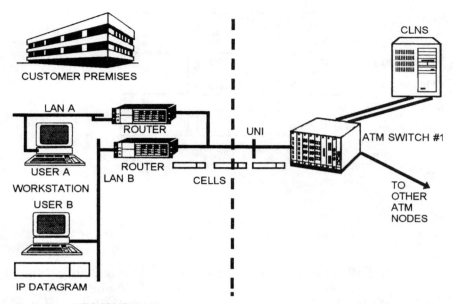

Figure 6.25 ATM CLNS arrangement.

the UNI to ATM network switch 1. Both cannot send connectionless cells at the same time on VPI = 0, VCI = 15 (but both will have separate VPIs by site for connection-oriented services). If they do, ATM switch 1 would have no idea who originated them or where they are to be sent, since the cells would be jumbled together as they were sent and the switch translation tables are all based on incoming VPI/VCI values. Yet this is exactly what happens. What table entry could switch 1 use to map VPI = 0, VCI = 15 to an output port when *all* the cells to everywhere else on the network for connectionless services are coming in with the same VPI/VCI values? This is the essence of the problem.

The whole scheme works because to deliver connectionless services, a local ATM network node *must* do more than just switch cells based on VPI/VCI values. This following discussion presumes AAL-3/4 as an AAL, since this is what AAL-3/4 was invented for, but other scenarios are possible, if not likely, today. What will happen when the routers on the UNI in Fig. 6.25 both try to send IP datagrams in a connectionless fashion through the ATM network? The exercise is worth exploring to point out a major difference between offering connectionless and connection-oriented services to the same user community on an ATM network.

The process begins with both user *A* and user *B*'s routers getting an IP datagram to send at the same time. The IP datagram, being connectionless, will have a unique IP source and destination address in the header. The AALs for both user *A* and user *B*, being configured for CLNS using

AAL-3/4, will add the proper CPCS-PDU headers and trailers (Btag, BAsize, etc.) and chop the resulting data unit up into a series of SAR-PDU payloads, all with their own headers (SN, ST, etc.) and trailers (LI, etc.). Each SAR-PDU will have a unique MID field, however, based on some distributed algorithm (since user A operates completely independently from user B) for assigning these values. The ATM layer (or layers, since the result will be the same) will interleave the resulting 48-byte SAR-PDUs as they are generated (or else a 64-byte user A datagram may be delayed behind a 6400-byte user B datagram), attach a cell header to each with VPI = 0, VCI = 15, and send them across to UNI to switch 1.

There is a set of actions that switch 1 must be able to perform to deliver connectionless services. There is a lot of extra work to do. First, switch 1 will indeed have a table entry on each UNI port for VPI = 0, VCI = 15. But this entry will not map to a "normal" output switch port. Rather, the entry will map to "CLNS," the device attached to switch 1 to deliver connectionless services. The CLNS device may be special software also running on switch 1, a separate box entirely colocated at the switch 1 site (most likely for public ATM networks), or even a central device to deliver CLNS to all ATM switches on the entire network (most likely for private ATM networks with no public CLNS requirement). One way or another, all cells arriving on VPI = 0, VCI = 15, whatever their ultimate IP address destination in the datagram, arrive at the CLNS.

Once at the CLNS, switch 1 will strip off the 5-byte VPI = 0, VCI = 15 cell header of each cell as it arrives. It will buffer the 48-byte payloads in memory based on the MID field value. Obviously, user A's MID *must* be different from user B's or else all the cells will be jumbled together. Once separated by MID value, the payload CRCs are checked for errors, and then the ST field in the SAR-PDU header is examined. A sequence must begin with a BOM segment or an SSM segment.

In the 44-byte BOM segment (or the SSM segment) is a vital piece of information: the destination IP address. This is extracted from the SAR-PDU header by the CLNS and used to index another table: the CLNS address routing table. This routing table entry will map the destination IP address to a "normal" VPI/VCI NNI format connection number. This connection number follows a path through the ATM network to the local switch that has the UNI for the destination IP address. If there is no entry for that particular IP address, then switch 1 must have some procedure for finding it. Endless debates rage about the proper and most efficient way for this to happen. Perhaps there will be one IP address server on the ATM network that supplies this information for all CLNS. Then the problem shifts to how the IP address server finds out ITS information, and so on.

Assuming the entry exists, the CLNS will make an entry in a table associating this particular MID with that particular VPI/VCI. The SAR-

PDU is then sent back to switch 1 with a new cell header. This header, however, may have VPI = 576,VCI = 1067 for user A's MID = 45 and VPI = 1002,VCI = 2098 for user B's MID = 87. Each subsequent cell SAR-PDU payload with ST = COM delivered to the CLNS will use the MID field value as an index into this routing table to map the COM segments to the same connection path. Naturally, the COM segment will still use the MID entry, but then the CLNS will delete it to prepare for the next sequence.

Once on their way across the network, away from switch 1, the connectionless cells are no longer connectionless at all. They follow a path just like any connection-oriented cell in the ATM network. They are all switched by a locally unique VPI/VCI value from input port to output port. However, these paths must be set up so that once these cells reach the ATM switch with the destination UNI, the cell headers will direct these cells *back* to the CLNS on that ATM switch (so CLNS must be supported on the remote switch as well). The CLNS screens the IP address, again making a MID entry, and sends the cells back to the switch with a "well-known" VPI/VCI value in the header. This time the table entry directs the cell to the UNI output port for the receiver and retranslates the VPI/VCI back to VPI = 0,VCI = 15.

Each ATM layer on the UNI must watch for all cells with VPI = 0, VCI = 15. The ATM layer will "copy" these cell payloads to each AAL supporting connectionless service (AAL-3/4) it is attached to. Each possible receiver AAL-3/4 on top of each ATM layer supporting connectionless service must check each BOM (or SSM) segment for each SAR-PDU for its own IP address as the destination. If it does not match, these SAR-PDUs are discarded. If it is a match, the MID field is used to associate subsequent COMs and a final EOM to rebuild the IP datagram as sent. This whole process is illustrated in Fig. 6.26.

If this sounds complex, it is. In fact, the cost in terms of effort (routing table maintenance) and equipment (CLNS hardware and software) has lead many to believe that offering connectionless services on an ATM network is (1) not worth the trouble and (2) the most expensive way of moving data around an ATM network. Ironically, the Internet people (IETF) have turned their backs on a service offering supposedly geared for them especially (connectionless ATM service = connectionless IP datagrams) and embraced connection-oriented service types (AAL-5) for IP router connectivity over ATM networks. It turns out that IP did not function very well with connections, which is not surprising. Thus the IETF simply started changing IP to accommodate ATM, which is very surprising.

A simpler, more efficient, and probably more likely arrangement for offering connectionless services on an ATM network is being discussed. In this arrangement, AAL-3/4 is not required, or even desired. AAL-5,

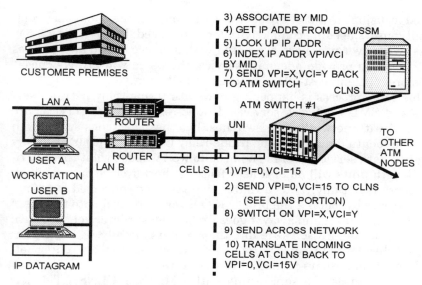

Figure 6.26 ATM CLNS arrangement.

with the lowest overhead and simplest AAL of all, is used to establish almost any VPI/VCI combination for connectionless services. In this case, the local ATM network node would just forward any cell arriving on a UNI with this VPI/VCI combination to a connection that lead to a network-central connectionless server. Once the cell arrived at the central switch, the destination IP address could be extracted easily and mapped via a table to a destination VPI/VCI. This cell would then be forwarded, along with all the subsequent AAL-5 body cells, directly to the destination ATM network node.

For efficiency, all switches would be connected directly to the central server switch. AAL-5 could be used universally for data on such an ATM network. The appeal of this whole second scenario is so great that the idea of a CLNS using AAL-3/4 appears to be in danger of disappearing entirely.

The DXI interface. One more topic is related to providing connectionless ATM network services but also has become important in its own right. This is the data exchange interface (DXI), a method originally invented to make the whole connectionless arrangement more cost-effective. Recently, the DXI has become a viable alternative for offering any ATM service at all.

The structure of the ATM protocol stack gave two main ways for providing data services: the class C connection-oriented method, mainly aimed at using AAL-5, and the class D connectionless method, mainly aimed at using AAL-3/4. These are both aimed at the same user community: users needing connectivity for high-speed, low-delay data services. Whenever users are presented with a choice of two alternatives that can each provide adequate service, the users will always choose the more efficient, cost-effective (cheaper) alternative.

This same process is happening now with frame-relay network services and SMDS network services. Frame-relay network services are provided with network node switches, but these switches still switch variable-length data units (the frame-relay frames). Since frame relay is only a data service, there is no need to worry about what these variable-length units will do to time-sensitive, shorter voice or video traffic—there is not any. Thus a router can easily be converted to frame-relay service by loading the proper ISO layer 2 protocol onto the WAN board of the router, and away it goes. In fact, most router vendors have started bundling FR software into their routers already. This is a simple and cheap way to convert from a private-line–connected router network to a frame-relay–connected router network.

However, to do the same thing with SMDS (or CLNS ATM networks), the process is not so simple. Since cell-based networks can only be fed with cells, the router must generate cells to be sent into the SMDS or ATM network. This is not a software process today; the SAR sublayer of the AAL to translate frames to and from cells is done by a chipset on a board. This tends to be expensive. To change a router today from a private-line interface to an SMDS interface requires not only new software (the CLNAP) but also new hardware (the SAR and ATM layer) on a board. However, this new board may cost more than the whole router itself.

Thus a means was sought by SMDS (and later ATM) service providers to make the transition from private router network to SMDS router network as simple and easy as the transition to a frame-relay router network. The DXI configuration, invented by BellCore, standardized by the SMDS Interest Group, and adapted by the ATM Forum, is shown in Fig. 6.27. In place of the SIP-3 PDU, the ATM Forum specifies the CLNAP-PDU from AAL-3/4. The whole concept revolves around putting the SAR

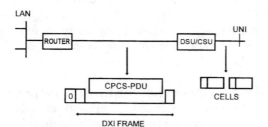

Figure 6.27 Data exchange interface (DXI).

sublayer and ATM layer into a separate device, the digital service unit/channel service unit (DSU/CSU) that interfaces with the SMDS or ATM network. Actually, the function is only in the DSU itself, but the effect is the same. It is the function of the DSU to make the cells. The entire SIP-3 PDU or CLNAP-PDU is sent from a router port inside a DXI frame invented for this very purpose. The DSU may have many ports, and the entire DXI specification allows many different configurations, but they are all basic variations on this theme.

Since the SIP-3 PDU or CLNAP-PDU is still a variable-length data unit, the DXI frame can be sent over any network port available on the router. Now the transition from private router network to SMDS/CLNS becomes a simple software swap in the router, just like frame relay. And the DXI frame is just another variation on HDCL, the same as frame relay at this layer. Thus the cost of the DSU/CSU may be spread between four or five departments instead of requiring each of them to buy a separate SMDS/ATM board for each router, which may not be affordable for any of the departments individually.

The structure of the DXI protocol stack and the DXI frame structure is shown in Fig. 6.28. The DXI physical layer may be V.35 or the newer high-speed serial interface (HSSI). The DXI link layer transfers the variable-length frames across the DXI interface. The DXI header varies in format but always includes the following fields:

Flag: Hex 7E, the HDLC standard flag byte.

DFA: DXI frame address of 10 or 24 bits. It is divided into a 4-bit VPI subset and a 6-bit VCI subset in the 0-bit version and forms a 24-bit extended VCI (from the ATM cell header's 16-bit VCI) in the 24-bit version.

RSVD: Reserved field, always set to 0.

CN: Congestion notification bit used to transfer the ATM EFCI bit in the cell header PTI field to the DXI user inbound from the ATM network on the DXI. It is always set to 0 outbound.

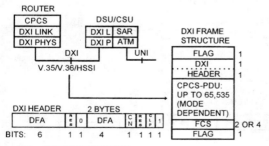

Figure 6.28 DXI protocol stack.

CLP: Cell loss priority bit used to transfer the ATM CLP bit in the cell header to the DXI user inbound from the ATM network on the DXI. It is always set to 0 outbound.

The ATM Forum specification on DXI allows three modes of operation:

Mode 1a: Up to 1023 virtual connections (10-bit DXI address field), AAL-5 only, a data unit up to 9232 bytes long (known as the DTE SDU in the DXI architecture), and a frame check sequence (FCS) 16 bits long (a CRC-16).

Mode 1b: Up to 1023 virtual connections (10-bit DXI address field), AAL-3/4 for at least one connection (e.g., VPI = 0,VCI = 15), AAL-5 for the others, a DTE-SDU up to 9232 bytes long for AAL-5, a DTE-SDU up to 9224 bytes long for AAL-3/4, and a frame check sequence (FCS) 16 bits long (a CRC-16). This is essentially all of mode 1a plus support for AAL-3/4.

Mode 2: Up to 16,777,215 virtual connections (i.e., a 24-bit DXI address field), either AAL-5 or AAL-3/4 for each virtual connection, a DTE-SDU up to 65,535 bytes (64K) long, and a frame check sequence (FCS) 32 bits long (a CRC-32).

A comparison of the three modes as implemented in a DXI arrangement is shown in Fig. 6.29.

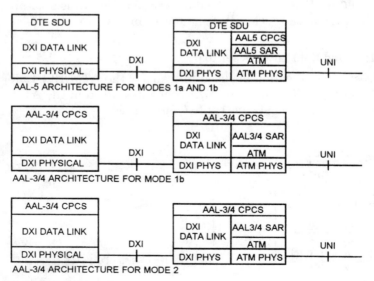

Figure 6.29 DXI modes.

ATM and TCP/IP. TCP/IP is a very widely used protocol stack that underlies the worldwide Internet and many corporate UNIX-based LANs. In fact, a large number of Novell Netware LANs use TCP/IP instead of Novell's proprietary IPX protocol for interoperability reasons alone. Therefore, it is essential that ATM take into consideration the pervasive nature of TCP/IP protocols and make an effort to accommodate TCP/IP connectionless *datagrams* (which are nothing more than the connectionless version of connection-oriented *packets*) in an elegant fashion inside ATM cells.

The TCP/IP developers, mainly the Internet Engineering Task Force (IETF), have already slightly modified the TCP/IP protocol stack for high-speed networks in general. But the immense installed base of TCP/IP networks makes the fit of ATM networks to TCP/IP at least as important as the fit of TCP/IP to ATM networks. The IETF and the ATM Forum have taken tentative steps to ensure the harmonious functioning of TCP/IP networks linked by ATM.

The essential problem is the venerable age of TCP/IP. The protocol stack is about 20 years old, and many of the mechanisms used by TCP especially are just too slow and verbose for efficient use on an ATM network. Incidentally, the same arguments hold true about TCP when TCP/IP is run on modern wireless data networks as well. The network layer protocol of the TCP/IP stack—IP itself—is better suited for ATM, but IP is connectionless and ATM networks are inherently connection-oriented. The transport layer protocol of the TCP/IP stack—TCP—is a better ATM match in the sense that TCP is connection-oriented, but TCP has all the overhead ATM networks would rather do without.

There is also the fact that TCP/IP has survived changes to the Internet structure no one foresaw 20 years ago. The IEFT has added voice and video capabilities to TCP/IP, although in a very limited fashion. Clearly, history shows that while some tinkering with TCP/IP is possible to accommodate ATM, wholesale change is probably out of the question.

Originally, developers saw ATM as just another type of transport for TCP/IP datagrams. Routers on a TCP/IP network would feed ATM switches transparently, and the two networks would be separate and independent, functioning as they did at different layers. All this scheme did was expose the basic conflict between ATM and TCP/IP. Both ATM and TCP/IP needed their own addressing structures and routing/switching methods. There was now a need to convert between them as traffic moved between TCP/IP and ATM network layers.

Unfortunately, the ATM and TCP/IP communities saw this conversion happening in two different ways. The IETF members favored a method known as "classic IP over ATM" and used a modified version of IP's address resolution protocol (ARP) to find ATM VPI/VCI connections corresponding to IP network addresses. The ATM Forum favored an extension of LAN emulation services (detailed below) to convert MAC layer addresses (which corresponded to IP network addresses) to VPI/VCIs. Both groups tend to view the other as well-meaning but misguided and spend much time trying to point out the errors of each other's ways.

In many respects, neither approach is flawless. Both fail to take full advantage of ATM's unique capabilities in regard to QOS parameters, since the ATM network is essentially a high-speed "leased-line replacement." They also shift a lot of work onto the routes feeding the ATM network. This may guarantee that no matter how fast the ATM network is, the TCP/IP networks may be slow and congested. Lastly, having two separate routing/switching structures each trying to determine the "best" path through a large network may cause nothing but confusion. This already occurs sometimes in hierarchical router networks running TCP/IP alone.

Both the IETF and ATM Forum are currently entertaining proposals for something called the *peer model:* TCP/IP and ATM would share addressing structures, and the IP routers and ATM switches would exchange routing information and updates. They also would share traffic management information. This task, however, will remain a long and difficult one. For now, the best ATM solution for supporting TCP/IP appears to be the LAN emulation service.

6.2.4   LAN emulation services (LES)

An important data service proposed by the ATM Forum to be provided by ATM networks will be the direct linking of local area networks (LANs) over an ATM network without the need for FR or SMDS/CLNS on a router to provide an interface for the LAN to the ATM network. This LAN emulation service (LES) differs from the other ATM data services, connection-oriented or connectionless, in one important fashion: It is totally transparent to the LANs themselves, not only the user applications on the LAN. In LES, the ATM network does not merely provide connectivity between LANs, as routers do today. LES actually emulates a LAN itself, making the two separate LANs think they are actually all one big LAN, whether they are separated by two floors or 2000 miles. Not only that, the LES definition includes the situation where two private ATM networks may be linked transparently over an existing LAN. But the wisdom and desirability of doing this second LES have been questioned, mainly because of ATM network deployment issues (why build more ATM when the LAN exists?). This section examines the use of LES to link two separate LANs across an ATM network.

What LES actually emulates is a LAN's MAC layer (ISO layer 2b) protocol so that the ATM network looks like just another media access control sublayer, similar to Token Ring or Ethernet's CSMA/CD. Existing applications interact with the MAC sublayer via protocols such as

NetBIOS, IPX, and so on. The applications can access any ATM-attached routers, servers, workstations, or other network devices. LES would still allow the underlying protocols and their drivers to interact with the ATM protocol that takes the place of the MAC sublayer. This allows all so-called legacy LAN adapters, using such protocol drivers as NDIS (network device interface specification) and ODI (open datalink interface), to function exactly as they did before. All this backward compatibility, from retention of LAN applications to the interfacing of protocols, is part and parcel of the LES specification. This means that even when there are no longer any Ethernet or Token Ring adapter boards left on the LAN, all the LAN protocols and applications run exactly as they did before.

One possible complication for LES is the fact that LAN protocols frequently multicast (or even broadcast) messages to more than one physical LAN address. Broadcasts are also frequently sent to every possible address on the LAN. This is not easy to do on a connection-oriented ATM network. However, the goal of LES is to offer this same capability by intercepting LAN multicast and/or broadcast messages and sending them directly to their destinations. Alternatively, broadcasts can still be sent with LES to all stations, as is done in today's LANs.

An ATM network may support more than one emulated LAN, but each will be totally separate, even if they are actually on the same physical network. Communication between them will only be possible through traditional bridges and routers. In other words, Ethernets can only talk directly to Ethernets, Token Rings to Token Rings, and so on (FDDI will work also, but only if FDDI frames are converted to Ethernet or Token Ring frames first).

Each emulated LAN consists of more than one LAN emulation client (LE client), a single LAN emulation service (LE server), a LAN emulation configuration server, and a broadcast and unknown server (BUS). All communications, whether from LE client to LE client or from LE client to LE service, are done via ATM virtual channel connections (VCCs). There must be one control VCC from an LE client to an LE service, although more may be established for efficiency. The VCCs may be SVCs, PVCs, or even a mixture of both. The client software has a number of functions, but the most vital is the mapping of physical MAC addresses to ATM addresses (known as *address resolution*).

The purpose of the BUS is an interesting one. On most LANs, the servers "listen" and the clients "talk," sending requests to the server to load software, transfer files, and the like. Obviously, the clients must know the MAC address of the server(s) in order to send frames to it. In many LAN protocols, such as Netware, the server broadcasts a *service advertising protocol* (SAP) message periodically so that all clients know the server's address. Since this mechanism must be supported in the connection-oriented ATM environment, the BUS software must have knowledge of the "unknown servers" to minimize the amount of broadcast and multicast traffic on the emulated LAN. Thus the LE client need only send to the BUS in order to send information to many destinations. This also cuts down the amount of time an LE client would have to wait while a data connection is set up to a given destination.

All three servers can be run on separate machines or as software functions on a single main ATM switch. They could even be distributed across an ATM network. The LES ATM Forum committee has been very flexible in implementation scenarios.

The architecture of the LAN emulation service is shown in Fig. 6.30. The connection management layer handles the setup and release of the VCCs, for both SVCs and/or PVCs. AAL-5 is used to transfer the LAN data over the ATM network. The LAN emulation clients on the user premises communicate with the ATM network LAN emulation service over the L-UNI, the LAN emulation UNI. This L-UNI provides the LES service with initialization information [finding the ATM addresses of the LE service(s) on the ATM network and joining or leaving an emulated LAN], registration functions (informing the LE service of an LE client's MAC address, source routing information, multicast addresses, and the like), and address resolution (mapping LE client ATM addresses to MAC addresses). The L-UNI also moves data from source to destination via AAL-5. Both end systems (workstations) or bridges and routers may implement the L-UNI, depending on the user's configuration preference. Note that the L-UNI does not directly support multiple multicast servers. All multicast, broadcast, and unknown traffic is handled by the broadcast and unknown server (BUS) on the emulated LAN.

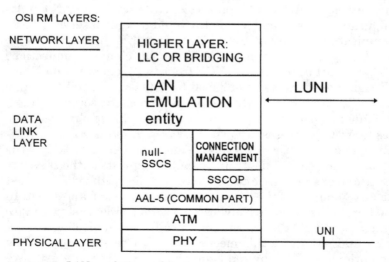

Figure 6.30 LAN emulation architecture.

There are several different frame formats used in LES. None have been finalized, but there will be at least the following:

1. *IEEE 802.3 CSMA / CD LE data frame.*   An IEEE 802.3 ("Ethernet") frame is packaged inside a fixed-length header of 2 bytes (LEH 1) and an optional frame check sequence for Ethernet (FCS-E).

2. *IEEE 802.5 / Token Ring LE data frame.*   An IEEE 802.5 Token Ring frame is packaged inside a fixed-length header of 2 bytes (LEH 2) and an optional frame check sequence for Token Ring (FCS-TR).

3. *Control frame.*   A 40-byte frame used to perform functions other than data transfer on the emulated LAN. Such functions include join the emulated LAN, register LE client information, and address resolution. (A special "flush a path on a VCC" message is sent on a data VCC.) Each of these control functions will have its own protocol and control frame format.

LAN emulation is a fairly complex scheme. Data transfer only takes place at the end of a complicated five-step process.

1. *Initialization.*   To join an emulated LAN, an LE client must establish an ATM connection (VPI and VCI) with the LE server. To do this, the LE client needs to find out the LE server's ATM address. LES allows this to happen in a number of ways. The LE client must first use the ATM Forum's ILMI (interim layer management interface) to try and obtain the address of the LE configuration server from the ATM switch. If this fails, another query for another LE configuration server address may be tried. Alternatively, the address of the LE server itself may be returned by the ATM switch.

If these queries fail, the LE client uses an agreed-on "well-known address" for the LE server specified by the L-UNI for every ATM network. Another option is to use a well-known VPI/VCI connection that should always be available for client-to-BUS communication. If all else fails, the LE client can try a previously known LE server address or other predefined VPI/VCI between the LE client and LE configuration server. The whole idea is to minimize the impact of devices being powered up and down, and joining and leaving, the emulated LAN.

2. *Configuration.*   The LE client uses the LE server address to determine what kind of emulated LAN it is joining and what the maximum frame size is. This information also may come from the LE configuration server. The LE client then tells the LE configuration server its ATM address, its MAC address, type of LAN it supports, and maximum acceptable inbound frame size.

3. *Joining.*   The LE client may now join the emulated LAN by creating a control connection to the LE server and sending a *join request*

with such parameters as its ATM address, LAN type, and maximum frame size to the LE server (in case this information is not available on the LE configuration server). The LE server sends back a *join response* which either registers the LE client on the emulated LAN or refuses to allow the LE client to join. If the client is refused, it must terminate the *request* and take down the connection, although it may repeat the initialization and configuration process and try again. The LE client also may try again (or abandon the *request* entirely) if the LE server does not respond in a given time interval.

4. *Registration and BUS initialization.* Once it has joined the emulated LAN, the LE client must request the LE server to send it the ATM address to be used for the LE client's broadcast MAC address. This is really the BUS ATM address (the BUS handles all broadcasts). The LE client then sets up a data connection to the BUS. The BUS adds the LE client to a point-to-multipoint connection or adds a separate point-to-point connection for the LE client.

5. *Data transfer.* Now the LE client has successfully joined the emulated LAN and may send data to any other LE client on the emulated LAN. It does this by taking packets from the existing layer 2 driver interface and checking the ATM address corresponding to the destination. The destination MAC address is either a broadcast indicator or a "unicast" individual MAC address. If it is a broadcast destination, the packet is packaged up as a series of AAL-5 cells and sent to the BUS. If it is not a broadcast packet, the LE client checks to see if it knows the ATM address that corresponds to the MAC address of the destination. If it knows the address and has a connection to the destination, the LE client again packages the packet as a series of AAL-5 cells and sends them. If it knows only the ATM address, the LE client sets up the connection with ATM signaling and then sends the cells. If even the address is unknown, the LE client sends a special LE address resolution protocol (LE-ARP) request to the LE server asking for the ATM address. While waiting, the LE client sends the cells to the BUS. If the LE server does not respond or does not know the ATM address of the destination, the LE client continues to send to the BUS, which essentially broadcasts the cells on all connections.

Currently, LAN emulation does not have its own service class or QOS parameters (the LES signaling protocol uses "QOS class 0," which is the "undefined" service class). The LES proposal itself recommends this be "class X" service, but "class Y" available-bit-rate (ABR) service is being considered, as well as class C (connection-oriented, variable-bit-rate, timing-insensitive) service. When finalized, the LAN emulation service promises to be a popular addition to ATM network service offerings.

6.2.5 ATM video and audio services

Sending video and the accompanying audio soundtrack on ATM networks is quickly becoming as complex an offering as data. Just as data can have widely varying requirements if the data are a file transfer or a real-time application, so video today relies on the answer to the question, "What *kind* of video?" All video used to be constant-bit-rate video, so AAL-1 was a nice fit. With compression and systems where only "changes" to a video scan picture are sent, however, it is now just a low-delay, variable-bit-rate service like many others, and AAL-2 is a good fit as well.

The Motion Picture Experts Group (MPEG) of ISO is the industry source of these compression standards. Although similar to data in bit rates, video is not meaningful in most point-to-point environments. True video services on ATM networks must wait for the development of fast and reliable "broadcast" or "multicast" ATM switches and multipoint signaling capabilities.

Video compression techniques have been around for a while. All video cameras, from the cheapest "palmcorder" to the most expensive television studio camera, are capable of producing "broadcast quality" video. The question of compression bandwidth required is answered by deciding what it should look like at the receiving end. The picture quality on a viewing screen ranges from a grainy security camera gray scale to a full-color broadcast-quality picture. Figure 6.31 shows the current range of video compression techniques available today.

Most ATM Forum activity has centered around the use of MPEG-2 for what the ATM Forum has called the *audiovisual multimedia service* (*AMS*). AMS would define a *video/audio service-specific convergence sublayer* (*VASSCS*) to run on top of AAL-5.

COMPRESSION TYPE	COMPRESSION RATIO	TRANSMISSION BANDWIDTH	VIDEO QUALITY
FULL MOTION JPEG	10:1-25:1	3 to 6 Mbps	S-VHS
MPEG 1	40:1-50:1	1.5 to 3 Mbps	VHS
"MPEG 1+" (Unofficial)	40:1-50:1	3 to 6 Mbps	S-VHS
MPEG 2	40:1-50:1	6 to 8 Mbps	BROADCAST

Figure 6.31 Video compression.

It is interesting to note, however, that MPEG-2 support on ATM networks is not limited to VBR services. MPEG-2 can be used with a CBR offering such as AAL-1. This may sound paradoxical, but it really is not. When MPEG-2 is generating fewer bits than the CBR connection will carry, the excess bandwidth is filled with special "idle" patterns. When MPEG-2 is generating more bits than the connection can handle, the receiver can "invent" bits or attempt to "predict" what the missing bits would have represented. The receiving application sees this effect as a "momentary" freezing of the screen, or perhaps some details will become extremely fuzzy.

There is another reason that putting MPEG-2 video into AALs other than AAL-2 makes sense. An MPEG-2 data stream consists of several different kinds of "packets." There is an MPEG-2 packetized elementary stream (PAS), a program stream (PS), and a transport stream (TS). The TS is the most important, and the data units for the MPEG-2 TS are fixed (*not* a maximum) at 188 bytes. This means that two of these TS data units of 376 bytes total would map very nicely into an 8-cell sequence in AAL-1 (376/8 = 47). Even AAL-5 could be used by padding the eighth cell (with 8 unused bytes) so that the AAL-5 trailer fell into the ninth cell in the sequence. Only AAL-3/4 is not a good fit. The 44-byte cell payload and 8-cell sequence will not map to an even number of TS data units, at least at low numbers of TSs. Lacking a firmly defined AAL-2, the delivery of MPEG-2 video over AAL-1 or AAL-5 seems almost certain.

6.2.6   ATM circuit emulation services (CES)

One of the nicest features of ATM networks is their ability to take existing DS-0, DS-1, or E-1 leased private lines and run them over the ATM network. This is the easiest way to bring ATM services into an existing network, but it represents far from optimal use of ATM features. Most voice (tie lines) will go ATM this way.

Because these leased lines *must* use the AAL-1 interface, however, no bandwidth is saved. Even if all channels in a T-1 are idle, the idle channels are all sent over the ATM network as cells. And AAL-1 will treat them as a constant bit rate, recover clock, and so forth. This is a big overhead bite just for ATM connections.

However, this may be desirable to do anyway. First of all, the IWU-to-IWU network is now all cells everywhere, so there is a compatibility benefit. Second, it offers a migration path until older, fully depreciated equipment is phased out. Third, the aggregate bit rates on ATM circuits using SONET are much higher than typical T-networks, meaning more efficient multiplexing *if* the user density is there. If not, access costs will rise.

The overwhelming requirement for carrying existing time-division multiplexed (TDM) circuits over a cell-based ATM network is that the

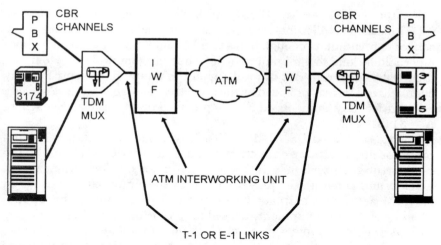

Figure 6.32 ATM circuit emulation services.

ATM must emulate circuit characteristics and that the performance delivered is just as good as that provided by the TDM circuit network itself. The ATM Forum proposes that CES cover these types of class A CBR service: channelized DS-1 and E-1 and an unstructured DS-1 and E-1. *Unstructured* means that the ATM network is just providing a constant raw bit rate at 1.544 Mbps (DS-1) or 2.048 Mbps (E-1). The channelized services will be *permissive,* meaning that any number of DS-0 64-kbps channels may be provided (known as "*N* × 64 kbps service"). This service applies to both the public and private UNI interfaces and supports both PVC and SVC types of service. Figure 6.32 shows a representative configuration for CES support on an ATM network.

What is *not* supported, at least initially, is also significant. CES will not currently support DS-3 (45 Mbps), E3 (34 Mbps), N-ISDN 64-kbps circuits, non-ATM Q-based signaling protocols (e.g., Q.931), analog voice (POTS, plain old telephone service), or direct digitized voice transport. CES also will remain undefined on the NNI for the time being.

CES will be delivered as a class A CBR service using AAL-1. The *N* × 64 CBR service is designed to support a point-to-point fractional DS-1 or fractional E-1 circuit. *N* may range from 1 to 24 for DS-1 and from 1 to 31 for E-1 emulation. For *N* × 64 CBR DS-1 emulation, the service provider must be capable of interfacing with the extended superframe (ESF) framing format, with older format support optional. E-1 interfaces must support the G.704 framing standard. Supported DS-0 channels can be contiguous (adjacent in the frame) or noncontiguous (optionally). Other issues, such as support for alarms and how typical TDM error measurements like errored seconds would translate from an ATM nonburst error environment, are still under study.

For the $N \times 64$ service, AAL-1 will use the structured data transfer (SDT) mode. The ATM network packetization delay (i.e., waiting at the sender to accumulate enough bytes to fill a complete cell payload) optionally could be kept to a minimum by introducing "dummy" bytes to fill up a partially filled cell. But full cell support is required. Support for fully channelized DS-1s is provided by the special case where $N = 24$ (24×64). Support for fully channelized E-1s is provided by the special case where $N = 31$ (31×64).

The unstructured DS-1/E-1 service provides a "clear channel" capability for any arbitrary data stream using the service. Optionally, the unstructured service may interpret performance information, detect alarms, and generate the proper signals in the emulated frames based on ATM network conditions. Clocking must be capable of being supplied by the CES equipment, traceable to a primary reference source. This is the synchronous mode of clocking. Optionally, the CES may take timing from the attached equipment and carry it through the ATM network. This is the asynchronous mode of clocking.

The unstructured service will use the unstructured data transfer (UDT) mode of AAL-1. No cell padding is allowed, as in $N \times 64$ service. With UDT, no framing information is preserved across the ATM network. That is, the receiver can make no assumptions about the alignment of bytes in a DS-1 frame and bytes in an ATM cell payload. If the emulated circuit is timed in the asynchronous mode, then the synchronous residual time stamp (SRTS) method of AAL-1 clock recovery must be used. Use of adaptive clock recovery is being studied.

CES is supported on the SONET (where the SRTS clock is recovered from the line rate) and DS-3 (where the SRTS clock is recovered from the DS-3 PLCP frame) ATM UNI physical layer transports. In fact, any synchronous physical framed transport could theoretically be used for CES. No support is proposed or planned for the asynchronous UNIs such as the FDDI-based TAXI or Fibre Channel.

For CES support on ATM connections, the peak cell rate (PCR) must be specified. The PCR for each service is set as follows:

1. Unstructured DS-1:

$$\frac{1{,}544{,}000 \text{ bits/s}}{47 \text{ AAL-1 bytes/cell} \times 8 \text{ bits/byte}} = 4106.3828 \text{ cells/s} < 4107 \text{ cells/s PCR}$$

2. Unstructured E-1:

$$\frac{2{,}048{,}000 \text{ bits/s}}{47 \text{ AAL-1 bytes/cell} \times 8 \text{ bits/byte}} = 5446.8085 \text{ cells/s} < 5446 \text{ cell/s PCR}$$

3. $N \times 64$ (K indicates the number of AAL-1 bytes filled per cell. $K = 47$ by default.):

K = bytes filled	N = 1	N = 6	N = 12	N = 24
K = 6	1333	8000	16000	32000
K = 12	666	4000	8000	16000
K = 24	333	2000	4000	8000
K = 47	170	1021	2042	4085
	(64 Kbps)	(384 Kbps)	(768 Kbps)	(1.536 Mbps)

Figure 6.33 $N \times 64$ peak cell rates ($8000 \times N/K$ cells/second).

$$\frac{N \times 64,000 \text{ bits/s}}{K \text{ AAL-1 bytes/cell} \times 8 \text{ bits/byte}} = \frac{8000 \times N}{K \text{ cells/s}} \text{PCR}$$

Some representative PCRs for various values of N and K are shown in Fig. 6.33.

When the AAL-1 SAR-PDU for CES is placed in the ATM cell, the CLP bit is always set to 0 and ignored by the receiver. The same applies to the PTI traffic bits (the last 2).

Building ATM Networks

The last section of this book deals with the issue of actually doing something with ATM, not merely inventing it or talking about it. There are organizations, both end users and service providers, that have begun to build ATM networks even now, at a relatively immature stage of the technology. This is probably as much good news as bad. Many ideas that seem good at a particular time and place prove difficult to implement in practice. Until someone actually goes out and tries to build something, however, some of these sticky problems tend to get lost in the shuffle. In ATM, AAL-3 is a case in point. It seemed like a good idea at the time, but it proved to be more trouble to implement than it was worth. So along came AAL-5.

Several aspects of ATM are like this. The good news is that these early implementers of ATM will quickly find out what works in practice and what does not. Another good aspect is that ATM is not just a paper standard that exists but no one has found the will or the way to make into a technology that people will accept or even pay for. The bad news is that as things quickly change, organizations that have spent time and effort supporting features such as AAL-3 are rapidly left behind in the ATM game.

Part 3 is a look at the problems and successes that various organizations have had in implementing ATM networks.

Chapter 7 begins this section with a look at things that will prove to be critical for ATM's success and acceptance. In every new technology, there are important considerations and questions that must be answered to everyone's satisfaction before the actual work of building a network or product can even begin. In Chap. 7, these questions revolve around network performance: Can an ATM network live up to the expectations that have been outlined for it? Can there ever be a single network technology that satisfies everybody for everything? The first part of Chap. 7 looks at the performance issues in depth.

The second part of Chap. 7 looks at another critical aspect of network deployment: network management. No one will ever build an ATM network if it cannot be managed at least as well as today's router-based networks are (some will argue that router networks are still to a large degree unmanageable). Regardless of current state-of-the-art network management techniques, ATM has staked out a very ambitious territory for its network management claims. Because of the fact that ATM networks are not just voice, or just data, or just video networks, they cannot be managed like voice, or data, or video networks. And even if it were possible to manage the whole as the sum of the parts, what network management tools are available for video networks (as an example)? Nevertheless, there are existing methods and proposals for ATM network management. They are explored in Chap. 7.

Chapter 7 ends with a series of "myths" and "unanswered questions" about ATM. The whole purpose and function of ATM is sometimes unintentionally distorted due to the newness of some of the concepts that are applied to ATM. However, there are still unanswered questions, not necessarily due to the lack of a standard way of doing something, e.g., ATM interoperability testing, but a lack of any way of doing something, e.g., VBR compressed video. There is even the possibility of multiple ways of doing something, and the hazard here is choosing the wrong one. ATM network flow control is an example.

Chapter 8 takes a long, hard look at the future of ATM. No technology is "futureproof," in the sense that something better may come along. For the immediate future, however, ATM is the most advanced network technology around. Chapter 8 explores some of the network technologies sometimes viewed as rival technologies to ATM. Technologies such as high-speed LANs (100 Mbps) are available now for building the same kind of performance for data users that ATM is capable of delivering. And it may be much cheaper to build these other networks today rather than using ATM.

The validity of these claims is explored in Chap. 8 not only from a technology standpoint but also from a service perspective. Users can now get advanced services for networking such *as frame relay and SMDS. Just what is the relationship between ATM and these other services? Should builders of ATM networks worry about the possibility that users may want or need frame relay instead of ATM? It turns out that ATM can offer these same services (perhaps under a different name) to end users.*

These issues are tied up with the "ultimate goal" of ATM: the deployment of a vast broadband-ISDN network (B-ISDN) as ubiquitous as the worldwide telephone network. ATM is the transport network for B-ISDN services, and B-ISDN services include literally everything. There is a profoundly disturbing implication in all this, which will be discussed in Chap. 8 as well.

Chapter 9 closes out the book and is divided into two sections. The first looks at the possibilities of building private ATM networks. These intrapremises ATM networks have a number of alternative ways to deploy equipment and build their networks. The issue here involves just where cells are made on the network. The vendor that controls the cell making controls the ATM private network market.

The second section looks at providers of public ATM networks. These interpremises ATM network service providers have taken a number of different approaches to the issue of cell making as well. The major players in the industry have different strengths and weaknesses, and the competition will be fierce.

The third section explores various ATM products and services available. The surprising fact is that many of the traditional networking industry leaders have lost a step when it comes to ATM technology. Newer companies and smaller companies have seen an opening and are exploiting it.

A sobering thought is that a new network technology has always meant a total turnover in the dominant service providers. The telegraph doomed the pony express and stagecoach mail delivery, and the telephone doomed the telegraph companies, which were absorbed by the phone companies in an astonishingly short amount of time.

Will this happen again?

ATM Network Considerations

If ATM sounds too good to be true, it probably is. This is still a new network technology, and as such, it suffers from its share of limitations and other things that will drive the initial implementers crazy. This chapter is a look at some considerations that must be addressed before anyone can build an ATM network.

First of all, ATM can be thought of as a greatly enhanced version of traditional statistical multiplexing (stat muxing) that has special considerations regarding network capacity. The whole point of ATM multiplexing is its *asynchronous* nature: the idea that an application that is generating no live traffic bits on a connection should not take up any bandwidth capacity on the connection. This means that ATM facilities may be massively oversubscribed. *Oversubscription* is the process by which an ATM network service provider (or builder of a private ATM network) can support, for example, ten 10-Mbps connections on a single 45-Mbps DS-3 interface. Of course, this means that special consideration must be given to the fact that there may actually be times when all 10 connections are actually generating live data at 10 Mbps.

Bit errors, as well as bit loss, are a factor in any network, and ATM is no exception. The issue is complicated in ATM networks because of the fact that information is packaged into fixed-length cells. This is combined with the fact that ATM is designed to run on very low bit error rate (BER) transports such as fiber. This has led to the stripping off of all "assured delivery" features in older technologies such as X.25, where the network resent errored packets transparently to the end user. But not in ATM. This assured delivery feature is up to the end-user application, not the network, to provide. Even if the resending of cells were made part of the technology, the low delay required end to end in ATM networks would prohibit the practice on all but the most error-sensitive connections.

This very issue of delay is another factor, but ATM networks are susceptible to a further complication: cell delay *variation* (CDV). A consistent end-to-end delay is critical for the proper functioning of many network applications that ATM networks want very much—and need very much—to support. This is much harder to provide on the packet-type network that ATM is rather than the circuit-type network that these delay-variation-sensitive applications are used to.

The subject of managing a network is always a crucial one in any network technology discussion. Adequate mechanisms must be built into the network standards to allow not only management of specific vendors' equipment but also management of *any* vendor's ATM equipment. Proprietary network management schemes are not acceptable to most organizations today. ATM networks, attempting many new things, will need network management standards that address these new capabilities and features.

Another issue is related to network management. The question of interoperability is a frequent requirement in building any new network. Interoperability of components is desirable for economic reasons, functional reasons, and industry reasons. If users are confident that a vendor's product will be compatible with other vendors' products, selling into a particular market (e.g., routers) becomes easier, competition is robust, and prices fall dramatically (e.g., Ethernet NIC cards). There is less of a concern on users' parts that "application X will not run correctly with box Y on the network," a worry that locked users in to a specific vendor in older times. Lastly, interoperability is good for the whole industry, in the sense that it creates a level playing field for all comers (theoretically, at least), which means that exploring better and more efficient ways to do something is always an advantage.

Finally, the fact the ATM is still emerging should be considered. Parts of ATM are firmly set in concrete. Other parts are as slippery as mud. An ATM network implementer or service provider must always keep an eye out for what is standardized today, what will be standardized soon, and what might not ever be standardized in order to keep expectations realistic and users happy.

These six main ATM performance issues and network considerations are summarized in Fig. 7.1. Each of these issues is explored in depth in this chapter.

- ATM MULTIPLEXING LIMITS
- BIT AND CELL ERRORS AND LOSS
- CELL DELAY AND CELL DELAY VARIATION
- ATM NETWORK MANAGEMENT
- ATM EQUIPMENT INTEROPERABILITY
- ATM STANDARDS INCOMPLETENESS

Figure 7.1 ATM network considerations.

7.1   ATM Multiplexing Limitations

For many years, there have been two philosophies for multiplexing digital data: *time-division multiplexing (TDM)* and *statistical multiplexing* [known under a variety of names: *stat muxing, asynchronous TDM* (ATDM), or even *statistical TDM* (STDM)]. Statistical multiplexing occurs where a network designer takes advantage of the fact that multiple inputs to a network node or special multiplexing device are seldom—if ever—active at the same time. There is only a probability (hence *statistical,* defined in this context as "based on probabilities, a stochastic process") of this maximum activity happening, and if it is remote enough, everyone can save money in the network. The more connections that a multiplexer can support, the less money spent from the network provider perspective, and the more money saved from the network user perspective.

With a straight time-division multiplexer, the sum of the inputs is *always* equal to the output speed: 2400 bps + 4800 bps + 2400 bps = 9600 bps (these speeds show how long this technology has been around). With a statistical multiplexer, the sum of the inputs is *always* greater than the output link speed: 2400 bps + 4800 bps + 2400 bps > 4800 bps. The saving on the reduced speed of the output link offsets the added cost of the statistical multiplexers needed at each end of the link. The user only needs to buy a 4800-bps link to support the same three circuit connections, i.e., if the user has determined that the input links are only in use about 50 percent of the time. This is shown in Fig. 7.2.

But statistics being the way they are, an average of 50 percent utilization of 4800 bps means that about half the time the link is sending less than 2400 bps (not really, but it is usually close enough) and the other half of the time the link is sending more than 2400 bps, but never more than 4800 bps (because of the physical line speed limit). It is this mixture of busy and idle periods that allows statistical methods to be used. What if all inputs happen to be busy (sending bits) at the same time? Nothing can really be done short of throwing the bits away except

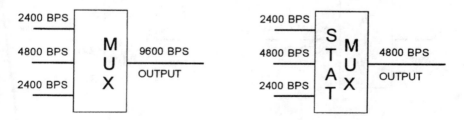

OUTPUT = SUM OF INPUT   OUTPUT < SUM OF INPUT

Figure 7.2 Multiplexing and statistical multiplexing.

to buffer the data. The data can only be buffered for so long, however, before the delay in the buffer becomes unacceptable for users or the fixed-length buffer itself overflows. Thus, if the condition persists, data ultimately will be lost.

ATM takes advantage of statistical multiplexing as well. Instead of the concepts of circuit input and output speeds, these terms must translate to cell rates instead. In the case of ATM, the multiplexers have to consider the average and peak bit rate, in terms of cells per second (CPS), of the user connections. This will apply not only to ATM switches with multiple input ports and output ports but also to ATM customer equipment arrangements, where many ATM connections will be multiplexed onto a single UNI in most cases.

In general, the ATM network node has to be configured so that the total capacity of the output link will be *greater than* the *average* bit rate in CPS of all the inputs. At the same time, the total capacity of the output link should be *less than* the *peak* bit rate of all the inputs. This is shown in Fig. 7.3, where, for the sake of simplicity, three equal average and peak cell rates are illustrated. These two parameters, average and peak cell rate, must be specified by the end user whenever an ATM network virtual channel connection (VCC) is established, either by hand as a PVC or via a signaling protocol as an SVC. Of course, these are tricky numbers to pin down. Given the "bursty" nature of much ATM traffic, how much lower than the sum of the peaks can an ATM go?

If the value is set too low (too close to the sum of the average cell rates), large buffers may be needed, and data may still be lost. Also, buffering will add to the delay through the network as cells have to wait longer and longer at each network node as the buffer size increases. On the other hand, if the value is set too high (too close to the sum of the peak cell rates), or even potentially *equal* to the sum of the peak bit rates, then the ATM network will be defeating one main purpose that ATM was introduced to solve in the first place: wasted bandwidth

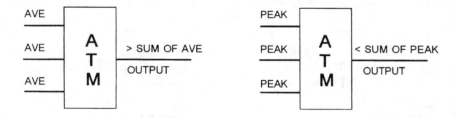

OUTPUT > SUM OF AVE
OF ALL USERS

OUTPUT < SUM OF PEAK
OF ALL USERS

Figure 7.3 ATM statistical multiplexing.

on networks. When set at a very high level, close to the sum of the peak cell rates, ATM becomes indistinguishable from straight TDM.

The average and peak cell rates are used for connection admission control (CAC) on ATM networks. If the CAC is too permissive, too many connections will be granted, and the performance of the entire network will be degraded. If the CAC is too restrictive, then the network may easily service more connections, and either network costs will be too high (in private ATM networks) or network revenues will be minimized (in public ATM networks). In any case, the average cell rate definition has come to mean an average over the entire lifespan of the connection. But connections may be SVC or PVC. They may last for minutes (SVC) or weeks (PVC). Obviously, a calculation of the average cell rate will vary widely over different time spans.

It would be nice if there existed a simple and straightforward formula or even a rule that could be applied to ATM networks to set the peak cell rate–to–output cell rate "ratio." This formula or rule could be used on customer equipment to figure out easily how many connections could be handled by a UNI and on ATM switches to figure out whether the switch is underconfigured in terms of trunks (links to another switches) to support a given number of UNIs (usually called *ports*). Actually, there are several formulas that have been proposed and explored. They range from the simple rule-of-thumb type, such as "an ATM network node cannot assign more than 80 percent of the output cell rate for connections based on average cell rate," to formulas so complex that even if they were correct, an ATM network node would be hard pressed to figure out whether the connection could be granted or not in enough time to keep users happy.

Several important results have emerged from research into the most frequently discussed CAC formulas, as uncertain as they are. The first result is that it quickly becomes obvious that the output link cell rate may be kept very low—extremely low and near to the sum of the averages—if the buffer space and long delay that go along with this extensive buffering are acceptable. The second result is that to minimize this buffer delay, it is necessary to set the peak/output cell ratio very high—extremely high and near to the sum of the peaks—to give performance in terms of stable network delays equal to those on circuit-based networks. In most cases, the "effective bit rate" of the cells is almost 95 percent of the peak cell rate itself, even though the average cell rate may be only 10 percent or less of the peak cell rate.

These results are sometimes surprising to those expecting the best of all possible worlds from ATM. Keep in mind that these formulas are mathematical exercises in many cases and that very few "real-world" traffic studies have been done on ATM networks. "Tuning" ATM networks to proper peak/output ratios is expected to be an important area of continuing research on ATM networks.

- ACCURACY AND DEPENDABILITY:
  CELL ERROR RATIO
  SEVERELY-ERRORED CELL BLOCK RATIO
  CELL LOSS RATIO
  CELL MISINSERTION RATIO (RATE)

- SPEED:
  CELL TRANSFER DELAY
  MEAN CELL TRANSFER DELAY
  CELL DELAY VARIATION

Figure 7.4 ATM performance parameters.

7.2 Bit and Cell Errors and Loss

The next two sections of this chapter deal with bit and cell errors and loss and with cell delay and cell delay variation. Both of these affect ATM network performance, but they are treated as separate issues here. This is done because the ATM Forum neatly divides the measurements of these two characteristics, errors and delay, into two types of performance measurements: accuracy and dependability for error characteristics and speed for delay characteristics. These ATM performance parameters are listed in Fig. 7.4.

Bit errors occur in all networks, not just ATM networks. In fact, however, they are much less a factor in ATM networks than in others. This is due to two considerations: the minimal cell length and the expected extensive use of fiber in ATM networks, both public and private. A single bit error will make a whole packet or frame invalid, making resending of an entire 1600-byte sequence (e.g., Ethernet) or even an 18,000-byte sequence (e.g., 16-Mbps Token Ring) necessary. In ATM, the small cell size limits the effect of these bit errors. Of course, the upper layers (applications) may still lose the whole packet or frame, but this many be an argument in favor of smaller packets and frames, or even generating ATM cells for cell-relay services, at the application layer as well.

Fiber has the best error characteristics of any medium available. ATM networks built on fiber are expected to have bit error rates (BERs) in the range of 10^{-10} to 10^{-12}. Early X.25 networks expected errors in the range of 10^{-3} to 10^{-6}. As an example, at T-1 speed (1.5 Mbps) and a BER of 10^{-6}, there is one bit error every 0.7 seconds. On fiber at 10^{-12}, this is now one bit error every 7.7 *days*. The error rate is 1 million times better. (Even a BER of 10^{-10} at 1.5 Mbps is one bit error every 2 hours or so.) Some network service providers have found that the BERs on their single-mode fiber backbones have been as low as 10^{-13} (1 in 10 trillion) in many cases. This translates to 1 bit in error at 64 kbps (normal digitized voice rate) on a connection running every 5 years.

Much discussion has revolved not around resending errored cells, since these have been rare enough to ignore on fiber-based ATM networks to this point, but rather around what to do at the receiver, since there is no way to even *ask* a sender to repeat a cell even if it is miss-

ing or errored. Data applications leave this up to the receiving application. For example, if an e-mail application running on a ATM network
that discards a sequence of errored-cell payloads (based on the AAL-5
CRC, presumably) needs a retransmission, it is up to the receiving
application to inform (via a return cell-based message, of course) the
sending application of this need. Generally, even real-time data applications will function with occasional resending of data.

However, class A and class B time-sensitive ATM connections for video
and audio applications may not be so tolerant. It has been seriously proposed that as part of the standardization process for these services there
should be included specification for the substitution of special dummy
cells that would fool the receiver into thinking that the data arrived
intact. This is something like supplying a letter *e* for any letter missing
in an e-mail message. This being the most common letter in use in
English, chances are pretty good that it is actually an *e* that is missing.
There is a good chance that the MPEG-2 class B compressed video service description will include a "predictive" dummy cell algorithm for
inventing cell payloads if one happens to disappear on the ATM network.

Total cell loss is the most serious impairment on ATM networks. This
is a different situation from errored-cell payloads that are discarded by
the receiver. There are two conditions that will lead to total cell loss:
ATM header errors that are uncorrectable and cell loss due to network
congestion at ATM network nodes. If an ATM node is unable to correct
a header error detected with the HEC field (*not* errors in the cell data
itself), the cell is discarded by the ATM switch to prevent cell insertions.
A cell insertion occurs when a cell arrives at the wrong connection termination point because of undetected VPI and VCI header field errors.

Also, if a node is congested (i.e., cell queues and buffers have exceeded a preset threshold), then cells with the cell loss priority bit (CLP) set
(low priority) may be discarded to service other cells with CLP = 0. The
user is expected to set this bit on "low-priority" network traffic. However, the ATM network node is allowed to set the CLP bit in cells on
some connections. This is part of the ATM network *policing function*
and is accepted practice.

The ATM network policing function monitors bit sources once a connection has been accepted into the network. This policing unit monitors
the connection for billing purposes but also to make sure that the quality-of-service (QOS) guarantees and parameters are respected. The
policing function is done at the network connection point, the local
ATM network node, and its main intent is to prevent switch overload
by making sure that users respect the bit-rate parameters they have
agreed to. If the actual bit rate exceeds the subscribed threshold, the
ATM network may tag the excess cells as low priority (CLP = 1) or may
even discard the excess cells at the entry point. Even if accepted by the

network with CLP = 1, these cells are obviously candidates for discarding along the way. In addition, the network service provider may be subject to billing penalties under the service contract.

7.3 Cell Delay and Cell Delay Variation

At an ATM switch, many cells may be directed to the same output port. At a customer premises on a single UNI, two or even more cells from different AALs may be ready to be sent by the ATM layer at the same time. Two may "collide" in either case, or three or more may be arriving at the same output port at the same time. The ATM network device must buffer all but one until a cell slot is available.

If the characteristic delay for the device without any buffering is T, then the other cell must wait $T + n$ time, where n is the slot time of the ATM device's output port. For example, at a DS-3 rate of 45 Mbps, cells can be sent at no more than 96,000 per second (12 cells/PLCP frame $\times$ 8000 frames/second). This works out to a per-cell time delay of about 10.4 µs (1/96,000 of a second). If there are more than two cells contending, then the delay will be more. Therefore, depending on the buffer length, cells will be delayed a variable amount of time on different occasions as they make their way through the ATM network. In fact, the general cell delay time per network node will be

$$T + (m \times n)$$

where T is the device cell delay, n is the cell slot time for the device, and m is the number of cells waiting when a cell arrives. ATM devices usually provide buffers of up to 64 cells or more on output ports. Delay in ATM networks is always defined as the sum of the propagation delays on each link plus the nodal processing delay for switching and queuing. This introduces a unique factor in ATM networks: cell delay *variation* (CDV).

Cell delay variation is actually a worse condition to deal with in ATM networks than absolute cell delay. A constant-bit-rate (CBR) service such as voice will tolerate cell delay as long as it is within bounds [less than 25 ms without echo cancelers, up to about 500 ms (0.5 s) even with] and does not vary much. Owing to the asynchronous nature of ATM, however, and the switching delay mentioned previously, these CBR services experience CDV or *cell jitter* along the way.

A real concern for early builders of ATM networks is the size of cell buffers allowed in ATM switches. Although nothing has been standardized yet, early work on ATM performance parameters seems to endorse the BellCore standard jitter allowance of 250 µs per network device. This is fine for TDM circuit switching, but a DS-3 output port with 10.4-µs cell time slots can only buffer about 25 cells before the last cell out exceeds this 250-μs maximum. Most ATM switch vendors, however, set cell buffers in groups of 64, meaning a buffer size of 0 is clearly too small, but a buffer size of 64 may be too high to offer acceptable class A and class B QOS parameters.

CDV has two effects on ATM data streams: If the cell delay suddenly increases, this is called *dispersion,* and if it suddenly decreases, this is known as *clumping.* Variable cell interarrival times can affect signaling or cell reassembly functions for other services as well. The concept of CDV is illustrated in Fig. 7.5. Clearly, something additional must be done at the receiver to compensate for the CDV.

Typical CDV values for some of the early ATM networks can be up to 5 percent of the minimum delay for uncontended cells. On a 25-ms TDM voice circuit, this would amount to 0.05×25 ms $= 1.25$ ms, which is not a lot. As ATM networks grow larger, however, and more network nodes are between a source and a destination, the greater are the chances that a cell will encounter one very large queue on the network. The ATM Forum has unofficially (lacking a better number) endorsed the BellCore and ANSI standard of less than 1 ms of nodal delay for each network element. Clearly, on a large ATM network with 10 nodes from coast to coast, this potential 10 ms of CDV will have to be dealt with for time-sensitive connections.

In ITU-T ATM documentation, the ATM adaptation layer may provide a service at the receiver known as *network conditioning,* which is a way of *adding* a known delay to the incoming cells to smooth out the CDV. Because ATM functions in a statistical manner, the cell delay will

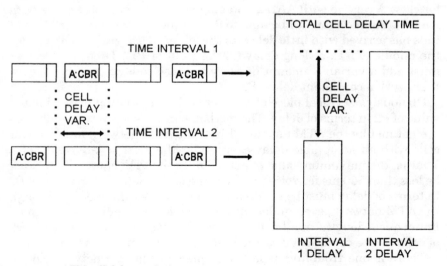

Figure 7.5 ATM cell delay variation.

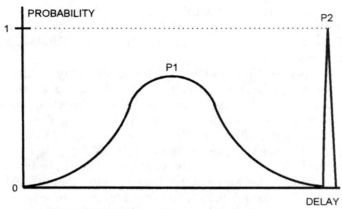

P1 = PROBABILITY DENSITY FUNCTION OF DELAY

P2 = PROBABILITY DENSITY FUNCTION OF DELAY AFTER
CONDITIONING AT THE RECEIVER ATM ADAPTATION LAYER

Figure 7.6   ATM network conditioning.

vary in a bell-shaped curve, with some with low delay, some with high delay, and most with average delay. This is shown in Fig. 7.6. The bell-shaped curve is a probability distribution function (PDF), labeled as $P1$.

If the receiver can add some delay at the endpoint, it will come up with another PDF, labeled $P2$, with probability 1 (certainty; the "curve" representing $P2$ should be a completely straight line), and minimize the effects of CDV. Using some sort of timing information derived across the network [perhaps the synchronous residual time stamp (SRTS) method for class A service with AAL-2 and maybe even for class B service with AAL-2], the receiver will be able to determine if a sequence or block of cells has arrived with little delay (to the left of $P1$), average delay (under the middle of $P1$), or long delay (to the right of $P1$). Then the receiver must add a variable amount of delay to these cells in order to deliver them with a consistent delay, $P2$.

Obviously, a critical piece of this network conditioning method is the value of $P2$ in terms of delay. The method will not work if two conditions are not met by the ATM network. First, the ATM network must deliver cells with an acceptable delay even under the most severe conditions. That is, the maximum value of delay under the PDF curve for $P1$ must be less than 500 ms for voice services, and so on. Second, the value of $P2$ in terms of delay must be set greater than the maximum delay through the ATM network, even under the most congested conditions (i.e., maximum queue lengths at all network nodes). If $P2$ is set at 30 ms, no block of cells can be conditioned correctly if they arrive in more than 35 ms.

There is one troubling aspect of implementing this network conditioning scheme. The value of $P2$ will be totally dependent on the longest path and longest buffer length allowed for a connection on the ATM network. However, there exists no easy way to find out what these parameters are for a given ATM network besides manual inspection of a network topology map and examination of ATM network node configuration parameter information.

Both may change with time. The network topology may change with the addition of ATM switches and network links. The network node configuration may change as the network is tuned or reconfigured for new topologies. This means that the network conditioning parameter must change as well, for every potential connection. Better methods and tools are needed for implementation of network conditioning to deal with CDV in ATM networks.

7.4   ATM Network Management

It almost goes without saying that network management is a vital part of any functioning network. Owing to asynchronous nature of ATM and the mix of traffic service requirements, ATM networks pose a unique challenge for network management systems. Although the B-ISDN protocol reference model and many ATM standards from the ITU-T all show and mention both layer management and plane management (B-ISDN consists of a user plane, control plane, and management plane), little work has been done addressing these needs in many respects. The ATM Forum has developed more specific recommendations and requirements for managing ATM networks.

All methods for managing ATM networks look at extending the use of the widely used and respected simple network management protocol (SNMP), developed for the Internet, for use in ATM network management. In fact, it is being put to work in some areas already. For instance, the ATM Forum uses SNMP version 1 (SNMPv1) to allow users to set up their own PVCs on an ATM network. SNMPv2 is being studied for use at some point in the future, but this may be very soon.

A management information base (MIB) for use with ATM SNMP has been developed called the *interim local management interface* (*ILMI*) from the ATM Forum. Since the concepts of SNMP and MIBs are relatively new ones, especially to organizations without TCP/IP protocols of Internet connectivity, some details on SNMP and MIB functioning are in order.

7.4.1   SNMP and the MIB

SNMP was developed in 1987 mainly to manage routers on the Internet. It addressed the fundamental need for a standard and nonproprietary ("open") method of managing equipment from different vendors with greatly different functions; it did so so effectively that it quickly became the de facto standard for managing *any* network device. Today SNMP is found in modems, CSUs/DSUs, hubs, and so forth, as well as, of course, in all TCP/IP router-based networks. A newer and even more powerful version of SNMPv1, known as SNMPv2, was standardized in 1993, but implementation and deployment of SNMPv2 hardware and software have been slow, at least in part because of the enormous success of the original SNMP in the network management arena. (When seen as SNMP, the version is always taken to be SNMPv1.)

SNMP works by providing network management software (called a *manager* in SNMP) with a database of information in the managed device. Described by a management information base (MIB), this database is accessed by the device's SNMP "agent" software, usually installed on the device by the vendor before sale to the customer. Technically, the MIB is just a piece of paper. The MIB defines various fields and values that the agent software must keep track of in the managed device. Once the MIB is "compiled" and running in an active network device and the fields of the MIB take on values unique to the device, the MIB should be called an *object*. However, use of the term *MIB* to describe both the database specification and its implementation in the managed device is so universal that the term *object* is rarely heard.

SNMP is essentially a TCP/IP protocol stack application that lets the agent know which "entry" in the MIB (really the object) the SNMP manager software wants the value of (all it gets are the *current* values). The manager software does this by sending, via the SNMP protocol (SNMP is both a TCP/IP application and a TCP/IP protocol), a message with an *identifier* for the particular MIB entry.

Humans using SNMP may use *labels*, an alphanumeric substitute for the identifier specified by something called the *structure of management information (SMI) tree*. For example, all Internet "objects" (MIB entries) begin 1.3.6.1... or (as labels) ISO.ORG.DOD.INTERNET....

The relationship between MIBs and objects and SNMP and agents is a bit confusing, but it is an important one. Figure 7.7 shows a sample look at how they work together for network management. The SNMP agent software runs in the ATM network device. It has access to the database objects, which are the current values of the database entries. The MIB is the *definition* of the database, but when it is running as software, the MIB forms a set of objects. MIBs may be *standard*, meaning their definition is published in some standard, or *private*, meaning only the vendor knows exactly what the structure of the MIB data field definitions are. The vendor may release these to buyers of the vendor's equipment or publish the private MIB themselves, but the private MIB usually addresses such things as power supply and device fan failures. In other words, private MIBs are for low-level, hardware-specific network management and, as such, really belong in the vendor's domain.

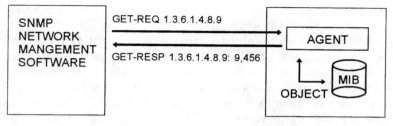

ATM NETWORK DEVICE

MANAGER: "NOW I KNOW THAT
THERE HAVE BEEN 9,456 CELLS
ON THIS PVC TODAY."

Figure 7.7 SNMP and the MIB.

Who but the vendor would know whether the device even has a redundant power supply or battery backup?

When the network management software issues an SNMP "get request" with an object identifier string (1.3.6.1.4.8.9 in the example), the receiving agent software accesses that object, which is defined by the MIB ("this is an integer field, read-only, counting the number of cells"). The agent software sends an SNMP "get response" back to the network management software with a value (called a *variable binding*): 9,459. Now the manager knows what the device knows.

Clearly, the MIB is the key to all this: no definition, then no object, and no information available about it. And a standard MIB is needed to make all vendors' equipment equally manageable. MIB definitions are written in a special language known as *abstract syntax notation 1* (ASN.1), which is an ISO standard layer 6 (presentation layer) construction. This is used so that any vendor can implement the MIB executable module in any language or code format as long as the MIB compiler used can understand ASN.1.

7.4.2 The ATM Forum interim local management interface (ILMI)

An important aspect of managing ATM networks is the development of the management plane (M-plane) of the B-ISDN protocol reference model. Unfortunately, very little work has been done on this, which is very bad news for the initial builders and users of ATM networks. Until such time as ITU-T international standard network management methods and protocols specifically for ATM networks are available, the ATM Forum requires using the interim local management interface (ILMI). It is considered *interim* in the sense that it eventually will be incorporated (or even phased out) in favor of standard M-plane network management once it is available.

ATM networks will eventually be fully switched systems, like the telephone network. Until standard signaling methods are designed, tested, and implemented, VP connections will be "static" resources on ATM networks. However, users must still be able to change them. The ATM Forum uses ILMI to allow users to set up their VP connections. ILMI will use SNMPv1 to access an ILMI MIB running on the ATM network device. Along with performance information, an important ILMI function is to allow user configuration of VP (and VC) connections. This makes the VP (and VC) connections into static "semipermanent" resources on the ATM network, in the sense that ILMI is not a true signaling protocol. ILMI VPs and VCs are PVC (permanent virtual circuit), not SVC (switched virtual circuit), connections.

The ILMI MIB tree structure (under the umbrella of the "master" SMI tree) is set up to allow users to set correlations between VPs and VCs and their ports on the ATM network device. There is available information on the physical layer and ATM layer as well. However, the accumulation of ATM layer statistics, such as number of cells dropped, operational status, etc., is *optional*. This means that some equipment manufacturers will implement this part of the MIB, and some will not. Unfortunately, network managers will be interested in doing more than just setting up connections and whether a particular physical layer link is in service or not.

The current ATM Forum ILMI MIB tree structure is shown in Fig. 7.8. The two rightmost groups, network prefix and address, are included for backward compatibility with earlier versions of the ILMI. In addition, although not shown in Fig. 7.8, the system group from Internet implementations of SNMP must be implemented as well. The system group includes information such as a description of the device (switch, CPE, etc.), the contact person responsible for the device, the network name of the device, the location of the device, the services provided by the device, and the identification of the vendor's private MIB location (beginning 1.3.6.1.4.1...).

Each of the MIB entries on the tree must be accessed by the object identifier string and an index. An index is required because network management information on, for instance, physical interfaces (ports) must be provided for each configured port. This index is usually just a simple integer sequence number indicating the first, second, and third ports and so on. But some objects are more complex. These need not only a numeric port index but also a "subindex" to indicate a further indexing structure to the MIB entry. For example, information on a particular VPI number is available but must be accessed by SNMP not only by port index but also by an additional index indicating the VPI number itself.

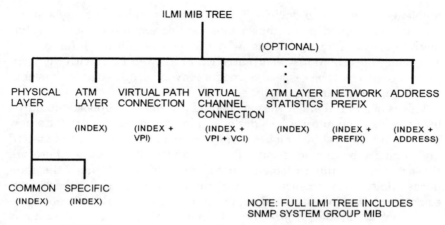

Figure 7.8   ILMI MIB.

- PHYSICAL LAYER:
  TRANSMISSION TYPE
  MEDIA TYPE
  OPERATIONAL STATUS

- ATM LAYER:
  MAXIMUM NUMBER OF VPCs
  MAXIMUM NUMBER OF VCCs
  VPI/VCI ADDRESS WIDTH
  ATM PORT TYPE (PUBLIC/PRIVATE)

- ATM LAYER STATISTICS:
  ATM CELLS RECEIVED
  ATM CELLS DROPPED ON RECEIVE SIDE
  ATM CELLS TRANSMITTED

Figure 7.9   ATM ILMI MIB
entries (representative).

A representative, but not exhaustive, list of the managed objects
included in the ILMI MIB is shown in Fig. 7.9. Note that the ILMI is
intended for use on the ATM UNI and does not address any network
management issues on the NNI interfaces.

Even though the MIB objects are software running in a device, they
usually just hold and record values for reporting to some network management software. However, because the ILMI MIB contains information about the relationship between ports and VPs and VCs, it can be
used to configure the connections if the agent software references them
for this purpose.

7.5   ATM Equipment Interoperability

Interoperability is always an important issue in any technology.
Interoperability simply means that equipment from vendor A can be
attached to equipment from vendor B without major problems, as long
as the functions supported by each correspond. There are always minor

problems, even among devices from the *same* vendor, but *major problems* in this context mean that a considerable amount of time is spent (perhaps days) figuring out just why the devices will not interoperate, and sometimes there just is no satisfactory answer, even with the technical experts from the respective vendors involved, although such events are, fortunately, rare.

This is one of the major reasons behind the rush to support standards in the vendor community. Besides giving instant market entry for a new product, interoperability makes it easy for customers to "mix and match" and compare equipment from different vendors (to a point—there are those worrisome minor problems that always crop up). Usually the standards implemented to ensure interoperability are "open" standards from some recognized international standards organization. But not necessarily. When a suitable *de jure* (by rule) standard is not available, many times vendors will seize on *de facto* (by fact) standards. De facto standards are standards based on large numbers of people doing things in the same way, not because of some standards organization's blessing or some inherent advantage that a particular method has over others. DOS and Windows have become de facto standards in the PC world, Unix in the workstation world. Neither is mandated, nor even particularly well suited for many tasks users wish to accomplish on either platform (Windows struggles to multitask, Unix is still text-based, and so forth).

Understandably, the ATM Forum, as a vendor consortium consisting of some 500 companies, has a real concern that the products and services developed and offered by their members compete on a more or less equal footing as far as features and interoperability. No member would want another to produce a proprietary method of performing some function that would give that vendor unfair advantage in the marketplace. The products and services must compete for market share based on their merits, not their exclusivity.

Accordingly, the ATM Forum has taken steps to ensure interoperability between the various vendors of ATM devices. Current proposals would require a member organization to submit the device (or software, or service implementation) to the ATM Forum for interoperability testing. Or an organization may carry out its own quality-control testing, including interoperability testing, if it so chooses. But how is anyone to be sure that ATM devices will interoperate, when the ATM network features and functions, and their various combinations, can form a long and elaborate list of things that two devices might do when they are internetworked? The ATM Forum used something called a *PICS proforma*.

7.5.1   The ATM Forum PICS proforma

The ATM Forum protocol implementation conformance statement (PICS) is a statement of exactly which functions and options have been implemented in an ATM device. The term *proforma* is Latin for "a declaration," so the PICS "declaration" forms a vendor's intentions regarding the capabilities of a particular product. The PICS is in the form of a questionnaire, usually many pages long (the PICS for ATM Forum signaling conformance is 30 pages long, with some 25 or so "questions" on many of the pages). The PICS will specify exactly which features are mandatory or optional, based on the relevant ATM Forum implementation agreement (e.g., the ATM Forum signaling specification). A conformance tester will simply check off the supported features one by one, with or without comments.

There are a number of ways that use of the PICS proforma will help customers with their ATM interoperability concerns. First, customers may be more willing to buy with confidence if the practice of PICS testing becomes common. Second, a customer may actually ask two vendors of ATM equipment for a copy their PICS proforma on a particular device. Interoperability may then be simplified by just comparing the two lists feature by feature to see if the devices do indeed support all the features and options the customer expects.

Most of the physical layer interfaces, the ATM layer itself, and the ATM signaling protocol all have their own PICS to date.

7.6   ATM Standards Incompleteness

The ATM Forum recently has been criticized for actually discouraging interoperability, not encouraging it. This puzzling statement does not mean that the 500 or so ATM Forum members are actively pursuing divergent paths; the truth is quite the contrary. It does, however, point out a very troublesome shortcoming of *all* ATM network standards today: They are necessarily incomplete.

The ATM Forum has quickly moved ahead on all sorts of issues that will be critical for ATM networking acceptance and success. Among these are lower-speed transports, network management issues, and so forth. But what has happened in the meantime is that the ATM Forum has moved far beyond the international standards community (the ITU-T, ISO, even ANSI) in terms of the intended scope of early ATM standards documentation. How will the international standards bodies ever catch up?

By extending existing ATM ITU-T documentation, for instance, the ATM Forum members risk being caught traveling down the wrong path, so to speak, when a group such as the ITU-T finally gets around to standardizing a certain way of performing some task in the ATM protocol stack. Then the ATM Forum organizations face the embarrassing situation of either changing their own specifications to conform to the de jure standard or staying their course, which would then diverge from the accepted practice, by definition. Never lose sight of the fact that the ATM Forum is a vendor consortium, not a standards-making body per se. Their specifications are actually *implementation agreements* binding *only* on their own members. Now it can rightly be said that if *everybody* is a member, this may be good enough. But not everybody *is* a member, and consortiums have a funny way of breaking apart or at least forming internal factions when an issue that is passionately championed by an important member becomes a rallying point for opponents following their own agenda. The rocky road to a "standard" version of Unix is a perfect example.

The ATM Forum points out that divisiveness and factions are not only characteristics of consortiums. Even the ITU-T member nations were divided over the decision to make the ATM cell payload 48 bytes as a compromise between 32- and 64-byte payload lengths. And a compromise is nothing more than a way of alienating two groups when a decision will at least make one party or the other happy with the outcome.

Examples of ATM standards incompleteness abound. But just to illustrate the potential for diverging standards in the most innocent of areas, not only with the international standards community, but even within the ATM Forum itself, the long saga of ATM network flow control will be briefly related.

7.6.1   ATM Forum flow control proposals

It was easy to talk about flow control in ATM networks: There wasn't any. There was a flow control *mechanism,* to be sure. Every ATM cell on a UNI has 4 bits set aside for a generic flow control (GFC) field. The trouble is that use of this field is not defined anywhere. There is a mechanism but no details available for the intended functioning of the mechanism.

The issue of flow control is closely related to the technically separate issue of congestion control. If an ATM network is congested, it may respond by discarding cells. For some classes of service (notably class A CBR and class B VBR), there is nothing that can be done about this; time-sensitive applications cannot effectively retransmit missing cells. However, discarded cells that have been broken down by the ATM SAR sublayer of the AAL from *data* application variable-length frames or data units are another story.

Existing data protocols all respond to errored data by resending the data in error. And because of the utter lack of ATM-specific data transport protocols (itself another example of incompleteness), end-data applications have really no choice but to resend the entire data unit, which may have been broken up into nearly 100 cells. For example, a 4500-byte, 4-Mbps Token Ring frame must be sent across an ATM network as a series of 95 cell payloads with AAL-5. Even if only one cell is discarded by a congested ATM switch, the entire 95-cell sequence must be resent to the destination. This only adds to the network congestion, of course. Thus the ATM network needs congestion control within the network to tie in to flow control for the users feeding the network to prevent this condition. Then the ATM network can inform senders to slow down, not because a receiver is being swamped with too much data arriving too fast (flow control), but because the ATM network is being swamped with too much data arriving too fast.

Proposals for doing this in a systematic rather than proprietary or ad hoc manner have been made. But there are proposals to the ITU-T, to ANSI, to BellCore, and other standards organizations. There are also ATM Forum proposals for ATM flow control. Thus the debate is not only among the organizations but within the organizations themselves. This section provides a brief overview of the separate proposals for ATM Forum flow control and the debate they generated until rate-based flow control was standardized in November 1994.

There were two main proposals debated at the ATM Forum. One was known as *rate-based* (RB) flow control, and the other was known as *credit-based* (CB) flow control. To further complicate matters, there were actually two different credit-based flow control schemes being considered. This section will group both CB methods together for simplicity.

Rate-based flow control basically recommends translating the frame-relay FECN and BECN bit functions into ATM equivalents. Some of this has been done already, but only for the specific case of a frame-relay service connection on an ATM network. There are even more elaborate variations on this method, proposed as part of the available-bit-rate (ABR) service definition.

Credit-based flow control is sometimes referred to as *virtual circuit flow control* (*VCFC*), but most proposals just break them down into rate-based flow control (RBFC) and credit-based flow control (CBFC) alternatives.

Both RBFC and CBFC methods had strengths and weaknesses. Normally, a data network based on private leased lines (or existing ATM data services) runs as an "open loop." That is, data traffic is sent from either end (full duplex operation) as fast as the links can carry it. The endpoints are the only pieces of the network that need to exchange flow control information. The network plays no real role in the process. An ATM network, however, given its variety of services and scope of applications support, needs a way to break into this loop to add information about the congestion within the network to this endpoint-to-endpoint conversation. This would make the duplexed connections into a *feedback loop*.

RBFC proposes to do this by setting the EFCI bit in the PTI field of the cell header. This bit is used for data applications using AAL-5 and is ignored by class A and class B applications on an ATM network. This corresponds to the FECN bit in the sense that it is sent along the same path as the data to the destination. It is up to the destination to inform the sender to slow down. FECN/EFCI schemes are used in data protocols such as TCP/IP, where the sender's data unit rate is controlled by the receiver's *window size,* a measure of the receiver's buffer allocation. BECN, which has no explicit counterpart in ATM (yet), would be used with data protocols that control data unit flow rates at the sending side of the network. Most of the functionality of the RBFC method must be built into the endpoints of the ATM network.

CBFC proposed to construct the required feedback loop with explicit, hop-by-hop (ATM network node to ATM network node) messages. These messages (the credits) would say, in effect, "VPI = 34,VCI = 776 may send 20 more cells." After the 20 cells have been sent from one ATM switch to the adjacent ATM switch, no further cells can be sent on the connection until further permission messages are received. The net result is a *very* tightly controlled feedback loop and very robust control down to the link level. Most of the functionality of the CBFC method must be built into the ATM switches themselves. Since ATM switches already have a lot to do, this has made some people nervous.

A comparison of an open loop and RBFC and CBFC feedback loops is shown in Fig. 7.10.

The two CBFC proposals differed as to how these credit messages would be sent between two network nodes. One proposal was to create

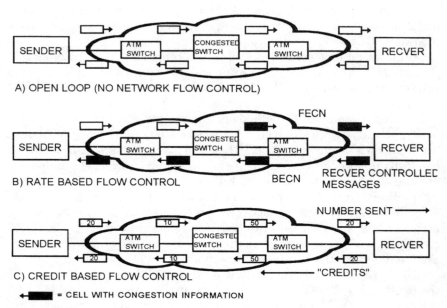

Figure 7.10   Flow control mechanisms.

RATE BASED:	CREDIT BASED:
Well Understood	Better for ATM
RB has long history	CB is only future choice
CB is long-range	CB is ready now
CB is too much for switches	Switches can do it
RB can be per hop too	CB is per hop now

Figure 7.11 Rate-based versus credit-based.

explicit cells, similar in format and function to OAM cells, that would circulate between endpoints on the ATM network to carry the FECN (now) and BECN (later) notifications. The drawback of this proposal was that it added traffic to what is supposedly an already congested network. In other words, it seems paradoxical to fix a network that is sending too many cells by sending more cells. The other proposal would somehow indicate credits by means of a mechanism in the cell headers themselves. The drawbacks of this method were that (1) there is not a lot of room in the cell header to begin with, and (2) the method's proper functioning depended on the availability of cells in which to send the credits. In a "gridlocked" ATM network, this may be asking a lot.

RBFC was a better fit with what has come before in this arena, but CBFC was probably better in the long run for ATM network's unique aspects. The worst thing that could possibly happen is that the ATM Forum might have standardized *both* and left the implementation optional for various vendors. This would satisfy no one and could actually slow ATM acceptance and deployment.

The core arguments for and against RBFC and CBFC are summarized in Fig. 7.11. Keep in mind that this issue was essentially a "sideshow" under the big top of ATM standardization. At any rate, it points out the current state of affairs in many areas of ATM, areas that in other networking technologies are fully understood and implemented in a consistent fashion already.

7.7 ATM Myths

ATM is so new that it would seem that all the information available about it should be accurate and up-to-date. Yet there are many misconceptions or myths about ATM throughout write-ups in the trade press and magazines. This section takes a look at some of the myths that have grown up around ATM even at this early stage of its life as a network technology. Some of the myths concern ATM limitations ("ATM does not..."), and

- NO ERROR CHECKING ON CELL DATA
- ATM DISCARDS CELLS WHEN CONGESTED
- ATM WILL RUN WELL ON ANYTHING
- ATM NETWORKS CARRY VOICE AND VIDEO TODAY
- ATM NETWORKS ARE MORE EFFICIENT
- ATM WILL EVENTUALLY BE ALL THERE IS
- SMDS AND ATM ARE VERY DIFFERENT

Figure 7.12   Seven myths about ATM.

some concern ATM capabilities ("ATM will..."). Unfortunately, there are some things ATM does that people sometimes say it cannot and some things that ATM just will not do that others insist it will.

So here is a detailed explanation of some of the more consistent and persistent myths about ATM performance and features and why they are distortions of the truth. For convenience, they are listed in Fig. 7.12.

7.7.1   No error checking on cell data

Myth 1: ATM does no error checking on the cell data, as in "ATM only does error checking on the cell header." This myth is actually a partial truth. It *is* true that ATM switches—the network nodes themselves—only do error checking on the cell headers. The reason is to prevent errored cells from being sent to the wrong destinations, a reasonable enough aim.

However, there *is* error checking on the payload, or information, inside an ATM cell. However, it is done at the endpoints of the ATM network. This error checking is a function of the ATM adaptation layer (AAL), which is very much a part of the ATM protocol architecture. AALs have cyclical redundancy checks (CRCs) on data all over the place, and with good reason. It makes no sense at all to pass data that may be in error to a computer, either to a hardware board chipset or to main memory. Errors may cause the system to hang, data to be lost, or even possibly both.

To claim there is no error checking on data by ATM is inaccurate at best and irresponsible at worst.

7.7.2   ATM discards cells when congested

Myth 2: ATM switches discard cells when congested, as in "ATM networks will throw cells away under congested conditions." This myth is also a partial truth and may even be strictly true. But it is rather like sending a car overseas by ship. The shipper will never say, "By the way, if the ship is in danger of sinking, we will have to throw cargo overboard, and this may just be your car." This may be undeniably true, but who would ever send cargo with these guys?

The same is true of ATM switches. If the switch is in danger of becoming swamped with traffic, and if there is a choice between crashing the switch and possibly taking all the switches it is attached to down or throwing some cells away, then the ATM network node will discard cells. But this is *only* a last resort. Cells in ATM are tagged with a cell loss priority (CLP) bit, a 1 bit meaning that the cell *may* be discarded if, to use the analogy, the ship is sinking. But generally speaking, the CLP = 1 traffic goes merrily on its way through the network with the "more important" CLP = 0 cells.

There are two very good reasons for this. First, the network service provider may get paid by the number of cells delivered or (if the charge is a flat rate) provide for a discount for undelivered cells. Discarding cells means lost revenues. And the danger exists that the cell will be sent 90 percent of the way across the network and discarded almost at the destination. All those network resources used for nought!

Second, discarding traffic is not a particularly effective means of combating congestion. Restricting input is usually more effective, and discarding usually *adds* to congestion. This is so because applications (users) are all poised to respond to missing data by simply resending the absent cells onto the already congested network. This, of course, defeats the whole purpose of discarding cells to being with.

Thus ATM networks have little to gain from discarding cells under any but the direst of circumstances. Add buffers, speed up links, redesign the backbone—anything is more desirable to both network and users than throwing cells into the bit bucket.

7.7.3   ATM will run well on anything

Myth 3: ATM can run well on any medium, as in "ATM networks may use unshielded twisted-pair (UTP) wiring, coaxial cable, microwave, or fiberoptic media." The key word in this myth is *well.* Nobody actually knows how ATM will perform on anything but fiber. ATM is designed to run on fiber, being essentially the switching strategy developed in 1988 for SONET (SDH to the ITU). SONET is a high-speed (gigabits again) trunking technology running on fiber, and only fiber.

ATM has many design characteristics that are optimized for fiber-based networks, which are in turn characterized by two qualities: (1) bit-error rates (BERs) literally thousands of times better than other media such as coax, and (2) the fact that when bit errors do occur, they are more than 99 percent of the time single-bit errors. That is, they do not come in bursts, as on all other media.

In fact, the error checking on the header is a direct by-product of this characteristic. Why check the whole cell for errors if the chances are so small? Just check the header to prevent misdirected traffic.

A concern is that ATM is no longer coupled to SONET and low-error fiber. ATM may now run on DS-1 (T-1 at 1.544 Mbps) and DS-3 (T-3 at 45 Mbps) and even other transports. But T-1 runs on two pairs of unshielded copper wire. T-3 may run on fiber, but it is also common over microwave links and coaxial cable. The error rates on these media are higher and bursty by nature.

Whether the error rates on these media will be compatible with ATM as designed is an object of intense debate. So far, results are promising, but only promising, not complete.

7.7.4 ATM networks will carry voice and video today

Myth 4: ATM networks will carry voice and video right now, as in "early ATM networks will be able to carry telephone, cable TV, and data traffic." This myth has far-reaching consequences, because ATM is being positioned in the marketplace as a technology that can "do it all": voice, video, data. Everything is just a bit stream to ATM, so why not?

The problem is that nobody has a standard way of putting video on ATM networks, and the methods proposed for voice are primitive at best. Consider voice first. Current networks generate voice samples at a continuous bit rate (CBR) of 64 kbps. This occurs whether someone is actually talking or not. Silence is just another bit pattern. Putting this stream of bits on an ATM network is self-defeating. ATM is essentially a sophisticated multiplexing technique that saves bandwidth when an application is not generating bits. But CBR applications *always* generate bits. There is no technical gain at all. And added to the fact that someone ultimately must pay to migrate all this older voice equipment to new ATM voice equipment, it will likely be years before voice ever appears on an ATM network, if at all.

Video has a different problem. Video today comes in uncompressed and compressed versions. Uncompressed video is a CBR application like voice, and the same arguments apply. Compressed video becomes a variable-bit-rate (VBR) application (since sometimes 1000 bytes may be compressed to 500, and sometimes to 250, and so on). But it is VBR with a special twist: It still matters how long it takes for the bits to get to the TV. And worse yet, the receiver has to know how long it took, because video bits that arrive too early or too late must be discarded; otherwise, the screen action will jerk and jump like old nickelodeons.

There is no solution today to this problem. In fact, it is actually worse. The audio portion of the video must be sent along. There is no way to coordinate the video and audio bits at the receiver. It may be years before telephone and cable television appear on an ATM network.

7.7.5   ATM networks are more efficient

Myth 5: ATM is more efficient than other network architectures, as in "ATM networks offer a more efficient use of network resources." This myth involves a misuse of the term *efficient*. It is undeniably true that ATM networks will be more flexible than other network architectures, in the sense that they can be adapted for a wide range of user requirements and applications. However, it is never a good idea to confuse *flexibility* with *efficiency*.

Right now television sets sold in the United States cannot be used in Europe; the European system uses a different scanning technique that cannot be received by U.S. sets. If a company added a device to each television it made that enabled it to receive both kinds of signals, the result would definitely be more flexible. But would it be more efficient?

The answer to the question involves more than just capabilities. It would have to include considerations of price, customer acceptance, and the percentage of television sets moved back and forth between the United States and Europe to answer that question. Right now the answer would have to be "no."

So it is with ATM today. While the promise of ATM is both flexibility and efficiency, there are other factors to consider before implementers will do more than just offer more of the same kinds of basic data services. People can buy a kitchen device that both slices and dices, but unless it is much more attractive to users in price and convenience than a slicer and a dicer separately, why bother?

7.7.6   ATM will eventually be all there is

Myth 6: All networks will eventually migrate to ATM, as in "ATM will be the network of networks for all services: voice and video as well as data." Someone once remarked that ATM must fail. It cannot succeed, the argument went, by its own definition. If ATM is designed to be an adequate network for voice, an adequate network for video, and an adequate network for data, all at the same time, then it is obviously doomed; no one in their right mind would ever use it.

Because there will always be a better way to build voice networks, and video networks, and data networks, why settle for second best? ATM cannot possibly be the best voice/video/data (pick one) network there is, because it must satisfy the other user nonvoice/nonvideo/nondata populations at the same time. Therefore, ATM cannot be the best solution for anything, by its own definition.

This argument is very seductive and probably more subtle than it seems. It actually ties together myths from the previous two sections. If ATM cannot do voice and video right now, and it is not more efficient than building separate specialized networks, then what is it good for?

It may seem that there is not even a good reply to this argument. But there is. The answer is that ATM is new and evolving. It is not finished yet, but that may be its strength and not its weakness.

Many technologies have taken years to grow up and shake out less viable alternate methods of doing things. Electricity came to homes as ac and dc until Tesla showed that it was much more economic (efficient) to deliver ac, even though dc was safer. A more pertinent example is the early automobile. No one thought the simple gas-buggies of the 1890s would be anything more than a toy for the rich. Horses pulled ice wagons, elegant carriages, heavy loads. Yet it was not long before the flexibility and efficiency of gasoline engines made horses obsolete.

ATM may be only adequate today for many services, but it may not remain that way for long.

7.7.7 SMDS and ATM are very different

Myth 7: SMDS is different from ATM, as in "users will not buy SMDS because they are waiting for ATM." This is more of an SMDS myth than an ATM myth, but it has an impact on ATM just the same.

Switched multimegabit data services (SMDS) was an early (1990) BellCore attempt to bring the benefits of ATM to the marketplace as soon as possible. As such, it is a full and complete implementation of all the ATM layers. Unfortunately, SMDS layers do not correspond one-for-one with ATM layers. For instance, the ATM cell appears in SMDS as the SMDS interface protocol layer 2 protocol data unit (SIP-L2 PDU).

Instead of emphasizing these differences, it would be better to emphasize what SMDS offers that ATM does not: a way of doing connectionless services over a connection-oriented transport network (ATM). This is the attraction of SMDS for a large community of data users faced with the problem of mesh-connecting high-speed LANs. This function is *not* provided by ATM itself. Connectionless services must be added on in ATM networks by means of a connectionless network access protocol (CLNAP). SMDS provides this today.

There is no reason why SMDS services cannot be offered over a pure ATM network. This would not affect the user interface at all, since it occurs above the normal connection-oriented transport services ATM provides. In fact, the ITU-T intends to merge SMDS and its European counterpart CBDS (connectionless broadband data services) into something called *connectionless network services* (CLNS) at some point in the near future. Then SMDS would become just another thing an ATM network can do.

There may be lots of reasons why people will not buy SMDS. It may be priced too high, not be available in many places, and even suffer from security issues. All these things are certainly true. But what is meant by the myth in this case is that users do not need a different implementation of ATM, which is what SMDS provides. They would rather wait for SMDS capabilities in a true ATM environment. Looking at the matter in this way would end the confusion.

These are the myths, and this is the reality. ATM is not too good to be true, nor is it so bad that it is awful. It is a tool for building advanced networks that match up with the requirements of the 1990s and beyond quite well. But it is only a tool. And like a tool, it is how well it is used that really counts.

7.8   ATM Unanswered Questions

Just to wind up the discussion of ATM performance and network considerations, there are some other concerns that do not seem to fall into any other category. There are some very critical items to be dealt with before ATM becomes as viable a network architecture as TCP/IP or even X.25. There are many minor ones, but four major issues threaten to stall ATM deployment before it even gets started.

First, it is just a fact of life that variable-length packets or frames or cells (call them either) are *better* for data. If the major applications on ATM networks remain bandwidth-greedy graphics, imaging, and multimedia applications, the whole rationale for cells is gone.

Next, for a true WAN-based ATM network, standards and methods for flow control and congestion management *must* be in place and used. This is not so critical for private ATM networks, but for ATM to become the next "telephone" network, it is crucial.

Also, the demand for switched virtual circuits will only intensify since users may not settle for "semipermanent" site VPI numberings. But signaling protocol implementations have always been difficult to do and even harder to make interoperable.

Most critically, ATM must be able to carry existing transport protocols (whatever layer) easily and efficiently. A lot of documentation has been prepared on interfacing TCP/IP protocols with ATM networks, but the fact remains that TCP/IP, on its twentieth birthday, was designed and intended to run on slower networks. Some organizations, particularly those represented in the ATM Forum, have bitten the bullet and decided to change the way their protocols, even proprietary ones, operate just to make it easier for them to run on ATM networks.

8

ATM and the Future

ATM does not exist in a vacuum. Although it is tempting to view ATM as the network of networks and the last network that will ever be built, there are many other technologies that users will consider along with ATM as a possible solution to their networking problems. Some of these are even seen as rival technologies to ATM. The term *rival* is used in this context to mean that if another network technology can solve a business problem as easily as ATM, the deciding factor will shift to some other aspect. Perhaps cost or ease of installation and operation will be the criterion by which a potential business solution will be judged under these circumstances. In any case, the decision to use ATM is not a foregone conclusion in many business situations, especially where data are concerned.

ATM is unique in its attempt to fold video, voice, and data networks into a single physical network. But users may not care in the short run—or even in the long run—about anything but data. This chapter is a look at the future of ATM in a world dominated by the overwhelming need for users to consider advanced networks not for their broadness but for their depth. It may turn out to be much more important for users to build and operate networks that will handle data in more and better ways in terms of delay and bandwidth than in terms of wide application among different needs. Will ATM be able to compete in this situation?

This chapter begins by looking at a number of different solutions that are often mentioned in the same breath as ATM in terms of advanced data network solutions. Three different environments will be examined: the LAN, the MAN, and the WAN. The rise of simple and cheap local area network (LAN) solutions has led to the rapid development of several technologies for a customer premises environment, so several different potential solutions will be considered in this section. These limited-distance solutions are newly proposed 100-Mbps IEEE LAN technologies, Switched Ethernet, which assigns a full 10 Mbps to each station on a LAN, and a variation on ANSI's FDDI standard known as FDDI-II.

The next technology applies to metropolitan areas. Only one is considered here, but it is important as both a forerunner and rival to ATM. This technology is IEEE 802.6 metropolitan area network (MAN) using a protocol called *distributed queue dual bus* (*DQDB*), which has many features in common (as well as important differences) with ATM. The last technology applies to the wide area (coast to coast). The accepted standard technology here is naturally ATM, but this chapter is meant to consider alternatives. Thus a proprietary method of building low-delay, high-speed wide area networks (WANs) is examined. The method chosen, just as an example, is a technology from IBM known informally as *packet transfer mode* (*PTM*). Although this is IBM's version, other companies have announced plans to support a very similar approach for data networks, even using these "packet" methods as an NNI combined with ATM Forum UNI support. The future of such hybrid schemes is uncertain, to say the least, but important nonetheless.

The next major section of this chapter examines the relationship of public service offerings to ATM. The two offerings most frequently mentioned as ATM alternatives or rivals are frame relay and SMDS. Their features and operational characteristics in relation to ATM are discussed in more detail, including a more detailed look at how frame-relay and SMDS networks might operate in an ATM world.

The chapter closes with a look at the whole environment that ATM is intended for: full broadband ISDN. The B-ISDN reference model is discussed in light of alternative networking possibilities, and a startling conclusion about the future of other networking technologies in the ATM world is pointed out. The ATM agenda is shown to be the only rational and natural approach for building literally any kind of network at all.

8.1   Local Area Network (LAN) Solutions

A very good argument can be made that if it weren't for LANs, there wouldn't be any ATM. This may sound strange, especially in view of the fact that ATM started out strictly as a WAN technology. The key to understanding the whole point, however, is realizing that it was the pressure on the LAN equipment vendors to provide higher and higher speed solutions that made these vendors turn to ATM in the first place. The LAN vendors essentially "hijacked" the entire ATM protocol stack away from the WAN groups (e.g., ITU-T, BellCore, among others) and gave it a new identity as a possible LAN solution.

This did not have to be the case, though. In fact, the traditional LAN standardization groups, such as the IEEE and ANSI, had already several customer premises LAN solutions that were supposed to solve all the data problems that users were encountering as applications and processors migrated more and more toward a client-server environment. The characteristic most identified with client-server architectures and applications is their *distributed* nature, meaning that more and more processing power is needed not in a stand-alone device but spread out among many devices on a network. These are the clients and the servers.

There are three parallel standards that have been mentioned frequently as solving the client-server need for high-speed data networks connecting PCs and workstations in a distributed environment. The first to be considered and the newest of them all is the IEEE's initiative to standardize a version of both Ethernet and Token Ring to run at 100 Mbps. The original versions of Ethernet ran at 10 Mbps, and the two original versions of Token Ring ran at 4 and 16 Mbps (on shielded twisted pair). The second method discussed is a technique known as *Switched Ethernet*, which enables each station on a 10-Mbps Ethernet to actually utilize a full 10-Mbps bandwidth instead of sharing a single 10 Mbps, as the original Ethernet specification mandated. The last method is a technique based on FDDI (which already runs at 100 Mbps) and known as FDDI-II. This will do pretty much all that FDDI does in the data world but adds some features for addressing the needs of isochronous channels for time-sensitive applications (such as voice). With this added capability, it is sometimes proposed that FDDI-II would rival ATM in terms of service and that FDDI-II would actually be cheaper to use than ATM.

The list could easily be expanded to include newer proposed technologies such as Fibre Channel, but earlier chapters have shown that technologies like Fibre Channel and FDDI can be used as ATM transports. The goal of this chapter is to detail methods and technologies that have not been discussed earlier. Thus the list will be limited to the alternatives listed in Fig. 8.1.

8.1.1 100-Mbps LAN solutions

When the first Ethernet LANs began to appear in the early 1980s, the PCs and microprocessors that existed were used in an overwhelmingly stand-alone fashion. LANs were used to connect minicomputers for the most part, with PCs only participating as terminal emulation devices

- LOCAL AREA NETWORKS:
  100 Mbps LANs
  Switched "Ethernet"
  FDDI-II

- METROPOLITAN AREA NETWORKS:
  IEEE 802.6

- WIDE AREA NETWORKS:
  PACKET TRANSFER MODE (PTM)

- PUBLIC NETWORK SERVICES:
  SMDS (MAN)
  Frame Relay

Figure 8.1 Alternatives to ATM.

on the LAN. That is, they became text-based teletype-equivalent terminals that depended on the locally attached minicomputer for all processing. PCs and workstations had their own operating systems and applications, but they were not generally used in the client-server environment initially.

This was probably just as well. Early PCs and even workstations were built around processor chips that were extremely modest in power and speed. Early PC chipsets ran at 8 MHz, executed about 4 million instructions per second (Mips), and had only 64K of memory. The common rule of thumb, then as now, is that a microprocessor chip can generate bits for a network attachment at about half the rate of the instructions per second it can execute internally. Thus a 8-MHz machine with 4 Mips of power could generate about 2 Mbps of data for a network, at its peak rate. Usually, the machine had much less of a bandwidth requirement.

Therefore, an Ethernet LAN running at 10 Mbps could easily accommodate 10, 50, or 200 of these early PCs when the time came to hook them up to LANs directly. This was done as the applications these PCs and workstations ran easily overtook in power and sophistication the applications that were earlier reserved for the mainframe and minicomputer environment. The need for PCs and workstations to share information and resources (generally, resources are considered physical entities, such as color printers, scanners, and other equipment an organization felt it could not afford to buy for each and every desktop) meant that they came to be deployed directly on the Ethernet and Token Ring LANs that were being built in the mid-1980s.

The PCs and workstations shared the bandwidth provided by the LAN. Since data applications were inherently "bursty," with long periods of silence ("think time") punctuated by a demand for high speeds and throughput, it was a very good match. Applications got all 10 Mbps of bandwidth on the Ethernet, but when the application was silent, other stations could use it, on a contention basis. LANs could efficiently parcel out the bandwidth available, and PCs and workstations had a very high-speed network available whenever they needed it. And since the stations could only generate 2 Mbps of data in one burst anyway, there was no danger at all that *any* station on the LAN would monopolize the bandwidth or demand higher speeds for any application.

By the late 1980s, however, there were signs that this situation would not hold true much longer. The newer 386 chipsets ran at 32 MHz and executed about 12 Mips, so they could churn out bits at about 6 Mbps, which exceeded at least one of the more common LAN architectures available: Token Ring. When a LAN suddenly became swamped with traffic from these higher-speed machines—and the applications that ran on them—the only choice a network manager had was to split the LAN into two parts. The need for formerly connected

LANs to still communicate (that was the whole point in the first place) was handled by adding an internetworking device—a bridge or router—to the now separated LANs. These LANs more and more frequently came to be built around "hubs" (Ethernet-based—really 802.3 CSMA/CD, the IEEE standard—network devices) instead of Token Ring solutions, mostly due to cost considerations.

By the 1990s, even this concept was running into problems in large LAN situations. The processors were now Pentium-type machines with 66 MHz and 100 Mips. These could pump out 50 Mbps and easily overwhelm not only a 10-Mbps Ethernet but a 16-Mbps Token Ring as well. Network managers found that their LANs were starting to show 30 percent utilization during busy hours and 50 percent during peaks. The idea of dividing the LANs up into smaller and smaller units with fewer and fewer stations connected by bridges or routers did not appeal to many of these network managers. This reluctance was mainly due to the uncertainty of the practice (it was not always clear just what the net effect would be) but also because the practice seemed so ad hoc and even "klugey."

Thus pressure began to mount on standards organizations, especially the IEEE as the source of all earlier LAN specifications, to invent the "second generation" of LANs. These would preferably run at 100 Mbps or higher and be similar to Ethernet and Token Ring LANs that most organizations were familiar with. The users generally did not want *new* technology, just *faster* technology.

But new technology was what they got initially. First, they got a 100-Mbps LAN technology—sort of. Around 1989, a technology called *fiber distributed data interface* (*FDDI*) was developed by ANSI. FDDI ran at the required speed, but on fiberoptic cable, a medium most organizations were not familiar with and which was generally more expensive than other media. It was designed to run over distances as great as 100 km, which did not really appeal to users who were concerned with the clients in the next office and the server down the hall. Eventually, FDDI was modified to run on copper-based media such as unshielded twisted pair (Ethernet and Token Ring had taken the plunge into UTP from coax and STP long before), but the damage was done. Users stayed away in droves.

Another possibility was being explored, and users liked this idea much better, for one very good reason: They had essentially proposed it. Users and user groups had flexed their muscles in the late 1980s and been very successful—and they liked it. The first example was with Ethernet itself. Users—really the network managers and implementers, but they are still users too—did not like the limitations in terms of size and weight of the coaxial cable Ethernet required. Cable television networks used much smaller and cheaper cable. It was more flexible than "thick" Ethernet coax and so much cheaper to have installed.

Thus, when a version of Ethernet was offered by a vendor that could use this cable television coaxial cable, users voted with their dollars. Soon the scramble was on the introduce "thin coax" products, which created such anarchy that the IEEE was forced to standardize this "Cheapernet" (as 10Base2) as well. It was still Ethernet in terms of speed, but the physical layout and distances were highly restrictive compared with classic Ethernet-based LANs.

Once users started building larger and larger "Cheapernet" networks, however, it became apparent that the new standard was totally unsuited for a general office environment. The stations had to be "daisy-chained" together from one to the other, making it next to impossible to insert or remove stations without recabling the LAN. There were other complaints as well, but all focused on the impracticality of wiring a building efficiently with thin-wire Ethernet.

What users ideally wanted was not something that looked like data cabling at all. They wanted data cable for LANs to look like UTP phone wire for telephones, for a number of reasons. First of all, it was dirt cheap. Second, installers had been working with it for years and were familiar with it. Third, it was a star-wired system radiating out from a central point, not a complicated bus (Ethernet) or daisy-chain ("Cheapernet") arrangement.

Of course, the same "Cheapernet" scenario happened again, with one vendor offering 10-Mbps Ethernet-based LANs over UTP wiring. This time, however, instead of scrambling with different flavors, the other vendors got smart. They went directly to the IEEE and insisted on a 10BaseT standard ASAP. These vendors argued that they could not wait years while a new standard was researched and debated, while one vendor dominated the market. They needed something immediately so that all vendors who wanted to sell 10BaseT solutions could do so on an even footing with the same technology. Thus in a mere 18 months—an astonishing speed—the 10BaseT (802.3i) specification became the overwhelmingly favorite LAN technology. This star-wired UTP LAN created the 10BaseT hub market almost overnight.

Needless to say, when the first user rumblings were heard from large users of LAN products about the need for 100-Mbps LANs that were as similar to Ethernet-based LANs as possible, the IEEE responded. (Never forget that most IEEE committee members are employees themselves of vendors of these products.) Two groups insisted that they knew best how to provide 100-Mbps data transfer over a UTP LAN.

The two groups were a startup company in California named Grand Junction and two of the largest and most respected companies in the data communication arena today: Hewlett-Packard (HP) and AT&T. It is a measure of how fast things change in the industry today that they were competing for 100-Mbps Ethernet-based LAN standards on more or less equal footing. The major appeal of Grand Junction's approach

ATTRIBUTE:	100BaseT (802.3u)	100VG-AnyLAN (802.I2)
MAC Layer	CSMA/CD	"Demand Priority"
Backward Compatible?	YES	NO
Media	Cat 5 UTP* (2 prs)	Cat 3 UTP* (4 prs)
Token Support?	NO	YES
Intended Distance	100 meters (328 feet)	100 meters (328 feet)

* Each group has promised to support both types

Figure 8.2 100BaseT and 100VG-AnyLAN compared.

was to retain all of 802.3's MAC protocol, known as *carrier sense multiple access/collision detection (CSMA/CD)*. HP and AT&T used a technique they called *demand priority*.

Today, both approaches are being standardized by IEEE committees. Demand priority, since it is *not* in any shape, manner, or form related to CSMA/CD, has its own committee: 802.12. Grand Junction is working under the Ethernet 802.3 committee as 802.3u. The main differences between the approaches are shown in Fig. 8.2. Most of the time HP and AT&T (and the newest partner, IBM) refer to their plan as 100VG-AnyLAN, referring to the fact that it runs at 100 Mbps, on "voice grade" wire (actually category 3 or better UTP), and that it is not just tied to 802.3 Ethernet-based LANs anymore. If the new 802.12 hubs distribute a token on some ports, these ports would make a Token Ring subset of the network.

A full standardization of either technique is imminent. These technologies will address only data in any case, with no concept of multimedia or video support built in. But since the costs for interface cards are only supposed to be twice that of existing 10-Mbps 802.3 Ethernet boards, there should be a good market for these products.

8.1.2   Switched Ethernet solutions

Perhaps it does not make sense to standardize LANs that run at 100 Mbps, as an extension to Ethernet or anything else. After all, FDDI runs at 100 Mbps, and it has been around for a while. No one seemed really excited about building FDDI networks, probably due to the fact that this fiber-based technology remained quite expensive until relatively recently.

Most users cannot even use up a significant portion of a full 10-Mbps 802.3 or Ethernet bandwidth as it is, despite the load on the networks in the aggregate. The 10 Mbps may not be enough for 100 users or even 50 users, but it is certainly enough for *one* user. Thus there are companies with products that keep the LAN speed at 10 Mbps but give each users attached to the hub a "segment" on the LAN. This segment forms a point-to-point data link running at a full 10 Mbps. It is still a LAN, and there is still CSMA/CD, but there are no other stations on the segment except the user's station and the hub port.

Inside the hub, instead of using the backplane bus to emulate an Ethernet-like bus cable, the input and output are linked by a switched fabric. This forms a LAN with network nodes that function almost exactly like ATM switches, but with 10-Mbps input and output port speeds only.

The advantage to this approach is that it requires no new standards at all. The network is still essentially an Ethernet or 802.3 LAN, but instead of many stations sharing one bus cable, exactly one station per segment is switching through the fabric. Since what happens inside a switch or network node is not really part of a standard protocol stack (the same holds true for ATM, of course), a vendor can implement Switched Ethernet in a number of ways.

There are several variations on the Switched Ethernet theme, including *full-duplex* Switched Ethernet, which allows a station to send and receive at a full 10 Mbps at the same time. This makes the throughput for each station a full 20 Mbps but, unfortunately, it is not compatible with other Ethernet protocol implementations and hardware.

But again, Switched Ethernet is a data-only solution. No multimedia or video support is part of the technology itself. So far Switched Ethernet solutions have been highly proprietary.

8.1.3   FDDI-II solutions

To this point, the two LAN technologies mentioned, 100-Mbps Ethernet and Switched Ethernet, have no allowance for multimedia or video in their specifications. What this means is that these solutions have no real way to guarantee a fixed delay for time-sensitive applications of this type while they are busily delivering variable-length LAN data frames. This seems to eliminate both of them as viable competitors with ATM or ATM LANs, unless multimedia and video applications are not important to a particular user community at all, either now or in the future. Now, support for these applications could always be added in the future, but then this would be an added-on function, almost an afterthought, and not a capability considered and planned for from the beginning, as in ATM.

However, there is at least one possible solution that *does* include support for time-sensitive traffic very similar to ATM's. This support is provided by FDDI-II, an extension and upward-compatible version of the original data-only FDDI LAN approach.

FDDI in its original form with variable-length data frames up to 4500 bytes or so long is unsuited for CBR, fixed-delay services that ATM supports as part of its service description. There is a "synchronous" traffic class in FDDI, but even this class of service only guarantees a minimum sustained data rate, not a fixed delay. This fixed delay is needed for applications that would typically be circuit-switched, such as voice and video.

FDDI-II adds this circuit capability while still supporting variable-length data frames. Two stations on an FDDI-II network establish a connection for these isochronous CBR services, either manually or by a messaging protocol. The only requirement is that the two end stations understand the method used.

What FDDI-II adds is a 125-µs frame structure to the FDDI ring architecture, which circulates along with the variable-length data units. A connection consists of regularly repeating time slots in this frame. In FDDI-II, these connections are supported in *hybrid mode*. A *basic mode* exists that is the equivalent of regular FDDI.

When in hybrid mode, the FDDI-II network uses a constantly repeating data unit called a *cycle*. The cycle is essentially a transmission frame, just like a SONET frame in concept. All stations can access the contents of the cycle as it circulates around the FDDI-II ring. The cycles are generated 8000 times per second (i.e., every 125 µs) by a special station on the network called the *cycle master*. Since the cycles in hybrid mode are generated 8000 times per second, each cycle is 12,500 bits long (100 Mbps/8000). The structure of this cycle is shown in Fig. 8.3. In hybrid mode, only these cycles circulate on the FDDI-II ring.

The cycle is organized into 96 rows of 16-byte units, with the exception of the first row, which has a 12-byte cycle header field following a nondata "preamble" symbol. The 12-byte cycle header describes the use of the cycle content. The remaining 95 rows all have 16 bytes for data and a special dedicated packet group (DPG) byte every eighth row. These 12 DPGs are numbered from DPG 0 to DPG 11 and are used for token-controlled frame transfer (FDDI-II calls them packets, but they

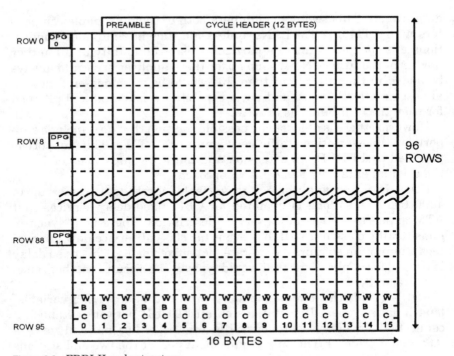

Figure 8.3 FDDI-II cycle structure.

are more similar to regular LAN frames). This always allows for at least 768 kbps of variable-length frames (12 bytes/cycle × 8000 cycles/second × 8 bits/byte) to be sent on the FDDI-II network, even in hybrid mode.

The bulk of the cycle is taken up by sixteen 96-byte units arranged in columns. These are the wideband channels (WBC), numbered from 0 to 15, each providing 6.144 Mbps bandwidth (96 bytes/WBC × 8000 cycles/second × 8 bits/byte). The term *wideband* just refers to the bandwidth of the channel: bigger than narrowband but smaller than broadband. Each of these channels can be used for a circuit "connection" or a normal frame-transfer channel. Any channels used for frames are merged and used with the DPG bytes to form one large channel for variable-length frame data transfer, essentially the same as FDDI. For example, one additional WBC used for token data transfer would merge with the DPG bytes to yield 768 kbps + 6.144 Mbps = 9.912 Mbps of bandwidth. The use of each WBC channel is indicated in a field in the cycle header called the *programming template.*

Any of the channels used for connections can support a single isochronous data stream, the same as ATM's circuit emulation capability, but running at 6.144 Mbps. This is not too useful, since few isochronous circuits run at this speed, so various substructures to the WBC are allowed to align FDDI-II connections with more common circuit speeds. Each subchannel scheme will use a different number of bits in the WBC and so support a varying number of subchannels in the WBC. For instance, if only 8 bits per cycle in a WBC is used, this would yield a data rate of 64 kbps (8 bits/cycle × 8000 cycles/second). There would be 96 of these 64-kbps subchannels in the WBC (6.144 Mbps/64 kbps), each connecting a different pair of stations on the FDDI-II network and possibly used for digitized voice channels. Many other structures are possible, as shown in Fig. 8.4.

All this sounds very impressive. FDDI-II certainly is not limited to data only, as the "fast Ethernet" techniques were. And if the network is to be used just for data, it can always operate in basic mode. The hybrid capabilities can be turned on when needed. This seems like not only a good data solution but a real potential competitor to ATM in wide area networks as well.

There is only one problem. The FDDI-II architecture is the same as "regular" FDDI. This means that the whole network is limited to about 100 km (62.5 miles). Over longer distances, some other technology is needed to send FDDI-II cycle contents from one network to another. Unfortunately, there is no standard way of taking the cycle subchannel

BITS/ CYCLE	CHANNEL RATE (Kbps)	APPLICATION/ EQUIVALENTS	CHANNELS/WBC
1	8	Compressed voice, data	768
2	16	Compressed voice, data	384
4	32	Compressed voice, data	192
8	64	Voice ISDN B channel	96
48	384	6 B channels, H0	16
192	1536	24 B channels. H11	4
193	1544	DS-1	3
240	1920	30 B channels, H12	3
256	2048	E-1	3
768	6144	Full FDDI-II WBC	1

Figure 8.4 Possible WBC subchannels.

structure over a wide area. Another protocol must be used, which is one of the advantages that ATM enjoys over almost every network protocol today: It is the same technology and protocol for networks linking desktops as for networks linking cities across the country.

8.1.4 IEEE 802.6 MAN (DQDB)

This section looks at IEEE 802.6 metropolitan area networks (MANs) and the associated media access control (MAC) protocol, distributed queue dual bus (DQDB). A look at DQDB slots shows how closely they are related to ATM cells (and why this should be so).

The primary objective of a MAN as envisioned by the IEEE is to provide a subnetwork that may be used as a public network for data. Most people see MANs as having two advantages over private networks: (1) ubiquity and (2) reliability. The first advantage means a user can send data to anyone that subscribes to the public service, the same concept as applies to the public voice telephone network. The second means users will presumably not have as many problems as a private network encounters.

Figure 8.5 shows a MAN operated by a local exchange carrier (LEC). XYZ Company uses the MAN to link its corporate network with its factory. Because it is a public network, XYZ Company can easily send data (orders and invoices) back and forth to ABC Supply Corporation. The only limitation is the fact that the MAN is limited to a span of about 100 km and is usually run entirely within the local exchange carrier's

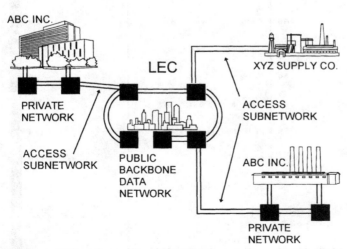

Figure 8.5 Primary objective of 802.6.

(LEC) LATA (local access and transport area; connections outside this area must use a "long distance" company such as MCI or Sprint).

What is the relationship between an 802.6 MAN and ATM? 802.6 MANs are seen as good candidates for being linked up via ATM wide area networks (ultimately). Private 802.6s and LEC 802.6s can all be linked together with ATM.

The IEEE sees MANs as giving coverage to an entire metropolitan area. The services are provided to multiple customers and businesses, which means security and privacy will be an issue. Both public and private subnetworks will feed the MAN, and it will integrate voice, data, and video services to these customers. IEEE 802.6 is seen as a logical extension to the 802 LANs of the 1980s.

An IEEE 802.6 MAN runs on a shared medium (like a LAN should), in this case dual buses at 45 Mbps (DS-3). Once SONET is available, it will run at 155 Mbps (STS-3c). The maximum distance is about 100 km (about 63 miles). Because both buses are accessible, the actual capacity is 90 Mbps (300 Mbps when STS-3c is available). It uses a fixed-length cell of 53 bytes. It would be very nice if this DQDB "slot" had the same format as an ATM cell—but it doesn't.

The MAC layer, which 802.6 has, employs a first-come, first-served shared medium access control strategy called *distributed queue dual bus (DQDB)*. An 802.6 MAN is as much a part of the 802 protocols as 802.3, 802.5, or any other. Just because 802.6 is not as familiar as the others does not mean it is unusual or exotic. In fact, it uses 802.2 logical link control (LLC) as the upper layer 2 just like the others. The media access control (all IEEE LANs use shared medium) is DQDB, which is more complex than CSMA/CD, but not inordinately so.

Figure 8.6 shows the structure of an 802.6 MAN. The two buses are bus *A* and bus *B*. It is *not* a ring. There is a "head" and a "tail" to each bus. Data starts at the head of one bus and flows through all intermediate access units (AU) at the nodes to the tail, where it is basically "turned around" and flows back. Servers, clients, hosts, and/or workstations are attached to the node AUs (multiples of each). The AU may write to *either* bus to go "upstream" or "downstream." And it may even do so in full duplex (FDX) mode, meaning the AU may write to both buses at the same time. When there are data to send, the AU simply reads the incoming stream, finds the proper "slot" to insert its data, and writes them.

The MAN can recover from two failure types: link loss and AU failure. In actual use, the MAN is a physical ring but logical bus; the head and tail are usually the same AU. *Link loss* means that there are now "real" head and tail AUs. An *AU failure* does the same, with the next adjacent AUs becoming the new head and tail.

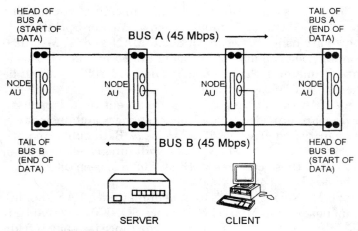

Figure 8.6 802.6 DQDB architecture.

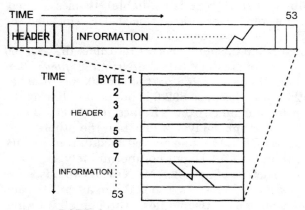

Figure 8.7 DQDB slot structure.

Figure 8.7 shows the structure of a DQDB slot on an 802.6 MAN. It is basically an ATM cell: 53 bytes, 5 for a header and 48 for information. Unfortunately, there are important differences between the ATM cell and the DQDB slot. The structure of a DQDB slot is a little awkward. The slot is still divided into a 5-byte header and 48 bytes of data, but there is also the concept of a *segment* and a *segment payload*. This comes about because the critical fields of the DQDB slot are all in the first header byte, called the *access control field*. Since it is so vital, the term *segment* (52 bytes) is used to refer to the other bytes. The segment is divided into a *segment header* (only 4 bytes are left now) and a *segment payload* (still 48 bytes).

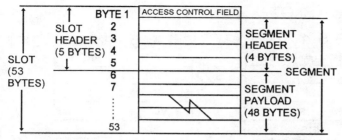

Figure 8.8 DQDB slot: segment and payload.

Figure 8.8 shows the DQDB slot header. Some of the fields even have the same names as the ATM cell. VCI is still virtual channel identifier. (But notice that there is no VPI, just a 24-bit VCI field with no structure similar to ATM's "static/dynamic" concept.) The HEC of an ATM cell is now the header check sequence (HCS), but it works the same. PT is payload type. There are important differences, of course, mostly in the first byte. The busy bit indicates to an AU that the slot is in use. The three request bits are used by the AU to ask that a vacant or idle slot be "reserved" for its use.

Initially, an IEEE 802.6 MAN will run on DS-3 at 44.736 Mbps. The IEEE is currently working on 802.6 running on STS-3c at 155.52 Mbps (times 2, of course), something called SDS3 (which stands for simplified DS-3 fiberoptic customer premises extension: DS-3 to your premises), and DS-1 at the regular T-1 rate of 1.544 Mbps. Planning is proceeding on the European ETSI levels as well, involving data rates that roughly correspond to the DS-1, SDS3, and STS-3c rates.

IEEE 802.6 MANs will provide for the transfer of voice and video as well as data, although not initially. This is done through a mechanism similar to ATM's provision of different rates for circuit emulation services (CES) through circuit mode cell assignments. In 802.6, there are prearbitrated (PA) slots and queue-arbitrated (QA) slots. PA slots are for the transfer of isochronous information: 64 kbps voice, CBR video, DS-1, and the like. The head of each bus will "launch" PA slots at regular intervals to support these services. QA slots are for everything else (e.g., packet data). The node AUs contend for these remaining slots using DQDB. Obviously, care must be taken to balance the PA and QA slots for services.

The key to using PA and QA slots is the slot type field in the access control field of the DQDB slot header. It works along with the VCI field as well. Slot type = 0 identifies a QA slot, and slot type = 1 is for a PA slot. The VCI coding is as follows: All 1s is for QA access to network connectionless service. PA access is by preassigned VCI numbers for various services. The other possible VCI numbers are available for QA connec-

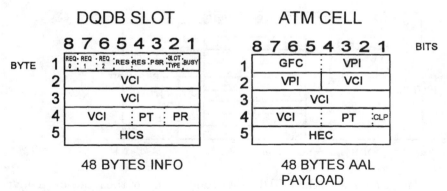

Figure 8.9   DQDB slot and ATM cell.

tion-oriented services, but only locally (since these numbers may be PA numbers elsewhere).

An important point is that PA slots do not have to take 48 bytes from a single AU; each of 8 different AUs may be set up to insert 6 bytes into PA slots of (for example) VCI = 27 which appear in the "slot stream" at a fixed interval. In this way, 8 AUs can "share" a PA slot and cut down latency.

The rest of the fields are still under study by the IEEE. They are for future enhancements, and while the function of some can easily be guessed, no standard mechanism for their use has yet been published.

Figure 8.9 shows the DQDB slot and the ATM cell side by side. The similarities are obvious, from the 5-byte header to the 48-byte information payload. Even some fields in the headers line up closely in position and function (e.g., HEC/HCS). There are important differences as well. These differences mean that DQDB MAN services may be transported over B-ISDN ATM-based networks, but the fit will require "massaging" of the headers between the two networks. However, the fit will be easier than, say, X.25 and SDLC.

8.1.5 Packet transfer mode (PTM)

So far the technologies mentioned supply data services over a local area or metropolitan area (802.6). But a much greater need exists today for data networks that connect company sites over a wide area, e.g., coast to coast. To effectively compete with ATM, even in the data arena only, an alternative technology must offer low delays and high speeds not just over a small area but over an arbitrarily wide area as well.

More than one technology has been explored that is capable of keeping data units in variable sizes and yet still delivering high bandwidths and low delays. In fact, based on research done on some of these schemes, the claim is often made that if the links are fast enough, and the switch is fast enough too, there is really no need to send everything through the network in cell form anyway.

Several companies have announced intentions to offer products based on variable-length data units for at least part of their overall architecture, even if the whole is still based on ATM. For example, the UNI may employ ATM-compliant cells, but on the "backbone" or trunk links connecting switches from the same vendor together, the "cells" could be packed into variable-length "packets" and sent to the other switch. This violates no current ATM Forum implementation agreement. As long as the two switches from the same vendor (which is the key) understand each other, it makes no difference to users what is going on internally in the network.

This approach has been followed by vendors for years. No one at all cared what X.25 switches sent to each other; X.25 defined a *user* interface with a network. It is only with the rise of real user concern over "open architecture" that the movement to use open interfaces between a vendor's own products gathered momentum. This is one of the main points of the ATM Forum, of course.

However, what happens when vendor A's equipment, with a particular variable-length data unit on one interface, needs to be connected with vendor B's equipment, with another variable-length data unit format? Obviously, this is a real customer concern. No problem, say these vendors. In such a case, the interface would be customer-configurable to comply with ATM Forum and/or ITU-T standards. Besides, these vendors point out, if cells can be modified internally to a switch from a vendor (e.g., the Fore switch internal cell format would not be the same as another vendor's internal cell format), why can't the cells be modified for internal use within a network segment?

Whether customers will buy these arguments is debatable, but the attraction of preserving variable lengths for data users (as opposed to voice and video users) through an ATM network is powerful enough that many vendors will try. These other voice and video users may, of course, configure their ports to support ATM Forum–compliant ATM cell interfaces. This mixing of cells and packets on one network has made some companies nervous about the whole plan. After all, ATM cell networks are new enough without the added complexity of supporting packets as well.

One of the companies willing to make a case for using variable-length units on at least some of its products' interfaces has been IBM. Many names for IBM's approach have been used both internally by the company and externally for marketing purposes. But the simplest name for it, and the one that points out the differences from ATM most clearly, is *packet transfer mode* (*PTM*). This term is used here strictly for descriptive purposes, not to imply its use to indicate an architecture or technology advocated by IBM or any other company.

Specifically, IBM says that PTM is much better for data than "plain" ATM and will in fact save the data user of PTM much of the overhead required by ATM. But just what is it about PTM that makes IBM confident enough to make such a statement? And if PTM is so much better than ATM, should potential investors in ATM network equipment worry about making the wrong choice? To answer these questions, more details about just how IBM's PTM operates in relation to ATM must be presented.

The first thing is that IBM is *absolutely correct.* PTM is much better for data users than pure ATM. And it does save considerable data overhead, bringing the overhead required for "cellifying" variable-length data packets down from 5 bytes in every 48 (10.4 percent) to the 3 to 4 percent range that data protocols have traditionally used.

PTM was born from Project Aurora, a joint venture by MIT, BellCore, the University of Pennsylvania, and IBM to investigate the hardware and software requirements of futuristic networks running not at megabits per second (Mbps) but at gigabits per second (Gbps), a full thousand times faster. Of course, fiberoptic transmission paths were fully capable of supporting such speeds, but transfer rate is only half the struggle of creating a network. There must be network nodes that operate at least as fast, and usually much faster, than the input and output line speeds. At very high line speeds, network switches must operate all the faster to create the necessary low end-to-end delays needed to go along with the high data rates. IBM developed a very high-speed packet switch for the Aurora network known as a *packetized automatic routing integrated system* (*PARIS*). This switch is entirely capable of switching ATM cells but also can handle PTM packets and in most configurations is capable of mixing both. Thus it is not pure ATM. In a PTM network, ATM now becomes an option that a user of the network chooses to configure or not. It is the use of packets that offends ATM purists. Here is why.

The ATM Forum and CCITT define a *cell* as the unit of information exchange in an ATM network. And a cell is, by definition, a fixed-length "packet." It is always, in ATM, exactly 53 bytes long: 5 bytes for a header and 48 bytes for a payload or information field. ATM networks never deal with anything else but a cell. If users can only generate variable-length data units, these units must be converted to a series of cells before they hit the ATM network. This function is provided by the ATM adaptation layer (AAL). The cells must be built up again into the original packet at the destination.

This is the first and most obvious distinction between ATM and PTM. In ATM, packets are always of fixed size and are called *cells,* while in PTM, packets may be of variable size, up to some maximum. (No maximum size has been published. In fact, since the length is determined by "delimiters" as in SNA, the maximum is in theory unlimited.) Note, however, that if the size of the PTM packet payload is always exactly 53 bytes, the result is indistinguishable from ATM.

Thus there is an important difference between PTM and ATM. And because of this difference, all PTM networks may be ATM networks as well, but no ATM networks can be PTM networks. (Of course, using PTM *only* to transport ATM cells would provide no added benefit at all.) But why should anyone care? It is all because of the ATM overhead.

The overhead in ATM is enormous. A protocol such as TCP/IP may add a 40-byte header to a PDU, but the PDU can be 64,000 bytes long. Even a 1000-byte PDU only gets 4 percent overhead from a TCP/IP header. But ATM adds 5 bytes to every 48 bytes of information. This is more than 10 percent additional overhead. Consider the 1000-byte PDU. It must be broken up into 21 cells, each of which carries 5 bytes of overhead for a total of 105 bytes. This is more than 2.5 times the TCP/IP overhead, and TCP/IP uses one of the more lengthy packet header formats. Thus PTM can potentially reduce this cell overhead to around 50 to 80 bytes, because larger packets need fewer headers per user PDU. PTM overhead varies with type of traffic and routing method used, so a direct comparison is not straightforward.

A straight apples-to-apples comparison of ATM overhead with PTM overhead is difficult to do in a general case. This is so because ATM has other overhead besides the 5-byte cell header overhead, and PTM allows various routing/switching schemes that have different overhead bytes for each.

ATM includes specifications for ATM adaptation layers (AALs) that have 1, 2, 4, or even 0 additional overhead bytes per cell. The least ATM overhead for data is provided by AAL type 5 (AAL-5), which adds at least 6 bytes and at most 53 bytes of AAL overhead to a frame-relay frame or IP datagram. IBM's PTM allows both encapsulation of ATM cells into PTM frames (which just adds more overhead) and switching of ATM cells with a "variant" cell header format. But the real promise of PTM as far as overhead goes is when PTM is used with automatic network routing (ANR) to transport variable-length frames.

In place of a general overhead comparison, some real-world examples may be more enlightening. Figure 8.10 compares ATM's AAL-5 overhead for various-sized "frames" with IBM's PTM ANR overhead. The ATM figures assume an average of 29 bytes of AAL-5 overhead, and the PTM figures assume a PTM network with a five-hop maximum path through the network and 1-byte switch ID (SID) addresses. The PTM overhead would be 16 bytes in this case. It is a further feature of PTM that the overhead actually diminishes as the frame passes through the network, but this aspect will be ignored for simplification purposes.

PDU Size	AAL5 Overhead (# Bytes)*	(% Of PDU)	PTM Overhead (# Bytes)	(% of PDU)
64 bytes (e.g. ACK)	39	60.9%	16	25.0%
1500 bytes (e.g. 802.3)	189	12.6%	16	1.1%
4100 bytes (e.g. FR)	464	11.3%	16	0.4%
9100 bytes (e.g. SMDS)	984	10.8%	16	0.002%

* Calculated as an average of 29 bytes plus cell headers

Figure 8.10 ATM/PTM overhead compared.

AAL TYPE	CELL PAYLOAD	AAL OVERHEAD	AAL PAYLOAD
AAL-0	48	0	48
AAL-1	48	1	47
AAL-2	48	3	45
AAL-3/4	48	4	44
AAL-5	48	(6-53)	48*

* AAL-5 overhead is added once in the last cell

Figure 8.11 AAL overhead by type.

Figure 8.11 shows the overhead bytes from the other AALs beside AAL-5. These all add even more overhead to the cell segmentation process, culminating with a whopping 20 percent or so with AAL-3/4. Even on PTM networks that mix ATM cells and PTM frames on the same links, which might limit PTM frame sizes to three to five times the size of ATM cells, the overhead savings would be in the 60 to 80 percent range.

Implementers of any network architecture always want less overhead sent per unit data, whether they are designing networks as service providers (carriers) or private networks for corporate use. Less overhead sent maximizes profits for service providers because the total network capacity is used more for paying customers' bits. Private networks will cost less if there is more capacity for data.

It sounds like a sure-win situation. Why would anyone *not* choose to save the overhead? The catch is that this savings applies to *data* only. ATM networks are supposed to be the network of networks, an unchannelized bit pipe not only for data but also for digitized audio and video as well. There are no channels anymore, as there are on almost all existing T-1 and T-3 digital transports today. Connections take their place in ATM. All services generate a stream of bits that are mixing together in cells at the physical layer of the network. The optimization available from PTM for data users will not generally apply to other services, especially ones characterized in ATM as continuous (or constant)-bit-rate (CBR) applications. CBR services include uncompressed voice, video, and the carrying of existing digital transports such as T-1s and T-3s over an ATM network.

In fact, ATM was designed with the cell size set at 53 bytes so that CBR applications could send bits on the network quickly, without waiting for a huge, 10,000-byte data packet to finish being sent. These delays due to large data packets are deadly for CBR applications, which must send and receive bits at the same rate constantly. ATM purists point out that PTM will make the multiplexing of data and CBR applications over the same physical link that much more difficult and is in fact no better than other multiplexing techniques that ATM was developed to improve.

PTM proponents answer in two ways. First, data users will be the most important user community on early ATM networks. They will probably pay for initial ATM network deployment, and it will likely be years before audio and video applications find their way onto ATM networks. If data users are turned off by ATM's overhead or inefficiency (as in the building up of cells back into PDUs at the destination), they will be reluctant to buy ATM, and the end result will be that the audio and video applications will never even appear on the ATM network. Thus PTM just makes good business sense.

The second part of the answer is that ATM was designed in 1988. The machines available were running 80286 processors and around 16 MHz. Now there are 486s running at 66 MHz. It is no longer necessary to design the cell size on the basis of older technology. If the CBR cells are delayed by 10,000-byte data packets, the answer is to make the switch and the transport faster. The PARIS switch used in Project Aurora showed that this was a completely viable strategy and that cells and packets could mix on a network. Unfortunately, most switch vendors today have focused on "cell-only" technologies and are not entirely pleased with alternatives to implement.

The PTM proponents may pick up an ally from the CBR application world as well: the cable television companies. ATM is one method of providing 500 channels to your home. Since CBR considerations apply only to uncompressed video, and most video in the near future will be compressed, video will look more and more like data to an ATM network. And as such, the newer MPEG compression standards make it more efficient for cable television companies to use 180-byte cells, not 53-byte cells. Thus it makes sense for the cable television companies to implement PTM rather than pure ATM for compressed video services. It is worth remembering that the 48-byte ATM payload size was a totally arbitrary decision. Voice specialists wanted a 32-byte payload, and data specialists wanted a 64-byte payload. The 48-byte size was a compromise that totally satisfied neither party.

Again, there is the worry that if early ATM networks are too costly or too slow for the first users to accept, there will never be any willingness to put other applications such as multimedia and "video on demand" on them. So why design the network node architecture to be optimal for CBR applications?

This is a potent argument, but one that goes far beyond technology and into the realms of corporate politics and social issues. ATM at heart is designed to be one unchannelized physical network capable of delivering different service characteristics (quality of service, or QOS) to all potential users of the network. It has acceptable video features for cable television companies, high bandwidth features for multimedia users, and so on. The key word is *acceptable*. Just because ATM is designed to be this network of networks, this does not mean it is in all cases desirable or even possible to move to ATM. And when the added requirement of profitability is added in (the new ATM network must cost less than the old X network, Y network, and Z network), the potential of making the network more efficient for the most important group of users becomes very attractive.

The whole ATM/PTM debate can be summarized by looking at how the "packet mode" time slots on an ATM link are utilized. Figure 8.12 shows how a variable-length data unit must be broken up into cells in order to be transmitted in the slots available between the class CBR "circuit" bytes on an ATM UNI. Figure 8.13 shows how PTM handles the same situation much more efficiently for data connections; there is just much less fragmentation involved.

One other point must be made about the use of cells and packets on the same network. ATM proponents insist that the whole reason cells were invented was to reduce the fixed-length cell packetization to a bare minimum on the sending side of the network. The goal: Reduce this component of overall network delay for class A and class B time-sensitive connections. However, ATM specifications include the con-

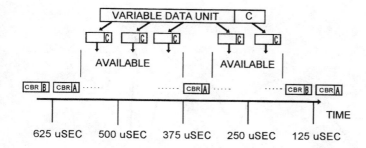

Figure 8.12 ATM: circuit and packet modes.

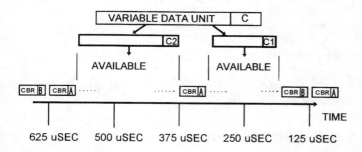

Figure 8.13 PTM: packet transfer mode.

cept of *network conditioning*. This adding of a variable delay at the receiving side of the network strikes PTM advocates as the height of hypocrisy. For what is the sense, they ask, of getting traffic out very rapidly on the sending side of the network only to be delayed at the receiving side? Both $2 + 10$ and $10 + 2$ are both 12. Figure 8.14 illustrates this argument. Even if cells *were* delayed in a network behind variable-length packets on a link or in a switch, as long as the $P2$ end-to-end delay is the same, it matters not at all if the actual distribution of network delay is $P1$ as in purely ATM networks or $P3$ as in PTM networks mixing cells and packets.

IBM has announced a network node as the switching device that will allow the mixing of both ATM Forum–compliant cells and PTM packets on the same network. Besides providing a means for backward compatibility, this would offer a customer a completely configurable choice between ATM and PTM, and the advantages for data connections the

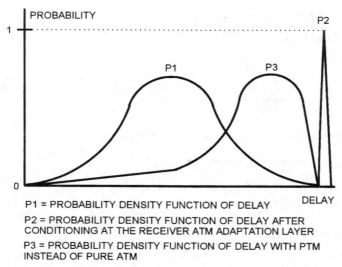

P1 = PROBABILITY DENSITY FUNCTION OF DELAY
P2 = PROBABILITY DENSITY FUNCTION OF DELAY AFTER
CONDITIONING AT THE RECEIVER ATM ADAPTATION LAYER
P3 = PROBABILITY DENSITY FUNCTION OF DELAY WITH PTM
INSTEAD OF PURE ATM

Figure 8.14   PTM network conditioning.

low PTM overhead would provide. The TNN is part of IBM's overall broadband network services (BBNS).

8.2   Switched Multimegabit Data Services (SMDS) and ATM

SONET and ATM are really just technologies. But what users want (and will pay for) are services. Switched multimegabit data service (SMDS) is a full service, not just a technology. LAN internetworking can be efficiently implemented with SMDS, which is also a public service like 802.6 MANs, rather than with partial-mesh networks made up of private point-to-point leased lines connecting routers.

SMDS is layered, as is ATM. The layers are the SMDS interface protocol (SIP) layers and they have similar functions to the ATM layers. This section will examine how SIP layers and their associated PDUs line up with ATM. Then a method will be detailed to allow SMDS networks to connect to both over an ATM network and to other users on the ATM network itself.

SMDS is the "first ATM service," as described by BellCore, and can be offered without ATM or SONET, expands existing LAN connectivity services, and is a public network offering (but anyone can *build* one).

Figure 8.15 shows the structure of an SMDS network. SMDS is a public WAN service extension of LAN and MAN services. The goal is to provide connectivity for MANs, FDDI subnetworks, and private LANs. Sharing data should be not harder than making a phone call. Multiple services (data, voice, video) will be supported. Initially, the SMDS services will be

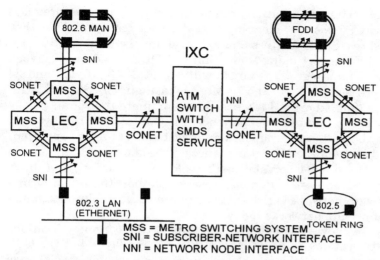

Figure 8.15 SMDS and ATM.

offered by the local exchange carriers (LEC) in a confined area through
"metropolitan switching systems" connected by SONET (or DS-3) links.
SONET, DS-3, or even DS-1 will connect to the customer sites as well.
Ultimately, the interexchange carriers (IEC, IXC) will connect it all.

Initially, SMDS networks will offer data transfer between subscriber's LANs, the same function as provided by private leased lines
and router-based networks today. There will be no voice or video. This
will come later. The data transfer will be at LAN speeds and delays
across the entire metropolitan area (e.g., 10 Mbps, 16 Mbps, at least on
a DS-3 access link). SMDS will be connectionless, like LANs, so there
will be no wait for an end-to-end connection. (The end-user applications
may be TCP-based connection-oriented services, but the network itself
is connectionless.) Thus SMDS will provide LAN internetworking easily and efficiently with public network penetration (theoretically, *anyone* will be able to get SMDS) and reliability.

SMDS is designed to provide an easy migration path to B-ISDN and
SONET in the near future. In fact, since it is the *carrier* equipment that
changes, the migration should be transparent to most users.

Here are some of the attributes of SMDS: Availability must be more
than or equal to 99.7 percent, which works out to 26.3 hours of down
time per year. If an outage occurs, it must be restored in less than 3.5
hours. The delay across the network should be less than 20 ms for 95
percent of the packets at DS-3 speeds. This compares favorably with
DS-1 delays and even with many hard disk drives. Less than 5 in 10^{13}
packets should be errored, and less than 1 in 10^4 packets will not be
delivered. These are design parameters, not suggestions.

Early SMDS implementations will feature single customer premises equipment (CPE) access, meaning that if a user has two LANs, they would need two SMDS ingress and egress channels. Later it will have multiple CPE support using some kind of DQDB 802.6 bus (maybe). SMDS ingress and egress channels will run at 4, 10, 16, 25, and 34 Mbps. The reason for 4, 10, and 16 Mbps is to align SMDS speeds with Token Ring and Ethernet LAN speeds to eliminate the router bottleneck that LANs frequently experience. Packets up to 9188 bytes in length may be sent, and group and multicast addressing is supported.

A crucial element to SMDS acceptance will be address validation and screening. There must be valid methods for both allowing *and* disallowing source and destination addresses. Together, these will form a virtual private network (VPN), primarily aimed at wooing users and builders of private networks today.

Figure 8.16 shows two 802.5 Token Ring LANs at remote locations running applications using TCP/IP at layer 3 and layer 4 of the OSI-RM. In this case, SMDS internetworking is provided by a special node on the LAN with both SIP and LAN protocol stacks. The IP layer is still present, but SIP layer 3 operates as a lower layer 3 protocol. The network providing SMDS interfaces the SIPs, forming the traditional LAN-WAN-LAN arrangement. The IP packets will form the payloads of the SIP L3 protocol data units (PDUs). Notice that the network details are hidden from the users and that SMDS may be provided by an ATM network or even frame relay. (This latter may actually happen, and it might even be a good match as far as services go.)

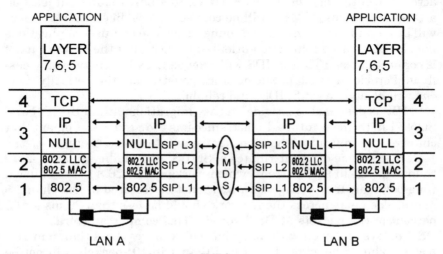

Figure 8.16 LAN internetworking with SMDS.

There is an interesting aspect to Fig. 8.16 that should be pointed out in more detail. The figure shows two 802.5 Token Ring LANs connected over an SMDS network. What would happen if the two connected LANs were not the same, but one was an 802.3 Ethernet-type LAN running at 10 Mbps and the other remained an 802.5 Token Ring? These LANs have different frame structures at layer 2a (the MAC sublayer) of the OSI model. Notice that there is an IP layer in the SMDS network interface device. This layer takes the IP datagram, an ISO layer 3 PDU, out of the LAN frame, Token Ring, or Ethernet and places it in an SMDS SIP layer 3 PDU. The reverse takes place at the other side of the SMDS network. Since the same unit is sent—an IP datagram—as received, this works. But the presence of layer 3 in the network interface device means that the SMDS network device *must* be a router if the LANs on each end of the network are different in any way.

A bridge links LANs at layer 2 (actually, the MAC sublayer). It makes two LANs behave as one and does extend node counts. The "relay" function of sending (forwarding) frames from one LAN to the other is provided by a processor in the bridge. For this reason, they are more complex than repeaters and in fact are usually PCs. Since there is no sense in forwarding frames for node addresses that are on the local LAN, the bridge will have memory for storing addresses of frames to be relayed.

Several types of bridges are used in different environments: IEEE 802.3 LANs use transparent bridges, while most 802.5 Token Ring LANs use source routing. Even though bridges connect LANs at layer 2, they are not often used to connect LANs of different types (e.g., 802.3 and 802.5). Although all IEEE LAN types use 802.2 LLC as an upper layer 2, the different MAC sublayers make it difficult to bridge them. There are different frame lengths, speeds, and frame types to deal with. There are other, more subtle differences as well (e.g., what is to be done with the 802.5 A/C bits?). The fact is that although bridges can be used to connect LANs with dissimilar MACs and bridges may be used with SMDS, it is far more common today to see a different device used to link LANs.

Although many LAN vendors have products they *market* as bridges for historical reasons, they are really routers. This is so because the IEEE-recommended way to connect LANs is with a router.

Much of the difference between a router and a bridge is that the router is a more intelligent device. It can route packets through multiple networks, can support several routing protocols such as the routing Internet protocol (RIP) or open shortest path first (OSPF), can reformat packets for different network requirements, and may even fragment or segment packets and put them together again.

Routers also can serve as "firewalls" between networks; although connected, they are still distinct LANs. And they have the intelligence to allow and use correctly multiple network paths, which can drive bridges crazy. They also serve as a focus for gathering network management information. Ironically, the first routers were marketed for their "firewall" capabilities. Everybody knew that *bridges* were used to connect LANs. SMDS will be implemented in routers or over DXI interfaces to a CSU/DSU.

8.2.1 The SMDS SIP protocol data units

SMDS is not only a data service that is very similar to ATM's CLNS using AAL-3/4, but even the data structures used in SMDS closely resemble those used in AAL-3/4. However, SMDS has its own three-layered protocol: SIP layer 3, SIP layer 2, and SIP layer 1. Layer 3 closely corresponds to AAL-3/4 in form and content. The SIP layer 2 closely resembles an ATM cell, but with significant differences. In preparation for examining exactly how SMDS can be provided over an ATM network, this section offers a more complete look at the SMDS protocol data units.

Figure 8.17 shows the SIP layer 3 PDU. The LLC PDU from a LAN is now the INFO field ($\leq$9188 bytes). The PAD field is used so that the INFO from header to trailer is an even multiple of 32 bits (so there are zero to three 0-filled PAD bytes). The X+ fields are for 802.6 MAN compatibility. These bytes are used with the higher layer protocol identifier (HLPI) field used in 802.6 and are sent end to end through the network unchanged. The header extension field is for interexchange carrier (IXC) selection, since SMDS is primarily aimed at local exchange carriers' (LEC) public networks. The length field in the trailer is calculated from destination address through to the end of information field.

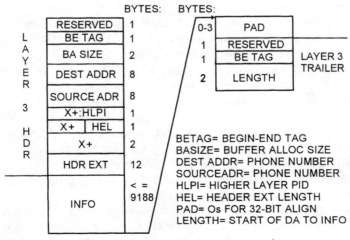

Figure 8.17 SIP L3 protocol data unit (PDU).

BYTES:

1	ADDRESS TYPE	O O O 1
2	DIGIT #1	DIGIT #2
3	DIGIT #3	DIGIT #4
4	DIGIT #5	DIGIT #6
5	DIGIT #7	DIGIT #8
6	DIGIT #9	DIGIT #10
7	1 1 1 1	1 1 1 1
8	1 1 1 1	1 1 1 1

Figure 8.18 SIP L3 PDU address format.

The destination and source address fields are just essentially phone numbers. Figure 8.18 shows how the digits are packed into the 8-byte destination address and source address fields. The address type field may be either 1100 (individual address) or 1110 (group address—*not* allowed in the source address, of course). The 10 digits are encoded using binary-coded decimal (4-bit) values.

Future SMDS addressing will use 15-digit addresses (all but the address type nibble will be used). The whole is based on the CCITT E.164 numbering plan first developed for ISDN.

The SMDS header extension (HE) field has a very critical function for a public switched network service; this is where carrier selection takes place. Up to five 2-byte-long carrier IDs may be encoded in the 12-byte field. Other functions can be selected as well, but carrier selection is the only one fully supported at the present time. The whole cannot exceed 12 bytes.

Figure 8.19 is an example of this use. It shows the element length set to 10 decimal (so 2 PAD bytes are added). The element type of 1 indicates the carrier selection function. The two carrier ID bytes encode the normal carrier identifiers (e.g., 288 = ATT = AT&T) with 4 bits to spare. The carriers are tried in order if one is unable to accept traffic. If an LEC cannot forward SMDS traffic from one metropolitan area to another over the user's carrier selection choices, the LEC may use the carrier of its choice.

The SIP layer 3 PDU is not put inside the SIP layer 2 PDU information field whole. Rather, it is split up into multiple layer 2 PDUs, which are very similar to ATM cells, but with important differences in the header fields. Figure 8.20 shows the structure of the SIP layer 2 "cell." The ACF field is borrowed from DQDB, at least in part. From the customer premises equipment (CPE) to the switching system (SS at the LEC level), both the busy and request bits are used. The interface from SS to CPE uses only busy bits.

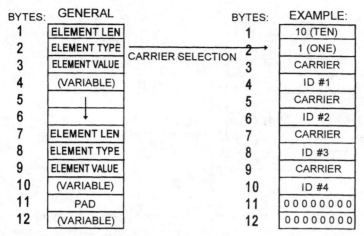

Figure 8.19 SIP L3 PDU header extension field.

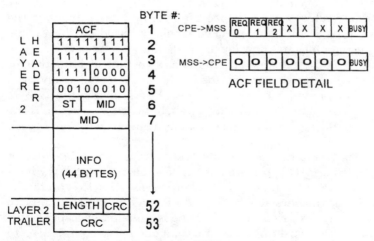

Figure 8.20 SIP L2 protocol data unit (PDU).

The 20-bit all 1s field indicates connectionless service, and bytes 2 through 5 form the network control information. ST is segmented type: BOM (beginning of message), EOM (end of message), COM (continuation of message), and SSM (single-segment message) are exactly as in ATM AAL-3/4. MID is multiplexing identifier, and length is the length of INFO used if not all 44 bytes, valid in an SSM or EOM segment. Their use is essentially the same as in ATM AAL-3/4.

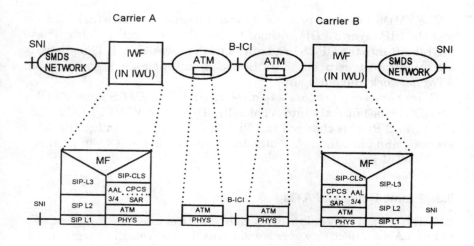

MF = Management Function

Figure 8.21   SMDS/ATM internetworking.

Figure 8.21 compares the structure of an SMDS layer 2 PDU and an ATM cell. Here are two separate protocols for high-speed networking (with important differences), but they both still look remarkably similar. They are supposed to, because ultimately they should merge under the B-ISDN umbrella as connectionless ATM service (CLNS).

8.2.2   Interfacing SMDS and ATM

Until this merging of SMDS and ATM connectionless service happens, how should SMDS networks and ATM networks interoperate? Most of the preliminary work has been done by the ATM Forum in the specification known as the *broadband-intercarrier interface (B-ICI) document*. This is being extended by a series of joint documents to be issued by the ATM Forum and the SMDS Interest Group.

Figure 8.21 shows the interconnection of SMDS networks with ATM. Although the figure shows an interworking function (IWF) architecture for interfacing SMDS and ATM networks, the IWF is no longer required in the latest ATM Forum proposals. The figure shows a B-ICI interface between two ATM networks in the middle, but the same scheme would work if there was only one ATM network connecting the two SMDS networks, of course. The mapping functions take care of translating such SMDS functions as routing and carrier selection into ATM connections. That is, a routing decision may follow one of two or more ATM connection possibilities. Carriers will be chosen by ATM connection as well.

The SMDS interface protocol for connectionless service (SIP-CLS) is just the SIP layer 3 PDU without the header and trailer fields. These are rebuilt into the CPCS header and trailer for AAL-3/4. Thus there is a complete restructuring of an SMDS data unit as it passes into an ATM network and out again.

There have been proposals to directly translate SMDS layer 2 PDUs ("SMDS cells") directly into ATM cells. The all 1s VPI/VCI field of an SIP layer 2 PDU is changed to VPI = 0,VCI = 15 inbound to the ATM network and back to all 1s outbound. This method has been finalized by the ATM Forum.

8.3   Frame Relay and ATM

SMDS is a high-speed, low-delay public network service aimed at providing LAN connectivity over a wide area. Frame relay is a high-speed, low-delay public network service aimed at providing LAN connectivity over a wide area. Two services provided by the same entities (public network service providers) marketed for the same user community. Surely there must be a difference. There is, and it is an important one. SMDS is a connectionless service, and frame relay is connection-oriented.

Since LANs are connectionless, it might appear that SMDS is a much better fit for LAN connectivity than frame relay. However, even though the LANs themselves are connectionless, most organizations today use routers to connect these LANs. And the routers are usually connected by point-to-point leased lines—circuits or physical channels. Now, in ATM, the place of physical channels or circuits is taken by connections, and so it would be with leased lines for router connectivity. Frame relay is a connection-oriented data service. Since the connections in a frame-relay network are essentially the same as the circuits in a router-based network, frame relay is actually as good a match (or better) as SMDS for LAN connectivity.

Frame relay has often been called "X.25 for the 1990s," and this is a very good description. The X.25 protocol operated at layer 3 and below of the OSI-RM and switched packets (layer 3 PDUs) through a network of switches by connection identifier. The packets were checked for errors, and a flow control function was provided by every switch ("hop by hop") in the X.25 network. The flow control function just referred to the fact that the X.25 switch made sure that a sender was not sending packets faster than a receiver could handle them. The X.25 switch did this by a number of methods, such as withholding acknowledgments for data already sent. This prevented the originator from sending more than a certain number of packets into the network at a given time, which is the whole point of flow control.

Frame relay takes this layer 3 and below architecture and makes it into a layer 2 and below architecture. It basically strips off all the layer 3 functions done on a packet-by-packet basis in X.25 and makes them into layer 2 frame functions. The frame, which is the official layer 2 PDU in the ISO-RM, now has the connection identifier. Frames are relayed through the network nodes instead of packets being switched. Any error checking on frame content and flow control must be done at the end-points (originator and destination) of a frame-relay network, if at all.

Again, the details of a frame-relay network interfacing with an ATM network are given in the ATM Forum's B-ICI specification. This is shown in Fig. 8.22. There are two scenarios, one in which the ATM network connects two frame-relay networks and one in which an ATM network forms one end of a frame relay–to–ATM connection. How can this happen with frame relay and not with SMDS? Simply because a full description of the frame-relay bearer service (FRBS) interoperation with a frame-relay network exists in ATM as part of the AAL-5 definition. This is lacking in SMDS.

There is one other reason that the relationship of frame-relay networks to ATM networks is so important. This has to do with the fact that AAL-5 is intimately tied in most documentation not only with frame relay, which can transport almost any kind of data traffic from SNA to Novell's IPX, but also with the transport of TCP/IP datagrams across an ATM network.

Typically, routers used in TCP/IP architectured networks will use a WAN protocol known as *point-to-point protocol* (*PPP*) on the ports connecting the routers over private leased lines. Many router vendors will bundle not only PPP for use of these links with the router software but

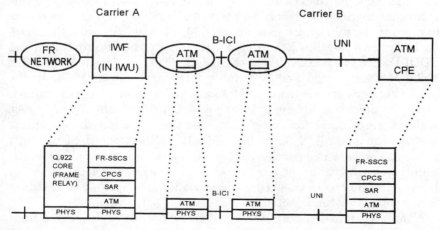

Figure 8.22 FR/ATM internetworking (I.555 scenario 2).

other protocols as well, such as X.25's LAP-B (link access protocol, balanced). Router vendors have now begun to bundle the frame-relay link layer protocol with the router as well. Hooking a router up to a frame-relay network can be as simple as swapping out the PPP link layer protocol for the frame-relay link layer protocol. (Of course, the leased lines must be replaced by a frame-relay network.)

As it turns out, TCP/IP datagrams may be sent across an ATM network in a variety of ways. They may be encapsulated inside a frame relay by a router and use a frame-relay network for connecting routers. Some of these routers may be on different frame-relay networks connected by an ATM network. In this case, both end users see only frame relay.

Another method would be to encapsulate the TCP/IP datagram inside a frame-relay frame but then use an ATM network with frame-relay bearer service (FRBS) and AAL-5 to connect the routers. Again, the users see only a frame-relay network.

A third method is to directly encapsulate TCP/IP datagrams inside an AAL-5 CPCS data unit. This time the ATM network is directly visible to the end users. That is, they see ATM connections (VPI/VCI), not FR connections (DLCI).

Much work remains to be done on the best way to send TCP/IP datagrams across an ATM network, with or without frame relay. The Internet Engineering Task Force (IETF) has tackled this, not the ATM Forum directly, but this is as it should be. The importance of TCP/IP as the dominant WAN protocol (and even in many LAN environments) makes its accommodation by ATM networks imperative.

8.4 The ATM Agenda

So far this chapter has looked at seven different data protocols and services that might conceivably be the basis of networks that customers may want to build or use instead of ATM. On the LAN side, the chapter looked at 100-Mbps Ethernet, Switched Ethernet at any speed, and FDDI-II. For more extended networks, the chapter detailed the IEEE 802.6 MAN standard and proprietary schemes such as PTM. In the public network service arena, SMDS and frame relay, were examined.

Notice something interesting, however. Even for data-only purposes, without the support for audio and video that ATM provides, not one protocol can do it all. No one can build a 100-Mbps Ethernet from coast to coast. The data will get there all right, but it cannot travel across the country as raw Ethernet frames, as it can within the local Ethernet LANs. And no one in their right mind would attempt to use SMDS or frame relay as a LAN protocol.

ATM is a LAN, MAN, and WAN protocol. So while each of these other technologies may threaten ATM in one arena, none of them can replace

ATM everywhere. Even if ATM LANs never arrive, ATM WANs may still appear, and vice versa. All other technologies have limitations when compared with ATM.

High-speed LANs such as 100-Mbps Ethernet and even Switched Ethernet are not "scalable"; they must run at a fixed speed. But ATM has no such limitation; the connections on an ATM network are completely fluid as far as speed goes, up to the physical limit of the link. And since the links are tied to SONET, they may be scaled up as future networks need even more than 100-Mbps speeds.

Networks based on IEEE 802.6 are still limited in area, so some other technology must be used to hook them together. In fact, the IEEE terminology of *subnetwork* applied to 802.6 implies that this will always be so.

PTM solutions are very promising for data applications, but they remain highly proprietary in functional details that are standardized in ATM. Thus it may be difficult for customers choosing a PTM solution to switch vendors or interconnect equipment from other vendors. This is exactly the situation that the ATM Forum was founded to prevent.

Public networks such as SMDS *are* standard and have real potential. However, the fact that SMDS is a connectionless service and so has to perform a routing as well as a switching function in many network nodes means that SMDS may be expensive for quite some time to come.

Frame relay is probably the most serious contender for an ATM rival technology in a data-only world. It is relatively cheap and very good at handling TCP/IP router-based network traffic. However, ATM can handle most situations, including TCP/IP transport, as effectively as frame relay. The price of converting all data to cells, despite the existence of the DXI interface, will mean that ATM will remain a higher-cost network service than frame relay for quite some time (maybe always).

However, since ATM networks can provide LAN emulation, SMDS connectionless, and frame-relay service all on the same network, and even interconnect existing LANs, SMDS, and FR networks, why not just build ATM networks and in effect build them all? No one will ever be able to deliver SMDS over a frame-relay network, or vice versa.

This is true because ATM has a unique agenda. ATM is ambitious, to be sure, with support for voice, video, and data all on the same network. But ATM is intended to

1. Use the same procedures and protocols at the LAN, MAN, and WAN levels.

2. Provide support for multimedia services.

3. Provide services at a wide range of physical media speeds.

4. Replace fixed physical channels with virtual connections.

None of the other protocols even comes close to these capabilities of ATM, real or intended.

It is sometimes claimed that almost any one of the other protocols and technologies mentioned above, from Switched Ethernet to SMDS, can be extended to provide exactly the same kind of support than ATM is intended to provide. For example, if the frame-relay standard some-day included a provision for time-sensitive connections for voice and video, could not a frame-relay network be used almost anywhere a more expensive ATM network might be built? This is not a trivial argument and should be addressed.

Consider a cable television network delivering a number of channels to a user's television set at home. The cable television network itself is a good vehicle for delivering the channels, but it is not a channel itself. Some of the channels are sports channels, comedy channels, and so on. But they are all delivered on the same cable television system to all "users" who watch whichever ones they would like to. The channel producers pay the cable television company to carry their channels, and the cable television company turns over some of the profits from subscribers to that channel.

Of course, the producers of these comedy and sports channels might look at this situation and think: What do we need the cable television network for? People don't watch *it*; they watch *our* channels. So one day the comedy channels build their own cable television network and entice the sports channels onto their system. The original cable television network eventually folds (no decent programming to be had), and the net result is—a cable television network.

The whole point is that, of course, SMDS or frame relay or something else can eventually do exactly what ATM was intended to do. But what-ever the result, anything new must look pretty much like ATM does today, no matter where this new network technology came from.

ATM and Network Service Providers

This book began with a survey of telecommunications networks from a historical and functional point of view. Various network technologies were examined in terms of their utility: what they could do to provide services for the people using them. ATM is a very promising technology when seen in the light of this historical and functional perspective. But a promise is not an actuality; a promise is only a potential. ATM must be used—and used well—by potential customers and service providers if it is to fulfill the promise.

There is still a question about the use of ATM by customers and service providers. It is by no means clear just where in a network is the best place to employ ATM. The term *employ ATM* essentially means: Where are the cells made and unmade in the overall process of moving information from a source to a destination? Ultimately, it makes perfect sense to just expect applications and end-user devices to generate and consume ATM cells in the same way that it is expected today that serial ports on computers generate 0s and 1s. This is just what they are set up to do best.

However, no network device in common use today is "set up" to do ATM (i.e., generate/consume ATM cells) yet. In view of this fact, once a user or service provider has been sold on the ATM concept (and the membership of the ATM Forum shows that many organizations have indeed been sold on the idea of ATM), the question becomes not *why* do ATM but rather *how* and *where* does ATM happen in a network?

This chapter looks at some of the possible ways that ATM can be deployed in both public and private networks. As mentioned earlier, when ATM is a mature technology, the question may well be answered by simply saying "everywhere." But in today's networking environment, this approach is neither feasible nor affordable for most organizations.

A similar process occurred during the transition period from an all-analog telephone network to an all-digital telephone network in the United States (a process which is still, after 30 years, not entirely completed). As soon as it made good economic and technical sense (and was socially acceptable) to digitize analog voice, the telephone companies began to explore ways to bring the new methods into the existing analog network. It was quickly apparent that it made perfect sense to digitize switches in central offices to take advantage of new computer processing power and to digitize the multichannel trunks between these offices to take advantage of the more efficient multiplexing techniques that digital transmission systems provided.

A funny thing happened, though. It turned out that it was much too difficult and expensive to convert large metropolitan area switches with 10,000 subscriber lines to digital central offices. It was better to start small with the less dense rural switching areas with a few thousand lines. These processors were less complex and easy to install and troubleshoot. When enough experience with these was gathered, the larger switches began to be converted.

On the other hand, it made no sense to digitize trunks in these rural areas where calls were less frequent and distances were relatively large between switching offices. The need for digital multiplexing to save facility space was much more urgent in urban areas where calls were substantial and distances were relatively short. Thus a situation developed and persisted for a number of years in which digital trunks were downtown and the digital central offices were out of town, and few connections between the two were needed or even seen.

It will be the same with ATM initially. But the issues will be much more complex. It will not be a matter of one entity (the telephone company) deciding where and when and how to deploy equipment internally. The bewildering array of vendors in the ATM Forum, coupled with the service providers and added to the growing number of "system integrators," means that there will be a lot of confusion for a number of years over the issue of just where in a network ATM in best employed.

Each component of this equation—end-equipment vendors and network service providers—has reasons to employ ATM in different parts of a network. The case may be simple: A hub vendor that uses ATM will use ATM in its hub, of course. Or it may be more complicated: A large network service provider may deploy ATM equipment internally for a variety of reasons, but should it offer ATM cell services directly to the customer? And which customers? And how should they be billed for it?

All these questions are further complicated by the fact that right from the start of initial vendor offerings customers may build their own private "intrapremises" ATM networks. They may eventually link their private networks with public "interpremises" ATM network service providers, but even this is not a foregone conclusion. In the "half-analog, half-digital" world of the telephone network, it was not unusual for a residential subscriber's analog call to be digitized at the end office, analoged for the trunk, digitized again at another office, and analoged yet again at the far end. In fact, five or more analog-digital conversions were not uncommon on long-distance calls. The same may happen, and probably will, with ATM cells.

This chapter looks at the implications of deciding on an ATM model. That is, just where is the best place in the network to generate and consume ATM cells instead of packets or frames or anything else? The stakes are high. Whoever's ATM model prevails will carve out a large slice of the ATM market immediately, leaving all the other players to scramble over the remaining segments of the ATM equipment and services world.

A discussion of specific vendors, products, and services is presented at the end of the chapter.

9.1   Private Intrapremises ATM Network Providers

When it comes to building private ATM networks, networks that will all be contained within an office complex or even a single structure, three groups are well represented within the ATM Forum and are actively pursuing their own vision of the ATM model. The three groups are the LAN hub vendors, the router vendors, and the multiplexer vendors. Each one has announced ATM products, some have even delivered, and a few are acknowledged leaders in their field.

This is not the place to debate product merits and descriptions, which change from week to week in any case. Rather, the three groups will be discussed in terms of their arguments that the "best" place to make ATM cells is (surprisingly) in the equipment that they happen to sell. All these arguments are, in a literal sense, self-serving. However, this section will not focus on arguments along the lines of "buy a Ford and not a Chevy" but more along the lines of "buy a car and not a horse." If a router maker is serious about ATM, the first task is to convince customers to buy ATM routers and then to compete with other ATM router makers.

All the groups discussed here will be represented by various vendors, and some will be mentioned by name. These corporations are not mentioned as any kind of product endorsement, but merely to place the product being discussed in a real-world context.

The hub vendors are represented by such companies as Bay Networks (formerly Synoptics) and Cabletron. These companies have built their businesses on selling mostly Ethernet-based hubs to connect unshielded twisted-pair star-wired PCs and workstations over a local area. The attraction of ATM to them is in its use as a high-speed switching matrix used internally in their product. These hubs can then support not only Ethernet-based ports but also Token Ring or FDDI ports with the same internal architecture, a real savings across the product line.

The router vendors are represented by such companies as Cisco and Bay Networks (formerly Wellfleet). These companies have built their businesses on selling routers to provide LAN connectivity conforming to the router-based networking paradigm that dominates the networking world toady. As such, routers are used as devices to bridge the gap between the LAN on one side and the WAN on the other. Another router provides this function on the other end of a point-to-point leased line or public network service offering (e.g., X.25). Thus LANs today communicate over wide areas via routers attached to each LAN. Router vendors are attracted to ATM because of the interest in ATM on the LAN side of their product (the hub vendors) and on the WAN side of their product (the network service providers). Also, there is a real speed and performance advantage to doing switching inside the router based on locally unique ATM connections over doing pure routing based on network-wide unique addresses.

The multiplexer vendors are represented by such companies as General DataComm (GDC) and Network Equipment Technology (NET). These companies have built their businesses on selling muxes to provide access to the channelized leased lines that end users employ to link their LAN routers, PBXs, and videoconferencing networks. Lately, these vendors have taken to calling their devices *bandwidth managers,* reflecting the newer generation of the devices' capabilities. Newer boxes do not just time-division multiplex traffic on the trunk side of the network anymore. Instead, they frequently perform dynamic bandwidth allocation in a highly proprietary fashion.

Mux vendors are attracted to ATM because of the potential savings and performance gain offered by ATM's asynchronous multiplexing nature. An unchannelized ATM link can carry many times more connections asynchronously than a simple time-division synchronous multiplexer can do over a channelized link running at exactly the same speed. And ATM offers a standard and very sophisticated way of doing this.

All three groups are busily trying to sell their version of the ATM model for building private intrapremises ATM networks.

9.1.1   The switching hub vendors' ATM model

Figure 9.1 shows the type of world that the vendors of switching hubs would like to see. The hub vendors are in a very strong market position, especially if ATM comes to be seen as a way of delivering interconnectivity between existing LANs. It is easily positioned as an "upgrade" to current 10BaseT or other LAN hubs.

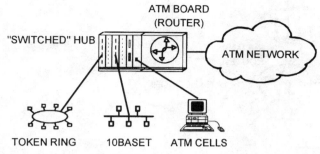

Figure 9.1 Hub vendors' ATM model.

In this model, there is no need to deliver ATM to the desktop, except for very high-speed data applications. All the existing Token Ring and 10BaseT LANs go on as before. But *internally,* the hub will convert everything to cells and use multiple high-speed backplanes or a distributed matrix to switch cells around between input and output ports. This now becomes an ATM switch in itself.

Notice that the variably sized LAN frame does not have to be converted to an ATM cell at a port with a standard AAL. As long as the cell is only used internally and a matching conversion is done at the output port, any mechanism, even proprietary, may be used to convert the LAN frames. Most vendors will employ AAL-5, however, for hub-to-hub connectivity considerations. If ATM boards in workstations become common, then these devices can be linked directly to a private UNI interface, and no AAL function is even needed for those ports.

Not all LAN hub traffic stays within a building though. In a world of readily available wide area ATM network services, the router disappears. Instead of a router handling traffic sent off premises, the separate router box becomes redundant. The router function becomes just a board in the hub (although it may be *supplied* by a router vendor).

This has actually been tried before by the hub vendors. They all announced a board for their pre-ATM Ethernet-based hub products that performed the router function and in many cases was even made by a router vendor on their behalf. But the effort failed. Users did not want to tie the router function to a hub but preferred a separate box for that function. This is a perfect example of technological and economic feasibility without the social acceptability. So the technology disappeared.

Naturally, the router vendors have their own model to build on.

9.1.2   The router vendors' ATM model

Figure 9.2 shows what the router vendors would like to see. Many organizations have hubs on every floor of a building. Some have several hubs on each floor. It would be prohibitively expensive to expect an early

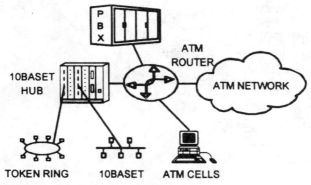

Figure 9.2 Router vendors' ATM model.

migration to ATM hubs when these products are relatively new. Yet there is a better way, say the router vendors, to enjoy the advantages of ATM in a private ATM network. Keep the hub, buy an ATM router, and plug the ATM cell-capable equipment right into the router. Hubs will have their familiar LAN interfaces to the router, the same as they do today.

Now the router becomes the creator and consumer of ATM cells for all devices hooked up to it. This is even a potentially more broadly applicable use of ATM also. ATM networks can carry voice connections as well as data. Thus a corporation or organization can put the PBX on it at some point in the future too.

Now the router does all the cell functions. What better place? The hub has enough to do. Users, the argument goes, do not need cells to the desktop. What is the sense of buying an ATM board for every device in the organization. Users need cells only for the ATM network, not for each and every workstation.

Router vendors will counter the hub vendors' approach of a router as a board in the hub by pointing out that users like having the router function in a separate box. However, ATM is different from normal LAN protocols in use today. There really is no separate router function to distinguish local LAN traffic from wide area LAN traffic. In ATM, there are only connections everywhere and anywhere. The connections are in no way distinguished by distance. Two workstations side by side or across the country are still exchanging cells based on a VPI/VCI connection number.

Connectionless services are a slightly different matter. A separate function must be added to ATM switching to route the cell traffic. There is a possibility that users will prefer to link LANs connectionlessly with ATM. However, the cost and complexity of adding this function to private ATM networks may always make it more expensive to implement and deliver than straight connection-oriented ATM. Thus routers will probably not devolve to providing connectionless ATM services in conjunction with connection-oriented ATM hubs. This makes as little sense as the analog-digital conversions in the telephone networks, especially since major players such as the Internet Engineering Task Force (IETF) and Novell have plans to change the way IP and IPX (which is a totally proprietary protocol) operate to make these connectionless protocols function more efficiently on a connection-oriented ATM network.

There is some consideration that needs to be given to the ATM Forum's intention of supporting a LAN emulation service. When a full implementation definition is finished, the role of hubs and routers and even bridges will be much better defined in a private ATM network. For now, this whole segment remains a constantly shifting playing field.

The whole router vendor argument may be a stretch. Do not be surprised to see, therefore, cells in hubs right to the desktop and the router vendors making the boards (a proprietary board for *each* major hub vendor).

9.1.3 The multiplexer vendors' ATM model

Figure 9.3 shows the kind of world the multiplexer vendors would ideally like to see. The manufacturers of T-1 multiplexers would like everyone to keep their existing hubs and routers and do all the cell conversion in the multiplexer. If there are cell boards in workstations, these would perhaps have a remote concentrator unit (from the same vendor, of course) on each floor to link up to the mux in the basement.

PBXs can hook up as well; in fact, the PBXs probably do already, along with the routers. Generally, a site will have only one mux, upgraded from time to time as the organization grows. Thus ATM need only come once, in one location. As the organization and the ATM industry grow in size and sophistication, the mux is still the last box

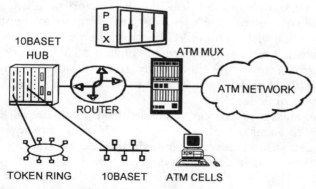

Figure 9.3 Mux vendors' ATM model.

encountered by traffic leaving the site and the first box encountered on the inbound side. This is a perfect place to incorporate ATM from the start. A very powerful argument.

There is another, more subtle argument that goes along with it. The argument goes along with: If anybody understands muxing, it is the mux vendors. And ATM is just fancy muxing at heart. How can LAN and router vendors ever hope to know enough about the demands of voice to give users PBX connectivity? They make data products. And the complexities of videoconferencing and networking will always remain beyond their expertise in any case. Users are going to need the mux vendors for that anyway.

The LAN hub and router vendors are banking on the demands of data to position them initially in the ATM equipment market. Mux vendors are counting on the long-term needs for voice and video; users can buy it now or buy it later, but they are going to have to buy it eventually.

9.2 Public Interpremises ATM Network Providers

The other major market segment competing for ATM dollars is the arena of public network service providers. The term *public* in this context describes an entity that is used to provide services to all comers who ask for and can afford a service. Public networks have subscribers to a service. Whether the public network is a voice network (telephone companies) or a television network (cable television companies) or even a power company, service cannot be denied arbitrarily.

There are potentially competing groups in this category as well. But it is only *potential* competition for a number of reasons. First, these companies sell services, not technology. They do not make a tangible product that can be shipped and delivered in a box. Services may be provided *by* an ATM network, or they may be delivered *on* an ATM network. The difference is significant. Services like the delivery of cells for customers with ATM equipment on site obviously will be more efficient and economical to provide with a public ATM network in place. But services such as frame relay can easily be provided *by* an ATM network, even though the customer only sees frame relay. In this case, the public network is an ATM network, but it is used as such only internally by the network service provider.

Second, it is by no means a foregone conclusion that public network service providers are as eager to build and deploy ATM as private organizations. Some organizations have an immediate need for the high bandwidths and low network delays that ATM provides. All this means, though, is that there are potential customers for the public network providers. The investment structure and technology considerations are different for service providers, who in many cases are struggling with regulatory restrictions and competitive issues as well.

This section assumes that ATM will happen in these groups, but only for the sake of argument and comparison. Five groups are discussed here, but this number is derived in an arbitrary fashion. The blurring of lines in the public service arena between what a local telephone company (for example) can and cannot do means that the divisions between these service providers are not as clearcut as they used to be.

There are five important players in a position today to offer ATM services on an interpremises basis. Whether the ATM cells are generated in a LAN hub, a router, or even a mux, there is still a need to transport these cells between user sites in a secure and structured manner. It makes no sense to "cellify" on the premises and then convert to something else over a MAN or a WAN. Each has different advantages and liabilities when it comes to convincing customers that they are the best source for ATM network access and connectivity.

The five groups distinguished here are the local exchange carriers (LECs), such as NYNEX or US West, the interexchange carriers (IXCs), such as AT&T and MCI, the competitive carriers (CAPs), such as Metropolitan Fiber Systems (MFS), the cable television companies, such as TCI and Cox, and the value-added network providers (VANs). This last group is especially hard to exemplify, because many organization in the other four categories have spun off subsidiaries or bought other companies outright to provide VAN services [sometimes called *enhanced service providers* (*ESPs*)] in addition to their other lines of business. But the best examples of this category are probably MFS Datanet, a subsidiary of MFS, and BT Tymnet, a subsidiary of British Telecomm. A list of the five groups is shown in Figure 9.4.

9.2.1 The LECs' Centrex ATM model

Local exchange carriers (LECs) have traditionally been granted a monopoly for providing telephone service in a franchise area. This monopoly franchise is given by some regulatory agency (usually at the state level in the United States) in return for regulation. Regulation is the compliance with certain rules on business conduct (mostly concerning profits and expenses) that are put in place to guarantee that

- LOCAL EXCHANGE CARRIERS
- INTEREXCHANGE CARRIERS
- COMPETITIVE CARRIERS
- CABLE TELEVISION
- VALUE-ADDED NETWORK PROVIDERS

Figure 9.4 Five interpremises ATM players.

the service is provided in the public interest. This is an enormous simplification of what an LEC is and does, and things are slowly changing to a competitive environment, but the definition is good enough for ATM purposes.

One of the services LECs offer on top of the basic provision of dial tone for telephone calls is a *Centrex* service. In a Centrex configuration, an organization does not buy a PBX (or multiple PBXs) to deliver voice services within the organization. Instead, a portion of the LEC's switch is bought or leased to the organization for the delivery of these services. The customer has no need to buy a PBX, configure it, or even maintain it. The Centrex cannot become obsolete (theoretically) like a PBX, and administration is done with a simple phone call to the LEC. The LEC gains by capturing a market segment for voice revenue that would have been lost to private PBX vendors.

Maybe this could work the same with ATM. A great barrier to buying private ATM equipment will be the initial costs. How much better to buy (lease) ATM services from the LEC.

The LECs (along with the others in this group) will point out that ATM is a full network architecture. It would be expensive and probably overkill for one organization to build either a hub, a router, or a mux-based ATM network with extensive connectivity needs. Better to offer an ATM Centrex service. The concept is illustrated in Fig. 9.5.

The LECs have the ATM network already, the argument would go. That is what the carriers are for: penetration and services. Therefore, customers are better off paying for an ATM Centrex, a little piece of the carrier's ATM switch all for the customer's own use. Let the LEC worry about cells and so on. Customers still have non-ATM hubs, routers, and muxes, and the customers would feed the newer cell equipment on the same speed links they have now. Who can afford DS-3 at 45 Mbps for ATM? Now a customer does not need to.

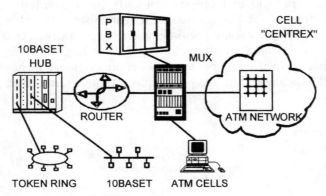

Figure 9.5 Centrex ATM model.

There are no management, performance, or security worries. It is the carrier's concern. If the carrier does not deliver what it promised, then get a new one; this is ATM, and it is the same for everybody. And even if an organization has an ATM "model" network based on one of the previous three private models, it can hook it up directly to the ATM Centrex.

9.2.2   The IXCs' ATM model

The only problem with getting ATM services from an LEC is that an LEC is exactly what the name implies: a *local* exchange carrier. Even if an organization with offices on both coasts gets Centrex services from a LEC in New York and a LEC in California, there is still a need to link them together with voice tie lines. Right now, neither LEC can do this. An IXC must provide the connectivity for these "long distance" calls. IXCs are usually barred from providing local services and LECs are barred from long-distance services, but this is slowly changing.

Data networks frequently span long distances, usually with point-to-point leased private lines like DS-1s. The IXCs are, of course, the traditional sources for networks; if users need to build an SNA or router network, they call an IXC and get some links. The IXC would even provide "local access coordination" with the LEC on each end. The customer paid them, and they paid the LECs.

There were attempts to sell users ISDN and X.25 packet services, but lately they have been just "bandwidth mongers." (Actually, they were not; a fish monger is someone who went down to the harbor and bought fish they hauled up the hill and sold to customers for more because they did not like the smell down at the harbor.) A customer needs a network? How many T's do they want? They got revenue from that. Until recently, the LEC had a dead solid lock on local access, but this is changing. The IXCs had a tight grip on long-haul connections, but only because they could depend on the user density to drive the need for new equipment investments. (But there was no T-1 in Montana for ages.)

Now all the IXCs want to sell services like ATM and SMDS. And with them supplying the bandwidth in the form of leased lines, if a competitor wants to supply ATM, it better be good, because it will be hard to beat the IXCs on price alone.

9.2.3   The competitive carrier ATM model

Companies in this category used to be called CAPs, for *competitive access providers*. Now they are getting into all phases of the business, and the newer term is to call them *competitive carriers*. These companies used to offer just "bypass" services; they would run wire (or use microwave) for customers to the IXC's point of presence (POP) directly for a user's PBX or SNA network or whatever. This spared the customers the sometimes considerable local access charges. Now these companies are being let into the LEC's central office itself. Soon users may see Centrex services (off-premises PBX) from these CAPs and may be even a whole CO itself (this has already happened in Texas). For urban areas, they are offering fiber rings (for backup) in high-density areas. These companies to date have been very aggressive but generally small. But so was MCI once.

These companies see ATM as the great leveler regarding their position with the LECs and IXCs. Everybody is a new player in the ATM network arena, so nobody has a built-in advantage in terms of experience or tradition. And these companies are not saddled with enormous switches and physical plant facilities that cannot be replaced overnight to provide new services that ATM networks would make possible. Regulations about the depreciation of telecommunications equipment make it less economically feasible for LECs and IXCs to replace older non-ATM equipment wholesale. Competitive carriers labor under no such restrictions.

The argument in favor of getting ATM network services from these companies runs as follows: The large LECs and IXCs are rooted in technologies of the past. They are incapable of taking advantage of all the possibilities of ATM because of this lack of imagination and willingness to change entrenched networking techniques rapidly. All they are interested in ATM for is to deliver to customers the same old stuff more efficiently, mostly to make bigger profits, not to offer services more cheaply.

The competitive carriers have a point. The LECs and IXCs failed to market X.25 services effectively and fumbled the narrowband ISDN ball repeatedly. They may be mishandling SMDS as well. The LEC and IXC sales representatives cannot even explain the new ATM-based services, having little idea of the possibilities themselves. And the pricing point is especially well taken. Both voice and data services are based on a digital T-carrier hierarchy today. All voice and data services are delivered on DS-1s and DS-3s. Prices from the LECs and IXCs for leased DS-1s and DS-3s come down all the time. But this is just bandwidth. The service delivered on DS-1s and DS-3s is voice dial tone. Yet the price of voice has hardly budged at all. Cost efficiencies gained from use of digital facilities are passed along for raw bandwidth but not for voice services. For services, the efficiencies mainly translate into greater profits.

It is just possible that these aggressive companies will offer the best hope for affordable public interpremises ATM services.

9.2.4 The cable television ATM model

The cable television companies in the United States want in on the ATM network scene also. If this sounds strange, remember that the Home Shopping Network generates millions of dollars for the *telephone* companies. If the cable box could be used to order merchandise, the cable television company could capture that revenue. And if one very special type of telephone call is possible, why not all? This whole concept of "cable-phone" is actually offered in many areas of the United States today.

In data applications, the cable television companies are attracted to the broadband-ISDN aspect of ATM with its "video jukeboxes" (movies on demand) and "interactive CDs" (the SEGA Genesis channel). There may be "interactive pornography" and other sexually oriented services, which are already a driving force behind dial-up bulletin boards and e-mail networks.

Ironically, there is bandwidth reserved in every cable television system in the United States today for transmission from the set-top cable box back to the cable company head end. But it is essentially useless because of the way cable television networks have been built to date. It is not unusual for a large cable television network to have 20,000 homes serviced ("houses passed" in cable television talk, only some of which are subscribers) off of one large branching cable trunk. Some of these homes are separated from the cable television head end by 30 or 40 analog amplifiers, all pointing outbound. Signals trying to make their way back to the cable television head end can only pass through three or four of these amplifiers. Besides preventing interactive services, these numerous analog amplifiers draw a lot of power and break down a lot (which contributes to the cable television companies' bad service reputation).

Thus the cable television companies are all busy running fiber to the neighborhood or curb or home because amplifiers cannot do two-way well at all. In a fiber cable television system, there may be only three or four digital regenerators for the same 20,000 homes. (Actually, there are many more branching fiber trunks as well.) Signals from a set top easily pass through these back to the cable television head end. And digital fiber regenerators draw much less power and seldom break down at all, being solid-state electronic devices.

In addition to offering entertainment and telephone service over this new cable network, the cable television companies are experimenting with data services as well. Already there are several cable television networks in the United States today providing connectivity to the Internet not by dial-up through the telephone network but by attaching the PC at home to a special port in the set-top cable television box. This "Internet channel" most often runs at 1.544-Mbps (DS-1) rates, but speeds up to 10 Mbps (Ethernet LAN speeds) have been tried. And the cost is much less than for a privately leased DS-1 from the LEC.

The ATM argument here runs along the same lines as that of the competitive carriers. Newer companies understand newer technologies better, are more willing to take risks, and so on. A real impediment to cable television companies' credibility in the network services arena is their abysmal service and reliability reputation. But early computers suffered from the same criticism and still ultimately prospered.

The question is not whether the cable television companies are interested in providing services besides 500 channels of reruns (clearly they are), but rather what role ATM will take in the cable television network of the near future. Several companies have expressed interest in placing compressed digital video using MPEG-2 inside ATM cells with AAL-2 or even AAL-5. Others have considered using a larger cell (190 bytes?) or even PTM instead. Plans change almost monthly, it seems.

The cable television companies already have a big advantage; by law, only the LEC, the power company, and the *cable television company* can use the utility poles in a neighborhood. This section has not discussed power companies as possible public ATM service providers, but this is possible too, especially in a "deregulated" market. In any case, the power companies would fall into the last category discussed in this section.

9.2.5 The VAN providers' ATM model

The value-added network (VAN) providers are in a very strong position to deploy and market public ATM services effectively. Many companies have subsidiaries that fall into this category. For instance, Hewlett-Packard, an equipment vendor, has a wireless heart monitor network that it builds on top of wireless services, thus "adding value" to the network's native capability.

Using a VAN for ATM service makes a lot of sense, these companies argue. They are already used to and expected to provide services, not bandwidth. They understand the whole game well: designing and building the network, managing it, security issues, and so forth. VANs offer their whole expertise to the client in many areas, not just one.

However, they must avoid the "me too" syndrome. Nobody buys "me too" services; a company must be the first to offer the service or be the best (or at least claim to be the best). It is not good enough to just offer something because someone else does; there must be a good reason to call them in the first place (it probably will not be price, due to the cost of adding enough value to a basic connectivity network).

But these companies are in a very flexible position; they can take the best from all worlds. If a customer is building ATM hub networks, that is okay, because there is no conflict there with a Centrex business. VANs can live with router-based ATM, or mux-based ATM, or just about anything else. They can sell the customer what the customer needs, not just what they sell.

Their interest in ATM emphasizes the "network of networks" aspect of ATM. A VAN can just build more network with ATM and not worry about building frame relay or SMDS or any other service-specific type of network.

9.3   A Real-World ATM Network: The MFS Datanet ATM Network

A frequent criticism of ATM is that it is not ready for "prime time." The technology may be impressive, but it is too early to build functioning networks entirely from commercially available ATM products, especially with live users on them. Early ATM networks will be for research and development, and even if there are actual users on them, they should expect long and unpredictable outages and problems. This is taken as gospel by many industry observers.

In view of this, it might be entertaining and enlightening to close the book with a look at a large, working, commercially viable ATM network service offering with paying customers on it. These ATM services come from company that is a mix of a VAN and a competitive carrier, which is in fact a more and more common configuration in these times of reduced regulation in the telecommunications industry. This relationship may be instructive in itself.

MFS Communications Company, Inc., was founded in 1987 by Peter Kiewit Sons, a construction, mining, energy, and communications company, and began operations in 1988. It went public in 1993 and announced its ATM network in August of that same year. MFS was founded with one eye on the increasingly competitive market for advanced telecommunications services, the philosophy being that there were opportunities for agile and aggressive companies to compete in new service areas with established and more traditional telecommunications firms. MFS is segmented into two major business sectors. One offers systems integration and facilities management services through a subsidiary called MFS Network Technologies. The other offers telecommunications through such subsidiaries as MFS Telecom, MFS Intelenet, MFS International, and most relevant here, MFS Datanet.

MFS Datanet, a member of the ATM Forum, offers high-speed data communications services to government and business end users. All the factors previously discussed regarding the use of ATM by service providers apply here. The flexibility of ATM in terms of bandwidth allocation, high speeds, low delays, and unified networking protocols all have had an effect on the decision to build ATM into a data network rather than some other technology.

MFS had already offered a LAN connectivity service for its customers over a metropolitan area with FDDI. In the process of operating the FDDI service, the company learned the serious management and availability problems inherent in trying to scale up FDDI rings into a national or global network. The company became convinced that only an ATM backbone network would be capable of evolving to meet its customers' high-speed communications needs. Of course, no one buys technology, and MFS customers are no exception. What MFS is selling through the MFS Datanet is LAN connectivity at native LAN speeds (4, 10, 16, and even 100 Mbps) across wide areas. MFS calls its service *high-speed LAN interconnect (HLI)*.

HLI allows customers to link LANs separated by large distances essentially transparently. The LANs appear to both end users and applications as simply bridged LANs, i.e., one big LAN instead of separate networks linked by routers, the most common way of linking widely separated LANs today. Since the LANs on the MFS Datanet appear to be locally bridged, they can be seen as virtual LANs. The virtual connections in ATM make it easy to configure a user network as a star, mesh, or ring depending on customer and application requirements. HLI is basically an early implementation of the ATM Forum's LAN emulation service.

The architecture of an HLI service connecting LANs is shown in Fig. 9.6. Users are connected to the MFS backbone network over fiber or an unchannelized DS-3 through a pair of concentrators. User hubs link up via fiber as well. The portion of direct interest in this section is the MFS backbone itself, a large network of ATM switches connected by DS-3 links (which will migrate to SONET). MFS also offers a pure cell-relay ATM service for customers with AAL-3/4 and AAL-5 VBR applications.

A network like this could be built using other technologies. MFS chose ATM for a number of reasons, which are probably worth enumerating. If the ATM approach makes sense for one company, it will probably make sense for others. The reasons for basing HLI on ATM

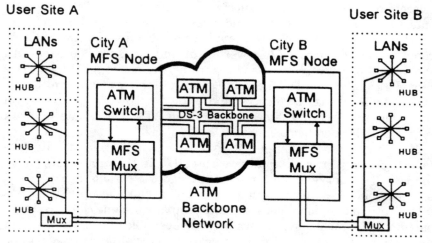

Figure 9.6 MFS Datanet architecture.

- ATM Forum, ANSI, and ITU Standards

- Allows mesh, star, or ring VCC configurations

- Universal LAN and WAN protocol

- High speeds and low delays on a national scale

- Scaleable transport to Gigabits

- Accepted by many vendors and suppliers

Figure 9.7   Reasons for ATM deployment.

MFS Datanet's Asynchronous Transfer Mode Network

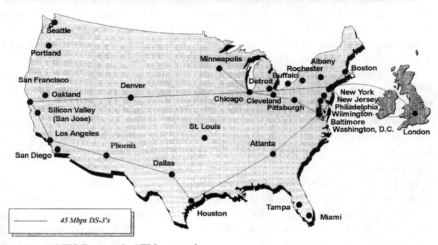

Figure 9.8   MFS Datanet's ATM network.

are listed in Figure 9.7. All are familiar from previous discussions and need no elaboration.

MFS Datanet is surprisingly large considering its youth. Fifteen U.S. metropolitan areas were in the initial service area, and an international ATM link now runs to London, England. Coverage in the United States is being expanded into an additional 16 areas. The MFS Datanet service areas are shown in Figure 9.8. Over the next 2 or 3 years, the company expects to expand the core network to 65 cities and 10 international financial capitals. Alliances will be established to bring services to outlying areas, much like the airline "hub and spoke" service agreements.

Some details on MFS Datanet's ATM network are in order here. The switches typically have from 4 to 32 ports and are configured to be fault-tolerant (i.e., if one fails, service is not disrupted). In view of the lack of standard ATM network management, a proprietary management scheme is used, but this is unavoidable. Most of the ports run at DS-3 speeds (45 Mbps), but there are already some STS-3c ports (OC-3c running at 155 Mbps). Other ports speeds are TAXI ports running at 100 Mbps and early "low-speed" implementations (below 45 Mbps). The switches are all currently using VPIs and VCIs configured as PVCs, but ATM Forum signaling standards for SVCs will be implemented soon. Most of the switches have priorities and policing capabilities, but the lack of strict ATM Forum implementation agreements in these areas has been felt.

The MFS Datanet network interfaces can adapt to many other protocols. Frame-relay and Ethernet LAN ports are available. FDDI will definitely be supported and perhaps even Token Ring. For nondata applications, the MFS switches can support circuit emulation service (AAL-1) at DS-1 speeds (currently) and both 56 kbps and $N \times 64$ (soon). Voice in the form of PBX traffic can be supported with this interface as well, and video support for full motion JPEG is available. MPEG and other video interfaces also could be added.

MFS Datanet brilliantly sells HLI speeds in terms of "fractional Ethernet." This subtly emphasizes that users do not really want a "fractional T-1" to link their LANs with routers; what they really want is the network to appear to be an extension of their LAN. There is intense competition from public frame-relay network providers, but (as has been pointed out) ATM can deliver frame relay easily if users really want and need it.

By basing its services on virtual Ethernets and Token Rings, MFS Datanet gains the flexibility of exploiting other telephony services such as SMDS, frame relay, and ISDN in those service areas where they are offered as a commercial service. This allows MFS Datanet to improve its economics and extend the reach of the ATM network without exposing its customers to technology risk or concerns about global availability of compatible telephony service offerings.

What are MFS Datanet's customers doing with HLI? After all, ISDN networks were built and no one could figure out what to do with them. MFS has released details on the kinds of things several organizations are doing with HLI on the ATM network.

A large international bank with offices in the United States used HLI's increased bandwidth and low delays to reduce its processing time from 9 hours at night to 30 minutes during the day. (Further potential savings: What became of the night shift?) Another company used MFS Datanet to concentrate its Novell servers where their technical staff was located. Because the network was fast enough to make servers across the country appear to be servers down the hall, all network mappings and menus could be uniform, an enormous advantage to users and applications. Finally, another company supplying commercial Internet connectivity used MFS Datanet to provide full 10-Mbps connectivity between its routers spread throughout the country. This would have been prohibitively expensive with other point-to-point private networking methods.

This section has given a view of the ATM networking future. Not only is the architecture of the MFS Datanet relevant, but so are the kinds of things users have employed MFS's service to accomplish. The simple fact is that ATM has advantages that no other network technology comes close to matching.

9.4   A Survey of ATM Products and Services

This book ends with a very useful and at the same time difficult subject. The quickly evolving nature of ATM standards and practices has meant that products and services that vendors have offered based on ATM have evolved rapidly as well. Thus it is extremely hard to be up-to-date and at the same time accurate when considering ATM products and network services.

Yet it is hoped that this section still has value. If nothing else, it is an indication of which vendors and service providers have made an early commitment to ATM. And even if the list of specific products and services will not be accurate for long, the companies and organizations mentioned are clearly the place to start for anyone interested in ATM as a networking technology.

The vendors of ATM products fall roughly into two categories: companies that have been around in the networking industry (some seemingly forever) and are expanding into the ATM arena and companies specifically formed to exploit the interest in ATM technology evident today. The older companies tend to have higher-priced, but better-supported products, although there are many exceptions. The newer companies tend to be very aggressive price-wise, but customers run the risk of being left with a dead-end product if disaster strikes the vendor. The smaller, newer companies generally do not have deep enough pockets to survive more than a few rough initial years. Fortunately, there are many exceptions in this category as well.

The providers of ATM services also fall into the same types of categories. There are older, experienced networking companies that matured with telephone services in the middle of the twentieth century, and then there are the newer service providers seeking to take advantage of the current environment of deregulation. *Deregulation* just refers to the fact that many factors, from economic pressures to government policy, have gradually lead to the opening up of many service areas and markets to a number of providers, not just one.

Pricing and support usually mirror the same pattern as with product vendors, with older companies generally offering stability in prices and support and newer companies generally being more aggressive and fluid. However, many potential customers have been more willing to experiment with products on a small scale than to take a risk with new service providers, which generally involve large projects and longer pay-off periods.

Older companies, both vendors and service providers, tend to have a kind of "instant credibility" with their ATM product offerings, mainly because they have been successful in the past. The implication is that if the company makes good Ethernet equipment (for instance), they will make good ATM equipment. This is by no means a foregone conclusion, of course, but it is real nonetheless. Newer companies sometimes are portrayed as "wanna-bes" because they dearly want to be as respected and profitable as their older competitors in the ATM market. Finally, some companies are just "me too" companies in the ATM market. They have no deep or abiding involvement with ATM development or research other than that they must offer ATM products and services because all their competitors are offering ATM.

Some companies mentioned below make product lines that will fit into small, private networks and larger, public networks. In that case, the company will be treated as a vendor of equipment for smaller networks, mainly due to the fact that a customer will not experience its products directly through a public network offering. It sometimes may happen that a "credible" vendor of small, private ATM products will be a "me too" vendor of public ATM products, but the whole field of ATM is too new for this to happen often.

This section is merely a survey, not an exhaustive product evaluation, which would be hard enough to keep up to date on a weekly basis, let alone in a book. However, it is representative of the status of ATM goods and services.

Please keep in mind, however, that the opinions expressed about corporations and their products are the subjective opinions of the author and apply only to the specific product lines mentioned, not the entire company in general. The whole industry benefits from strong companies and products, and many a less-than-perfect "version 1.0" has been corrected in spectacular fashion by a gotta-have version 2.0.

This section begins with a survey of vendors of products for private ATM LANs. Many of these products are also useful for building ATM WANs as well, which is the topic of the next section. In some cases the decision to place a vendor's product in one category or another is entirely arbitrary. This is not capricious but merely an indication of the applicability of ATM technology to both LANs and WANs with equal ease.

9.4.1 ATM products for private ATM LANs

This section will explore various offerings that would be useful for an organization interested in implementing ATM on a site-by-site basis without necessarily worrying about how to link all the sites together. Or perhaps the organization itself is small enough to consist of entirely one site.

In either case, the attraction of ATM is as a "next generation" LAN implementation. Remember that one of the distinguishing features of ATM is that it employs exactly the same hardware, software, and protocols whether the network extends down the hall or around the world.

This section will not examine vendors of ATM chipsets for one reason. Usually, customers will not be buying the chipset directly, but rather on or in some product from some other vendor. Vendors of ATM NIC cards will not be examined in detail either, because the products in many cases are custom solutions or little more than prototypes. The companies most often mentioned in this area are Adaptive, Fore, and Synoptics (now Bay Networks). Also respected are boards available and planned from IBM (with a *very* aggressive pricing strategy), Trancell, DEC, SUN, and Hewlett-Packard.

Here is a brief look at some of the current players in the ATM product and services marketplace.

Private ATM LAN vendors with instant credibility

Synoptics. Synoptics (now Bay Networks) rates very highly in anyone's survey of private ATM products because the company has taken a leadership position in the field of ATM switch development. While many companies' R&D divisions were exploring ATM switching in a laboratory, Synoptics was partnering with Washington University in St. Louis, Missouri, to build working ATM switches. (Interestingly, Synoptics was the prime mover behind the wildly popular 10BaseT LAN standard, which they called *LattisNet*. They are either extremely foresighted or extremely lucky.) As a result, Synoptics' offering, the Lattiscell switch, is marketed as a "second generation" product, which it is.

The Lattiscell switch comes in one basic shape and size: 16 ports running at 155-Mbps, 12 over shielded twisted pair, and 4 over fiber. The price is excellent, and it is a distributed matrix switch with multicast capabilities. Synoptics' commitment to ATM is second to none, and the recent merger with Wellfleet will only broaden the appeal of Synoptics' products.

Fore. This book has already examined the ForeRunner switch family from Fore Systems. A startup specifically formed to offer ATM products, it seems strange to list Fore in the "instant credibility" category.

But this is because Fore is a startup company founded by members of Carnegie-Mellon Institute's faculty. CMI has always been a respected source for ATM theory and research.

Fore switches have been a mainstay of many service providers' networks (whether they want to admit this fact is another issue, especially if they have their own ATM products announced). In addition to low pricing, Fore products offer advanced features such as redundant power supplies and hot-swappable modules, features that have not found their way into many other vendors' offerings.

Fore is also one of the few vendors to make its products available for independent testing. An ASX-200 switch has a nodal delay of about 40 μs with a port running at 45 Mbps (DS-3).

Newbridge. Newbridge's VIVID (from voice, image, video, and data) switch has been a respected ATM product. But its most widely acclaimed ATM product is known to Newbridge customers as a *Ridge* or *Atomizer.* Newbridge products have proved indispensable for early implementers of ATM networks for a very good reason: There are lots of ATM switches but very few good ways to get *to* the switches.

A 12-port ATM switch, for instance, will support exactly 12 workstations or any other computer with ATM interface cards. This way of building networks is hardly efficient or cost-effective. What is really needed for ATM network feasibility is a way to interface *existing* LANs with ATM switches. This is what the Ridge does: 12 Ethernet ports in and 1 ATM port out.

FiberCom. FiberCom's Enterprise Access Server 8000 is another possible Ethernet in, ATM out concentrator switch. Capable of routing, bridging, and switching, the FiberCom 8000 has proved to be a popular choice for the premises portion of a public ATM network service provider's equipment.

Private ATM LAN vendor "wanna-bes."

IBM. Some observers would be surprised to find IBM listed here, given IBM's enormously active presence in the ATM Forum. (Practically no meeting happens without IBM in the room, and several committees were suggested and founded by IBM.) In fact, IBM arguably has more cell networking experience than anyone else in the world.

So what's the problem? It's twofold. One, IBM's *N*-ways switch and product line, including interface cards, must fight several battles. Several aspects of *N*-ways operations depart from accepted ATM Forum specifications, and IBM must sell its own particular way of doing things. Second, this very approach has raised the SNA/Token Ring issue all over again. That issue revolved around IBM's inability to support *anything* that the rest of the industry seemed to want.

DEC. Digital Equipment Corporation has been very active in the ATM standards process and is seeking to develop a whole array of products for ATM networks. Three products have been announced: a 13-slot (52-port total) premises ATM switch known as the GIGAswitch, a 155-Mbps SONET adapter for DEC's TURBOChannel on the DEC 3000 APX systems, and a 2-port ATM line card.

If the GIGAswitch is anything, it is big. All 52 ports running at 155.52 Mbps gives an aggregate bit rate of 10.4 Gbps. This, coupled with DEC's longevity and support structure in the industry, makes the GIGAswitch an important product. Ironically, the huge capacity will be massive overkill for most potential customers, at least initially.

3COM. 3Com is widely respected in the LAN world and would like nothing better than to continue the trend with ATM. Its ATM products will be part of the SuperStack network hub line. Until then, 3Com will resell the widely respected Fore switch line.

Cabletron. Cabletron has been sharing the Ethernet 10BaseT hub marketplace leadership role with Synoptics for the past few years. In the ATM marketplace, its 9A000 Switch Module for the multimedia access center family of hubs is one of the few hubs available with ATM switching. But its stature in the ATM industry is mainly upheld by its close relationship with Fore.

Hughes LAN Systems. GM-Hughes has been a major presence in the ATM Forum and as a corporation has been singing the praises of ATM for years. Whether this will translate into ATM products that sell is anyone's guess at this point. Its Enterprise Hub product is low-priced and has the latest ATM features.

Lightstream. Lightstream is another active ATM Forum participant. A startup with high hopes out of Ungermann-Bass and BBN (Bolt, Baranek, and Newman), the Lightstream 2010 is yet another ATM switch. The only thing that saves Lightstream from the "me too" category is its close attention to ATM Forum standards even before they have been approved. Lightstream is one of the prime movers and shakers behind the P-NNI.

Private ATM LAN vendor "me-toos." A number of companies have announced ATM products and support for ATM interfaces. Many are current leaders in various LAN markets and see ATM as both a blessing and a curse—a blessing because ATM may mean more customers for their ATM products, but a curse because the company has no special expertise or experience in building or applying ATM technology.

This list of vendors is not exhaustive nor meant to be critical. In several respects, it is better to be in the mainstream of a technology revolution than on the "bleeding edge." All these companies have announced ATM "strategies," but mainly because they have had to. The feeling is that more potential customers will buy today knowing ATM is supported when the customer requires it.

ADC Fibermux

Cisco (now Bay Networks)

Kalpana

Lannet

Madge

Network Systems

Proteon

Retix

Synernetics

Xyplex

9.4.2 ATM products for private ATM WANs

The products in this section fall into a different category. There will be organizations whose ATM network needs are not so much concerned with on-premises networking but with linking sites around the country (or even the world) into one large internetwork. Much the same is done with router-based networks today. Who will provide the switched-based ATM networks of tomorrow? If history is any judge, it will *not* be the same organizations as today.

Thus the traditional vendors in the private WAN arena, the T-1 multiplexer vendors and the X.25 switch vendors, have embraced ATM as a second lease on life. Their growth has been much slower than for the LAN hub/router group, but since ATM is ATM, no one has a built-in edge in the market anymore.

Here is a brief look at some of the players, along the same lines as the preceding section.

Private ATM WAN vendors with instant credibility

Ascom Timeplex. Ascom Timeplex has been very active in ATM trials, including the Washington University ATM project. Its product, the INP, offers many WAN interfaces (frame relay, SMDS) along with LAN interfaces (Ethernet, Token Ring), all in an ATM package. The company plans a full range of ATM products for workgroups to large enterprise networks.

Digital Link. Digital Link has found its niche in the ATM world. Few ATM prototype networks or pilot projects, which generally have different board, switch, and other vendors involved, do *not* have Digital Link equipment. The simple reason for this is that Digital Link specializes in interface-to-interface ATM connectivity. That is, its equipment takes ATM cells off an HSSI interface and puts them onto a DS-3, and so on. This is hardly an overwhelming capability, but it is a necessary one.

GDC (General DataComm). GDC's APEX ATM switch is one of the largest ATM switches available today. It has a nice mix of features and is probably the richest of all the ATM switches in this category. The DV-2 is a very large, very fast (40-µs) ATM switch for large corporate ATM networks.

Newbridge Networks. Newbridge's ATMNet products also have received high marks from early users and evaluators of ATM products. They have an excellent mix of features and about a 40-µs nodal processing delay. The 36150 MainStreet product is aimed at customers needing to build networks larger than a site or two, and the switch has proven to be very easy to set up and configure.

GTE Government Systems. GTE's SPANet switch is really aimed at large central office operations, but smaller versions are available at very reasonable prices. GTE's willingness to expose its switch to any test, anytime, anywhere and to generally pass these tests with flying colors has earned the SPANet switch a deserved reputation for reliability and speed (in the 40-µs nodal delay range). GTE expects to be a large vendor of ATM products for the U.S. government.

Private ATM WAN vendor "wanna-bes."

AT&T Network Systems. As surprising as it is to see IBM as a "wanna-be," it is more surprising to see AT&T in the same category. AT&T Bell Labs is very active in developing and researching ATM theory and evolving ATM prototype switches, but this has yet to translate into market credibility. The BNS-2000 is an impressive switch, but AT&T has been reluctant to expose it to the scrutiny needed to gain a reputation as a market leader.

ADC Kentrox. ADC has been active in developing products for use by ADC Telecommunications. It has established relations with Loral Data to provide ATM switches for large data networks.

Alcatel Data Networks. Alcatel has impressive plans for ATM switch products. Its product will be a real central office switch and will probably be used by Sprint in its public ATM service offerings.

Motorola Codex. Motorola Codex's 6950 SoftCell ATM network node has been criticized for using proprietary schemes in addition to standard ATM architectures. Regardless of the merits or liabilities of this approach, Motorola faces a hard sell for this scheme despite its "practical migration path" campaign.

Northern Telecom. The Magellan Passport switch from Northern Telecom is an attempt give NT a presence in the ATM product marketplace. Northern Telecom has been active in the ATM Forum and has made efforts to be more visible at ATM demos and trials.

Stratacom. Stratacom deserves special mention due to their early efforts to "packetize voice" a la X.25. They provided a real push to ATM. They hold several key ATM patents as a result, which they have leveraged effectively. Although recently emphasizing frame-relay products, the latest ATM offerings on their BPX switch have been impressive.

Private ATM LAN vendor "me-toos." As in the market for ATM LAN products, the vendors of ATM equipment for WANs have all been pressured to announced an ATM strategy, whether ATM is really in their plans or not. Again, inclusion in this category is not a criticism of the corporation's product line but merely an acknowledgment of its more cautious approach to ATM technology.

NET (Network Equipment Technologies)

Cascade Communications

Gandalf

9.4.3   ATM public network service providers

Many organizations, especially smaller ones, will not be willing or able to afford building their own ATM networks, especially with initial product prices. These organizations will turn to others as providers of the ATM services they need.

Owing to the nature of the companies described in this section, which offer services rather than products, no details will be explored. The categories are established by such factors as commitment to ATM equipment deployment and offerings of related network technologies such as frame relay and SMDS. Both these services may be delivered on ATM networks.

A key issue is commitment to expand service areas. Many companies will deploy only enough ATM to claim a presence in the ATM service arena but not expand the service areas enough to make it worthwhile for many customers to consider.

ATM public service providers with instant credibility

MFS Datanet. As should be clear from the previous description, MFS Datanet has a leadership position in the ATM service marketplace.

Bell Atlantic. As the first Bell Operating Company (BOC) to offer tariffed ATM service, Bell Atlantic has a natural market in the Washington, D.C., area: the federal government.

NYNEX. NYNEX has extensive trials and other projects under way throughout New England and New York State. These started in 1993.

Pacific Bell. PacBell has been experimenting seriously with SMDS since 1992 and intends to deploy ATM service extensively.

WilTel. Wiltel has had an ATM service available for a while. But for the longest time customers were confused because WilTel did not specifically *call* it ATM. Their Channel Networking Service tended to get lost among WilTel's many frame-relay customers.

ATM public service provider "wanna-bes."

Ameritech. This particular BOC has ambitious plans to offer ATM services throughout its service area.

Bell South. Bell South has been particularly active in deploying fiber throughout its entire service area.

US West. US West has considered many switch vendors for its anticipated ATM service offerings.

GTE. GTE is in a very good position to deploy ATM services nationwide.

AT&T. AT&T's plans regarding ATM deployment have been enigmatic. It has said and done all the right things. But its reluctance to offer SMDS on other than a trial basis in metropolitan areas is not a good sign for future ATM deployment.

ATM public service providers "me-toos."   Again, inclusion is this category is not a criticism. Service providers here have announced plans, but mostly in reaction to the plans of others.

Southwestern Bell

MCI

Compuserve

9.4.4 Summary

This section has been a very brief tour of ATM products and services. Again, an organization's inclusion or categorization is purely a subjective judgment and not an endorsement or condemnation. Likewise, exclusion may not be a reflection of any lack of interest in ATM technology on the part of any organization but rather a reflection of exposure to a particular company's products and/or services.

Selected ATM and Related
Broadband Networking Standards

Asynchronous Transfer Mode (ATM)

ATM Forum

Generally available networking standards

DXI 1.0 (1993)	ATM Data Exchange Interface (DXI) Specification
UNI 3.1 (1994)	ATM User-Network Interface (UNI) Specification
B-ICI 1.1 (1994)	BISDN Inter-Carrier Interface (B-ICI) Specification

Subcommittee networking standards

M4 NM Interface	Interface Between Network Management System and the ATM Network
M5 NM Interface	Interface Between Public and Private ATM Network Management Systems
P-NNI Phase 0	Private Network-to-Network Interface
LAN Emulation 1.0	LAN Emulation for ATM Networks
100-Mbps PICS	Testing Specification for 100-Mbps Multimode Fiber Physical Interface
DS3 PICS	Testing Specification for DS3 Physical Interface
OC-3c PICS	Testing Specification for 155.52-Mbps SONET Physical Interface

BellCore

TR-NWT-000233 (1993)	Wideband and Broadband Digital Cross-Connect Systems Generic Requirements and Objectives
TR-TSY-000301 (1990)	Public Packet Switched Network Generic Requirements (PPSNGR)
SR-TSY-000857 (1987)	Preliminary Special Report on Broadband ISDN Access
FA-NWT-001109 (1990)	BISDN Transport Network Framework Generic Criteria
TA-NWT-001110 (1993)	Broadband ISDN Switching System Generic Requirements
TA-NWT-001111 (1993)	Broadband ISDN Access Signaling Framework Generic Criteria for Class II Equipment
TA-NWT-001112 (1992)	Broadband ISDN User to Network Interface and Network Node Interface Physical Layer Generic Criteria
TA-NWT-001113 (1993)	Asynchronous Transfer Mode (ATM) and ATM Adaptation Layer (AAL) Protocols Generic Requirements
TA-NWT-001114 (1993)	Generic Requirements for Operations Interfaces Using OSI Tools: Broadband ATM Network Operations
TA-NWT-001115 (1993)	BISDN Inter-Carrier Interface (B-ICI) Requirements
TA-TSV-001117 (1993)	Generic Requirements for Exchange PVC CRS Customer Network Management Service
TA-TSV-001238 (1992)	Generic Requirements for SMDS on the 155.520-Mbps Multi-Services Broadband ISDN Inter-Carrier Interface (B-ICI)
TA-NWT-001248 (1993)	Generic Requirements for Operations of Broadband Switching Systems
SR-NWT-002076 (1991)	Report on the Broadband ISDN Protocols for Providing SMDS and Exchange Access SMDS

IETF (Internet Engineering Task Force)

RFC 1483 (1993)	Multiprotocol Encapsulation over ATM Adaptation Layer 5
RFC 1577 (1994)	Classical IP and ARM over ATM
RFC 1595 (1994)	Definitions of Managed Objects for the SONET/SDH Interface Type

ITU-T (formerly CCITT)

F.811 (1992)	Broadband Connection-Oriented Bearer Services
F.812 (1992)	Broadband Connectionless Data Bearer Service
I.113 (1991)	B-ISDN Vocabulary of Terms
I.121 (1991)	Broadband Aspects of ISDN
I.150 (1992)	B-ISDN ATM Functional Characteristics
I.211 (1992)	B-ISDN Service Aspects
I.311 (1992)	B-ISDN General Network Aspects
I.321 (1991)	B-ISDN Protocol Reference Model and Its Applications
I.327 (1993)	B-ISDN Functional Architecture Aspects
I.361 (1992)	B-ISDN ATM Layer Specification
I.362 (1993)	B-ISDN ATM Adaptation Layer Functional Description
I.363 (1992)	B-ISDN ATM Adaptation Layer Specification
I.364 (1992)	Connectionless Network Access Protocol
I.371 (1992)	Traffic Control and Congestion Control in B-ISDN
I.413 (1992)	B-ISDN User-Network Interface
I.432 (1992)	B-ISDN User-Network Interface-Physical Layer Specification
I.555 (1993)	Frame Relay and ATM Interworking
I.610 (1992)	B-ISDN UNI Operations and Maintenance Principles

Frame Relay Standards

ANSI (American National Standards Institute)

T1.602 (1990)	Telecommunications-ISDN-Data Link Layer Signaling Specification for Applications at the User-Network Interface
T1.606 (1990)	Frame Relaying Bearer Service—Architectural Framework and Service Description
T1.617 (1991)	DSSl-Signaling Specification for Frame Relay Bearer Service
T1.617a(1991)	Frame Relay Bearer Service—Architectural Framework and Service Description on Congestion Management Principles
T1.618 (1991)	DSS l-Core Aspects of Frame Protocol for Use with Frame Relay Bearer Service

BellCore

TA-TSV-001240 (1993)	Generic Requirements for Frame Relay Access to SMDS
TA-NWT-001248 (1993)	Generic Requirements for Operations of Broadband Switching Systems
FA-NWT-001327 (1992)	Framework Generic Requirements for Frame Relay Network Element Operations
TA-NWT-001328 (1992)	ISDN Exchange Termination (ET) to Frame Handler (FH) Interface Framework Generic Criteria
TR-TSV-001369 (1993)	Generic Requirements for Frame Relay PVC Exchange Service
TR-NWT-001370 (1993)	Generic Requirements for Exchange Access Frame Relay PVC Service
TA-NWT-001371 (1993)	Generic Requirements for Phase 1 Frame Relay PVC Customer Network Management Service

IETF (Internet Engineering Task Force)

RFC 1315 (1992)	Definition of Managed Objects for Frame Relay DTEs
RFC 1490 (1993)	Multiprotocol Interconnect over Frame Relay
RFC 1573 (1994)	The New Interfaces MIB
RFC 1604 (1994)	Definitions of Managed Objects for Frame Relay Service

ITU-T (formerly CCITT)

I.122 (1988)	Framework for Providing Additional Packet Mode Bearer Services
Q.922 (1992)	ISDN Data Link Layer Specification for Frame Mode Bearer Services
Q.931 (1988)	ISDN Signaling Specification for Frame Mode Bearer Services
I.233 (1992)	Frame Mode Bearer Service (FMBS)
I.370 (1991)	Frame Mode Bearer Service (FMBS) Congestion Management
I.372 (1993)	Frame Mode Bearer Service (FMBS) Network-to-Network Requirements
I.555 (1993)	Frame Mode Bearer Service (FMBS) Interworking

Frame Relay Forum

FRF. 1 (1991)	User to Network Interface Implementation Agreement
FRF.2 (1992)	Frame Relay Network-to-Network Interface Implementation Agreement
FRF.3 (1993)	Multiprotocol Interconnect over Frame Relay
FRF.4 (1993)	Switched Virtual Circuit (SVC) Description
FRF.5 (1994)	Frame Relay/ATM Interworking Implementation Agreement
FRF.6 (1994)	Frame Relay Customer Network Management Implementation Agreement

Switched Multimegabit Data Service (SMDS)

BellCore

TR-TSV-000772 (1991)	Generic System Requirements in Support of Switched Multimegabit Data Services
TR-TSV-000773 (1991) Revision 1 (1993)	Local Access System Generic Requirements Objectives, and Interfaces in Support of Switched Multi-Megabit Data Service
TR-TSV-000774 (1992) Sup. 1 (1993)	SMDS Operations Technology Network Element Generic Requirements
TR-TSV-000775 (1991)	Usage Measurement Generic Requirements in Support of Billing for Switched Multi-Megabit Data Service
TA-TSV-001059 (1992)	Generic Requirements for SMDS Networking
TR-TSV-001060 (1991) Rev. 1 (1992) Rev. 2 (1993)	Switched Multi-Megabit Data Services Generic Requirements for Exchange Access and Intercompany Serving Arrangements (SMDS)
TA-TSV-001061 (1991)	Operations Technology Network Element Generic Requirements in Support of Inter-switch and Exchange Access SMDS
TR-TSV-001062 (1993)	Generic Requirements for Phase 1 SMDS Customer Network Management Service
TR-TSV-001063 (1992) Rev. 1 (1993)	Operations Technology Generic Criteria in Support of Exchange Access SMDS and Intercompany Serving Arrangements
TR-TSV-001064 (1992)	SMDS Generic Criteria on Operations Interfaces—SMDS Information Model and Usage
TR-TSV-001239 (1993)	Generic Requirements for Low-Speed SMDS Access

TR-TSV-001240 (1993)   Generic Requirements for Frame Relay Access to
                             SMDS

IETF (Internet Engineering Task Force)

RFC 1209 (1991)   The Transmission of IP Datagrams over the
                             SMDS Service

RFC 1304 (1992)   Definitions of Managed Objects for the SMDS
                             Interface Type

RFC 1406 (1993)   Definitions of Managed Objects for the DS1 and
                             E1 Interface Types

RFC 1407 (1993)   Definitions of Managed Objects for the DS3/E3
                             Interface Type

SMDS Interest Group

SIG-TS-001 (1991)   Data Exchange Interface (DXI) Specification

SIG-TS-002 (1992)   Local Management Interface (LMI) Specification

SIG-TS-003 (1992)   DECnet over SMDS Specification

SIG-TS-004 (1993)   Connectionless OSI over SMDS Specification

SIG-TS-005 (1993)   DXI/SNI Specification

SIG-TS-006 (1993)   SIP Relay Interface (SRI) Specification

SIG-IS-002 (1993)   Guiding Principles for Ordering and
                            Provisioning of Intercarrier SMDS

SIG-IS-003 (1993)   Guiding Principles for SMDS Intercarrier
                            Operations Management

More Books About ATM Networking

DePrycker, Martin, *Asynchronous Transfer Mode: Solution for Broadband ISDN,* 2d ed.
    (Ellis-Horwood, 1994).
Flanagan, William A., *Asynchronous Transfer Mode User's Guide* (Flatiron Publishing,
    1994).
Handel, Rainer, and Huber, Manfred N., *Integrated Broadband Networks: An
    Introduction to ATM-based Networks,* 2d ed. (Addison-Wesley, 1994).
Lee, Byeong Gi, Kang, Minho, and Lee, Jonghee, *Broadband Communications
    Technology* (Artech House, 1994).
McDysan, David E., and Spohn, Darren L., *ATM: Theory and Application* (McGraw-Hill,
    1994).
Onveral, Raif O., *Asynchronous Transfer Mode Networks: Performance Issues* (Artech
    House, 1994).
Saito, Hiroshi, *Teletraffic Technologies in ATM Networks* (Artech House, 1994).
Viniotis, Yannis, *Asynchronous Transfer Mode Networks,* Raif O. Onveral (ed.) (Plenum
    Press, 1993).

Index

ABOUT THE AUTHOR

Walter Goralski is a data communications and telecommunications specialist and an expert on LAN program development. He has more than 25 years' experience in the field, including 14 years with AT&T. In the past he has worked at Wang Laboratories as manager of wide-area, local-area, and specialized networks; at New York Telephone as technical support specialist for one of the largest electronic mail networks in the Northeast; and at Bell Telephone Laboratories. He is currently a professor and technical specialist at Pace University's Graduate School of Computer and Information Sciences in White Plains, New York. He is a frequent contributor of articles on communications technology and a member of the ATM Forum.